NAMES & NICKNAMES OF PLACES & THINGS

NAMES &
NICKNAMES
OF PLACES
& THINGS

Edited by
LAURENCE URDANG

A MERIDIAN BOOK

NEW AMERICAN LIBRARY

NEW YORK AND SCARBOROUGH, ONTARIO

Copyright © 1987 by Laurence Urdang

All rights, including that of translation into other languages, reserved.
Photomechanical reproduction (photocopy, microcopy) of this book or
parts thereof without special permission of the publisher is prohibited.
For information address G. K. Hall and Company, Division of
Macmillan Publishing Company, 70 Lincoln Street, Boston,
Massachusetts 02111.

Published by arrangement with G. K. Hall and Company

 MERIDIAN TRADEMARK REG. U.S. PAT. OFF. AND FOREIGN COUNTRIES
REG. TRADEMARK—MARCA REGISTRADA
HECHO EN FAIRFIELD, PA., U.S.A.

SIGNET, SIGNET CLASSIC, MENTOR, ONYX, PLUME,
MERIDIAN and NAL BOOKS are published *in the United States* by NAL
PENGUIN INC., 1633 Broadway, New York, New York 10009, *in Canada*
by The New American Library of Canada Limited, 81 Mack Avenue,
Scarborough, Ontario M1L 1M8

LIBRARY OF CONGRESS
Library of Congress Cataloging-in-Publication Data

Names & nicknames of places & things / edited by Laurence Urdang.
   p. cm.
   ISBN 0-452-00908-1
   1. Names, Geographical. 2. Names. I. Urdang, Laurence. II. Title:
Names and nicknames of places & things.
[G105.N36 1987b]   87-31513
910'.01'4—dc19   CIP

PRINTED IN THE UNITED STATES OF AMERICA

BOMC offers recordings and compact discs, cassettes
and records. For information and catalog write to
BOMR, Camp Hill, PA 17012.

Contents

Foreword

It must be emphasized that *Names & Nicknames of Places & Things* does not reflect an attempt at completeness: there are far too many candidates for entry, and it is unlikely that such a book could ever be complete. The attempt has been made to select for coverage such names and nicknames as might qualify for consideration as being universal or, at least, important. Yet, the choice is largely a subjective one, as it must needs be tempered and shaped by the cultural background and prejudices of its compiler. Being of the Eastern (and Western European) "Establishment," I have probably paid too little attention to other areas of the world, which would undoubtedly yield up thousands of valid entries. Suggestions from contributors did, indeed, cover territories not given space in this book, and if important entries have been omitted, responsibility for their nonappearance must be laid at my door.

This is the sort of book about which almost any reader or reviewer will say, "But it doesn't contain—," naming one of those places or things left out either deliberately or inadvertently. It is hoped that some readers will find interesting, informative, and useful the material that is here and not judge me too harshly for omissions. Suggestions for entries will be welcome for another edition, should such a phenomenon ever come to pass.

In order to attempt some sort of balance, I appealed to members of the American Name Society for suggestions, and they flooded in. In some cases, perhaps because I failed to make clear exactly the kind of entry being sought, the suggestions had to be rejected; in other instances, they were rejected either because they covered places and things that were too specialized for such a general work or had already been treated. Nevertheless, I should like to express my gratitude to those scores of members who did respond and whose names I have listed below. In addition, I should like to thank the mayors of major cities of the United States and Canada who either responded personally to my requests for help and suggestions or passed on my request to officials who replied.

vii

I am particularly grateful to Bob Perlongo, who helped with material about Chicago and the Midwest. The most prolific contributor has been John Ayto, of England, who prepared entries on the British Isles, much of Europe, and points beyond. Jacquelyn Goodwin is owed a deep debt of gratitude for helping me in every aspect of the preparation.

At bottom, though, while all of the good, useful, and interesting material in *Names & Nicknames* must be credited to these contributors, its shortcomings are attributable entirely to me,

Laurence Urdang

Old Lyme, Connecticut
August 1986

Members of the American Name Society who contributed material that formed the basis for many of the entries in *Names & Nicknames of Places & Things*:

Hugh Akers
Jeannette G. Blumengarten
Dwight Bolinger
Margaret M. Bryant
Danielle Chavy Cooper
Charlotte Downey
Stephen P. Holutiak-Hallick, Jr.
Charles E. Joubert
Alla Ktorova
Gabriel Lasker

Richard M. Lederer, Jr.
E. Wallace McMullen
Frances R. Perry
Robert Rennick
Alfred M. Silvia
Louis Stein
Robert Throckmorton
Glenys A. Waldman
Stephen Walker
Nelly Weiss-Füglister

Especial thanks are owing to:

Leonard R. N. Ashley
Thomas L. Bernard
Ralph Bolton
J. L. Dillard
Gary S. Dunbar
Steve Farrow
Barbara Rainbow Fletcher
Ira Freedman
Thomas J. Gasque
Erik Gunnemark
Eric P. Hamp
Marion O. Harris
Walter Herrscher

Betty J. Irwin
Donald B. Lawrence
Frederick Manfred
Arthur Paul Moser
Ozark Folk Center
Roger L. Payne
Peter E. Raper
Karl Rosen
Mary Schiflett
Sol Schoenbach
James K. Skipper, Jr.
Virgil J. Vogel
L. Zgusta

Names and Nicknames

AAA, the

An abbreviation for the Agricultural Adjustment Administration, established in the United States in the 1930s to administer measures for soil conservation and for the relief of farmers, as provided for by the Agricultural Adjustment Acts of 1933 and 1938.

Aardvark

The nickname of the F-111, a United States fighter-bomber aircraft, prior to its being fitted with infrared targeting and a laser guidance bombing system.

Abbey Road

A road in the St. John's Wood area of London which contains the EMI Recording Studios. It achieved wider fame when the Beatles gave its name to one of their albums (1969).

Abercrombie & Fitch

A department store, formerly headquartered at 45th Street and Madison Avenue, in New York City, known mainly for its sporting goods and, especially, for having fitted out a number of safaris and polar expeditions. It went bankrupt in 1977; its name was bought by another company, which opened twenty-five new stores and established a mail-order catalogue division.

Abu Simbel

A set of three temples to sun-gods, hewn out of sandstone cliffs in the time of Ramses II in about 1250 B.C.. On the west bank of the Nile at Aswan (ancient Nubia), they are known chiefly for four 65-foot-high colossi of the king. The entire site was threatened in the late 1960s by the creation of a huge reservoir, resulting from the construction of the Aswan Dam; in response to a drive by UNESCO, sufficient funds were raised to pay for the cutting of the colossi from the cliff face and their relocation on a 200-foot cliff above.

Abyssinia

A former name for Ethiopia, a country in northeastern Africa. As a word, the name enjoyed a certain vogue in the 1930s as a jocular farewell, based on its phonetic similarity to "I'll be seeing you."

Academy, the

A public pleasure-ground on the Cephissus, about one mile northwest of ancient Athens, on land said to have belonged, in the time of the Trojan War, to the hero Academus. It was surrounded by a wall by Hipparchus and further adorned by Cimon, the son of Miltiades, who bequeathed it to the citizens of Athens. It was the resort of Plato, who taught in its groves for nearly fifty years, till his death in 348 B.C., and gave its name to the Platonic school of philosophy.

Acadia

A former French colony in Canada, covering an area approximately that of modern Nova Scotia. Settled by France in 1604, except for Cape Breton Island, it was ceded to Great Britain by the Treaty of Utrecht (1713). Cape Breton Island was a French possession till 1763. The British deported the French in 1755, an event that was the theme of the poem *Evangeline* (1847), by Henry Wdsworth Longfellow.

accidental war, the

A nickname for World War I, so called because the German high command, obsessed with what analysts have called the "cult of the offensive" (in contrast with the "power of a strong defense"), misinterpreted the mobilization by Russia following the assassination of the Archduke Franz Ferdinand of Austria-Hungary by a Serbian extremist on June 28, 1914, at Sarajevo, and attacked and overwhelmed Belgium. Had Germany seen the event in its proper context of a minor political disturbance, the war, in which eight million were killed, could probably have been avoided. Also called **the war to end war, the war to end all wars, the war to make the world free for democracy** (Woodrow Wilson), (facetiously) **the war to make the world free for the Democrats**, (in Britain) **the Great War.**

Acemannes burh

An Old English name, meaning 'sick man's town,' for Bath, England. An ancient Roman road connecting Bath with London is called Akeman Street.

Addled Parliament

A nickname of the second Parliament of James I (April–June 1614). It was dissolved without having passed any acts when it refused to grant supplies till the king's imposition of customs and till the restoration of the nonconforming Anglican clergy ejected in 1604 had been considered.

Adelphi, the

A former fashionable area of London between the Strand and the Thames River, designed in neoclassical splendor by Robert Adam and his brothers in 1768. Its elegant terraces housed many glitterati of the times, including the actor David Garrick, the caricaturist Thomas Rowlandson, and, later, the authors Thomas Hardy and Sir James Barrie; it was demolished in 1936.

Adonai

The name used by the Jews in place of the ineffable name Yahveh, or Jehovah (from YHWH), wherever it occurs in the Scriptures.

Adventure

The name of Captain Kidd's pirate ship.

Aetolia

An ancient district of Greece, bounded by Epirus and Thessaly on the north, Doris on the northeast, Locris on the east and southeast, the Corinthian Gulf on the south, and Acarnania on the west.

Afghan, the

A name for Afghanistan.

Aganippides, the

An alternate name for the Muses of ancient Greek mythology, so called because the fountain Aganippe, near Mount Helicon, in Boeotia, was sacred to them.

Agora, the

A large irregular area in ancient Athens, part of which was a marketplace, part an area for political meetings.

AIPS

A nickname for AIDS-Induced Panic Syndrome, coined by scientists to dispel fears of the contagious nature of AIDS (Acquired Immune Deficiency Syndrome) by casual social contact.

Alamo, the

The name of a former mission church in San Antonio, Texas, that served as the site in 1836 of what is considered to be one of the most heroic of U.

S. military battles, although none of the Texan defenders survived and the battle was lost. Texan settlers living in Mexican territory decided to sever their relations with Mexico because of dissatisfaction with the Mexican government. About 150 men, under William Barret Travis, and including James Bowie and Davy Crockett, retreated to the Alamo at the unexpected arrival of Mexican General Antonio López de Santa Ana with an army of about 5,000 men. After ten days of siege, the Texans ran low on ammunition, Santa Ana was able to scale the walls, and the battle was over. "Remember the Alamo" became a battle cry and enabled General Sam Houston to gather troops; two months later he defeated Santa Ana at San Jacinto and forced him to sign a treaty granting Texas its independence. Also called the **"Thermopylae of America."**

Alamo City
A nickname of San Antonio, Texas. See also **Alamo.**

Albany
An exclusive apartment building on Sackville Street, in the Piccadilly area of the West End of London. It was converted from Melbourne House, the London residence of the Duke of York, in 1802, and in its early years Lord Byron and Thomas Macaulay, George Canning, and W. E. Gladstone lived there. Its fashionable heyday was probably in the Edwardian era; at that time its tenancies were still restricted to bachelors, and one of its most noted (fictional) occupants was Raffles, the celebrated gentleman burglar. It used to be a touchstone of high caste to know that to say "the Albany" was decidedly Non-U, a sure sign that one was not quite top-drawer.

Albany Regency
A clique of New York politicians who controlled the Democratic Party in New York State from about 1820 to about 1854. Among its members were Martin Van Buren (president of the United States 1837–41), John A. Dix, and William L. Marcy.

Albion
A poetic term for England, cited as early as Pliny (*Natural Histories*) IV. 102, ca. A.D. 77), popular particularly from the 16th to the 18th centuries|William Blake, for example, often used it. The word may be a reference to the white cliffs that fringe much of the southeast corner of England, *albus* being the Latin word for 'white.' Nowadays it crops up only in "perfidious Albion" (a French view) and, curiously, in the names of English soccer clubs, such as Brighton and Hove Albion, and West Bromwich Albion.

Al Borak

A legendary animal, between a mule and an ass in size, with two wings and of great swiftness, on which Muhammad is said to have made a nocturnal journey to the seventh heaven.

Alcan Highway

A highway, about 1600 miles long, built in 1942– 43, between Dawson Creek, British Columbia, and Fairbanks, Alaska.

Alcatraz

An island in San Francisco Bay, site, from 1934 to 1963, of a federal prison known for its security: it is said that in its entire history only one convict escaped from there. The prison became well known especially during the 1930s mainly through a number of Hollywood movies dealing with crime and prisons, and in the ensuing years it became a symbol of the harsh severity that awaited evil-doers. The island was named by the Spaniards for its large colony of pelicans (*alcatraz* means 'pelican' in Spanish), the name stemming originally from Arabic *al qädäs* 'bucket of a water wheel.' For a short time after the closure of the prison, Alcatraz Island served as the site of a hippie commune (in the 1960s) but has been largely deserted since the early 1970s.

Aldebaran

The ancient name for the red first-magnitude star alpha Tauri, forming the eye of the bull.

Aldermaston

A village in Berkshire, to the west of London, which is the home of the Atomic Weapons Research Establishment, an obvious target for anti-nuclear demonstrators. It became famous for giving its name to the "Aldermaston marches." At Easter, 1958, under the aegis of the so-called "Committee of 100," protesters marched in strength from London to Aldermaston, and for some years subsequently the annual event was a familiar part of the British Easter scene. In 1959 the route was reversed, starting at Aldermaston and ending with a big rally in Trafalgar Square. In its early years it never failed to draw enthusiastic support; however, as the '60s wore on, public concern dwindled, the number of participants fell away, and finally the march was discontinued altogether.

Aldershot

A town in northeastern Hampshire, about 34 miles southwest of London; the site of a large military camp since 1855 and thoroughly imbued with the traditions and lore of the army. It figures in the opening lines of Rudyard Kipling's poem, *Gunga Din*:

> You may talk o' gin and beer
> When you're quartered safe out 'ere,

An' you're sent to penny-fights an' Aldershot it;

Alexiad, The

A biography of Alexius I (Comnenus) (1048–1118), Byzantine emperor (1081–1118), written by Anna Comnena (1083–1148) and covering the period from 1069 to 1118.

Alhambra

A Moorish citadel and palace on the outskirts of Granada, Spain, built during the 13th and 14th centuries by the Moorish kings. Its name means simply 'red' in Arabic and, from the exterior, it appears to be a solid fortress of red brick. The interior, however, is a maze of alcoves, halls, archways, and courtyards with pools and fountains, all entirely covered with intricately carved and polychromed stucco decorations. The beauty of the palace captured the imagination of Washington Irving who, as a diplomatic attaché in Spain, lived in part of the building and wrote *The Alhambra*, a collection of tales of medieval Moorish Spain.

Alice Springs

A town in the southern part of the Northern Territory of Australia. It began as a telegraph station set in a wilderness, and resembles in many ways the frontier towns of America during the 19th century. The Alice, as it is frequently referred to, tends to be dry and dusty, its wooden houses roofed over with galvanized corrugated iron. Although there are no springs, as such, and water is not abundant during most of the year, it is nonetheless available from wells. It is named for the wife of Sir Charles Todd, Superintendent of Telegraphs, for whom the Todd River, dry for most months, was named. See also **Center.**

Alligator Alley

The nickname for the west-east section of the Tamiami Trail (US 41), which runs from Tampa to Miami, in Florida, so named because it passes through parts of the Everglades that are infested with alligators.

Alligator State, the

A nickname of Alabama, Florida, Louisiana, Mississippi, and Texas.

Ally Pally

A nickname for Alexandra Palace, an imposing Victorian structure built on an eminence to the north of London. It was erected in 1873, "to refine and elevate the public taste," but only sixteen days after its opening it burned down; nothing daunted, the builders built anew. It was put to considerable use for exhibits, but it really came into its own and began to acquire its nickname, from 1936 onward, when the BBC used it as Britain's first television studios. Although the last entertainment program was broadcast from there in 1954, it continued to be used for news broadcasts for a further quarter of a century. It partly burned down again in 1980, but lavish plans were thereafter formulated to rebuild it as an arts, sports, and exhibition center.

Aloha State, the

The official nickname of Hawaii.

Alsatia

An area of medieval and early modern London that was off limits to those who wished to remain sound of body and purse. Situated between Fleet Street and the Thames River, it retained until 1697 the power of the former Whitefriars monastery to grant sanctuary. It consequently acted as a magnet for all the rogues and felons in London, who turned it into a notorious "rookery"|a maze of disreputable tenements, dives, and brothels. Its name comes from Alsace, a border area between France and Germany which was famous for harboring the disaffected. See also **Whitefriars**.

Amazonia

A name applied to the Amazon basin, the vast (about 1.5 million square miles) plain in Brazil through which the Amazon River flows to the sea. Most of it is occupied by huge tracts of tropical rain forest, although many areas are now being cleared, causing concern to environmentalists. The river itself got its name from some long-haired warlike tribesmen encountered on its banks by early Spanish explorers, who evidently thought they had met with the legendary Amazons, fierce female warriors.

Amen Corner

The nickname given by W. J. Chamberlain of the *New York Sun* to that part of the main corridor of the Fifth Avenue Hotel in New York City where the managers of the Republican Party met (1859–1908) to discuss plans and platforms. In churches, it refers to the section near the altar where the devout sit and shout "Amen!" in approval of what the preacher is saying.

American Nile, the

A nickname of the St. John's River in northeastern Florida, so called because the reeds and tropical vegetation growing along its banks resemble those along the Nile.

American Workhouse, the

An ironical nickname coined by London taxi drivers for the Park Lane Hotel, with reference to wealthy American tourists' predilection for its luxurious appointments. In British English, a *workhouse* is a poorhouse.

America's Bermuda

A nickname claimed by Block Island, Rhode Island.

America's Cup

A racing trophy, first given in 1851 to the *America*, a yacht owned by J. C. Stevens. In recent times, the class of yachts allowed to compete, called "12-meter," has drawn entrants from France, Australia, and other countries; all the races, which are held every two to four years, now organized as sedate affairs around a closed triangular course, had been won by the American vessel till 1983, when the Australian yacht, *Australia II*, with a uniquely designed hull, captured the huge silver trophy which, in arrogant confidence, had been "permanently" bolted into its display case at the New York Yacht Club, on West 44th Street, in New York City. The 12-meter class is established by a complex measuring rule, its name having little to do with over-all length, beam, waterline length, sail area, or any of the other individual dimensions customarily used in naming classes of racing sailboats. The competing boats are usually built by a syndicate of wealthy yacht-racing enthusiasts, because their cost, maintenance, and crewing are far too expensive for any one aficionado, no matter how fervent or wealthy. Although the vessels' sponsors regard the quadrennial competition as a national symbol, because sailboat racing is scarcely a spectator sport and because the costs of participation are so far outside the reach of any but a handful of avid millionaires, the average person's association with the event is quite remote. The race is officially held at the port designated by the winning team.

America's Dairyland

A nickname of Wisconsin.

America's Great Winter Garden

A nickname of the Imperial Valley, California.

America's Ice Box

A nickname of Alaska.

America's Little Switzerland

A nickname of Tuscarawas County, Ohio.

America's Most Historic City

A nickname claimed by Charleston, South Carolina, and Fredericksburg, Virginia.

America's Oldest City

The nickname of St. Augustine, Florida, founded in 1565.

Anatolia

An oblong plateau of mountainous land bounded on the north by the Black Sea and on the south by the Mediterranean. Anatolia forms the Asian part—and indeed by far the major part—of Turkey. The European part, on the far side of the Bosporus, is only about three per cent of the total area of the country. In ancient times, Anatolia was the same as Asia Minor.

anatomist's snuffbox
The small hollow formed on the back of the hand at the root of the thumb when the thumb is bent back strongly, so called because those who take snuff use it as a temporary repository before sniffing it up the nose.

Angel, the
A road junction in northeast London, where the City Road meets Pentonville Road and Islington High Street. It is named after a famous former coaching inn on the site.

Angora
Before 1930 Ankara, the Turkish capital, was known as Angora; today the name survives only as a designation for certain long-haired breeds of rabbits, cats, and goats.

Angostura
From 1764 to 1846 the name of Ciudad Bolívar, a town in Venezuela. Angostura bark, from certain South American trees, provided some of the secret ingredients of Angostura bitters, an astringent potion first concocted in the 19th century as a stimulant for people suffering from loss of appetite, but now much used for adding bite to mixed drinks.

Antelope State, the
A nickname of Nebraska.

Antipodes, the
Antipodes comes from a Greek word meaning 'with feet opposite,' and so literally refers to areas on the opposite side of the world—that is, where people "stand on their heads." The word became particularly popular with British speakers to refer specifically to Australia and New Zealand, which are almost diametrically opposite Britain on the globe. In addition, *the Antipodes* is the official designation of a small group of uninhabited islands to the southeast of New Zealand.

Apache State, the
A nickname of Arizona.

Appalachia
A name that immediately calls to mind great poverty and an almost total lack of hope. It refers to that part of the Appalachian Mountains in West Virginia, Tennessee, and Kentucky, where the terrain is too steep and rocky for farming or for road, highway, or airport construction, and

where mountain streams often flood valley settlements. Coal mining was the major industry, but many mines have closed because the stringent enforcement of anti-pollution laws has reduced the use of coal, leaving most of the area's inhabitants with no alternative means of employment.

Appalachian Mountains

Named for the Apalachee Indians, these mountains are the oldest in North America and the second largest after the Rockies. They extend about 1500 miles from the Gaspé Peninsula in Quebec, Canada, to Birmingham, Alabama. They include the Notre Dame mountains in Quebec, the White Mountains in New Hampshire, the Green Mountains in Vermont, and the Catskill Mountains in New York. Southwest of the Hudson River Valley they divide into three main sections: the Blue Ridge, which extend into Alabama; the Great Valley, from Pennsylvania to Tennessee; and to their west, the Ridge-and-Valley Province which, in turn, is bordered on their west by the Cumberland and Allegheny mountains. These last, together with the Blue Ridge and Great Smoky mountains make the Appalachians one of the great divides in North America, separating rivers that empty into the Atlantic Ocean from those that flow into the Gulf of Mexico.

Appalachian Trail, the

A two-thousand-mile-long footpath through the Appalachians from Mount Katahdin, Maine, to Springer Mountain, Georgia. It passes through fourteen states, two national parks, and eight national forests.

Apple Isle, the

A nickname given by Australians to Tasmania; apples are the mainstay of the island's agricultural production.

Aqueduct City

A nickname of Rochester, New York.

Arabia

A huge peninsula in the shape of an ax-head, at the southwest corner of Asia. To its west is the Red Sea, to its east the Persian Gulf; and its vast, almost trackless interior, the Arabia Deserta of the ancients, is a burning desert beneath which repose highly lucrative reserves of oil. It is comprised of the modern states of Saudi Arabia, Yemen, South Yemen, Oman, Bahrein, Qatar, and the United Arab Emirates. Less specifically, *Arabia* has in the past been used as a term for the Arab world generally, much as we might use Middle East today. Shakespeare no doubt had its oriental mystery in mind when he wrote "All the perfumes in Arabia will not sweeten this little hand" (*Macbeth*, V.i.). The archaic, poetic version *Araby* (as in *The Sheik of Araby*) has the same associations.

Aragon Ballroom

A slightly shabby Chicago dancehall that, in its glory days beginning in the late 1920s, and continuingly popular during the 1930s and '40s, was a picturesque mecca for couples and singles eager to socialize and appreciative of the big-name bands that often played there. Located in the North Side's Uptown area, near Lake Michigan, the Aragon in its prime was noted for its grandly romantic decor, a heavily Hollywood-influenced imitation of Moorish architecture. Radio "remotes"—on-location broadcasts—helped spread the ballroom's fame across the Midwest and a fair portion of the rest of the country. Perhaps best known of those who broadcast from there were Wayne King, "The Waltz King", and singer/bandleader Eddy Howard. With the advent of television and changing musical tastes, the Aragon began a long decline through a series of such dubious reincarnations as a psychedelic disco, a rock-band auditorium, a boxing-match arena, and, most recently, as the occasional host to Latino "salsa" bands.

Arcadia

An area in southern Greece. In modern times it is officially a Greek department in the central Peloponnese, but its fame rests firmly on its reputation as a paradisaic land of pastoral peace and revelry—a reputation incongruous in the light of the bleakness and mountainousness of its actual terrain. It was the ancient Greek poet Theocritus, following on from references in Vergil's *Eclogues*, who first peopled the landscape with amorous shepherds and nymphs; but the setting was eagerly seized on during the Renaissance by revivers of classical bucolics, who created anew the never-never land of *Arcady* (as they called it) and filled its long golden afternoons with lovesick Elizabethan swains. The most famous example of the genre is probably Sir Philip Sidney's long prose romance, *Arcadia.* A more chilling use of the name is in the tombstone inscription *Et in Arcadia ego* (literally 'I, too, in Arcadia'), not uncommon in medieval and early modern times; its import is enigmatic, but it may mean 'Even in Arcadia death is present.'

Archway

An area in London, to the northwest of Hampstead Heath. Through the middle of it runs Archway Road, which gets its name from a large viaduct, razed in 1900. When a London Underground station was opened nearby in the early 20th century it was called Archway station, and, as very often happened in such cases, the station's name became established for the surrounding district.

Arctogaea

In the scientific study of the distribution of animal species around the world, the name given to the vast landmass that includes Europe, Asia, and Africa, with the addition of North America. Compare **Neogaea, Notogaea.**

Arden

An area in the western part of Warwickshire, once part of a large forest that may have extended from the Severn to the Trent across the English Midlands. In English literature of the 16th and 17th centuries, it was often used as the scene of pastoral revels in shade-dappled glades and sylvan grottoes, and large parts of Shakespeare's *As You Like It* are set there. The association with Shakespeare, strengthened by the fact that his mother's maiden name was Arden, has led to a well-known modern edition of his works being called the *Arden Shakespeare.*

Army & Navy Stores

Originally an outlet for surplus army and navy goods and apparel, today a large department store, in Victoria Street, in London, known as outfitters for safaris and explorers and, formerly, for those posted to colonies in India, Africa, etc.

Artesian State, the

A nickname of South Dakota.

Ascot

A village in Berkshire, to the west of London, famed for its racecourse on Ascot Heath. The race meeting held there every June, known as Royal Ascot, was founded by Queen Anne in 1711; it is one of the focal points of the summer season in British high society. Competition is keen, not to say ruthless, for places in the Royal Enclosure that afford an opportunity to mingle, or at least seem to mingle, with such royalty as is present. It is a bonanza for couturiers, whose talents provide ammunition for a spectacular display of ladies' high fashion. Gentlemen turn up more soberly and uniformly attired in morning coat and topper, sometimes set off with a species of cravat known as an ascot.

Ashes, the

A nickname for the championship in test cricket between England and Australia. (The term "test," as in "test match," is similar to "world series" in the United States.) In 1882, the England [sic] side lost to the Australian side, and the *Sporting Times* published an "obituary." Since that time *the Ashes* has been used in referring to all series of test matches between England and Australia. Later, when the Australian team was defeated, some ladies from Melbourne burned a bail (a part of the wicket used in the game) and collected the ashes in an urn which was presented to the England team captain in a red velvet bag. *The Ashes* are today at Lord's Cricket Ground, in London. [Adapted from *English English*, by Norman W. Schur, Verbatim, 1980]

Asia Minor

A now rather dated or literary name for Anatolia, the part of Turkey that is in Asia. See also **Anatolia**.

Atchison, Topeka, & Santa Fe

The name of a major transcontinental railroad, between Chicago and the southwestern states of the U. S. (though it never passed through Santa Fe); it followed generally the old Santa Fe Trail.

Athenaeum, the

A London club, founded in 1824, situated in a large, white, Greek Revival building in Waterloo Place, just off Pall Mall (in **Clubland**, *q.v.*). In 1830, the members passed the following Resolution:

> The Athenaeum was instituted in 1824 for the association of individuals known for their scientific or literary attainments, artists of eminence in any class of the fine arts, and noblemen and gentlemen distinguished as liberal patrons of science, literature or the arts.

As the Committee acknowledges, "over the years these categories have been considerably widened and now extend to persons of attainment in any field where their work is of an intellectual nature and of substantial value to the community." This presumably accounts for the abundance of bishops among the membership, which is limited to about 2000.

Athens of Alabama, the

A nickname of Tuscaloosa.

Athens of America, the

A nickname of Boston, Massachusetts, so called after its many educational, literary, and cultural institutions.

Athens of Arkansas, the

A nickname of Fayetteville.

Athens of Texas, the

A nickname of Waco.

Athens of the North, the

Edinburgh, the capital of Scotland, acquired this epithet in the 18th and early 19th centuries, when it was the center of a great cultural and literary flowering, fostered by such distinguished citizens as James Boswell, David Hume, Sir Walter Scott, and Thomas Carlyle. But it could almost as well have been inspired by the elegant Georgian buildings of the New Town, which are of an Athenian refinement.

Athens of the Northwest, the

A nickname of Faribault, Minnesota.

Athens of the South, the

A nickname of Nashville, Tennessee.

Athens of the West, the

A nickname claimed by both Abilene, Texas, and Lexington, Kentucky.

Athens of Virginia, the

A nickname claimed by both Lexington and Westmoreland County, Virginia.

Atlantic Provinces, the

A name for the four Canadian provinces of Newfoundland, New Brunswick, Nova Scotia, and Prince Edward Island, though the last three are sometimes called the Maritime Provinces. They have been a major fishing center since the 1400s, providing more than three-quarters of Canada's fish, and include the Grand Banks, southeast of Newfoundland, one of the world's richest fishing grounds.

Atlantic States

A nickname for those states south of New England which border on the Atlantic ocean or are economically tied to it. The Middle Atlantic States are New Jersey, New York, and Pennsylvania; the South Atlantic States are Delaware, Florida, Georgia, Maryland, North and South Carolina, and Virginia, though West Virginia is sometimes included.

Atlantis

A legendary island in the Atlantic Ocean, just beyond the **Pillars of Hercules** (*q.v.*), mentioned by Plato in the *Timaeus* and the *Critias* as a major power in the entire Mediterranean area; it was destroyed by a cataclysm and sank beneath the sea thousands of years ago. Throughout history, similar legends pervaded the European cultures. Attempts to rationalize the existence of Atlantis have persisted to the present, the most recent theory placing its site on the island of Santorini (modern Thera), in the Aegean Sea, which evidence shows disappeared beneath the sea as a result of a gigantic eruption of a volcano in the 15th century B.C., obliterating all but traces of the Minoan Cretan colony that flourished there. Although such a theory is not impossible, it would place Atlantis thousands of miles east of its legendary site; besides, it is well known that there were many active volcanoes in the Mediterranean (and there still are—Vesuvius, Etna, Stromboli, etc.)—so there is no necessary justification to identify Atlantis with Santorini.

Auld Reekie

A nickname given in former times to Edinburgh, Scotland, on account of the pall of smoke, or "reek," that hung above the city in the days before clean-air legislation. *Auld* represents the Scottish pronunciation of "old."

Auntie

A nickname for the British Broadcasting Corporation, coined in a spirit of exasperated affection. It refers to the BBC's attitude toward its audience, and toward its employees, which is seen as being kindly but often fussy and old-fashioned. Compare **Beeb, Portland Place.**

Australasia

A vague collective term incorporating an indefinite number of territories in the southwest Pacific Ocean. In its most restricted use, it can refer simply to Australia and New Zealand, although it usually includes the nearby islands of Melanesia. It can also, however, embrace the farther-flung islands of Micronesia and Polynesia, when it becomes almost a synonym for Oceania. In addition, it is often used to refer to the British Commonwealth countries of the area: Australia, New Zealand, Fiji, and Western Samoa. See also **Oceania**.

Automobile Capital of the World, the

A nickname of Detroit, Michigan.

Auto State, the

A nickname of Michigan.

Avebury

A village in Wiltshire, England, site of one of the most extensive ceremonial locales in Europe, encompassing more than 28 acres. The ceremonial structures are, in some respects, similar to those at Stonehenge; on the other hand, the area is much larger than Stonehenge and involves structures that, successively, span more than 2000 years, up to the end of the Bronze Age, or about 1000 B.C.

Avenue of the Americas

The official name given to Sixth Avenue, in New York City, in the 1940s to honor the Latin American countries. Few New Yorkers use the name, which is inconveniently long for a people who are always in a hurry, and (as in this book) it is habitually referred to as Sixth Avenue. Its southern end is at Canal Street; its northern terminus at 59th Street, where it ends at Central Park. During the past three decades, since the removal of the elevated "subway" that blighted most of its length, the upper part, from 40th Street northward, has seen a revitalization through the erection of modern office buildings, some of which are part of **Rockefeller Center** (*q.v.*). **Radio City Music Hall** (*q.v.*) stands at the corner of Sixth Avenue and 50th Street.

Ayers Rock

A huge, red sandstone rock, about 1100 feet high, two miles long, and eight around, situated in the southwestern part of the Northern Territory of Australia, southwest of Alice Springs. Long a favorite of rock-climbers and vacationers, the caves at its base were long the habitation of aborigines, and rock paintings can be seen there. The nearest towns are some distance away, and Ayers Rock is regarded as being beyond the frontiers of civilization.

Azania

A name given by African nationalists to the territory occupied by the Republic of South Africa. It was applied to a fictitious African nation by the English writer Evelyn Waugh in his novel, *Black Mischief* (1932).

Aztec State, the

A nickname of Arizona, so called after the old ruins erroneously believed to have been built by the Aztecs because they had Aztec names.

B, the

A nickname for Bridewell, the former London prison, closed in the mid 19th century; it has become a metonym for prison in general, especially in Liverpudlian slang.

Babylon

The capital of ancient Mesopotamia, and a name that has come to be used symbolically for the corruption and depravity of great metropolises. In Protestant polemic of the Reformation and later times it was applied to Rome and to the Roman Catholic church in general, and more recently it has been adopted by the Rastafarians to refer to the oppressiveness and wickedness of western (white) society.

Baby State, the

A former nickname of Arizona, so called because until the 1959 entry of Alaska and Hawaii, it was the last state to join the Union (1912).

Back Bay

The name of the area west of downtown Boston along the Charles River from the Public Garden west to the suburb of Brookline, where until the 1920s lived the wealthiest families, often referred to as the *Boston Brahmins* (from *Brahmin caste*, the highest class in the Hindu religion). When they began to move to the suburbs in the 1920s, the long rows of beautiful townhouses on tree-lined streets were converted into apartments, which are now occupied by college students and young, upwardly mobile, white-collar workers. Many of Boston's finest stores and best restaurants are to be found here, as well as the Museum of Fine Arts, the Institute of Contemporary Art, Symphony Hall, the New England Conservatory of Music (the country's oldest music school), and Fenway Park, home of the Boston Red Sox baseball team. Two modern high-rise complexes are also here: Prudential Center has apartment buildings, a hotel, a civic auditorium, many shops, and the 52-story Prudential Tower Office building; in Copley Square, a few blocks northeast, is the tallest building in New England, the 60-story John Hancock Tower, in the glass sides of which are reflected Trinity Church and the main branch of the Boston Public Library, which has over 3½ million volumes.

Backbone of England, the

An epithet for the Pennines, in England, a range of hills from the Cheviot Hills, near Scotland at the north, to the Trent, the main river in the Midlands.

Backbone of the Confederacy

A nickname of the Mississippi River during the Civil War when most of the supplies for the Confederate forces had to be shipped on it, through the port of New Orleans, after Union ships blockaded the east coast.

Backs, the

A series of lawns running down to the Cam River in the center of Cambridge, on the opposite bank of the river from Queens', King's, Clare, Trinity, and St. John's Colleges. Particularly attractive in Spring, they offer an unrivaled vista of many of Cambridge's finest buildings; the view of King's College Chapel is especially famous.

Baden-Baden of America, the

A nickname of Hot Springs, Arkansas.

Badger State, the

The official nickname of Wisconsin, so called because the early lead miners lived underground, as badgers do.

Bad Lands, the

A depressingly grim region of southwestern South Dakota, extending into northwestern Nebraska, that is the result of deforestation and natural erosion.

Bagshot

Perhaps it is the connotations of the name—bagging anything that moves within the sights of one's shotgun—but the town of Bagshot inevitably suggests peppery comic-strip retired colonels, mustaches abristle. This part of Surrey, southwest of London, is indeed army country, with

Camberley (home of the Royal Military Academy) just a few miles down the road.

Baked Bean State, the

A nickname of Massachusetts. See also **Beantown.**

Bakerloo

One of the lines of the London Underground. When it was opened in 1906 it ran only between Baker Street and Waterloo—hence its name, originally a nickname—but it has since been extended out to Watford in the north and **Elephant and Castle** (*q.v.*) in the south.

Baker Street

A large thoroughfare in central London that leads down from Regent's Park to Oxford Street. It is a rather drab, nondescript street, its most noteworthy building probably being the monolithic headquarters of Marks and Spencer, one of Britain's leading department stores. But its most famous address does not exist and never existed: 221B, fictional address of the rooms let by Sherlock Holmes, the paragon of literary detectives. Here he would meet his clients and conduct experiments, and from here he would sally forth with Dr. Watson in pursuit of murderers, jewel thieves, kidnappers, and spies, or deploy his band of "Baker Street irregulars," young street urchins, in search of clues. It is no doubt more than a coincidence that his creator, Arthur Conan Doyle, a doctor, once had his consulting rooms in Devonshire Place, off Harley Street, just a few blocks from Baker Street.

Balkans, the

The area occupied by the countries of the mountainous Balkan peninsula in southeastern Europe: in the present day, Yugoslavia, Rumania, Albania, Bulgaria, the European part of Turkey, and Greece (although many people would feel that only the northern and northeastern parts of Greece—Macedonia and Thrace—are truly Balkan). Until the early 20th century, however, the region was divided into a far larger number of states, including Bosnia, Herzegovina, Serbia, Montenegro, Croatia, Moldavia, and Transylvania. As the area where the Turkish, Russian, and Austro-Hungarian empires jarred against each other, the Balkans became one of the great political flashpoints of the later 19th century, and many statesmen and diplomats retired defeated by the famously irresoluble "Balkan problem".

Balmoral Castle

A residence of the British royal family, in Aberdeenshire, Scotland, built in 1856 on the site of a former, smaller castle, which had belonged originally to the Farquharsons. Prince Albert acquired it in 1847. It is today occupied by the Queen during the summer months; it is rumored that the other members of the royal family dislike Balmoral, but the Queen insists. . . .

baloney dollar

The nickname of the devalued dollar when the U. S. went off the gold standard in 1933, so called because no matter how thin baloney is sliced, it still retains its basic characteristics.

Baltic States

Three states, Estonia, Latvia, and Lithuania, bordering the east coast of the Baltic sea and part of the Soviet Union. Prior to becoming independent countries in 1918, they had been ruled variously by the Danes, Swedes, Poles, Germans, and Russians and were part of the Russian czar's empire before World War I. In 1940 they were annexed by Russia.

Bamboo Curtain, the

A name used to characterize the ideological and cultural barrier between Communist China and its satellites, and the West. It was coined in imitation of the Iron Curtain, the boundary of East European Communism, and was used particularly in the 1950s and '60s, when China pursued a policy of hostile insularity. Compare **Iron Curtain**.

Bananaland

A not very polite nickname for the state of Queensland, Australia, where bananas are a prominent crop. Queenslanders are known uncomplimentarily as Bananalanders or banana benders.

banana republic

A derisive nickname, infrequent in current usage, for any of several Central or South American countries. The name was used especially in reference to those countries that were under the economic influence (hence, political control) of the United Fruit Company, a combine that purchased much of the produce of those nations.

Banbury Cross

The original of the nursery rime that begins, "Ride a cockhorse to Banbury Cross," was destroyed by Puritans in 1602; it was replaced in 1859. The borough of Banbury, in northern Oxfordshire, England is known mainly for its spiced currant cakes but also for its ale and cheese.

Bank, the

A road junction at the very heart of the City of London, which takes its name from the **Bank of England** (*q.v.*), on its north side. Also to be found here are the Royal Exchange and the Mansion House, official residence of the Lord Mayor of London. Seven heavily congested roads converge on the

Bank's triangular space, including Threadneedle Street, Cornhill, Lombard Street, and Poultry.

Bank of England, the

The central bank of England and Wales, which acts as the British government's bankers and helps to implement many aspects of its fiscal policy. It was founded in 1694, and nationalized in 1946. It is lodged in a suitably monolithic building in the City of London, on the north side of the Bank; particularly impressive and evocative of hoarded bullion is its massive blank outer wall, through which no ray of light or prying eye can penetrate. See also **Old Lady of Threadneedle Street**.

Bankside

In the late 20th century, this road, on the south bank of the Thames in London, just across the river from St. Paul's cathedral, is probably best known for its power station, which dominates the surrounding scene. But it was once much more lively. In Elizabethan times and later, Bankside was a bustling, thriving area that teemed with slightly disreputable joie de vivre; there were taverns, theaters (including Shakespeare's *Globe*), gardens, brothels, and abundant public entertainments of the bull- and bear-baiting variety. (A lane nearby is still called Bear Gardens.) In those days, prostitutes were often known as "sisters of the Bank."

Banner State, the

A nickname of Texas, probably because it polls the largest vote in national elections.

Banzai Pipeline

A tube-like configuration of a large, slow-breaking wave at the beach at Waikiki, in Hawaii, regarded as an idyllic opportunity for surfing enthusiasts. The name *banzai* comes from a Japanese cry (meaning 'ten thousand years') used by Japanese attacking soldiers in World War II. The association is between their reckless, suicidal spirit and the extreme danger in surfing through the Pipeline.

Barbary Coast, the

A historical name for the Islamic lands along the north coast of Africa, from the Egyptian border to the Atlantic. The Barbary States were Tripolitania, Tunisia, Algeria, and Morocco. The Barbary Coast was notorious in ancient and medieval times as a haunt of pirates. The name comes from the same source as the word *barbarian*, since the Saracens who lived there were regarded by Christians as heathens.

Barbican, the

A site in the City of London, to the northeast of St. Paul's Cathedral. The area lies just outside the site of the ancient city walls (part of the original

Roman wall is on display there), and the name *Barbican* comes from a word meaning 'watchtower or gateway in a wall.' In the 19th century it was London's garment district. Devastated by bombing in World War II, extensive postwar redevelopment plans led first to a grouping of luxury apartment blocks and finally to the Barbican Centre, an amalgam of theaters, cinemas, galleries, and a concert hall, opened in 1982. This building, usually known simply as *the Barbican*, was derided initially for its mazelike complexity, but quickly established itself as an essential part of London's cultural scene.

Barrio, the

The name given to any American city neighborhood the residents of which are mainly Hispanic, especially Puerto Rican.

Barset

Also known as Barsetshire, it is probably the most famous fictional county in English literature. Anthony Trollope wrote a series of novels in which it is featured, from *The Warden* (1855) to *The Last Chronicle of Barset* (1867), many of which are concerned with back-stairs ecclesiastical intrigue in the cathedral city of Barchester (modeled on Winchester).

Bart's

A nickname given to St. Bartholomew's Hospital and Medical School, in the City of London to the south of Smithfield. It was founded in 1123 and is the oldest hospital in London still on its original site.

Battersea

An inner-city suburb of London, on the south bank of the Thames, opposite Chelsea to the north. It has a rather grimy image, probably because it is firmly linked in the public imagination with Battersea Power Station (see **Nine Elms**), a powerful icon of urban industrialization; but in fact in the 1980s it is something of an up-and-coming area, with people moving in and renovating. Other well-known Battersea landmarks are the Funfair, which opened in 1951 as part of the Festival of Britain celebrations but no longer survives, and Battersea Dogs' Home, London's main dog pound.

Battle above *or* in the Clouds

Lookout Mountain, the site of the Battle of Chattanooga in 1863, is so high that it was said the soldiers were obscured by the clouds.

Battle-Born State, the

A nickname of Nevada, so called because it was admitted to the Union during the Civil War.

Battlebridge

Until the 1830s, the name for the area of north London now known as King's Cross. It is preserved in *Battle Bridge Road*, near King's Cross Station. See also **King's Cross, 1**.

Battleground of Freedom, the

A nickname of Kansas, so called in reference to the ten years of arguments, after passage of the Kansas-Nebraska Bill in 1854, as to whether slavery would be permitted.

Bay Horse

A nickname of Boston, Massachusetts.

Bayreuth

A city in Bavaria where, in the mid 18th century, the Margravine Wilhelmine, sister of Frederick the Great of Prussia, sponsored the building of a magnificent opera house as a focal point for her interest in the arts. The composer Richard Wagner (1813–83) settled there in 1872 and was present at the dedication of the Festival Theater. In 1876, the first complete performance of *The Ring* was given there, and 1882 saw the first performance of *Parsifal*. In the past century, Bayreuth has become firmly associated with Wagner, and his music and operas are performed there regularly, attended by devotees from all over the world.

Bay State

A nickname of Massachusetts.

Bay Street

The name for the financial district of Toronto, Canada.

Bayswater

A district in west London, to the north of Kensington Gardens and the west of Paddington. Like Earl's Court to the south, this is essentially an area of one-room apartments—a "bed-sitter-land," as the British call it—with a largely floating population of young people starting out on city life, and it has an appropriate air of slightly scruffy liveliness and impermanence. The grand houses of former generations are dowagers in decline.

Beachy Head

A 575-foot chalk cliff near Eastbourne, on the south coast of England, atop which is a favorite area for picnics when the weather permits. Its name comes from the French *beau chef* 'beautiful headland' and was spelt *Beuchef* in the 13th century.

Beacon Hill

North of Boston Common rises a hill where beacon fires were lit in the 1600s to signal ships, and which, since the 1700s, has given its name to a fashionable neighborhood of narrow cobblestoned streets, brick sidewalks, and gaslights. The first white settler in Boston, William Blackstone, was the first to build a home there in 1620. Its elegant brick townhouses are home to some of Boston's oldest and most distinguished families. The State House is located on the southern edge, and brick apartment buildings line the northern slope.

Bean, L. L.

See **L. L. Bean.**

Beantown

A nickname of Boston, Massachusetts. See also **Baked Bean State.**

Bear State, the

A nickname of Arkansas and Kentucky.

Beautiful City by the Sea

A nickname of Portland, Maine.

Beaver State, the

The official nickname of Oregon.

Bedlam

In 1247 the priory of St. Mary of Bethlehem (or Bedlam, as it was often known then) was founded in the Bishopsgate area of the City of London. As early as 1402 it is mentioned as being used as a lunatic asylum. It was burnt down in the Great Fire of 1666, and in 1676 a new Bedlam asylum was built a few streets away to the west. Finally, in 1815, it was moved south of the Thames to Lambeth. It has long since given place to more enlightened institutions (its former buildings now house the Imperial War Museum), but echoes of the chaos and terror that prevailed in mental hospitals of the not so distant past remain in the current application of the term *bedlam* to any scene of noisy confusion.

Bedloe's Island

From 1758 the name of the twelve-acre island in Upper New York Bay southwest of Manhattan Island (since 1956 officially named Liberty Island), on which the Statue of Liberty stands. The land was privately owned until 1800 when it was given to the U. S. government; in 1841, a fort with the plan of an eleven-point star was built there and named Fort Wood, after an officer killed in the War of 1812. The foundations of the fort are the base on which the statue stands. The island was named after Isaac Bedloe, its first owner.

Beeb, the

A nickname for the British Broadcasting Corporation, based on the pronunciation of its initial letters, BBC. Compare **Auntie, Portland Place.**

Beef State, the

A nickname of Texas.

Beehive of Industry

A nickname of Providence, Rhode Island.

Beehive State, the

The official nickname of Utah.

Belgravia

A fashionable residential area in the West End of London, to the south of Hyde Park. It was laid out in 1825 on land owned by the Grosvenor family, whose country estate in Leicestershire is called Belgrave. It assumed its position as the high-rent place to live in London as **Mayfair** (*q.v.*) was given over more and more to commerce, and it continues to hold its place, even though in the 1980s one's neighbor is more likely to be an Arab oil merchant than an English duke. See also **Sloane Square**.

Belisha beacon

A black-and-white-banded pole topped with a yellow glass globe which is placed on both sides of pedestrian ("zebra") crossings in England as a warning to motorists. It was introduced during the mid 1930s by Leslie Hore-Belisha, the Minister of Transport.

Belle City of the Bluegrass Regions

A nickname of Lexington, Kentucky.

Belle City (of the Lakes)

A nickname of Racine, Wisconsin.

Bellevue

A major hospital of the City of New York, situated below 34th Street on First Avenue. Although it is a large general hospital, it is best known for its psychiatric ward where violent psychotics, would-be suicides, and intransigent criminals are taken, often under restraint by the police, for confinement and treatment. Its name has become a symbol of uncontrollable behavior and insanity and has given rise to expressions like, "You're ready for Bellevue." See also **Bloomingdale's.**

Benelux

In 1948 three northwest European states, Belgium, the Netherlands, and Luxembourg, formed a customs union to which the name *Benelux* was given. In 1960 this was expanded to a more general economic union, allowing free circulation of people, goods, money, etc., among all three, and over the years they have come to be known collectively as the *Benelux countries*. Compare **Low Countries**.

Berkeley Square

A square (pronounced "Barkly") in Mayfair, in the West End of London, to the southeast of Grosvenor Square. In former times it contained many elegant town houses, but since World War II several of these have been replaced by rather bleak modern office blocks. There are still trees in the square, but in the 1980s it is less likely than ever that a nightingale would ever sing there.

Berlin Wall, the

In August 1961, the German Democratic Republic (East Germany) erected a barrier, then a concrete wall six feet high, with barbed wire on top, to seal off the part of Berlin it had occupied since the end of World War II from that occupied by the Federal Republic of Germany (West Germany). Prior to that, millions of people from Soviet-controlled countries had passed through Berlin to settle in the West. After the Wall was completed, such passage from east to west was virtually brought to a halt, and it was not uncommon for those who attempted it to be shot dead by the guards who man the turrets set above the Wall. Officially, East Berlin did not become a part of East Germany till 1966.

Bermondsey Market

A street market, formerly the Caledonian Market, now officially the Bermondsey and New Caledonian Market, situated in Bermondsey Street, on the south bank of the Thames, near Tower Bridge, in London. All sorts of wares are sold in its stalls, mostly antique and rummage, and it is open only on Fridays. There is also a large indoor area of stalls. See also **Caledonian Market.**

Bermuda Triangle, the

A roughly triangular area of the western North Atlantic Ocean, off the eastern seaboard of the U. S., that is notorious for the unexplained disappearance of planes and ships that venture into it. It covers a very large extent of sea (about one and a half million square miles in total, with its three corners at the tip of Florida, just below New York, and a point to the east of the island of Bermuda), and records of ships missing there or being mysteriously abandoned by their crews stretch back to the mid 19th century. Since that time about fifty vessels and twenty aircraft have been reported as the Triangle's victims. Perhaps the most celebrated case is that of five bombers that set out from Fort Lauderdale Naval Air Station, Florida, in 1945: after radioing back that they were lost, they were never seen or heard of again.

Bernese Oberland, the

The foothills and lower northern slopes of the Alps in south-central Switzerland, to the south of Interlaken. It is the quintessential Switzerland of mountain chalets, cowbells, alpenhorns, Emmenthaler (Swiss) cheese, and edelweiss. It lies mostly in the southern part of the canton of Bern.

Bessarabia

A region at the extreme southwest of the Soviet Union, on the borders of Romania. As a frontier area it was long the subject of disputes between the Russians and the Ottoman Empire, changing hands several times during the 19th century, until at the end of World War I it was occupied by Romania. It was ceded to the Soviet Union in 1947 and is now mostly in the Moldavian Soviet Socialist Republic.

Beverly Hills

A small city (1980 population 32,367) surrounded by Los Angeles. Mostly a low-density residential area with large houses on large lots, it has a commercial area in the southern part along and near Wilshire Boulevard. The population was only 674 in 1920, but it grew 250% in the next decade as it became a favored residence of people associated with the motion-picture business in nearby Hollywood. The relative affluence and notoriety of its citizens have given it a worldwide fame out of all proportion to its size.

Beverly Hills Hotel

The name of a hotel located in the heart of the residential area of Beverly Hills, California, on Sunset Boulevard. One of its dining rooms, the Polo Lounge, is a favorite haunt of people in the entertainment business at breakfast and lunch.

Bhopal

A city in the heart of India, the capital of the huge state of Madhya Pradesh, which lurched into unwanted fame in December 1984 when a calamitous leak from a tank of methyl isocyanate in the Union Carbide chemical plant there brought death and suffering to many thousands of its inhabitants. From being a pleasant but anonymous industrialized city, Bhopal turned overnight into a symbol of the uncaring exploitation of cheap Third World labor by rapacious Western capitalists—or of the ramshackle safety procedures in Indian factories, depending upon one's point of view. Compare **Flixborough.**

Bible Belt, the

An area of the United States, chiefly in the South and Southwest and including Tennessee, parts of Kentucky, Arkansas, Oklahoma, Texas, etc., characterized by fervid religious fundamentalism. Its name derives from the success of itinerant Bible salesmen in the region.

Big Apple, the

A nickname of New York City.

Big Ben

As most British schoolboys know, Big Ben is not really the gothic clock tower at the northern end of the Houses of Parliament in London; it is the huge 13-ton bell that hangs inside it and rings out the hours after the famous Westminster chimes. It was installed in 1859 and gets its name from the nickname of Sir Benjamin Hall, who was Commissioner of Works at the time. Gradually over the years the tower, a potent symbol of parliamentary democracy around the world, has taken over the bell's name.

Big Bend

The epithet for the extreme western portion of Texas, so called because its southern and western boundaries are formed by a natural bend in the Rio Grande, which separates Texas from Mexico.

Big Bend State, the

A nickname of Tennessee, a translation of the Indian name for the Tennessee River.

big Bertha

The nickname of a World War I German long-range gun, a reference to the daughter of the manufacturer, Friedrich Alfred Krupp.

Big Board, the

The nickname for the listing of companies with stocks sold on the New York Stock Exchange, especially in contradistinction to the listings of the American Stock Exchange and other stock exchanges in New York and elsewhere.

Big D

A nickname for Dallas, Texas.

Big Dipper

An American name for a part of the constellation Ursa Major, so called from the outline formed by seven of its stars.

Big Hole, the

The nickname of a huge, funnel-shaped crater, some 1500 feet in diameter, situated at Kimberley, South Africa. Its core was formerly a diamond-bearing volcanic plug, or pipe, of kimberlite, the portion above ground called *Colesberg Kopje*, or *Colesberg Hill*. Mining removed the core to a depth of 3600 feet and yielded three tons (14,504,375 carats) of diamonds. The crater served as a place of refuge during the siege of Kimberley; since 1921 it has been used as a reservoir.

Big Inch

A pipeline for conveying natural gas from Texas to the Northeast, constructed in the 1950s and actually 24 inches in diameter.

Big Mac, the

The nickname for a hamburger-shaped formation of quasars, discovered through the four-meter mapping telescope at Pisco Elqui, Chile, by Arturo Gómez. Its formal name is the Gomez Object, and it is so referred to in scientific journals.

Big Sky Country

A nickname of Montana.

Big Tex

The nickname of a statue, some eighty feet tall, used at the annual Texas State Fair, held in October at Dallas. Dressed in western attire, Big Tex is wired to speak greetings to fair visitors.

Big Town

A former nickname of Chicago.

Billingsgate

London's largest fish market, which took its name from one of the old gates of the City of London. It was formerly situated in Lower Thames Street, near the Tower of London, but in 1982 it moved to a new site further east, on the Isle of Dogs, near the old West India Docks. Billingsgate porters were famous for the colorfulness of their language. This led to *billingsgate* being used as a synonym for 'coarse abuse': "We disapprove the constant billingsgate poured on them officially," wrote Thomas Jefferson in 1799. The word is now used infrequently.

Billy Goat Tavern

A short-order café and bar in Chicago just north of the Loop, popular with newspaper people who work nearby. The Billy Goat's colorful owner, Sam Sianis, recently achieved national celebrity of a sort as the model for a character portrayed on television by the late comedian John Belushi; although neither the Billy Goat nor its owner was referred to by name, to patrons the setting and the distinctively accented calls for a "chizzborger, chizzborger" were unmistakable references.

Biograph Theater

A classic "Art Deco" moviehouse on the Near North Side of Chicago, famous for having been patronized on July 22, 1934, by "Public Enemy Number One," bankrobber John Dillinger, just before dying in a volley of FBI bullets, in an alley a few yards south. Dillinger had been hiding out nearby in the apartment of Anna Sage—the notorious "Lady in Red"—who, with another woman, had accompanied him to the Biograph after first alerting the FBI, which had then set up an ambush. (The movie that Dillinger and his companions saw was *Manhattan Melodrama* starring Clark Gable, William Powell, and Myrna Loy.)

Birdland

A former nightclub theater, opened in 1948 on Broadway, in New York City, mainly to provide a setting for bebop, the style of jazz then in its emergent phase. It was named for Charlie "Bird" Parker, the saxophonist regarded, along with Dizzy Gillespie and others, as a chief proponent of the genre.

Birmingham of America, the

A nickname of Pittsburgh, Pennsylvania.

Birthplace of American Liberty, the

A nickname claimed by Lexington, Massachusetts, and Philadelphia, Pennsylvania. The first battle of the Revolutionary War was fought on the Lexington Commons by the Minute Men in 1775 ("the shot heard round the world"), while Philadelphia is the location of Independence Hall, the seat of the Continental Congress, and the site of the signing of the Declaration of Independence.

Birthplace of Aviation, the

A nickname of Dayton, Ohio, so called because it was the home of Wilbur and Orville Wright. See also **Cradle of Aviation.**

Birthplace of Baseball

A nickname of Cooperstown, New York, based on an erroneous belief that it was the site of the first baseball diamond designed by Abner Doubleday in 1839. Nevertheless, Doubleday Field there is baseball's official home, and the Baseball Hall of Fame is there.

Birthplace of California, the

A nickname of San Diego.

Birthplace of Canada

A nickname of Charlottetown, Prince Edward Island.

Bison City

A nickname of Buffalo, New York.

Blackbird

A United States spy plane capable of flight at Mach 3 at extremely high altitudes.

Black Country, the

In the 19th century, the southern part of Staffordshire, to the northwest of Birmingham in the West Midlands of England, was a concentrated center of coalmining and iron-founding. The noise and smell of heavy industry were ever present, and the resulting slow drizzle of soot built up a black patina on the Victorian buildings of Wolverhampton, Wednesbury, Walsall, Dudley, and West Bromwich that gave the area its name. More ecologically acceptable light industry has since moved in, but the Black Country is still far from being one of England's beauty spots.

Black Death, the

An epidemic, probably of bubonic plague, that killed about one third of the population of Europe, Asia, and north Africa in the middle of the 14th century and is generally regarded as the greatest disaster ever to have affected western Europe.

Black Diamonds

A nickname for coal.

Black Forest, the

A mountainous area east of the Rhine, in Germany. Its name, translated from German *Schwarzwald*, derives from those regions covered with dense forests of pine trees. In western lore, it is associated with cuckoo clocks (which are, indeed, made there, along with toys and other products) and with Black Forest cake, a rich chocolate layer cake made with cherries (which is probably named for its color rather than its place of origin).

Blackfriars

An area of central London on the north bank of the Thames, to the south of the eastern end of Fleet Street. From 1276 to 1538 the Dominicans (or Black Friars) had a monastery here, and since at least the 16th century their name has been applied to the district. Shakespeare refers to it in *Henry VIII*. It is the site of a busy rail terminus bringing commuters from the southern suburbs to work in the City. Compare **Whitefriars**.

Black Friday

1. In England, December 6, 1745, when a financial panic was caused in London on the news that Charles Edward Stuart ("Bonnie Prince Charlie" or "the Young Pretender") had marched into Derby.
2. In England, May 11, 1866, when the failure of Overend and Gurney, a London banking house, occasioned financial panic.
3. In the United States, September 24, 1869, when a panic in the securities market in New York was brought about by the government's release of gold bullion into the market, which Jay Gould and James Fisk were illegally trying to corner. That day, the price of $100 in gold dropped from $163½ to $133 in paper money, wiping out many speculators.

Black Gold

A nickname for oil.

Black Hills, the

A mountain range in eastern Wyoming and western South Dakota, so called because its forested slopes have a dark appearance when viewed at a distance. It is an area rich in minerals.

Black Hole (of Calcutta)

A barracks room about 14 by 18 feet at Fort William, in Calcutta, India, where 146 Europeans were incarcerated by the Nawab of Bengal, on June 20, 1756. It was reported that by the following morning only twenty-three had survived but later research showed that only forty-three were unaccounted for. Ever since, however, the name has been used as a metaphor for a confining, dark, dungeon-like place.

Blackpool

The quintessential seaside resort of northern England, on the Lancashire coast. From Victorian times onward it was working people's great vacation magnet. Its attractions have become almost proverbial: donkey rides along the seven miles of sand; amusement arcades on the Golden Mile; the Tower built in 1895 in imitation of the Eiffel Tower, with the ballroom below it; vaudeville shows; and of course the famous Blackpool illuminations, a spectacular display of colored lights in various fanciful patterns representing anything from animals and birds to spacecraft. With the increasing cheapness of foreign travel after World War II, Spain's **Costa Brava** (*q.v.*) and **Costa del Sol** (*q.v.*) began to replace Blackpool as a holiday mecca, but the English resort retains its position in Northern folklore.

blackthorn winter

An English nickname for a period of cooler than normal weather in May, associated with the days of the "ice saints," Mamertus, Pancras, and Gervais, on May 11, 12, and 13, respectively.

Blackwall Tunnel

A vehicular tunnel beneath the Thames, east of London, recently connected with the M-25, an orbital motorway around the city. It is known as the site of frequent traffic jams.

Blackwater State, the

A nickname of Nebraska, so called because its streams are colored by the black prairie soil.

Bleeding Kansas

A nickname for Kansas in the mid 19th century, when it became a battle-ground between Abolitionists and pro-slavery partisans. The Abolitionist stronghold of Lawrence was attacked in 1855 and 1856 (when some impor-tant buildings were burnt), and again in 1863, when William Quantrill led a raid in which the men were massacred and many buildings were de-stroyed.

Blenheim Palace

A magnificent palace given by the Parliament of Great Britain to the Duke of Marlborough in gratitude for his victory at Blenheim, August 13, 1704, on the Danube, in Bavaria, defeating the Bavarians and the French in a decisive battle of the War of the Spanish Succession. It is said that the arrangement of the trees in the park of the palace match the formation of the troops at the battle.

Blighty

A slang term used by British servicemen abroad to refer to Britain. It originated with the British army in India, and comes from the Hindi word *bilyati* 'foreign land.' It is associated particularly with World Wars I and II, but remains in use in the second half of the 20th century.

Blizzard State, the

A nickname of South Dakota and Texas.

Blonde Beauty of the Lakes, the

A nickname of Milwaukee, Wisconsin.

Bloomie's

A nickname for Bloomingdale's department store, between 59th and 60th streets and Lexington and Third avenues, in New York City. Formerly, just another large department store, it recast its image entirely in the 1950s by an extensive program of interior redecoration and by promoting itself as the "in" place to shop for a new generation of the young at heart and the upscale in pocket. During the 1960s, when the upwardly mobile were moving into the new apartment buildings sprouting up along upper Third Avenue and the side streets of the **Upper East Side** (*q.v.*), it acquired its affectionate nickname. Any associations its formal name might have had with **Bloomingdale's** (*q.v.*) belongs to a generation long gone.

Bloomingdale's

A former lunatic asylum at 116th Street near the Hudson River in New York City, replaced in part by Columbia University when it moved from 50th Street and Madison-Fifth avenues to its present site early in the 20th century. Widely known at the time, the asylum gave rise to expressions like, "You're ready for Bloomingdale's." See also **Bellevue.**

Bloomsbury

An area in central London, to the northeast of Oxford Street, in which the British Museum and many of the buildings of London University are situated. At its northeast corner is Gordon Square, where in 1904 the novelist Virginia Woolf and her sister Vanessa Bell came to live. The coterie of writers and artists that gathered around them in the ensuing years has become universally known as the Bloomsbury Group, an avant-garde assault on Victorian stuffiness in art and morality that stressed above all else the search for the good, the true, and the beautiful. It included, among many others, the essayist Lytton Strachey, the novelists E. M. Forster and David Garnett, the painters Roger Fry and Duncan Grant, and the economist John Maynard Keynes.

Bluegrass Capital, the

A nickname of Lexington, Kentucky, so called because of the abundant grass of that type on which their Thoroughbreds thrive. See also **Bluegrass State.**

Bluegrass State

The official nickname of Kentucky. See also **Bluegrass Capital.**

Blue Hen State, the *or* Blue Hen's Chickens State

A nickname of Delaware, so called in reference to an incident during the Revolutionary War: two game cocks of a blue hen that belonged to a Captain Caldwell, of Kent County, fought so furiously and courageously that one of the Captain's men cried, "We're sons of the Old Blue Hen and we're game to the end." Thereafter, the regiment was known as "Blue Hen's Chickens."

blue laws

Originally, a series of stringent regulations, printed on blue paper, imposed on the citizens of some New England colonies in the 17th century by the Puritans based at New Haven, Connecticut. From a history of the state published in 1781, the laws seem unduly harsh in terms of today's standards, e.g.:

> The judge shall determine controversies without a jury.
> Married persons must live together or be imprisoned.
> A wife shall be good evidence against her husband.

But it must be remembered that contemporary laws (in England) provided for amputation of the hand upon conviction of the theft of a loaf of bread. The term *blue law* has come into modern use to designate any regulation felt to be unwarrantedly strict or severe.

Blue Law State, the

A nickname of Connecticut.

blue-light district

In Cartagena, Colombia, the name for the "red-light" district.

Blue Ridge Mountains, the

The main eastern range of the Appalachian Mountains that runs from southern Pennsylvania to northern Georgia, their name deriving from the blue tone that their forested slopes have when seen at a distance. The most famous section is in Virginia, separating the Shenandoah Valley from the Piedmont region. The outstanding beauty of their high peaks and valleys attracts thousands of tourists every year, and they are immortalized in the song *The Trail of the Lonesome Pine*, by Ballard MacDonald and Harry Carroll (1913), which begins, "In the Blue Ridge Mountains of Virginia . . ."

Bluff City

A nickname shared by Hannibal, Missouri, Natchez, Mississippi, and Memphis, Tennessee.

Boardwalk, the

A 60-foot-wide, wooden platform built several feet above the sand alongside the Atlantic Ocean in New Jersey, stretching for 4½ miles along the beach at Atlantic City and a further two miles along that in Ventnor. Originally constructed in 1870, the present one was completed in 1896. It borders the entrances to many of the hotels and of the casinos that have sprung up since the state enacted legislation allowing gambling, in 1976. Atlantic City has long been a favorite holiday spot, especially during the 1920s and '30s, and the Boardwalk, a focal point for amusement, entertainment, shopping, and eating, formed a promenade along which generations of visitors have been wheeled in the traditional high-back chairs, once pushed by hand, now usually pedaled or powered by battery. The inventor of the popular board game, Monopoly, came from Atlantic City and named the positions on the board after streets and places in the city. As all players in America know, "The Boardwalk" is the most expensive "property" in the game, and an opponent whose token lands on the Boardwalk must pay the highest "rent."

Bodleian Library

A major resource library at Oxford University, named for its founder, Sir Thomas Bodley (1545–1613) who, after his retirement from foreign service, devoted his efforts and his fortune to the expansion of the library, which had been established in 1327 but almost ruined under Edward VI by those bent on university "reform."

Bognor Regis

A salubrious seaside resort on the Sussex coast of England, to the west of Brighton. Its heyday was probably in the late 18th century, when it was a favorite watering-place of the aristocracy. Its splendor has faded since then, particularly with the decline of the Great British Seaside Holiday, but it retains its fair share of retirement bungalows (see **Costa Geriatrica**). Its title *Regis* 'King's' was conferred on it in 1929 by a grateful King George V after convalescing there, but it seems his private view of the place was not always so charitable: a few years later, when he was in fact in his last illness, a courtier, thinking to cheer him up, remarked, "If your Majesty continues to make such excellent progress, he will soon be able to enjoy a few weeks' holiday at Bognor"; muttered the king, under his breath: "Bugger Bognor!"

Bohemia

An area in central Europe, which now forms the Czech-speaking part of western Czechoslovakia. In the early Middle Ages it was an independent kingdom; then in 1526 it became absorbed into the Hapsburg Empire, and remained in German hands until World War I. Its name has come to be used, without a capital letter, for a resort of the artistic and unconventional because in former times the gypsies, who had a rather vagabondish reputation, were thought to come from Bohemia.

Bonanza State, the

A nickname of Montana.

Bondi Beach

Australia's most famous beach, on the Pacific coast of New South Wales, to the south of Sydney. Always crowded, it is a mecca for surfers.

Bond Street

A road in the West End of London, running north and south between Oxford Street and Piccadilly. The southern section is known as Old Bond Street, the northern part New Bond Street. Often nicknamed *the high street of* **Mayfair** (*q.v.*), it is proverbial around the world for its dazzling array of exclusive and expensive boutiques, art dealers' galleries, jewelers, and perfumers. Indeed, it seems that any establishment that wishes to be fashionable only has to add *of Bond Street* to its name to achieve instant cachet.

Boomer State, the

A nickname of Oklahoma.

Boot Hill

The name of a hill in Dodge City, Kansas, so called because only people who were killed in gunfights were buried there, said to have "died with their boots on."

Border, the

In Britain, an epithet conventionally used for the boundary between England and Scotland. *North of the Border* is understood to mean Scotland;
South of the Border, England. In addition, the hilly area of Scotland contiguous with the boundary is generally known as *the Borders*. The name was
made official in 1975 when the Borders region was formed from the
former counties of Berwick, Peebles, Roxburgh, Selkirk, and parts of Midlothian. The area's literary fame rests on the *Border Ballads*, a collection of
local songs and verses compiled by Sir Walter Scott in the early 19th
century; Scott also set many of his novels here. Compare **Marches**.

Border Eagle State, the

A nickname of Mississippi.

Border State, the

A nickname of Maine, so called because it is situated on the Canadian
border.

Border Town

A nickname of Rye, New York, so called because it was founded (1660) on
the border of what are now Connecticut and New York, and for many
years controversies moved it between the two states.

Borough, the

The familiar name for the former south London borough of Southwark,
particularly the part of it immediately to the south of London Bridge. (The
new London borough of Southwark, created in 1965, covers a far larger
area.) It is mainly a commercial and industrial area, much damaged by
bombing during World War II, but it is relieved by some attractive Georgian squares. Through the middle of it runs Borough High Street, a gateway to southeast England and the Continent, especially in the Middle Ages.
The area was crowded with inns to accommodate travelers, including the
Tabard, where Chaucer's Canterbury pilgrims lodged. See also **Old Kent
Road**.

borrowing days

An English nickname for a period of colder than normal weather in April.

Borscht Circuit

Collectively, a nickname for the resort hotels in the Catskill Mountains,
about 100 miles north of New York City, that have been popular with
mainly Jewish guests since the 1920s; many of the guests were of eastern
European origin, hence the "Borscht." The other part of the appellation,
"Circuit," reflects the viewpoint of entertainers—singers and singing
groups, dancers, comedians, and other performers who were hired to
amuse the guests and who combined bookings at several hotels in one

tour. Another nickname for the area is **Borscht Belt**, but that does not emphasize the entertainment aspect.

Boston Common

The name for the oldest public park in the United States, covering 45 acres in downtown Boston. It was originally set aside in 1634 as a military training field and public cattle pasture. In the 1600s women found guilty of witchcraft were hanged here; today it is a favorite spot for open-air political rallies and is much used and enjoyed by those escaping city noise and heat.

Boston Post Road

An old road, stretching from New York City about 250 miles to Boston, Massachusetts, originally developed for the transportation of mail and people via coach. For many years, until the opening of the New England Thruway (US I-95) in the 1960s, it was the main road through coastal New England and, as it passed through a large number of cities, towns, and villages, became the Main Street of many of them. Along most of its length it is largely commercial, with filling stations, retail shops of every description, eating places, and (latterly) office buildings abounding. The first major road in America, as a federal highway it was designated "US1," and, as such, it extends south from New York to Key West, Florida, and north from Boston into Maine, a total length of almost 1500 miles.

Botany Bay

An inlet to the south of Sydney, Australia, discovered by Captain James Cook in 1770 and named for the variety and profusion of plant life he found there. Because of its notorious penal colony (which was, in fact, a little further north at Port Jackson), Botany Bay became synonymous in the 19th century with transportation, and many a British felon feared being *sent to Botany Bay* scarcely less than the death sentence.

Bourget, le

The name of the small airport which was the first place in Europe where Charles A. Lindbergh set down his *Spirit of St. Louis* in his record-breaking, single-handed transatlantic flight from New York, in 1927. It is the site of an aeronautical museum, and now serves private planes only.

Bournemouth

A seaside resort in Hampshire, England, on the English Channel, with about six miles of beach and a promenade. Popular as a middle-class retirement retreat, it is associated mainly with the elderly, who now live there all year round. See also **Torquay.**

Bourneville

A suburb of Birmingham, in the West Midlands of England, which is intimately associated in the British public's imagination with chocolate, particularly dark chocolate. The district was laid out to provide houses for the workers in Cadbury's chocolate factory in the 1870s. The name was coined because it sounded French, French chocolate possessing a particular cachet.

Bow

An area of the East End of London, to the north of Limehouse. It has no connection with the famous Bow Bells, which are to be found in the church of St. Mary-le-Bow (often also known as Bow Church) in the City of London.

Bowery, the

A broad avenue between the Canal Street area to East 14th Street, where it meets Third Avenue, on the lower east side of New York City. As its name ("Bouwerie"), bestowed by Dutch settlers in the 17th century when the city was still called New Amsterdam, suggests, it was once a tree-lined thoroughfare, and was till the late 19th century, a major attraction for the promenaders and boulevardiers of the time. It was the subject of a song, popular at the time and since then a traditional air, the opening lines of which are:

> The Bowery, The Bowery
>
> They do strange things and they say strange things
>
> On The Bowery, The Bowery,
>
> I'll never go there anymore.

About the turn of the century, it became rather run-down and has never since recovered from its decline. Its condition was not improved by the construction of the Third Avenue elevated railway, originally a steam train, which created a noisy, dark, sooty, and dingy atmosphere in the street below. The "el" was torn down in the 1940s; but today, as for the past fifty years or so, The Bowery has remained a skid row, the haunt of down-and-outers known as Bowery bums, who panhandle from passersby and offer, for a handout, to "clean" the windshields of the cars of embarrassed motorists who have been "trapped" in their domain by a traffic light. Most are men who live in "flophouses" and in "shelters" that are operated by church groups and the Salvation Army, which also provide free meals for the indigent. However, because there are so many of them, a lack of facilities forces some to sleep in doorways or on the sidewalk gratings, through which heat rises from below. Although The Bowery is a blight that could be renovated by the City, it is low on the list of priorities if only because its drifting inhabitants might be left with no place to go.

Bowie State

A nickname of Arkansas, so called because during its early days many of the residents carried a bowie knife. See also **Toothpick State.**

Bow Street

A street in the West End of London, just to the east of Covent Garden. It has always had close associations with the administration of the law; in the present day it contains a police station and the Bow Street Magistrates' Court, the chief magistrates' court of the Metropolitan Police area, and in former times it housed the headquarters of the famous "Bow Street Runners," who preceded the modern police, and functioned from 1749 to 1829.

Boyhood Home of George Washington

A nickname of Fredericksburg, Virginia.

Boystown

The nickname of West Hollywood, California, where a large number of homosexuals have settled from various parts of the United States. Incorporated in 1984, the city in 1985 became the first in the U. S. to elect a city council a majority of which was openly gay or lesbian.

Bozeman Trail

A trail begun in 1863 by John M. Bozeman and used by travelers to reach the gold fields in Montana and Idaho. It ran for about 600 miles between what are now Fort Laramie, Wyoming, and Virginia City, Montana. The Sioux Indians continually attacked its travelers because the trail crossed their main hunting grounds, and it was finally closed in 1868. However, in 1877, the Indians having been subdued, Texas ranchers opened it again to move their cattle into Montana and Wyoming.

Bray

A village on the Thames River in Berkshire, to the west of London. It is famous for its former vicar, immortalized in an anonymous 18th-century song, who boasted of having held on to his job through the reigns of five different monarchs, from Charles II to George I, which involved his having to switch from the Catholic persuasion to the Protestant twice, and back again in the other direction twice. Thanks to the legend of this enterprising parson, the name of Bray evokes the notion of timeservery.

Bread and Butter State, the

A nickname of Minnesota.

Bread Basket of the World, the

A nickname of Minnesota.

Breakfast Food City, the

A nickname of Battle Creek, Michigan, so called because the Battle Creek Sanitarium pioneered the development of ready-to-eat breakfast foods. See also **Cereal City.**

Brenner Pass

The name of the most accessible pass through the Alps, crossing the border of Italy and Austria and linking the Mediterranean region with the northern part of Europe. It begins near Bolzano, Italy, and descends to Innsbruck, Austria. The ancient Romans used it; the Teutons crossed it in the 6th century to invade Italy; medieval traders used it to carry products from the Near East and India; and the U. S. Army crossed it in 1945, during World War II.

Bride of the Sea

A nickname of Venice, Italy.

Bridge of Sighs

1. The name for a bridge built about 1600 that crosses the canal in Venice between the Doges' Palace and the state prison, so called because of the sighs of prisoners who had to cross it. It is probably best known from Byron's poem, *Childe Harold's Pilgrimage.*
2. In New York City, the nickname for a covered bridge-like structure between the Tombs prison and the former criminal courts building across Centre Street. It was used so prisoners could be taken directly to courtrooms out of the view of the public.
3. In Cambridge, England, the nickname given to a bridge over the Cam River; it connects one building of St. John's College with another containing the dining room.
4. A nickname of a bridge in Oxford, England, that connects two buildings of Hartford College, so called because it resembles the bridge in Venice.

Brighton

A large seaside resort in Sussex, on the south coast of England. It first achieved popularity in the late 18th century, when it became a favorite watering place of the Prince of Wales, later George IV; his patronage led to its being frequented by fashionable society. When, in the 19th century, the railroad reached the town, it became instantly accessible to ordinary working people and has never really looked back as a popular destination for day-trippers and vacationers alike. Its heyday was perhaps in the 1930s, and since World War II the expansion in the foreign holiday trade has meant that its amusement gardens, piers, and pebbly beaches are no longer so claustrophobically crowded in summer as they were; but it makes up the numbers with the conference trade and English language students from abroad, and it remains the quintessential coastal holiday resort in southern England. Its proximity to and easy accessibility from

London have contributed a lot to a rather risqué reputation it has gained as a venue for dirty weekends [a Briticism for clandestine rendezvous], much frequented by businessmen and their secretaries (or "secretaries"). See also **Dr. Brighton, Kemp Town, Lanes.**

Britain

The standard everyday name for the country formally called the United Kingdom of Great Britain and Northern Ireland. Some British people are slightly squeamish about the term Great Britain, feeling that it sounds immodest, but in fact it arose originally in order to distinguish Britain from Little Britain, a name used in medieval times for Brittany (in those days Britain and Brittany were frequently spelt identically). It began to take on new significance in the 16th century, as moves for the unification of Scotland with England and Wales got under way; in this context it is intended to denote the entire country, in contrast with individual bits of it, in much the same way as Greater London refers to the whole area. It first came into official use with the union of Scotland with England and Wales in 1707, and for a time after that England and Scotland were referred to in Acts of Parliament as South Britain and North Britain, respectively. The other main constituent of the British Isles, Ireland, was sometimes humorously known as *West Britain*. Of the three names, only *North Britain* survived for any length of time. See also **England, United Kingdom**.

Brixton

A district of south London, to the south of Lambeth. It is a downtrodden working-class residential area, and has a rather negative image; its most famous building and institution is probably Brixton Prison, and it rose to notoriety in 1981 when tensions between the police and the local population, a large proportion of which is of West Indian origin, erupted into violence on the streets. Since then Brixton has been synonymous with racial riots.

Broad, the

Just as Oxford's High Street is known as *the High*, Broad Street is usually called *the Broad*. Amongst its occupants are Trinity and Balliol Colleges, the Sheldonian Theatre, and Blackwell's bookshop. See also **High**.

Broad Acres, the

A now rather clichéd epithet for Yorkshire, the largest county in England. In the popular imagination, Yorkshire may conjure up chiefly industrial rather than rural scenes—in particular, the soot-grimed towns and cities around the Aire River such as Leeds, Bradford, and Huddersfield, that were once at the heart of the mighty woolen industry, and further south the steel-making area centered on Sheffield—but in fact large areas of unspoiled countryside still exist. As the name *Broad Acres* implies, this is open, rolling, large-scale country, from the beautiful but sometimes bleak

North York Moors to the Dales that extend away to the south and west. See
also **Ridings.**

Broads, the

Just below the northern shoulder of the bulge of East Anglia in eastern
England stretches a low-lying area of watery land, where reedy swamps
give place to quiet stretches of open water, which are in turn succeeded by
grazing pastures. These are the Norfolk Broads, 50,000 acres of wetland
crisscrossed by six rivers that open out into 52 shallow lakes, or *broads*,
that give the area its name. They owe their existence to peat diggings that
were begun by the Saxons in the 9th century and were flooded 600 years
later when the sea level changed. Since Victorian times they have been a
very popular venue for boating vacations, but more recently, with both
commercial over-exploitation and changing agricultural techniques, including extensive drainage, there is concern for their survival as both a place
of outstanding beauty and a home for many rare species of animals and
plants.

Broadway

1. Said to be the longest street in the world, New York City's Broadway
extends from Bowling Green, at its southerly terminus, the site where
17th-century Dutch burghers played at bowls when the City was New
Amsterdam, north into Yonkers and, some maintain, beyond, a distance of
more than twenty miles. At its lower end it is a focus of the financial
world, associated with nearby Wall Street; like a river that has eroded its
way into a canyon between walls of tall office buildings, it passes through
commercial areas of a characterless nature, past Union Square, Madison
Square, and Herald Square (where it borders Macy's), to emerge at Times
Square, where it acquires a tawdry dignity because of its long traditional
association with the world of entertainment—vaudeville, the legitimate
theater, and the not-so-legitimate theater, once represented by burlesque,
now by the sleazier bars, dance-halls, massage parlors, and "private" clubs
that offer the voyeur, the depraved, and the lustful topless and/or bottom-
less dancers and waitresses. Broadway's passage through Times Square,
though brief, has provided it with much of its reputation. Even though
there are few legitimate theaters actually on Broadway—most are on the
side streets, east and west of Times Square—"Broadway" *means* the theater
world to most people, both in and out of the profession. It also symbolizes
brash promoters in loud suits and boasts a variegated, floating population
of drifters, grifters, runaways, panhandlers, conmen, pimps, prostitutes,
vendors of corsages and of every other conceivable item, gofers, tourists
from far away who speak little English, tourists from nearby whose English is difficult to understand (even for a native speaker), and a cadre of
indigenous people, mostly men, who just "hang out." It is always crowded,
and at times of a special event, like V-E day, V-J day, or any New Year's
Eve, its traffic is closed off and the density of population increases to about

one person per square foot. Before it was closed by Mayor Fiorello H. La Guardia, in the mid 1930s, burlesque flourished along Broadway, especially at the Gaiety Theatre, near 46th Street. Across Duffy Square (the official name for the north end of Times Square, where Seventh Avenue has already crossed over to the east of Broadway) stands the Palace Theatre, renowned as the place where a performer can realize the zenith of his ambition for recognition by his peers and receive the accolades of an adoring public. The Palace in the mid 1980s was a legitimate theater. This image of Broadway has been sustained through songs that remain ever popular ("Give My Regards to Broadway"), associated with songwriters and performers whose legends never die (George M. Cohan), and through the perpetual romanticization of the theater by Hollywood, especially in musical comedies produced during the late 1920s, and in the 1930s and '40s. Broadway became the center of first-run motion-pictures in New York, and huge theaters catered to enormous crowds during the 1930s and '40s when the Paramount, Strand, Capitol, Rivoli, and other movie theaters flourished. Many of these offered stage shows as well, with "Big Bands" and singers of great fame: headliners in those days were Frank Sinatra, who was besieged by thousands of screaming bobby-soxers when he appeared at the Paramount; Vaughn Monroe; Benny Goodman; Spike Jones; Artie Shaw; Tommy Dorsey; Glenn Miller; and other bandleaders, including Phil Spitalny and his all-girl orchestra. Always gaudy, Broadway and Times Square turn night into day by means of huge neon and incandescent extravaganzas; not only are the streets lit up by the coursing, flashing lights of the theater marquees, but enormous electrical billboards—some a full city block in length—burst forth their colossal displays to create a glow over the area that is visible from miles away. Totally brazen and indecorous, these gigantic displays move, flash on and off, scintillate, blow smoke rings, and perform in the most incredible ways to engage the attention of passersby: atop a clothing store, there were even two huge, seemingly nude statues of a man and a woman separated (at a distance of about 150 feet) by a genuine waterfall, about thirty feet high. Broadway does not run parallel to the other north-south thoroughfares in Manhattan, and at those avenues it crosses squares are created, like Union, Madison, and the others mentioned. After it wends its way north of Times Square, it crosses Eighth Avenue (which then becomes Central Park West) at Columbus Circle (59th Street), the site of the New York Coliseum, a major convention center. At 65th Street, it crosses Ninth Avenue (which becomes Columbus Avenue) and forms Lincoln Square, where the Metropolitan Opera House, Symphony Hall, the Juilliard School, the New York City Ballet, the New York City Opera, and other public entertainment facilities form Lincoln Center. Finally, it crosses Tenth Avenue (which becomes Amsterdam Avenue) at 72nd Street. North of Lincoln Center, Broadway acquires the character of the main street of the many neighborhoods it traverses, with wall-to-wall retail shops, restaurants, movie theaters, and the like along its entire length. These establishments are set into the ground floors of apartment houses and, occasionally, hotels. Except for an area several blocks north of 114th Street, where the brick and granite buildings of Columbia University offer relief from the commercial atmosphere, this character remains unrelieved for the rest of its length. At 125th Street, it passes west of Harlem; north of 135th Street through the western reaches of Spanish Harlem; above 155th Street through a mixed neighborhood, Washington Heights, which was once settled mainly by Jews and, after the mid 1930s, by Jewish refugees from Europe; it crosses the Harlem River at 225th Street (at Spuyten Duyvil Creek), where it is joined by the elevated subway that goes as far as 242nd Street, runs alongside Van Cortlandt Park in The Bronx, and on to the City line at 260th Street. Beyond that point it remains "Broadway" technically, but its association with New York City is lost. From **Columbus Circle** (*q.v.*) north to 168th Street, it is a roadway divided by a central mall which once offered trees and a grassy lawn to relieve the unremitting atmosphere of asphalt and concrete. In recent years, owing to neglect, it has more closely resembled a rubbish dump than the elegant greensward its designers intended. Over its entire length of some twenty miles, Broadway's reputation derives mainly from the short stretch between 42nd and about 50th streets.

2. A section of San Francisco, centered on Broadway, characterized by cabarets, bars, and theaters featuring nude women and by its honky-tonk atmosphere.

Brooklyn

A borough of New York City on Long Island, south of Queens. After New York City (Manhattan) itself, it is probably the best known part of New York, having figured widely in national and world culture, especially as the result of books (*A Tree Grows in Brooklyn*, by Betty Smith) and dozens of motion pictures in which people from Brooklyn have been characterized mainly as being fervently, uncompromisingly loyal to their home county (technically called Kings) and to their (former) baseball team (the Brooklyn Dodgers, whose home was Ebbetts Field). Natives of Brooklyn are somewhat caricatured for their accent, which, in fact, carries traces of an earlier pronunciation of English in New York City, still heard among the older residents, with slight remnants of Dutch, especially in the pronunciation of certain vowels. Thus, the caricatured pronunciation of "Third Avenue and 33rd Street" as "Toid Avenya 'n' Toidy-Toid Street," heard less often than formerly, is actually a simulation of a pronunciation in which the vowels of "Third" and "Thirty" are uttered closer to the front than the back of the mouth. Like the other boroughs of New York City (The Bronx, Manhattan, Queens, and Staten Island), Brooklyn is an agglomeration of neighborhoods, some of which are well known to non-natives. Brooklyn Heights, south of the eastern tower of the Brooklyn Bridge and overlooking the East River and lower Manhattan, was once occupied by writers and artists, but, as typical elsewhere in the City, most of them have been driven out by the increased rents in recent years, to be replaced by upper-middle-class residents who have bought the pretty, quaint old townhouses and reconverted many of them from small apartment houses back to single-family dwellings. Coney Island, a famous amusement park along an ocean beach, has, in later years, become known for its gaudy, raucous atmosphere; Flatbush, an area in the southern part of Brooklyn, was long (and incorrectly) identified with the Brooklyn Dodgers baseball club, which is associated with Ebbets Field, actually to the northwest; the Williamsburgh section is known chiefly as an area inhabited by a large colony of Hasidic Jews; and Park Slope, once a wealthy neighborhood near Prospect Park, went through a long decline only to be revitalized, beginning in the 1960s, by young, upwardly mobile middle-class residents who have bought the old Victorian houses and have restored them to their former elegance. At its eastern end, near the Atlantic Ocean, is the huge John F. Kennedy Airport, formerly called Idlewild. The Brooklyn Dodgers have long since moved their baseball club to Los Angeles, and Ebbets Field has been demolished. Yet the firmly incised impressions of Brooklyn linger on, little changed from years ago, and many people, though they may never have ventured there, retain for it a vicarious nostalgia.

Brooklyn Bridge

A suspension bridge linking lower Manhattan Island with Long Island, at Brooklyn. It was designed by John A. Roebling and completed in 1883 by William A. Roebling after the death of his father and at the cost of permanent injury incurred during a fire in one of the caissons while he was working on the foundation. Aside from its industrial beauty, somewhat marred by the later construction of a steel-trussed roadway, it figures in the folklore of New York in a number of tales. One centers on Steve Brody, a brawling resident of Irish descent, who is said to have won a bar wager that he would survive a leap from the bridge into the East River below; the other concerns the "sale" of the bridge by confidence men who dupe naive visitors to the city.

Brooks Brothers

A department store at 44th Street and Madison Avenue, in New York City, known chiefly for its conservative men's wear. Never renowned as a style-setter, Brooks has outfitted business executives in traditional clothing—narrow-lapel suits, button-down collars, and striped "old-school" ties—and was for many years (before the trend changed to blue jeans) supplier of clothing to the ivy-league college crowd.

Brother Jonathan

The first known nickname for Americans, used derisively by British soldiers and Tories during the American Revolution. It later became a comic Yankee figure in plays and gradually came to symbolize simplicity, forthrightness, honesty, and common sense. The original Jonathan is thought to have been Governor Jonathan Trumbull of Connecticut, whom

George Washington frequently consulted because of his solid common sense. A study of the American character by that name, written by Joan Neal, published in 1825 and intended primarily for foreign consumption, emphasized the alleged vulgarity of New York, the greed of New England, and the ignorance of the Quakers. See also **Uncle Sam.**

Brown Bess

The nickname, referring to its color, for an 18th-century British army flintlock musket, still in use at Waterloo in 1815.

brownstone

Literally, a reddish-brown sandstone, widely used in New York City as a facing on private dwellings built in the late 19th century. It became (and remained) so prevalent throughout the city that the name has become generic for private homes of a particular design: typically, the brownstone has a high exterior brownstone staircase (called a *stoop*) leading upward from the sidewalk to the parlor floor; a semi-sunken ground floor below that is reached by a door that is below the top landing of the exterior stairs. These homes, usually four storeys tall, were built on the standard 20' x 100' city lot, usually to a depth of 50' with a garden at the rear. Thousands of almost identical houses of this design were built in rows along the side streets of the residential areas of Manhattan and Brooklyn, especially. The increased property values and the construction of apartment buildings that characterized the development of residential housing in New York City after the turn of the century made private homes too expensive to maintain, and most brownstones were converted to small apartments and rooming houses. By the 1940s, the neighborhoods—chiefly the side streets where these houses were numerous—had deteriorated, and, in the poorer sections of the city, had become slums. The real estate boom following WW II and the subsequent housing shortages of the 1950s and '60s prompted many middle-class families to purchase old brownstones and renovate them, returning a large number of them to single-family occupancy. In wealthy neighborhoods, such houses cost about $75,000 in the 1950s; by the 1980s, renovated, modernized brownstones brought prices in the millions. Despite the fact that the truly luxurious townhouses, especially in Manhattan, are faced with limestone, the term *brownstone* has become generic for all such houses.

Brownstone State, the

A former nickname of Connecticut.

Brum

A nickname for Birmingham, Britain's second largest city; the local people are known as *Brummies*. The word is a shortened version of Brummagem, itself a local dialect variation, no longer much used, of *Birmingham*. In the 19th century the city gained such a reputation for the vast production of cheap manufactured goods, especially knickknacks and jewelry, that *brummagem* became a synonym for 'tawdry' or 'tatty.' The tower of Birmingham Council House is known by the local nickname *Big Brum*, in mock imitation of Big Ben.

Buckeye State, the

The official nickname of Ohio, so called in reference to the buckeye tree (*Aesculus glabra*) and to an Indian nickname for a Colonel Sproat who impressed them as he led the settlers into the first court session held there (1788).

Buck House

A disrespectful but on the whole affectionate nickname for Buckingham Palace, the official London residence of British monarchs since 1837. It was built in 1703 for the Duke of Buckingham and Chandos, when it was in fact called Buckingham House; George III bought it in 1761, and since then it has been much added to and enlarged.

Buffalo Plains State, the

A former nickname of Colorado.

Bug-eating State, the

A nickname of Nebraska, so called in reference to the bats found there.

Bughouse Square

A park on the Near North Side of Chicago, and the locale for numerous political and philosophical debates, particularly during the 1920s and '30s, when speakers espousing primarily radical causes would stand on boxes or crates in order to be better seen and heard above the heads of the many listeners and participants who gathered about. Though the tradition of these debates has survived, their former frequency and passion are things of the past. Washington Square Park, the official name, is rarely used.

Bull City

A nickname of Durham, North Carolina, so called because Bull Durham tobacco is manufactured there.

Bullion State, the

A nickname of Missouri, so called after the sobriquet, "Old Bullion" of Senator Thomas Hart Benton, for his defense of the use of gold and silver in preference to paper currency.

Bullring, the

A huge multi-level shopping area in the center of Birmingham, in the West Midlands of England. It is on a 23-acre site, and includes markets, restaurants, parking lots, and a bus station.

Bunker Hill

The site of one of the most important battles in the Revolutionary War, which actually took place on Breed's Hill on June 17, 1775. Both hills are in Charlestown, across the Charles River from the north shore of Boston, and it was here that the colonists repelled three British attacks in a bloody battle to defend Boston. The colonists lost the battle and were forced to flee, exhausted and without ammunition or reinforcements; but their fighting ability so raised the spirits and confidence of the Americans that in March of the following year George Washington and his troops were able to rout the British from Boston and the harbor. A memorial commemorating the battle was erected some fifty years later on the site.

Burbank

A city in California located within the Los Angeles metropolitan region at the eastern end of the San Fernando Valley. Because the largest concentration of movie and television studios is now found in and around Burbank, the city is frequently mentioned, often in a derisive or deprecatory manner, on television talk shows or comedies: the phrase "beautiful downtown Burbank" was often heard on the Rowan and Martin "Laugh-In" show in the late 1960s, and more recently, Johnny Carson has poked fun at Burbank on his "Tonight Show."

Burlington House

A grand edifice in Victorian-renaissance style, in Piccadilly Street, London, the home of the Royal Society, the Royal Academy (of Arts), and several other organizations. The nearby Burlington Arcade, an attractive regency covered promenade extending from Piccadilly Street to Burlington Gardens, has many fine shops known for the luxury of their wares.

Burma Road, the

A highway 2100 miles long from Lashio, northeast of Mandalay in Burma, to Chungking in southern China, which was used by the Allies from 1940 to 1942 to supply military equipment to Chiang Kai-shek, whose forces were fighting the Japanese.

Burton upon Trent

A town in Staffordshire, in the West Midlands of England. The water of the Trent River is said to be particularly suitable for the making of fine beer, and over the centuries Burton became known as the brewing capital of Britain. In the 19th century there were forty breweries there, and Burton became synonymous with beer: "Burton and biscuit and cheese he had, which indeed, is Burton in its proper company," as H. G. Wells wrote. Many of the Victorian breweries have since closed down or been amalgamated with others, but beer continues to be produced there in substantial quantities. In the days of biplanes and dogfights, when an RAF pilot was killed or went missing in action he was euphemistically said to have *gone for a Burton*—that is, gone out to get a drink of beer. The phrase later passed into general use in British English, meaning 'to be broke or ruined.'

Buzzard State, the

A nickname of Georgia, so called because of its stringently enforced protective laws.

Cabrini-Green Public Housing Project

The nation's first high-rise public housing complex, on the Near North Side of Chicago, commonly known as, simply, "Cabrini-Green." Gang-ridden, beset by a high crime rate, and with many of its 14,000 predominantly black residents on welfare and unemployment, the project constitutes a stark contrast to the affluent dwellings of the **Gold Coast** (*q.v.*), slightly over a mile away.

Cactus State, the

A nickname of New Mexico.

Caledonia

The Roman name for Scotland, much used in neoclassical poetry but today surviving virtually only in its adjectival form, as in the *Caledonian Canal*, a canal linking the Atlantic and the North Sea through the north of Scotland, and *British Caledonian*, an airline.

Caledonian Market

A street market, formerly held off Caledonian Road, southeast of Hampstead, north London. It has been moved to Bermondsey Street, on the south bank of the Thames, near Tower Bridge. See also **Bermondsey Market.**

Camargue, the

A desolate triangle of marshy land that forms the delta of the River Rhone on the southern coast of France. It is famous for its beef cattle, herded by lance-carrying cowboys on horseback, and for its abundance of waterbirds, particularly flamingos. It used to be sheep country, too, but much of its brackish water has been drained and replaced by fresh for the large-scale production of rice, and the sheep have been edged out.

Camberley

A genteel military town set amongst the sandy heaths and pinewoods of west Surrey. Its development started in the early 19th century, when the Royal Military Academy was set up at nearby Sandhurst; it aimed to attract army families and retired officers to its salubrious villas, and succeeded so well that it is now pigeonholed as the haunt of bristly colonels and their sporty daughters. Its original name was Cambridge Town, but this seems to have caused a certain amount of confusion, and in 1877 the new name of Camberley was found for it, invented by a certain Dr. Atkinson.

Cambodia

A state in Southeast Asia that has had something of an identity crisis in the latter part of the 20th century. With shifts of political status have gone many changes of name: in 1970, when the former monarchy was ousted and a republic declared, it became the Khmer Republic; then in 1975 its name was officially declared to be Democratic Kampuchea; and in 1979, when the blood-soaked Pol Pot regime came to an end, it metamorphosed again into the People's Republic of Kampuchea. Over and above these events it has continued to be widely known by its original name of Cambodia.

Cambria

The Roman name for Wales. In modern times it is preserved in the Cambrian Mountains, a range which runs north and south along mid Wales, and in the names of ancient geological eras: the Cambrian Period is so called because its characteristic rocks and fossils were first described from specimens found in Wales. The name *Cambria* derives ultimately from Welsh *Cymry* 'Welshmen.'

Camden and Amboy State

A nickname of New Jersey, so called after a former railroad.

Camden Lock

An open-air market situated where Chalk Farm Road crosses Regent's Canal, in north London. All sorts of merchandise—jewelry, clothes, hardware, antiques, crafts, etc.—are sold here on Saturdays and Sundays.

Camden Town

A district in north London, to the northeast of Regent's Park. From being rather a poor area before World War II, with many Greek and Irish immigrants, it has moved steadily upmarket until in the 1980s it is a very fashionable and expensive place to live. In its midst, Camden Lock, part of the Regent's Canal, is at the center of a well-known artists' colony, with many trendy and rather high-priced craft shops. Its name is easily confused with Camden, a new London borough formed in 1965, which covers a very large area from Holborn in the south to Hampstead in the north and includes Camden Town. Nor is it to be confused with Camden Passage, well known for its antiques shops, which is further east, in Islington.

Camelot

1. The town where, according to Arthurian legend, the court and castle of King Arthur were situated. It has been identified with an array of real places in England, most of them in the Southwest: Sir Thomas Malory, the most famous of Arthurian authors, thought it was in Winchester, Hampshire; Camelford, South Cadbury, and Queen's Camel, all in Somerset, have been candidates; and the 20th-century Arthurian scholar R. S. Loomis suggested that its name was an amalgamation of Avalon, legendary site of Arthur's last battle, and Caerleon in South Wales.

2. A nickname given to the White House during the presidency of John F. Kennedy, mainly because of the charismatic behavior of the president, the king-like power he exercised, and the queen-like beauty of his wife, Jacqueline.

Camino Real, el

'The Royal Road,' running from Chihuahua, Mexico, to Santa Fe, New Mexico, was first used in 1581, making it the oldest road in the United States. It is now US 85. The name is roughly equivalent to "Main Street" (*q.v.*) and is used in many places in the southwestern and western United States that were originally settled by Spanish speakers.

Campagna, the

A plain, about 800 square miles in extent, surrounding Rome. In classical times it was a rich and fertile area, and many ancient monuments remain to bear witness to its former glories. In the Dark Ages it declined to a malaria-infested wilderness, but in the 20th century much land reclamation has taken place.

Camp David

An area in the Catoctin Mountains of Maryland, about seventy miles from Washington, D. C., established as a retreat in 1942 by President Franklin Delano Roosevelt to allow him relief from the un-airconditioned summers in the capital, and which he named Shangri-La. It became the president's official retreat under Harry S. Truman. The scene of a number of important conferences between world leaders, including Roosevelt's meeting with Winston Churchill in 1943 and President Dwight D. Eisenhower's meeting in 1959 with Nikita S. Khrushchev, the Premier of the Soviet Union, it is especially noted for the talks President Jimmy Carter organized between President Anwar el-Sadat of Egypt and Prime Minister Menachem Begin of Israel, which resulted in a major peace agreement between their two countries, referred to as the Camp David Accords. See also **Shangri-la, 3.**

Canary Islands

A group of thirteen mountainous islands belonging to Spain in the Atlantic ocean about sixty miles off the coast of northwest Africa. The people of Gomera, one of the islands, are famous for their ability to communicate over large distances with a whistled language that imitates spoken Spanish. Although canaries were first discovered in the islands, its name comes not from birds, but from Latin *canis* 'dog,' because the ancients found fierce, large dogs there.

Cape, the

A nickname for Cape Cod, a hundred-mile-long narrow peninsula that sticks out eastward into the Atlantic Ocean like a beckoning finger. Properly part of Massachusetts and lying at its southeast corner, it is situated due east of Rhode Island. The towns of Woods Hole, site of a world-renowned oceanographic institute, and Hyannisport are on its south shore, on Vineyard Sound; Cape Cod Bay is formed on its northern and western shores by the crook of the finger; Chatham is at its southeasternmost point. Cape Cod may, technically, begin at Hyannisport, but many natives consider it as reaching northward from Chatham, where it is little more than a narrow sandbar, fringed by dunes, vegetated by razorgrass and by low, scrub-like trees and shrubs, and populated, except in the summer season, by more seagulls than people. At its very tip is Provincetown, in some respects a free-swinging beach resort town, in others, especially during the winter, a New England village. Provincetown is well known for being an artists' and writers' colony and almost equally famous for its open morality, a place where visitors of every sexual persuasion can enjoy themselves and each other unfettered by restraint. Once an area of quiet retreat for Bostonians and other New Englanders, the Cape has become, since World War II, a resort for those who enjoy long, open stretches of ocean beaches that are occupied only by the inhabitants of the relatively few homes scattered along its length. In the 1950s, it was designated a National Seashore by the U. S. government, a move that restricted the building of houses, hotels, and other facilities and, by that token, effectively increased the property values substantially.

Cape Cod turkey

A sobriquet for codfish. Also called **Marblehead turkey.**

Capital City

A nickname of the District of Columbia.

Capital of Houses without Streets,

A nickname of the District of Columbia.

Capital of the Highlands, the

Epithet for Inverness, in the north of Scotland, the chief town of the Scottish Highlands. See also **Highlands**.

Capital of the World, the

A nickname of New York City.

Capital of Vacationland

A nickname of Newport, Rhode Island.

Capitoline, the

The most important of the Seven Hills of ancient Rome. In earliest times (when it was known as the Saturnine or Tarpeian Hill) the Roman citadel was built on its northern summit. Subsequently the main national temple of Rome, dedicated to Jupiter, was erected on its southern summit; this temple was known as the *Capitol* (Latin *caput* 'head' or 'summit'), and eventually gave its name to the hill. The term has passed down the centuries to the building, itself on a hill, occupied by the U. S. Congress for its sessions.

Carey Street

A street to the north of the Strand in London, once the location of the Bankruptcy Department of the Supreme Court. Hence the now rather dated British slang expression *be in Carey Street*, meaning 'have no money.'

Carlsbad of America, the

A nickname of French Lick Springs, Indiana.

Carlton Club, the

A club in London, founded in 1831 by Conservative Members of Parliament and their supporters. Occupying a building of some architectural importance, its name is often used metonymically for the Conservative Party.

Carnaby Street

A road in the West End of London, to the east of and parallel to Regent Street. It leapt to fame in the mid 1960s, when boutiques sprang up there selling the products of the booming British teenage fashion industry, and the road became strongly associated with the culture of the "swinging '60s." In the 1980s the action has moved elsewhere, but Carnaby Street remains a popular tourist attraction and is still lined with clothing shops. Compare **King's Road**.

Casa Oscar Romero

A sanctuary sponsored by the Roman Catholic church in San Benito, Texas, about fifteen miles from the Mexican border. Named for an archbishop who was assassinated while saying Mass in El Salvador in 1980, it offers temporary sanctuary to those fleeing Central America and is thought by many to serve as an underground railroad helping refugees to enter the United States illegally.

Castro, the

An area in San Francisco typically frequented by homosexuals.

Cathay

In medieval and early Renaissance times China was known in the West as *Cathay*. The name survives today only as an archaic or poetic term—with associations of Oriental mystery and remoteness, penetrated by the daring Marco Polo—and in the name of Hong Kong's airline, *Cathay Pacific*.

Cavalier State, the

A nickname of Virginia.

Celery City

A nickname of Kalamazoo, Michigan.

Celestial Empire, the

A name used in former times for China. It is a translation of one of the many epithets the Chinese themselves used for their empire. Compare **Middle Kingdom**.

Centennial State, the

The official nickname of Colorado, so called because its entry into the Union (1876) occurred one hundred years after the signing of the Declaration of Independence.

Center, the

A name given to the arid, desolate plains that cover more than half the continent of Australia and particularly to the area in the middle surrounding Alice Springs. The flat desert of the outback supports little life and is only occasionally relieved by hilly outcrops and salt lakes. The area is also known as the Red Center, from the predominant color of the sand and rocks, and as the Dead Heart, a name taken from J. W. Gregory's book *The Dead Heart of Australia* (1906). In former times the name Centralia was coined, but it never really caught on.

Central State, the

A nickname of Kansas.

Centre Point

A 33-story office building in central London, at the junction of Tottenham Court Road and **Oxford Street** (*q.v.*). It was erected in the mid 1960s, in the confident expectation that it would become a symbol of the age of thrusting new technology. However, the office space proved to be too expensive at the time of its completion, and its owners gained considerable financial advantage, through tax relief, by refusing to rent out smaller units. Derelicts and hoboes began to take it over for nighttime accommodations, and it rapidly achieved a dubious celebrity as a white elephant.

Cereal City

A nickname of Cedar Rapids, Iowa, so called because the two largest cereal factories in the U. S. are situated here. See also **Breakfast Food City.**

Ceylon

A large island at the southern tip of India. The nation which occupies it has been officially known as Sri Lanka since 1970. The ancient Arabic name for the island is Serendip, from which we get the word *serendipity*, meaning 'the knack of making fortunate discoveries'; the connection is that this was an aptitude possessed by the heroes of the Persian fairy tale, *The Three Princes of Serendip.*

Champion City

A nickname of Springfield, Ohio.

Champs Élysées, the

Probably the most famous street in Paris, and one of the most renowned in the world, the Avenue des Champs-Élysées sweeps majestically up from the Place de la Concorde at its southeastern end toward the Arc de Triomphe, presenting a tree-lined vista that never fails to take one's breath away. At its northwestern end it is lined with shops, offices, movie theaters, and sidewalk cafés ideal for sitting and observing the passing scene. Not far away, at the southeastern end, is the Élysée Palace, official home of the French president; *Élysée* is frequently used as a shorthand name for the French government.

Chancery Lane

A street in central London, which runs north and south between Holborn and Fleet Street. Its name is firmly linked with the legal profession. It houses the Public Record Office, the headquarters of the Law Society, and many offices and shops connected with the law: patent agents, for example, and law stationers. Just to the west is Lincoln's Inn, one of London's Inns of Court (societies of lawyers), and turning right at the foot of Chancery Lane one comes to the Law Courts. See also **Inns of Court and Chancery.**

Channel, the

To an Englishman, the Channel, pure and simple, is always the English Channel, that narrow stretch of water that separates the British Isles from the continent of Europe (see also **Continent**). The French call it *la Manche* (literally, 'the sleeve'), while the Germans are content with *der Kanal.* Traditionally viewed as a powerful bastion of defense against potential invaders from Europe (although the idea didn't work out too well in 1066), the Channel has increasingly come to be seen as symbolic of the gulf in understanding between Britain and its supposed partners in the European community. "Europe" starts on the other side of the Channel, and significantly none of the projects to link the two sides physically has yet come near completion (see **Chunnel**). Bridging the gap continues to be left to the Channel swimmers, who crawl or dog-paddle along in ever greater numbers in the wake of Captain Matthew Webb, who first made it to the other side in 1875. Scores now have a go every year, and a record of 7 hours 40 minutes for the 21 miles was set in 1978 by Penny Dean. The Channel has witnessed some of the most notable episodes in the island's history, from that typically British glorious defeat, the evacuation from Dunkirk, in 1940, to a genuine naval victory over the Spanish Armada, in 1588.

Chappaquiddick

A tiny island, part of the island of Martha's Vineyard, Massachusetts. A more or less exclusive summer resort, it sprang into national—even international—prominence in 1969 when Senator Edward Kennedy, brother of the late president John F. Kennedy and U. S. Attorney General Robert F. Kennedy, was involved in an accident in which a young woman, Mary Jo Kopechne, was trapped and drowned when the car he was driving ran off a small bridge. There was an attempt, at first, to conceal the entire episode, and, although Kennedy was exonerated at an inquest in January, 1970, from which the press was barred and the testimony of which was sealed, the presiding magistrate, in April 1970, released the transcripts with a report in which he stated that he could not accept as truth key parts of Kennedy's testimony: he concluded there was probably cause to believe Kennedy had been driving negligently and had contributed to Miss Kopechne's death. The Massachusetts attorney general's office declined to prosecute and said the matter was legally at an end. But many still felt that the entire event was whitewashed because of Kennedy's social and political power. For many years, the name Chappaquiddick continued to crop up in oblique references to Kennedy as well as in macabre, black humor, and there is no doubt that the publicity surrounding the incident effectively stymied his aspirations for the presidency of the United States.

Charing Cross

A small triangular open space at the northern end of Whitehall in central London, forming the southern part of Trafalgar Square. The area was originally called Charing; the *cross* part of its name comes from the so-called Eleanor Cross erected here in 1291, the last of a series put up by Edward I to mark the funeral procession of his wife Eleanor from Nottingham to Westminster Abbey. In 1675 it was replaced with a statue of Charles I. Charing Cross is officially at the center of London; distances from the capital are measured from it. To the north runs Charing Cross Road, well known for its secondhand book shops. Charing Cross is also the name of a major railroad terminus here, from which trains go to the southeast of England. The local Underground station used to be called

Trafalgar Square, but is now *Charing Cross*; confusingly, the station that used to be called *Charing Cross* is now known as *Embankment*.

Charles's Wain

A British name for Ursa Major, so called from the outline formed by its stars.

Charter Oak City, the

A nickname of Hartford, Connecticut, so called after the tree in which the early settlers hid the Charter of the Colony of Connecticut in order to avoid surrendering it to King James II.

Checkpoint Charlie

A famous crossing point between the West and East zones of Berlin, situated on the Friedrichstrasse. It has been the scene of some brave escapes to the West.

Cheddar

The production of hard tangy Cheddar cheese has now spread around the world, far from the little Somerset village of Cheddar where it first started. Less susceptible to exportation is the spectacular Cheddar Gorge, a popular tourist spot with its series of limestone cliffs that rise to more than 450 feet.

Chelm

An imaginary town of eastern European folklore, peopled by foolish citizens who do outlandish things. See also **Gotham, Kocourkov, Mistelbach.**

Chelsea

1. An area in west London, on the north bank of the Thames, the status of which has undergone a cyclical change. In the 17th and 18th centuries it was a fashionable residential district, and many attractive streets and squares from the period help to give it its character. From the mid 19th century onward it became something of an artists' quarter: J. M. W. Turner lived there in his later years, and after him Dante Gabriel Rossetti, James McNeill Whistler, Wilson Steer, Augustus John, and John Singer Sargent. By the early 20th century it had acquired a distinctly bohemian reputation, but as property prices moved relentlessly upward, impecunious artists could no longer afford a Cheyne Walk address; they moved out westward, and the area reverted to fashionable society. Its slightly raffish air has never completely left it, however; its main street is the trendy King's Road, and its occupants have always tended to be younger and livelier than those of the more staid Kensington to the north (with the exception, that is, of the celebrated Chelsea Pensioners, red-coated British Army veterans who occupy Chelsea Royal Hospital). Chelsea is famous for its buns (first referred to in 1711), its boots (a sort of elastic-sided shoe), and its porcelain (first manufactured in the 18th century). But perhaps most of all it is known for the sort of youthful lightheartedness and high spirits typified by the annual Chelsea Arts Club Ball, a lively frolic at which London's *jeunesse dorée* lets its hair down: it was discontinued at one point for being too rowdy, but in the 1980s has been revived. See also **Royal Borough**.

2. A nondescript area on the West Side of New York City, bounded roughly by 14th and 34th streets on the south and north, and Fifth and Tenth avenues on the east and west. It is mainly commercial, from the large ofice building at Fifth Avenue and 24th Street, where the toy business is centered, to the flower mart in the mid 20s west of Sixth Avenue. There are some Greek and Armenian restaurants, some featuring bellydancers, along Eighth Avenue, and what residential neighborhoods exist are largely run down. The Chelsea Hotel, a baroque residential hotel on 23rd Street, once figuring in the reminiscences of the writers and artists who lived there during their years of penury, remains more as an architectural landmark than as a focal scene of the arts.

Cheltenham

A town in Gloucestershire, in the West of England. It first rose to fame in the early 19th century as a spa town, where fashionable folk came to take the waters. As the century progressed it came increasingly into vogue as a place of retirement for crusty old colonels and others whose livers and tempers had been impaired by prolonged service in Britain's tropical colonies. As a result, the town achieved, and has retained, something of a reputation as a redoubt of conservatism. Part and parcel of its image is Cheltenham Ladies' College, a famous private girls' school founded by the formidable Miss Beale, a model of forceful Victorian womanhood.

Chemical Capital of the World, the

A nickname of Wilmington, Delaware.

Chemical City

A nickname of Berlin, New Hampshire.

Chicago of the South

A nickname of Okeechobee, Florida, so called because of its location on a lake and on the southern edge of the cattle-range country of south Florida.

Child of the Mississippi, the

A nickname of Louisiana, which is built on land deposited at the mouth of the Mississippi River in the Gulf of Mexico.

Chiltern Hundreds, the

In former times, most English counties were divided up into areas known as *hundreds*, for the purpose of judicial administration. The Chilterns, an area of wooded hills in Oxfordshire and Buckinghamshire, to the north-west of London, comprised eight such hundreds. The manorial rights of three of these, Stoke, Desborough, and Burnham, all in Buckinghamshire, belonged to the Crown, which meant that the king or queen appointed stewards or bailiffs over them. Since 1707 it has been forbidden for a British Member of Parliament to hold an office of profit under the Crown: to do so brings instant disqualification. And herein lies a neat solution to a curious anomaly of Parliament, namely, that members are not allowed to resign from it. The Stewardship of the Chiltern Hundreds is such an office of profit, so any MP appointed to it immediately ceases to be an MP. To *apply for the Chiltern Hundreds* is therefore now the standard way for a member to leave Parliament if he or she does not wish to wait for a dissolution. The Stewardship is a purely nominal office, with no duties, and the holder resigns it immediately in order to leave it open for the next applicant.

Chimneyville

A nickname of Jackson, Mississippi, so called because nothing was left but the chimneys after a fire burned the city to the ground during the Civil War.

Chinatown

1. The name given to the section of any large western city occupied entirely or largely by Chinese. Most of the large cities of the western world have a Chinatown, notably San Francisco, whose Chinese inhabitants set-tled during the late 19th century, imported mainly to construct the rail-roads in the western United States. Typically, in addition to living quarters, such districts have retail shops and restaurants, owned and operated by Chinese, and many visitors are attracted by the exotic wares and foods offered. There is a large Chinatown in New York City, on the Lower East Side, just east of Foley Square and the court buildings on Centre Street and extending north to Canal Street. In a whimsical mood, the telephone com-pany has installed in the streets public telephone booths that have pagoda-shaped roofs.

2. London's original Chinatown was in Limehouse, the Dockland district to the east of the Tower of London. It came into being as Chinese sailors who had worked in the tea trade began to settle in the area. The oriental community here flourished in the 19th century, albeit under the cloud of opium trafficking and rumors of mysterious secret societies, which fueled fears of the "yellow peril"; and up until World War II it was all but an autonomous enclave. At its center was the small road known as Pen-nyfields, but some of the surrounding streets give the flavor of the area better: Oriental Street, Canton Street, Ming Street, and Pekin Street. In the

1980s Soho, and particularly the area around Gerrard Street, house London's chief Chinatown, but Limehouse still contains some of the best Chinese restaurants in London.

Chinook State

A nickname of Washington.

Chisholm Trail

An important route between San Antonio, Texas, and Abilene, Kansas. The original Trail, laid out by Jesse Chisholm (*ca* 1805–68) in 1832, was a wagon road between Fort Smith, Arkansas, and Fort Towson, in Indian Territory (later Oklahoma). In the mid 1860s, it was the main road for transport of goods and cattle to Abilene, the nearest station of the Kansas Pacific Railroad. Today, US 81 follows the route of the old Trail.

Christiana

A self-governing section of Copenhagen, consisting of a block of abandoned government buildings around what was previously a parade ground. It is occupied by about 1,000 people who deal openly in hashish and other hard drugs, though its residents maintain that users among them are exiled till cured of their habit. Regarded by many as a "free city," its inhabitants have adamantly refused to comply with government offers to rehabilitate the area, a sentiment in which they are supported by a majority of Danes.

Christ of the Andes

The name given to a bronze statue, 26 feet tall, that symbolizes peace between Argentina and Chile. At the conclusion of a treaty in 1902 that established their common border, money was raised by popular subscription for the statue. Created by Argentine sculptor Mateo Alonzo, it was cast from ancient cannons and erected in 1904 at the summit of Uspallata Pass, between Mendoza, Argentina, and Santiago, Chile, 12,674 feet above sea level. The left hand holds a cross and the right is raised in blessing. In 1937 a tablet was affixed to its pedestal which translates "Sooner shall these mountains crumble into dust than Argentinians and Chileans break the peace sworn at the feet of Christ the Redeemer."

Chrysler Building

A New York City skyscraper office building, completed in 1930, and, for the brief time till the opening of the Empire State Building, in 1931, the tallest building in the world. Situated at Lexington Avenue and 42nd Street, it is a notable example of architectural design in the Art Deco style: the first few floors are faced with black marble decorated with aluminum window frames, and the tower, which comes to a sharp spire, is also decorated with aluminum. There are stylized decorative gargoyles projecting from corners at various setbacks.

Chunnel, the

The name Chunnel, a blend of *Channel* and *tunnel*, is first recorded in 1928, but the idea of linking Britain and France with a tunnel under the English Channel goes back much further in time. It was first proposed by a French engineer as long ago as 1802, but, with the lethargy that has overcome all Chunnel projects, no one actually started digging a hole until 1880. Shortly afterwards, British interests backed away from the project, apparently for security reasons, so the scheme was canceled. Interest began to revive in the 1950s, and by 1964 it had been agreed to construct a railway tunnel between Folkestone and Calais. After nine years a treaty to this effect was signed, only for Britain to pull out again, in 1975, because of rising costs. The idea of a Channel tunnel never seems to die completely, though: in 1986, the governments of Britain and France announced plans for a joint project to construct a dual railway tunnel, to be completed by 1993.

Cincinnati oyster

A nickname for a pig's foot, used as food.

Cinque Ports, the

In medieval times, before England had a navy, five southeastern harbor towns were charged with the defense of the realm against attack from the sea. In return for this responsibility, these Cinque Ports (from the French *cinq* 'five') were granted considerable privileges, including complete jurisdiction over the southeast coast of England. To the original five, Hastings, Sandwich, Dover, Romney, and Hythe, were later added Rye and Winchelsea. Evolution both in methods of coastal defense and in the actual physical nature of the coastline (although Dover is still a thriving port, the others are now silted up, and Rye and Winchelsea are two miles from the sea) has removed the Cinque Ports' role and with it their historic privileges, but they are proud to retain the title.

City, the

The City of London is the germ from which the sprawling modern metropolis grew. In location and extent it more or less corresponds to the walled city of Norman London. In the present day, sandwiched between the West End and the East End, it is still a self-governing administrative unit, run by the Corporation of the City of London, which is presided over by the Lord Mayor. It is always familiarly known as *the City*, but this name has particular overtones; it refers especially to the eastern part of the area, which is one of the world's major banking and financial centers. It contains the Bank of England, the Stock Exchange, the headquarters of the British clearing banks, Lloyd's, and the offices of many other insurance companies and of all the main merchant bankers, foreign banks, and of other financial and commercial institutions. Those legendary accoutrements of the "City gent," the bowler hat and the tightly furled umbrella, are no longer much in evidence on the streets; in the 1980s when the City has become computerized and high-rise buildings prevail, during working hours, at least, there is little time for superannuated traditions. See also **Square Mile**.

City Beautiful in the Land o'Lakes

A nickname of Fergus Falls, Minnesota.

City Built by Hands

A nickname of Rochester, New York.

City by the Sea

A nickname of Newport, Rhode Island.

City *or* Cradle of Secession

A nickname of Charleston, South Carolina. See also **Game-cock State.**

City of Beautiful Churches, the

A nickname of Louisville, Kentucky.

City of Black Diamonds, the

A nickname of Scranton, Pennsylvania.

City of Brick

A nickname of Pullman, Illinois.

City of Brotherly Love, the

A nickname of Philadelphia, Pennsylvania, a loose translation of its Greek name.

City of Churches, the

A nickname claimed by Brooklyn, New York, and Anniston, Alabama. Also, a former nickname of Chicago.

City of David, the

A name given in the Bible to Jerusalem, in allusion to King David.

City of Dreaming Spires

A somewhat idealistic nickname for Oxford, based on the line from Matthew Arnold's poem "Thyrsis" (1866): "that sweet city with her dreaming spires." The skyline of Oxford is dotted with the steeples, towers, and cupolas of churches, chapels, and colleges. The adjective *dreaming* may also suggest a certain self-absorbed detachment.

City of Elms

A nickname of New Haven, Connecticut, (even though disease has destroyed most of those trees).

City of Executives

A nickname of Birmingham, Alabama.

City of Firsts

A nickname of Kokomo, Indiana, so called because it was the first to introduce the mechanical corn-picker, the push-button car radio, the commercially built car, and canned tomato juice.

City of Five Flags

A nickname of Mobile, Alabama, so called because it was in territory under the successive sovereignty of France, Spain, Great Britain, the Confederate States, and, finally, the United States.

City of Flour

A nickname claimed by Buffalo, New York, and Minneapolis, Minnesota.

City of Flowers and Sunshine

A nickname of Los Angeles, California.

City of Health, the

A nickname of Dawson Springs, Kentucky.

City of Homes, the

A nickname claimed by Dallas, Texas, and Louisville, Kentucky.

City of Isms

A nickname of Syracuse, New York, so called because in its early days it was the meeting place of abolitionists and reformers.

City of Kind Hearts, the

A nickname of Boston, Massachusetts, so called by Helen Keller because her teacher, Anne Mansfield Sullivan, and many of those who helped and inspired her were from there.

City of Light, the

A nickname sometimes given to Paris, France.

City of Lilies, the

A name given to Florence, Italy, which includes lilies in its coat-of-arms.

City of Magnificent Distances, the

A nickname of the District of Columbia, given to it in 1816 by the Portuguese Minister to the United States, José Correa da Serra, a jocular reference to the proposed distances between public buildings, parks, and avenues.

City of Oaks
> A nickname of Raleigh, North Carolina.

City of One Hundred Hills, the
> A nickname of San Francisco, California.

City of Opportunities
> A nickname of Miami, Florida.

City of Palms
> A nickname of Fort Myers, Florida.

City of Peace, the
> A nickname of Salem, Massachusetts, the name of which is a variant spelling of Arabic *salaam* 'peace.'

City of Receptions, the
> A nickname of the District of Columbia.

City of Roses, the
> A nickname claimed by Portland, Oregon, and Little Rock, Arkansas.

City of Soles
> A nickname of Lynn, Massachusetts, so called because of the thriving shoe manufacturing business there.

City of Steel, the
> A nickname of Pittsburgh, Pennsylvania.

City of the Angel
> A nickname of San Angelo, Texas.

City of the Plains, the
> A nickname of Syracuse, New York.

City of the Saints
> A nickname of Salt Lake City, Utah. See also **Land of the Saints.**

City of the Seven Hills, the
> A nickname for Rome. See also **Seven Hills.**

City of the Sun
> An epithet of ancient Rhodes, so called because Apollo was its tutelary deity.

City of the Violet Crown

A nickname of Austin, Texas. See also **violet-crowned city.**

City of Towers

A nickname of New York City.

City of Witches

A nickname of Salem, Massachusetts, a reference to the twenty people executed there for witchcraft in 1692.

City that is a Mile High and a Mile Deep, the

A nickname of Butte, Montana.

City That Lights and Hauls the World, the

A ponderous nickname for Schenectady, New York, where General Electric maintained its home office and a factory that made generators and where the American Locomotive Company was situated.

Clam State, the

A nickname of New Jersey.

Clapham

A district in southwest London that has three main claims to fame: its train station, Clapham Junction, which is at the center of a criss-cross of railroad tracks from the South and Southeast of England, distributing them to the London termini; it gave its name to the Clapham Sect, a 19th-century group of highly evangelical Anglicans who were filled with missionary zeal; and perhaps most notably, the "man on the Clapham omnibus," often cited as the type of the ordinary English person with average opinions and tastes. Like many another formerly grimy inner-city area in London, Clapham has seen the process of gentrification well under way in the 1980s.

Classic City

A nickname of Boston, Massachusetts.

Clink Street

A street in London on the south bank of the Thames, just to the west of London Bridge. In former times a prison stood here—hence the dated British slang expression *in the clink* for 'in prison.' In the Middle Ages and on into Tudor and Stuart times this was the center of a celebrated red-light district known as the Liberty of the Clink.

Clinton's ditch

A derisive nickname given to the Erie Canal that De Witt Clinton advocated building from lakes Erie and Champlain to the Hudson River, which was completed in 1825 during his term as governor of New York.

Clock at the Astor/Biltmore

A once-elegant, latterly commercial hotel, the Astor formerly stood on the west side of Times Square, between 44th and 45th streets, in New York City. In its Art Deco, black-glass-and-chrome lobby was a wall-mounted clock, where people often met by appointment before going on for an evening's entertainment. On the East Side of New York City, the Biltmore Hotel stands at 44th Street and Madison Avenue. It, too, had a clock where couples would meet. In the early 1980s, the Biltmore clock was removed during a general renovation of the hotel, and many thought it had gone the way of the Astor clock. But the hotel owners returned it, fully refurbished, when the renovation was completd, and people can again meet "under the clock at the Biltmore."

Clubland

1. Not so much a specific location as a general term for London's gentlemen's clubs and their members, Clubland is to be found in the St. James's and Pall Mall areas of the West End. Here and nearby are such august institutions as White's and the Carlton, the Reform, the Athenaeum, the Savage, Boodle's, and Pratt's. Traditionally they have provided facilities for professional men and men about town to meet, dine, or perhaps simply sit in a comfortable armchair with a newspaper, all in a congenial atmosphere of quiet elegance.

2. Northern England has a Clubland, too. Throughout the industrial areas of the North, a tradition has built up of working men's clubs, where after a hard day at work the lads repair to hoist a few glasses of ale, play darts or dominoes, and perhaps be entertained by a singer or comic. Many of these clubs have grown to such an extent that they provide a full cabaret, and the Clubland circuit has replaced the defunct music halls as a tough proving-ground for aspiring entertainers.

Clydeside

The area on the banks of the Clyde River, southwest Scotland, particularly the industrial and shipbuilding territory from Glasgow westward toward Greenock. Its name is sometimes confused with Clydebank, which is a town in its own right, now virtually a western suburb of Glasgow.

Coal Metropolis of the World

A nickname of Cardiff, Wales.

Coal State, the

A nickname of Pennsylvania.

Coat Hanger, the

An Australian nickname for Sydney Harbor Bridge, based on its distinctive shape.

Cobble Hill

A section of Brooklyn, near Brooklyn Heights. A residential neighborhood, its buildings are mainly 19th-century brownstones which were renovated during the 1960s and '70s when the area became an important adjunct to Brooklyn Heights, which had become too expensive for many to afford. It is bounded by Atlantic Avenue on the north, Court Street on the east, the Brooklyn-Queens Expressway on the west, and (roughly) Union Street on the south.

Cockade City

A nickname of Petersburg, Virginia, so called after the cockades worn by the soldiers recruited there during the War of 1812. See also **Cockade State.**

Cockade State, the

A nickname of Maryland, so called after the cockade worn by the soldiers of the Old Line during the Revolutionary War. See also **Cockade City.**

Cockpit Country, the

An area of desolate limestone plateau in the northern central part of the island of Jamaica. It is riddled with caves and hollows and striated with fissures and ridges. Behind its forbidding barriers live the Maroons, descendants of fugitive slaves of the Spanish. They are a law unto themselves, and Jamaican officialdom largely leaves them alone. In former times their reputation was such that any government officers entering the Cockpit Country rode back to back to guard against ambush, whence the area's nickname, the *Land of Look Behind.*

Cockpit of Europe, the

A nickname given to Belgium because its exposed position as a buffer between France and Germany has so often led to its being turned into a battlefield—from Ramillies in 1706, through Waterloo in 1815, Mons and Ypres in World War I, to the German invasion of World War II. The term *cockpit* refers to the sense of 'a place where cockfights are staged.'

Cockpit of the Revolution, the

A nickname of New Jersey.

Collar Capital of the World, the

A nickname of Troy, New York. See **Collar City.**

Collar City

A nickname of Troy, New York, so called for many years because it was the home of Cluett, Peabody Company, manufacturers of Arrow collars and shirts.

Colossus of Rhodes

One of the Seven Wonders of the World, this bronze statue of the god Helios was said to have been more than 100 feet tall and to have been built from bronze weapons and armor left behind by the army of Demetrius I of Macedon when they lost their siege of Rhodes. It was designed by Charus of Lindus (a city on the island of Rhodes) and erected at the harbor between 292 and 280 B.C. It is traditionally believed that ships could sail between its legs. An earthquake in 224 B.C. destroyed it and in the 8th century A.D. the bronze fragments were sold to the Saracens. The publicist's word *colossal* is said to derive from this gigantic figure.

Columbus Circle

A junction, at 59th Street and the southwest corner of Central Park, in New York City, where Broadway, 59th Street, and Eighth Avenue cross, the last to continue northward as Central Park West. At its center is a circular plaza with a fountain and a tall pedestal from the top of which Christopher Columbus gazes down on the frequent traffic jams below. Its west side is dominated by the Coliseum, a large convention center; at its south side stands the marble-faced New York City Visitors Center, formerly the repository of the Huntington Hartford collection of art, one of the last imposing agglomerations of some of the worst work by the best artists ever to have been accumulated in one place. Over its north rim towers the Gulf & Western building, a modern monolith to multinational conglomerates. It is, generally, a characterless area, though many years ago a nearby barber shop, at 58th Street, offered "Physiognomical Haircutting," perhaps the only distinctive feature seen for blocks around. It is said that Columbus Circle is the benchmark for all road distances shown on signs approaching the city.

Combat Zone

A nickname for an area in downtown Boston, bounded, roughly, on the west by Tremont Street, on the south by Boylston Street, on the east by Washington Street, and on the north by Temple Place. It is a section of theaters, but its name derives essentially from its unsavory atmosphere, created by sleazy bars, "adult" book and porno shops, "adult" movie theaters, and the patrons and people associated with them. It has assumed the character and function of the former **Scollay Square** (*q.v.*).

Commercial Metropolis of Western Tennessee, the

A nickname of Memphis.

Commonwealth

Only four states of the fifty in the United States call themselves a commonwealth rather than a "state": Kentucky, Massachusetts, Pennsylvania, and Virginia. Puerto Rico is officially designated as one but in this case it is a description of its status as a self-governing territory associated with the United States.

Coney Island of Boston, the

A nickname of Revere, Massachusetts, so called because it is the beach for Boston as Coney Island is for New York City.

Congregation of Spires, a

A former nickname of Chicago.

Connecticut Avenue

An attractive, wide street in Washington, D.C., where many of the embassies of foreign countries are situated. Most of them are large mansions, some in a park-like setting with iron fences about them, giving the area an air of sedate opulence, which, in time of international stress, belies the skulduggery assumed to be plotted behind the ivied walls.

Conservative Cincinnati

A nickname of Cincinnati, Ohio, so called because very little development took place there after the Civil War.

Constable Country

A name given to Dedham Vale, the valley of the lower Stour on the borders of Essex and Suffolk, in East Anglia. The landscape around here was immortalized by the painter John Constable (1776– 1837), and has changed very little since he put it on canvas. Places particularly associated with him are East Bergholt, where he was born, and Flatford, which figures in some of his most famous paintings, including "Flatford Mill" and "The Haywain."

Constitution State, the

The official nickname of Connecticut, so called because Fundamental Orders were drawn up there (1639) that are believed to be the first constitution written by the people. They were largely the work of Thomas Hooker. The Constitution of the United States is said by some to be more nearly like this constitution than that of any of the other colonies.

Continent, the

The British Isles are technically part of the continent of Europe, but when Britishers speak of *the Continent*, they do not include themselves in it. A "continental holiday," for example, definitely involves going abroad. The usage arose at a time when continent meant 'mainland,' as opposed to any islands near its shores, but there is no doubt that nowadays it is reinforced by the British people's feeling of separateness from the rest of Europe. In spite of Britain's joining the European Economic Community in 1973, the English Channel still represents a considerable cultural gulf. See also **Channel**.

Continental Divide, the

The main ridge of high land in North America that separates waters flowing into the Atlantic Ocean and the Gulf of Mexico from those flowing into the Pacific. In the Rocky Mountains, it crosses New Mexico, Colorado, Wyoming, Idaho, Montana, British Columbia, and Alberta. In Canada it joins the Height of Land and separates Pacific and Arctic Sea drainage on the west from the Arctic and Atlantic drainage on the east. It also runs through Mexico and Central America. Also called **the Great Divide.**

Continental Shelf

A geologic configuration along the shores of continents, where the water is somewhat shallower before dropping off to the greater ocean depths.

Convention City

A nickname claimed by Denver, Colorado, Louisville, Kentucky, and Syracuse, New York.

Coonskin Library

The nickname given to those books in the Ames, Ohio, library that were obtained from Boston in exchange for racoon and other animal skins.

Copacabana

1. A great sweep of silvery-white sand that constitutes the main beach of Rio de Janeiro, Brazil. Overlooked by the Sugar Loaf Mountain and the gleaming white tower blocks of the city, it is a magnet particularly to foreign tourists; the local smart set tend to prefer the beach at nearby Ipanema.

2. A nightclub in New York City, on 60th Street between Fifth and Madison Avenues. Operated for many years by the showman and impresario, Billy Rose, it featured a small chorus line of girls, selected for their height as well as their beauty, and advertised as "Billy Rose's Long-stemmed American Beauties."

Copper Belt, the

A region of central Africa containing vast deposits of copper. Most of it is in north-central Zambia, but it also stretches across the border into Zaire. Its mining provides the mainstay of the economy of Zambia, the world's third largest copper producer.

Copper State, the

A nickname of Arizona and Wisconsin.

Corn City

A nickname of Toledo, Ohio.

Corn-cracker State, the

A nickname of Kentucky, thought to be a corruption of *corn-crake*, a species of crane found there. See also **Cracker State.**

Cornhuskers State, the

The official nickname of Nebraska.

Cornish Riviera, the

Situated at the very southwestern tip of the country, and warmed by the Gulf Stream, Cornwall has the mildest climate in England. The long sandy beaches, the little harbor towns, and the frequently luxuriant subtropical vegetation have combined with the balmy weather to suggest the name *Cornish Riviera* for the stretch of southern coastline roughly between Falmouth and Looe. Like its inspiration, the French and Italian rivieras, it is a favorite vacation area. In spirit it extends further east along the coast as far as the elegant resort of Torquay; but this is actually in Devon, and the area is more correctly known as the *Devon Riviera.* See also **French Riviera, Italian Riviera.**

Corn State, the

A nickname of Iowa and Illinois.

Coromandel Coast, the

The southeast coast of India, from Point Calimere in the south (just to the north of Sri Lanka) to the mouth of the Krishna River in the north. Its fame is due not least to its identification as the home of the Yonghy-Bonghy-Bo by the 19th-century English nonsense poet, Edward Lear, but more probably to Coromandel work, a style of decoration consisting of black-lacquered wood, incised and painted gold or other colors, and frequently inlaid with semi-precious stones, mother-of-pearl, or porcelain. Though made in northern or central China, in the late 17th and early 18th centuries, it was transshipped from the Coromandel coast to Europe by merchants of the French and English East India companies. It is also called Bantam work because Dutch traders transshipped from Bantam in Java. Compare **Malabar Coast.**

Costa Blanca

A stretch of Mediterranean coast in eastern Spain, extending from Cartagena to Cape La Nao. It challenges the Costa del Sol as a vacation area; the resorts of Alicante and, in particular, Benidorm attract countless visitors every year.

Costa Brava, the

A stretch of Mediterranean coast in northeastern Spain, extending from Barcelona to the French border; the name means literally 'wild coast.' Its attractions were first "discovered" in the 1920s, and it played an early and leading role in the postwar boom in which Spain became northern Europe's vacation playground, providing guaranteed sunshine at bargain prices. Resorts, such as Lloret de Mar, with their rows of concrete hotel blocks, dot the coastline here, and although the Costa del Sol, the Costa Blanca, and Majorca have since come on the holiday scene, the Costa Brava, with its chip shops, fake pubs, and "afternoon teas" that pander to the British holidaymakers' desire to avoid foreignness, remains quintessential "packaged Spain" in most people's imagination.

Costa del Sol

A stretch of Mediterranean coast in southern Spain, extending eastward from Gibraltar to Málaga. It is popular as a vacation destination among British sunseekers, and many of the resorts there, such as Marbella, Torremolinas, and Fuengirola, have become so anglicized, with their pubs and chip shops, that only the climate reminds one that this is not Brighton or Blackpool.

Costa Geriatrica, the

A humorous nickname for the coast of southeast England, and particularly of Sussex, coined because of the large number of elderly people who tend to retire to seaside bungalows in the resorts there. Worthing, to the west of Brighton, is probably the quintessential senior-citizen territory, though Eastbourne shares the same character.

Costa Smeralda

A stretch of sybaritic vacation territory along the northeast coast of the island of Sardinia, centered on the resort of Porto Cervo. The name (*smeralda* is Italian for 'emerald') reflects the glinting colors of the Mediterranean that laps against the many bays and inlets of the coastline, but may also contain a passing reference to the proverbial wealth of the Aga Khan, who took a leading part in developing tourism there.

Côte d'Azur

The Mediterranean coast of France east of Marseilles; English speakers generally refer to it as the French Riviera. The name *Côte d'Azur*, which so aptly suggests the color of the Mediterranean, was coined in 1887 by the poet Stephen Liégeard.

Cottonopolis

A 19th-century nickname for Manchester, a city in northwestern England. It was the hub of the Lancashire cotton industry, which in those days earned Britain more in exports than any other product, and consequently brought much wealth and power into Manchester.

Cotton (Plantation) State, the
A nickname of Alabama.

Cottonwood City
A nickname of Leavenworth, Kansas.

Country of the Thousand Lakes
An epithet for Finland (which has some 60,000).

Court of St. James's, the
See **St. James's.**

Covent Garden
An open space in the center of London, to the north of the Strand, which has long been famous for two things: fruit and vegetables, and opera. There was a market on the site, for the sale of fruit and vegetables, and later flowers, from 1661 to 1974, when it was moved south of the Thames, to Nine Elms. The old market buildings have subsequently been restored to create an attractive pedestrian precinct, with many cafés and shops, and the new Jubilee Market has been opened, featuring craft stalls and a variety of street entertainments. In the 1980s it is one of the liveliest centers of London's city life. Just to the north is the Royal Opera House, familiarly known as *Covent Garden*, or, to initiates, simply as *the Garden*. There has been a theater on this site since the 1730s, and it is now the prestigious flagship of opera and ballet in Britain. Originally, this area was a garden belonging to the monks of Westminster and was known as Convent Garden. In the mid 17th century an elegant housing project was built here by Inigo Jones, in the central square of which the market was first held.

Coventry
A city in Warwickshire, in central England, well known in legend and, more recently, in fact. The legend goes back to the 11th century, when Lady Godiva, wife of Leofric, rode naked through the streets of the town on her palfry to protest a punishing tax that her husband had imposed on the people. As the story goes, all averted their eyes as she passed save for one voyeur, "Peeping" Tom, whose eponymic fame is scarcely exceeded by that of the object of his gaze. Coventry also figures in the idiom, chiefly British, *send to Coventry*, 'to ignore; refuse to have anything to do with'; if the speculators are right, this phrase had its origin some 600 years later, when the Royalists were incarcerated by Cromwell at the Coventry Gaol, essentially putting them out of commission for a considerable period. Coventry again emerged some three centuries later, when it was almost

entirely destroyed in a bombing raid by the Nazis, in 1940, during the Battle of Britain. As the British high command had knowledge of the impending attack, it is said that the citizens could have been warned and many lives saved. To have issued the warning would have revealed that the intelligence had been received by the breaking of the code of the Enigma machine, a Nazi coding device, and it was not deemed expedient to let that be known by the enemy. Modern Coventry is best known for its ultra-modern cathedral, designed by Sir Basil Spence and completed in 1962, built to replace the ancient one that was devastated in the 1940 air raid.

Cowboy Capital, the

A nickname of Prescott, Arizona.

Cowes Week

The first week in August, when the Royal Yacht Squadron, which is head-quartered at Cowes, Isle of Wight, England, joins with other local yacht clubs for an annual regatta.

Coyote State, the

A nickname of South Dakota.

Cracker State, the

A nickname of Georgia. There are three versions of the origin of this nickname: the sound made by the whips that the early settlers snapped over their mules; a shortening of *corncracker*, since the poorer settlers subsisted mainly on corn; and their dialect, which sounded to some like something being cracked. See also **Corn-cracker State.**

Cradle of Aviation

A nickname of Hammondsport, New York, so called because of the pio-neering aviation work done there by Glenn Hammond Curtiss. See also **Birthplace of Aviation.**

Cradle of Civilization, the

A nickname of Greece.

Cradle of Industry, the

A nickname of Springfield, Utah.

Cradle of Liberty, the

A nickname of Boston, Massachusetts.

Cradle of Texas Liberty

A nickname of San Antonio. See also **Alamo.**

Cradle of the Confederacy

A nickname of Montgomery, Alabama.

Cradle of the Union, the

A nickname of Albany, New York.

Cream City

A nickname of Milwaukee, Wisconsin, so called because many of its buildings were faced with a cream-colored brick that was made locally.

Creole State, the

A nickname of Louisiana.

Crescent City

A nickname for New Orleans, Louisiana, commonly used within that area. It came from the location of the city on the Mississippi River where a series of river bends gave the community a crescent shape. It is reflected in the badge of the New Orleans Police Department, which consists of a crescent positioned above a star.

Crescent City of the Northwest

A nickname of Galena, Illinois.

Crewe

A town in Cheshire, in Northwest England. Its reputation rests mainly on its status as a railroad junction. Lines converge on it from all points of the compass, and it figures largely in many rail journeys: "Change at Crewe" is a familiar watchword.

Crown City of the Valley

A nickname of Pasadena, California.

Crystal Palace

A district in southeast London which gets its name from the Crystal Palace, a huge metal and glass pavilion originally put up in Hyde Park in 1851 for the Great Exhibition. It was re-erected here in 1854, and eventually burned down in 1936, but not before the name had attached itself to the area (reinforced, no doubt, by the fact that the well-known local soccer team is called Crystal Palace).

Cumberland

In the Northwest of England, a former county on the Scottish border. In the local government reorganization of 1974 it became part of Cumbria.

Cumberland Gap

The name of a high pass through the Appalachian Mountains, near the junction of the boundaries of Tennessee, Virginia, and Kentucky, known as "the gateway to the West" to many early pioneers.

Cyclone State, the

A nickname of Kansas.

Dakota

1. A former term for 'any very remote place,' akin to the use of *Siberia* today.

2. The Dakota. A luxurious cooperative apartment building on Central Park West from 72nd to 73rd streets in New York City. Built in the early 20th century by William Randolph Hearst as an investment for his mistress, Marion Davies, it became a cooperative after World War II. Till about 1965, several tennis courts were maintained for the tenants who more recently included the Beatle, John Lennon, and other famous people. It was so named because at the time of its construction, its site was considerably remote from any other major buildings—residential or otherwise—in the city. (See definition **1**, above.)

Dales, the

Dale is a poetic word for 'a valley,' but in Britain *the Dales* has a very specific meaning. A series of rivers drain from the Pennine Hills through Yorkshire to the North Sea, and the valleys they flow through are known as *the Dales*. They range from Teesdale in the north, through Swaledale, Wensleydale (where a famous cheese is produced), Wharfedale, and Nidderdale to, just northwest of Leeds, Airedale. The Dales carve their way through a starkly beautiful landscape of craggy fells and high moors, most of which has been turned into a national park, known as the Yorkshire Dales.

Dallas Book Depository

A warehouse in Dallas, Texas, where, it was determined, Lee Harvey Oswald took up his position with a rifle and assassinated President John F. Kennedy, on November 22, 1963, as his motorcade passed nearby.

Dalmatia

The coastal area of Jugoslavia that borders on the Adriatic Sea.

Dark and Bloody Ground State, the

A nickname of Kentucky (a literal translation of its Indian name), so called in reference to the battles fought there between the Indian tribes of the north and south.

Dark Continent, the

An old nickname for Africa, evocative of a 19th-century colonialist attitude toward the continent as a relatively unexplored and mysterious place whose inhabitants were dark-skinned. It first seems to have been used by H. M. Stanley in the title of his book *Through the Dark Continent* (1878). Twelve years later he wrote *In Darkest Africa*.

Dartmoor

A wild, desolate area in Devonshire, England, the site of England's main prison (since 1850) for long-term convicts.

Davy Jones's locker

A nickname for the sea, used by sailors, a reference to the final resting-place of the dead, possibly from the biblical story of Jonah and the whale.

Deccan, the

A vast plateau which occupies much of India to the south of the northern plains. Beginning at the Narmada River (which is roughly on the same line of latitude as Calcutta), it extends southward in an ever-narrowing V as far as the Nilgiri hills and Ootacamund.

Deep South, the

In the United States, an area encompassing those states in the southeastern part of the country that were generally associated with a slave economy before the Civil War, namely, South Carolina, Tennessee, Louisiana, Mississippi, Alabama, and Georgia. Compare **South, 1.**

Delmarva Peninsula

The name for that part of the Atlantic Coastal Plain that juts south about 180 miles between Chesapeake Bay on the west and the Atlantic Ocean on the east, so called because it consists of parts of the states of Delaware, Maryland, and Virginia.

Denver of South Dakota, the

A nickname of Rapid City.

Derry

A city and county in Northern Ireland. Since 1613 they have been officially known as Londonderry, because in that year the city and surrounding district was given to the City of London as a place for English people to go and settle. Not surprisingly, the new name has never been particularly popular with the locals, and since the resurgence of Nationalist feeling in the late 1960s resistance has grown. In the 1980s, therefore, the old name of *Derry* has been approved for use again by the Post Office.

Deseret State, the
> A nickname of Utah, meaning *honeybee*, from the *Book of the Mormons*.

Deutsch-Athens
> A nickname of Milwaukee, Wisconsin.

Deux Magots, les
> A café, or brasserie, on the Left Bank, in Paris, on the Boulevard St. Germain. It has long been a popular lounging- and meeting-place of the writers and artists who frequent or inhabit the area.

Devil's Island
> A small island off the coast of French Guiana, South America, (one of a group of three, known as the Îles du Salut) which achieved notoriety as a French penal colony of proverbial severity. In earlier times it had been a leper colony, but its isolated position made it an ideal prison, and its function was changed in the late 19th century. Its most famous occupant was probably Alfred Dreyfus, and it is memorably described in the novels *Dry Guillotine*, by René Belbenoit, and *Papillon*, by Henri Charrière. It ceased to be a prison in 1938.

Devils Nest
> An area of wild terrain in the United States covered by a forest on the Nebraska side of the Missouri River between the towns of Crofton and Niobrara. Robbers, outcasts, Indians, trappers, and outlaws lived in the draws between the top of the very high hills and the river front.

Diamond City
> A nickname of Amsterdam, the Netherlands.

Diamond State, the
> A nickname of Delaware, because though small in size, it is great in importance. The sobriquet is also claimed by Arkansas and Maryland.

Diddy wa Diddy
> A name for a legendary place of abundance, superficially of food but essentially of all good things, notably of sexual fulfillment. The term stems from the Black culture of blues and early jazz musicians; though no reliable etymology is available, it might have originated in an African language.

Dimple of the Universe
> A nickname of Nashville, Tennessee.

dinosaur of darkness
> A nickname given to a prehistoric reptile of Antarctica, fossil evidence for which was discovered in 1986.

Dismal Swamp, the

One of the largest swamps in the United States, covering about 750 square miles, in southeastern Virginia and northeastern North Carolina, in which black bears, wildcats, a multitude of fish and other wildlife exist amidst a tangle of vines and a variety of valuable trees. Part of it has recently been cleared for farming. In 1974 Congress established a section of it as the Great Dismal Swamp National Wildlife Refuge. It is part of the Atlantic Inter-Coastal Waterway, but droughts in the late 1970s and '80s have made it unnavigable.

Disneyland

A large (184-acre) amusement (or "theme") park in Orange County in southern California, opened in 1955. Developed under the direction of Walt Disney (1901–1966), who had gained fame and fortune with his animated cartoons of Mickey Mouse, Donald Duck, and other characters, Disneyland was an immediate commercial success, and it has been widely imitated. Its focal point is a large "castle," which is modeled after the folly built by ("Mad King") Otto I of Bavaria in the mountains of his desmesne, and which is similar to a structure at Disneyworld, Disney's other "theme" park, in Orlando, Florida. The amusements, rides, exhibits, and other activities presented are of interest to adults as well as children, though some cynics view Disneyland as symptomatic of the false values placed on popular culture in America.

Dixie

The words *Dixie* and *Dixieland*, referring to the southern states, is said by some to come from the Creole pronunciation of the name of Jeremiah Dixon, who, with another astronomer, Charles Mason, were hired to survey the border between Pennsylvania and Maryland. See also **Mason-Dixon Line.**

Dockland

London probably owes its existence to its potentialities as a port. It is the first place upstream where the Thames is bridgeable, and its tidal waters there are deep enough to have served as a harbor for merchant vessels in Roman times. Seaborne trade lay at the heart of London's development over the best part of the next two millennia, culminating in the building of a vast 700-acre series of docks from about 1800 onward. Behind high prison-like walls, they occupied the area stretching eastward from the Tower of London, mainly on the north bank; this is London's Dockland, which for nearly two centuries provided a livelihood for a significant proportion of East Enders (see **East End**). Furthest upstream is St. Katherine's Dock, a small dock almost in the shadow of the Tower; next door, in Wapping, came London Dock, noted particularly for its huge bonded warehouses and vaults for the storage of liquor, tobacco, etc.; then, on the peninsula called the Isle of Dogs, came the East and West India Docks and the Millwall Docks; and furthest east lay the enormous Royal Docks, comprised of the Royal Victoria, Royal Albert, and King George V Docks, the last built as recently as 1921. On the south bank of the Thames, between London Dock and the Isle of Dogs, were the Surrey Commercial Docks, a great center for timber importation. For more than a century and a half Dockland throbbed with life—improvements were being made to it up until the late 1930s—but then in the 1960s, with the advent of containerization, a sudden and drastic decline began; not deep enough to accommodate the new generation of merchant ships, by 1981 the last of the docks had closed down. Redevelopment in the area has been rapid, much of it under the aegis of the London Docklands Development Corporation: St. Katherine's has become a noted tourist attraction, with a popular exhibit of ships; London Dock has disappeared, and amongst the tenants of its site are the new headquarters of *The Times* newspaper; much of the Surrey Docks area, too, has been filled in and used for housing; ambitious plans are afoot for development of the Isle of Dogs site as an upmarket residential area, for various recreational and commercial activities, and, not least, as an overspill area for the financial institutions of the City; and part of the huge acreage of the Royals may be put to use as a STOL airport. So although its role as a port has now been taken over by Tilbury, 26 miles downstream, Dockland remains a buoyant part of London's life. See also **Pool of London**.

dog days

A period of extreme heat and humidity in the temperate latitudes, in August, usually about the middle of the month, so called because they were attributed to the rising of Sirius, the Dog Star, which occurs at that time.

Dog Star

A name for the star Sirius.

Dogwood City

A nickname of Atlanta, Georgia.

Doldrums, the

An area of the world's oceans around the equator, characterized by light variable winds and long periods of flat calm. It is a sort of corridor between the trade winds, which blow toward it from north and south, and it was responsible for becalming many a vessel in the days of sail. A *doldrum* was originally a fit of depression; only later did it come to mean the state of being becalmed, hence a region where this was likely to happen. See also **Horse Latitudes**.

Domus Aurea

Literally, the "Golden House," a palace built by Nero in a park-like setting of about 200 acres, in the center of Rome, after the great fire of A.D. 64. In its grounds were pavilions, fountains, an artificial lake where the Colosseum later stood, and a 120-foot-tall bronze statue of the emperor.

Donner Pass

The name of a pass, 7088 feet above sea level, through the Sierra Nevada Mountains in eastern California, much used by westward migrating pioneers. It is named after George and Jacob Donner who led a party of 82 settlers through it in the winter of 1846–47 and became snowbound for three months; only forty settlers survived. According to some accounts, the survivors resorted to cannibalism to remain alive. In 1869, the first transcontinental railroad system went through the Pass, and it is now a national historic landmark.

doodlebugs

A jocular nickname used by the British during World War II to offset the terror and devastation of the German V-1 flying bombs. Their passage could be tracked by the sound of their motors; when the noise ceased, those below knew the eerie silence meant the bomb was dropping toward them. Also called **buzz bomb.**

Dormitory of New York, the

A nickname of Brooklyn, New York, so called because many of the people who work in Manhattan live there.

Dorset

A county in southwest England, along the English Channel. It is known mainly as the setting of the 19th-century novels of Thomas Hardy (1840–1928) in which the area was called Wessex after the Anglo-Saxon kingdom in the same general area.

double nickel

A scornful nickname for the 55-mile-per-hour speed limit imposed nationally in the United States at the beginning of the petroleum shortage in 1974.

Dover

A town and seaport in Kent, in southeast England. It commands the Straits of Dover, the narrowest section of the English Channel, and since earliest times has been England's gateway for traffic to and from the continent of Europe. Its artificial harbor is one of the largest in the world. See also **White Cliffs**.

Down East

A New England term for Maine. The "East" is obvious, as Maine is the easternmost part of the United States; the "Down" part probably comes from sailors' talk: first, because examination of a sailing chart that is not constructed on a Mercator projection shows Maine to be more easterly than its northerly appearance on conventional maps; second, because the prevailing winds along the Atlantic coast are westerlies, allowing a sailing vessel to go "easting down" (the *down* meaning 'downwind'); and third, because the shortest route (on a great circle) to northern Europe would take a vessel along the New England coast, past Labrador and Newfoundland.

Down East State, the

A nickname of Maine. See also **Down East.**

Downing Street

A street in central London, a turning to the left off Whitehall from Parliament Square. It contains the British Prime Minister's official London residence, and like **Number 10** (*q.v.*) itself has become synonymous with the office of Prime Minister, or indeed with the British government as a whole.

downtown

A general designation in the United States for the busy, commercial hub of a city, often where the entertainment facilities are centered. See also **uptown.**

Down Where the South Begins

A nickname of Virginia.

Drain, the

A derogatory nickname for the Waterloo and City Line, an underground railroad linking Waterloo station with Bank station on the London Underground. Built between 1894 and 1898, it is the oldest of London's "tubes." It operates only on weekdays, when countless thousands of commuters are conveyed by it to and from the City.

Dr. Brighton

A nickname for Brighton popularized in the Regency period, in the early 19th century, when the seaside town was celebrated as a health resort with seawater that had a most salubrious effect.

Druid City

A nickname of Tuscaloosa, Alabama, from its numerous oak trees.

Drury Lane

A road in the West End of London, linking High Holborn with the Aldwych, just to the north of the Strand. It contains Drury Lane Theatre (officially called the Theatre Royal, Drury Lane), and with many other theaters in the streets around it, it is at the heart of London's theatrical district.

D.S.N.C.O.

An acronym used for designating the towns of Duberger, Les Saules, Neufchâtel, and Charlesbourg-Ouest, which were annexed to the city of Quebec, Canada, in the 1970s.

Dukeries, the

In the 18th and 19th centuries no fewer than four dukes bought estates in the northern part of Sherwood Forest, including Wellbeck Abbey, Thoresby Hall, and the Duke of Newcastle's place at Clumber Park; this part of Nottinghamshire has been known as the Dukeries ever since.

dundrearies

A nickname for side-whiskers down to the chin, worn (1858) by the British actor Edward A. Sothern (1826–81) as Lord Dundreary in *Our American Cousin*, by Tom Taylor. Also called **Piccadilly weepers, weepers.**

Durgin Park

A well-known, popular restaurant in Faneuil Hall, Boston, famous for its generous portions, especially of roast-beef dinners, its informal, family-style service and plain decor, and its gruff waitresses.

Dusky Diamonds

A nickname for coal.

dust bowl, the

The name given to the area severely affected by drought during the 1930s, west of the Mississippi River to the Rockies, and south of Canada to the Mexican border.

Dynamic City, the

A nickname of Detroit, Michigan.

Dynamite Decade

A nickname given by the French to the 1890s, so called because anarchists often threw bombs into cafés in Paris.

Ealing

A suburb of London toward the west, identified mainly with the film studio established there and with the kinds of movies produced, typically *The*

Lavender Hill Mob, comedy productions starring Alec Guinness, Alastair Sim, etc.

Earl's Court

A district in west London, to the west of Chelsea. It is an area of single-room apartments whose occupants quickly come and go but give it a lively cosmopolitan feel. It is particularly popular with Australians—hence its nickname, Kangaroo Valley. It also contains Earl's Court Exhibition, a huge concrete building which houses several national exhibitions and shows every year.

Earthquake City

A nickname of Charleston, South Carolina.

East, the

1. In the United States, an area encompassing those states in the northeastern part of the country, namely, Maine, New Hampshire, Vermont, Massachusetts, Rhode Island, Connecticut, New York, Pennsylvania, and New Jersey, as well as the District of Columbia. Compare **Deep South, Midwest, New England, South.**

2. Geographically, the term *the East* is all-embracing but vague. In broadest terms it is synonymous with Asia, or at least the more southerly and easterly portions of that continent; many people would feel Soviet western and central Asia to be excluded from the notion of *the East*. It cannot be said to be the sum of its parts—the Near, Middle, and Far East—for the Near East teeters on the brink of Europe and Africa, and even the Middle East is perhaps a little too far west to be wholeheartedly the East nowadays. What can be stated with certainty is that the Far East is the East, and that the Indian subcontinent is included in that category too; these are the areas for which anyone going "out East" in colonial times was destined. In more romantic or literary contexts they are referred to as the Orient. Paradoxically, Australia and New Zealand, which are as far or further east than Asia, are usually not thought of as belonging to the East. This may arise from some overlap of the geopolitical connotations of *the East*. In this context it refers to the Communist countries of the world—the Eastern bloc, or Communist bloc—and particularly perhaps those in the Soviet rather than the Chinese sphere of influence: "East-West talks" essentially involve the USSR and the USA. In this sense Japan, confusingly, belongs to the West, even though geographically it is in the East.

East Africa

An area of eastern Africa occupied by the states of Kenya, Uganda, and Tanzania. In 1967 they combined to form the East African Community, which was designed to foster closer economic and social links between them, but it was dissolved ten years later.

East Anglia

A region of eastern England that in broad terms occupies the rounded
bulge of land at the lower right-hand corner of the country. It contains the
counties of Norfolk and Suffolk, the northern part of Essex, and the eastern part of Cambridgeshire. Its name can be traced back to the 6th century, when the Angles founded their kingdom there, and has continued in
use since, without the need for an artificial or literary revival (unlike, for
example, Wessex or Mercia). It is used in certain official designations; the
local area of the National Health Service, for example, is known as the *East
Anglia Region.*

East End

An epithet for the eastern part of London, north of the Thames. Its exact
boundaries are vague, but its western edge is probably marked by a line
going north from the Tower of London, and it extends eastward through
Whitechapel, Spitalfields, Shoreditch, Mile End, Stepney, Bow, Limehouse,
Poplar, Millwall, and Canning Town out towards West Ham and Plaistow.
Throughout London's history this area has been the home of the working
masses and of the poor, although the term *East End* does not appear
before the early 19th century. The powerful image remains of Victorian
slums huddled round the teeming docks (see **Dockland**), of cheerful
Cockneys making light of the Dickensian squalor of their surroundings, of
the low life recorded by HenryMayhew in his *London Labour and the
London Poor* (1849–64) and by Gustave Doré in his drawings. But in fact
much of this was obliterated by bombing in World War II. The slums have
been replaced by high-rise apartment buildings and the docks by light
industry; but the chirpy spirit of the East Enders remains undulled. Compare **West End**.

East Indies, the

A dated term for the islands of the Malay Archipelago, including Java,
Sumatra, Borneo, Sulawesi (Celebes), Timor, usually the Philippines, and
hundreds of smaller islands. As a name, *East Indies* recalls the days when
most of the area was colonial territory controlled by the Netherlands,
Britain, and Germany; not surprisingly, in an era of new independent
states like Indonesia and Malaysia, its continued use is not encouraged. In
earlier days still, its use was less specific: the *East Indies*, or *the Indies*, as
they were often simply called, frequently meant the same as East India, the
eastern part of the Indian subcontinent, and Southeast Asia, with which
the famous East India Company traded.

East Midlands, the

The eastern part of the Midlands, in England, including Lincolnshire, Leicestershire, Northamptonshire, and the southern part of Nottinghamshire.
It is not the legal name of a specific area, with its own local authority, in
the way that the West Midlands is, but it is used as part of more or less

official designations: for example, the airport serving the region, which is situated just to the southwest of Nottingham, is called East Midlands Airport.

East River

The swift-flowing river that separates Manhattan Island, on the west, from Long Island, with Brooklyn, at the south and Queens at the north, below **Hell Gate** (*q.v.*). See also **Harlem River.**

East Side

In New York City, the East Side is, technically, the part of Manhattan lying to the east of Fifth Avenue. It is more commonly associated, however, with the area south of 96th Street to 14th Street and east of Fifth Avenue. Its eastern boundary is the East River. The northern part of this district, especially that north of 46th Street along the river and north of 57th Street a few avenues further west, is usually referred to as the "Upper East Side" (see also **Lower East Side**) and is characterized by luxurious town houses and expensive apartments, especially those between Fifth and Lexington avenues and along the East River. Below east 57th Street lies Sutton Place, a short street with houses and apartments which, if anything, are even more expensive than those elsewhere in the area. The nickname of this part of the city has long been the "Silk Stocking District" from those pre-nylon days when only the wealthy women wore silk stockings. Its main thoroughfare is Park Avenue, beneath which rumble the trains arriving at and departing from Grand Central Terminal, at 42nd Street. Between 46th and 60th streets, Park Avenue once boasted fine apartment houses and residential hotels, like the Marguery. As elsewhere in New York City, after World War II the vast increases in property values caused these to be replaced by high-rise office buildings, notably Lever House, at 53rd Street and Park Avenue, the first "glass skyscraper" to be seen in the city, and, later on, the nearby Seagram Building, also largely of glass with continuous bronze mullions, designed by Ludwig Mies van der Rohe. At 50th Street, occupying an entire city block, is the Waldorf-Astoria Hotel, with its Waldorf Towers, where a suite may cost thousands of dollars a day. Overlooking the East River at 54th Street stands River House, a prime example of luxurious living. See also **Fifth Avenue, Grand Central, Lower East Side, Park Avenue.**

East Village, the

A neighborhood on the Lower East Side in New York City, roughly north of Houston Street, east of Second Avenue, and south of 14th Street, with its eastern boundary more or less at Avenue B. For many years it was a slum, which became only slightly improved in the 1950s when those who were displaced or put off by the higher rents in the West Village (see **Greenwich Village**) rented apartments there. The more adventurous bought the small, unpretentious houses that are characteristic of the area and renovated them. These aspiring "new bohemians," many of whom, though writers, artists, and other professionals, were essentially from the middle class, succeeded in making changes along the western reaches of the district, but Tompkins Park, the focal point of the East Village, remained a barrier beyond which few ventured eastward into the still dangerous slums. Vandalism, drug trafficking, and other crimes continued to dominate these slums, often spilling over into the more genteel streets west of Tompkins Park. By the mid 1970s, many of the pioneers of the 1950s, now twenty years older, tired of the continuing struggle to improve the neighborhood and moved away.

E-boat alley

A World War II nickname for the shipping lanes off the east coast of England where cargo ships were prime targets of German E-boats, which carried torpedoes as well as guns.

Eddystone Light

A lighthouse on the Eddystone rocks in the English Channel, about 12 miles from Plymouth. Built in 1698, it was the first such offshore structure, and it became legendary, memorialized in the folksong, "The Keeper of the Eddystone Light."

Edinburgh of America, the

A nickname of Albany, New York.

Egypt

A nickname of Illinois, so called because Cairo (pronounced KAY-ro) was named after the city in Egypt, and because since the northern part was settled after the southern, the settlers would say, "We must go down into Egypt to buy corn." See also **Egypt Land.**

Egypt Land

A nickname of Chickasaw County, Mississippi, so called because it produced an abundance of corn during the Civil War. See also **Egypt.**

Eire

The Gaelic name for the Republic of Ireland. It was officially introduced as the name of the country in 1937, replacing the Irish Free State. See also **Erin**.

Eisenhower Platz

A nickname given in World War II to Grosvenor Square, in the West End of London, where the American embassy is situated. During the war years most of the other buildings on the square housed the headquarters of the American military forces in Europe, which were commanded by General Dwight D. Eisenhower.

El Dorado

A mythical city or country in South America sought by the Spanish explorers of the 16th century for the fabulous wealth in gold and precious stones it was supposed to contain. Its name, which in Spanish means 'the gilded one,' has since come to be used to characterize any place or situation that holds out the (perhaps illusory) promise of great riches.

El Dorado State, the

A nickname of California.

Elephant and Castle

A working-class district in southeast London, to the south of London Bridge. Despite attempts to show that it is named after the Infanta de Castile, the simple explanation is that its name comes ultimately from that of a pub. There has been a tavern called the Elephant and Castle in the area since at least the 16th century, having as its sign an elephant surmounted by a *howdah*, or "castle." This is the crest of the Cutler's Company, a medieval trade association of those who made knives and similar implements and used a lot of ivory in the process. From the inn, the name has been transferred to the nearby crossroads, now a busy road junction, and finally to the surrounding area.

Embankment, the

All along its course through London, the banks of the Thames are shored up against possible flooding at high tide, and many stretches have broad thoroughfares along them, called embankments—Chelsea Embankment, for example, and Albert Embankment. Mention "the Embankment," however, and it will be generally assumed that reference is to the Victoria Embankment, which runs along the north bank from the Houses of Parliament eastward to Blackfriars Bridge. Its abbreviated name is in such common usage that the former Charing Cross Underground station is now officially called *Embankment Station*. About halfway along the Embankment is the well-known London landmark, Cleopatra's Needle.

Embarcadero, the

The name for the waterfront in San Francisco. See also **Fisherman's Wharf.**

Embassy Row

A section of Massachusetts Avenue, between Sheridan and Observatory Circles, in Washington, D. C., where many foreign embassies are situated.

Emerald Isle, the

A poetic name for Ireland, referring to the perennial lushness of its pastures and woodlands. It is first recorded in *Erin* by William Drennan (1754–1820), who later claimed to have invented it.

Empire City

A nickname of New York City.

Empire State, the

The official nickname of New York.

Empire State Building

A skyscraper office building at 34th Street and Fifth Avenue, in New York City. It was completed in 1931 and was for many years, at 1250 feet with 102 stories, the tallest building in the world, surpassing in height the recently opened Chrysler Building. As 1931 was the depth of the Great Depression, there were few tenants for many years, whence its nickname, the "Empty State Building." It was originally planned to use it for mooring dirigibles, an idea that was never greeted with much favor for reasons of safety, especially after the Hindenburg disaster. It figured in the climax of the motion picture, *King Kong* (1933), in which the gigantic ape climbed to the top only to be shot down and killed by a squadron of U. S. Army fighter planes. In 1945 a U. S. bomber crashed into the 86th floor killing 13. A television tower, 200 feet tall, was added to it in 1950, but the building later lost its record for height to the Sears Tower, in Chicago, which is 1454 feet tall. A number of people have attempted suicide by leaping from its upper floors, but only a few have succeeded. In the 1970s a man who jumped was blown onto a setback below by a strong wind with injuries no more severe than a broken leg. See also **Sears Tower.**

Empire State of the South, the

The official nickname of Georgia.

Empty Quarter, the

A name given, especially in former times, to the desolate area of sand dunes, barren plateaus, and low arid plains that together constitute the southern part of the Arabian peninsula. Its Arabic name is Rub' al Khali, and in English it is usually known as the Great Sandy Desert.

England

England stops about 30 miles north of Hadrian's Wall. It is not the same as Scotland; nor does it include Wales. British people tend to get slightly miffed when foreigners refer to Britain as *England*; the Scots and Welsh get absolutely furious when the English do so. See also **Britain, United Kingdom.**

Epsom

A town in Surrey, in southeast England, which is noted chiefly for its racecourse on Epsom Downs, where the Derby and other famous races are run. It has also given its name to Epsom salts, a preparation of magnesium sulfate, much used in former times as a laxative and naturally occurring in mineral springs which rise near Epsom.

Equality State, the

The official nickname of Wyoming, so called because it pioneered in women's suffrage.

Erechtheum

A temple to Athena on the Acropolis in Athens. Built about 400 B.C., it is known chiefly for its Ionic columns and for a porch, on the south side, with a roof supported by caryatids, which are relatively rare (compared with atlantes). Also, **Erechtheon.**

Erin

A poetic name for Ireland, taken from Gaelic and most often encountered in the motto, *Erin go bragh* 'Ireland forever.'

Eternal City, the

An ancient epithet for Rome, first used in classical times by such authors as Ovid and Tibullus.

Eton

Properly, *Eton College*, an internationally famous school for boys (founded 1440) in the town of Eton, Berkshire, a southwest suburb of London. See also **Harrow.**

Etruria

A district of Stoke-on-Trent, in the Potteries in the West Midlands of England. Josiah Wedgwood had a pottery works there (established in 1769), and built houses for his workers in the surrounding area; the name chosen for it was an allusion to Etruria in Italy, where the ancient Etruscans lived and produced their celebrated pottery.

Eurasia

A portmanteau word used for the continents of Europe and Asia considered as a single landmass. The term was coined in the 19th century, and is used chiefly in scientific contexts. In addition, *Eurasian* is a dated word for someone of mixed European and Asian blood, particularly in India.

European Economic Community, the

The official name for an association of Western European countries formed in 1958 to promote economic cooperation between its members. It is usually used in its abbreviated form, *EEC*, or simply referred to as "the Community." Of alternative, unofficial, names, the *Common Market*, once very widespread, is no longer so much in favor except in America, and

Euromarket is seldom heard. There has always been a certain tendency to refer to it by the number of its members: thus, at its inception it was *the Six* (Belgium, France, Italy, Luxembourg, the Netherlands, and West Germany); in 1973 Denmark, Ireland, and the United Kingdom joined, and it became *the Nine*; with the advent of Greece in 1981 it expanded to *the Ten*; and it became *the Twelve* in 1986 when Portugal and Spain came in.

Everglade State, the
A nickname of Florida.

Evergreen City
A nickname of Sheboygan, Wisconsin.

Evergreen State, the
The official nickname of Washington.

Excelsior State, the
A nickname of New York.

Executive City, the
A nickname of the District of Columbia.

Falkland Islands, the
A group of islands in the South Atlantic, about 400 miles northeast of Cape Horn. A British colony, they are also claimed by Argentina, and the Argentinian invasion and subsequent British recapture of the islands in 1982 gave prominence to their alternative Spanish name, *Islas Malvinas*.

Faneuil Hall
A public market and meeting-place in downtown Boston, built in 1742. Often called the *Cradle of Liberty* because of the many meetings held and inspired speeches given by colonists before the Revolutionary War, it now houses, in addition to its restaurants and shops, historical paintings, a library, and a military museum. Its giant grasshopper weathervane is a landmark. Also called **Quincy Market.**

Fannie Mae
A nickname for the FNMA (Federal National Mortgage Association) and for the bonds issued by that U.S. agency. See also **Ginnie Mae.**

Far East, the
The concept of the Far East, comprising all the countries of eastern Asia, including China, Japan, Korea, eastern Siberia, the Malay Archipelago and Indo-China, has remained relatively stable, unlike the associated terms *Middle East* and *Near East*. However, there is variation in that *Far East* is

sometimes taken to include the Indian subcontinent as well. See also **Middle East, Near East**.

Far North, the

A collective term applied to the regions of the world around and beyond the Arctic Circle: northernmost Scandinavia, the frozen Eurasian tundra, Greenland, the maze of islands to the north of Canada, northern Alaska, and the Arctic icecap itself.

Farther India

An archaic name for the region now known as Southeast Asia or Indo-China.

Far West, the

In the United States, an area encompassing those states that are the farthest west, namely, Nevada, California, Oregon, and Washington. Compare **Pacific Northwest, Southwest, West.**

Fashion Avenue

An official nickname, which appears on the street signs along Seventh Avenue between 35th and 40th streets, in New York City's Garment District. See also **Garment District.**

Faubourg St.-Honoré, Rue du

The fashionable and exclusive shopping street of Paris, which runs parallel to and north of the Champs-Élysées. It is lined with elegant houses and smart shops and is the center of Parisian haute couture and parfumerie: Lanvin, Yves St. Laurent, and Courrèges are all to be found here.

Feast of Lanterns

A name sometimes used by outsiders for the Japanese Buddhist festival Bon, held 13–16 July, when it is believed that the souls of the dead return to earth. Graves are cleaned, and lanterns are hung at graves and house-gates to guide the souls.

Featherbed Lane

A street near Jerome Avenue, in The Bronx, New York, a continuation of Mt. Eden Avenue. Its name is said to derive from the efforts of housewives who supplied General George Washington with featherbeds to enable his men to move their cannons silently during the night across the Harlem River to Washington Heights to surprise the British.

Federal City

A nickname of the District of Columbia.

Fens, the

A low-lying area to the south and west of the Wash in eastern England, including parts of Cambridgeshire, Lincolnshire, and Norfolk. The rivers Nene, Great Ouse, Witham, and Welland flow through it to the North Sea, and in former times much of it was desolate marshy land. Then, from the 17th to the 19th centuries, as drainage techniques improved, the waters were gradually pushed back, and in the present century the rich alluvial soil thus reclaimed has proved invaluable for the growing of vegetables and flowers.

Fertile Crescent, the

A name used to characterize the area from the Persian Gulf, along the Tigris and Euphrates rivers, to the eastern Mediterranean coast. Its well watered plains allowed for the growing of relatively abundant crops, while the Mediterranean allowed access to important trade. It formed the cradle of many ancient civilizations, including the Sumerian, Babylonian, Assyrian, Phoenician, and Hebrew. The term was coined by archaeologist James H. Breasted. See also **Mesopotamia**.

Fifth Avenue

A north-south avenue in New York City, beginning at Washington Square Park and extending to about 135th Street, in Harlem. It has always been associated with wealth: for many years before World War II, much of its length was graced by the mansions of millionaires. Most of these are now gone, the rise in property values having made it impractical to retain them and the difficulty of obtaining servants impossible to maintain them. The few that remain have been acquired by professional associations and institutions. They were replaced by high-rise office buildings and, below 59th Street, by department stores and fashionable retail shops. Most of the swanky retail businesses in the world are represented: Saks Fifth Avenue, Bergdorf Goodman, Gucci, Buccellati, Cartier, Tiffany, Dunhill, and others. At 58th Street is the Plaza, a square with a fountain, alongside which is the Plaza Hotel. From 59th Street northward, where Fifth Avenue borders Central Park (to 110th Street), the buildings are mainly expensive high-rise cooperative apartment houses, though here and there can be found the occasional private townhouse. The Temple Emanuel, at 65th Street, is the largest Reform synagogue in the world. There are a number of museums, too, among them the Museum of the City of New York (105th Street), the Guggenheim Museum (89th Street), and, facing Fifth Avenue from the Park at about 81st Street, the Metropolitan Museum of Art. North of 96th Street the neighborhood begins to deteriorate, especially above 105th Street, near Mt. Sinai Hospital. Above 110th Street, the northern end of Central Park, Fifth Avenue passes into east Harlem, where it assumes the character of that area. From its starting point at Washington Square, for its entire length, Fifth Avenue serves as the demarkation point between the East and West Sides of Manhattan, all buildings being numbered starting there.

Filene's Basement

The basement shopping facility at Filene's, a Boston department store, is associated with sales at which the prices of merchandise are greatly reduced; and it seems probable that the expression *bargain basement* was given currency by Filene's Basement as well as by Macy's and Gimbels' basements (in New York City) which have offered similar good buys. See also **Gimbels, Macy's.**

Financial Capital of the Midwest, the

A nickname of Chicago.

Fire Island

A barrier beach (also known as Great South Beach, but never called that), little more than a sand bar, 32 miles long and half a mile across at its widest point, running east and west, parallel to the south shore of Long Island, New York, east of New York City. Robert Moses (formerly Fire Island) State Park is at its western end, Captree State Park is at its eastern end, at Moriches Inlet; its southern shores are on the Atlantic Ocean; between its northern shores and Long Island lie Great South Bay and part of Moriches Bay. Although two bridges connect its extremities to Long Island, there are no longitudinal roads on the island, and motor vehicles, except for emergency vehicles and certain service trucks, are prohibited. There are some taxis available, but they and most of the other cars use the beach as a roadway. A number of communities are dotted along its length, each with its own character. The oldest and largest is Ocean Beach, which has paved streets, frame houses, mostly traditional in design, and a number of restaurants and other facilities. Farther east is Point o' Woods, an older, elegant community characterized by its large homes and, especially, by its trees and shrubbery, which contrast with the beach plums, stunted pines, blueberry bushes, and generally scrubby plant life seen elsewhere on the island. Cherry Grove, farther east, has many modern houses; it and Fire Island Pines (called "The Pines"), to the east, have had much to do with giving Fire Island its reputation for being a summer focus of homosexual life in the New York area. While it is true that homosexuals have for many years gravitated to these communities, most of the others on the island—Ocean Bay Park, Seaview, Saltaire, Davis Park, etc.—are occupied by families, many with young children who, because of the general absence of cars, can roam about with a freedom not accorded them by any but a few resorts of comparable character. With no cars, residents and visitors get about by bicycle, along the wooden boardwalks in many communities or paved walks in others. Children's wagons, often brightly painted and decorated, are widely used to transport groceries, baggage, and other goods, and scores can be seen, chained and locked against unauthorized appropriation, at the quays where the ferries dock. Many who own houses on the island rent them, at appropriately exorbitant rates, often to a group of beach-lovers who share the expense. These are called "groupers," for obvious reasons, and there may be as many as four occupying each bedroom in a house on alternate weekends from July 4th to Labor Day, in early September. From the point of view of those on Fire Island, Long Island is "the mainland," and access to the various communities is gained by ferry from different towns along its southern shore. The barrier beach itself, on the ocean side, is relatively empty, even on a holiday weekend at the height of the season—that is, although crowds may clump together at the beach near certain hotels or other facilities, one need stroll only a few hundred yards to have an acre of beach entirely to himself. There are wooden walks and stairs for crossing the high dunes, which afford the only protection against storms and where walking is prohibited. There is also a "Sunken Forest" that lies on a part of the beach below sea level and that is protected by the dunes. A slightly elevated boardwalk meanders through the 73 acres of holly, tupelo, and sassafras trees, permitting bird watching and a view of the abundant ground level growth. The winds and blowing sand shear off the tops of the trees when they reach a height of about 35 feet and are no longer protected by the dunes. Hurricanes have occasionally devastated certain areas of Fire Island, destroying expensive homes and wreaking havoc. Yet, those enamored of the beauty and the free life on the Island persistently rebuild.

First Atomic City, the

A nickname of Hanford, Washington.

First State, the

The official nickname of Delaware, so called because it was the first to ratify the Constitution.

Firth of Forth Bridge

A cantilever railway bridge about one mile long, built in 1889 across an inlet (firth) of the North Sea west of Edinburgh, Scotland. Painting it has become a symbol of a never-ending task, for, as soon as painting has been completed, the workers move to the other end and start over again.

Fisherman's Paradise of the North Atlantic

A nickname of Block Island, Rhode Island.

Fisherman's Wharf

A section of the waterfront of San Francisco, famous for its restaurants and especially for the stalls where crabs and other seafood specialties may be purchased, to be eaten with the sourdough bread for which northern California is known. See also **Embarcadero.**

Fitzrovia

The unofficial name for an area of the West End of London, to the north of Oxford Street and the east of Tottenham Court Road, that in the 1940s was a somewhat bohemian quarter, rivaling Chelsea as a haunt of hard-living, hard-drinking artists and littérateurs. Augustus John, Dylan Thomas, and Wyndham Lewis were among its more noted denizens. It probably got its name from the Fitzroy Tavern, a favorite watering-hole in Charlotte Street, just to the south of Fitzroy Square.

Five Points

An intersection on the Lower East Side, in New York City, at the south end of the Bowery. In the late 19th century, when the area declined, it was the gathering-place of toughs and criminals, from whom passersby were not safe. Notable was the Five Points Gang, a collection of hoodlums who caused the police great trouble before they were finally apprehended, at about the turn of the century.

Five Towns, the

Today there is only one town—Stoke-on-Trent—which has reached out and made suburbs of its former neighbors Tunstall, Burslem, Hanley, and Longton; but in former times these were the five autonomous corner-stones of the **Potteries** (*q.v.*), the great china- and earthenware-manufac-turing center of England, in Staffordshire in the northwest Midlands. They and their inhabitants were vividly dissected in the novels of Arnold Ben-nett, notably *Anna of the Five Towns* (1902), in which they go under the pseudonyms Knype, Turnhill, Bursley, Hanbridge, and Longshaw.

Flanders

An area in northwest Europe which in medieval times was a powerful self-governing principality; its territory is now divided up among Belgium, France, and the Netherlands. Flemish towns such as Ypres and Armen-tières saw some of the bitterest fighting in World War I, and the area gave its name to the Flanders poppy, used as a symbol of those who died there in both World Wars.

Fleet Street

A busy street in the City of London, which extends from the eastern end of the Strand to Ludgate Circus. In former times it was famous for the large number of booksellers' shops it contained, but since the late 19th century it has become firmly associated, indeed synonymous, with the British newspaper industry. Most of the national newspapers have had their premises on or near the street, and many provincial ones have offices there, too. However, toward the end of the 20th century, with the need to introduce more modern computerized methods of production, the publish-ers are beginning to move elsewhere, most of them to redeveloped sites in London's Dockland, and it remains to be seen whether the name *Fleet Street* will follow them or fall into disuse. A rather dated nickname for Fleet Street is *the Street of Ink*; more recently, it has been called *the Street of Shame,* apparently in reference to the proliferation of lurid and sensational stories in some sections of the British press.

Flickertail State, the

The official nickname of North Dakota, so called in reference to the Richardson ground squirrel, found only in this state.

Flixborough

A village near Scunthorpe in Lincolnshire, in eastern England, which entered modern folklore on the first of June 1974 when a chemical plant there exploded and burned down, killing 29 people. Its name has been firmly associated ever since with the hazards of large-scale manufacture of flammable chemicals. The plant was actually reopened in 1979 but finally closed down in 1981. Compare **Bhopal.**

Florida Parishes

The collective name for the part of Louisiana lying east of the Mississippi River and north of Lake Pontchartrain, so named because this part of the state was once under Spanish rule. In 1810, the settlers there rebelled against Spain and briefly established an independent republic.

Flower City

A nickname of Springfield, Illinois.

Foggy Bottom

A section of downtown Washington, D.C., where a number of office buildings of the Department of State are situated. The phrase, first used by James Reston in *The New York Times* in 1947, has become a metaphor for the State Department.

Foley Square

A large, open plaza in downtown New York City, behind City Hall, north of the Brooklyn Bridge, with Chinatown to the east. It is the site of a number of municipal and state office buildings, but it is known principally as an area where there are many courthouses—municipal, state, and federal. The name, *Foley Square,* has become a metaphor for these courthouses and for the legal activities associated with them.

Folies Bergère

A theater-nightclub in Paris, famous throughout the world for its Busby-Berkely-like extravaganzas, lavish costumes, risqué entertainment, and its *tableaux vivants,* which are carefully costumed and posed "living pictures" that duplicate well-known classic paintings by peopling them with performers. Its star for many years was the Chicago-born emigrée Josephine Baker. In these liberated times, it may be considered anachronistic, but the *tableaux* tradition was begun in days of Victorian prudery, when the

(French) law allowed women to appear on stage in the nude as long as they did not move. Still an attraction after so many decades, the *Folies* continues as a symbol of Parisian profligacy, eliciting a sly wink among those who are of a conservative turn of mind. See also **Moulin Rouge.**

Fontainebleau

One of the most famous chateaux in France, located southeast of Paris, Fontainebleau, originally a medieval hunting lodge, is an excellent example of French Mannerism (after Italian Mannerism), having been almost entirely rebuilt and completely redecorated in the 16th century by such artists as Benvenuto Cellini, at the direction of Francis I. It is set in a beautiful wood, about 65 square miles in area; the village of Barbizon, at its edge, has given its name to the school of bucolic painting that originated with depictions of the forest.

Fontainebleau Hotel

A resort hotel in Miami Beach, Florida, regarded as the epitome of garishness and poor taste, visited mainly by sunseekers from the North, especially New York City. Although it is named for **Fontainebleau** (*q.v.*) in France, it bears that lovely edifice no resemblance, even in name, for many refer to the hotel as "the Fountainblue."

Foothill City

A nickname of Calgary, Alberta, Canada.

Forbidden City, the

A name given to a city to which access is restricted, usually for religious reasons. It has two specific applications. First, to Lhasa, the ancient political and religious capital of Tibet; as a strict stronghold of Buddhism, it was virtually closed to foreigners in the 19th century. And second, to the inner sanctum of Peking, China. It is at the center of the Chinese boxes that constitute the former imperial capital. At the circumference is the Outer City; within, the walled-off Inner City; beyond this again, the Imperial City; and at the heart of it all, behind its purple walls, the Forbidden City, containing the former imperial palace and various temples, halls, and gardens.

Ford's Theater

A theater in central Washington, D. C., where President Abraham Lincoln was assassinated (April 14, 1865) by John Wilkes Booth.

Foreigner State, the

A nickname of New Jersey, so called in reference to Joseph Bonaparte, king of Spain, who fled to New Jersey about 1812 and lived in palatial splendor on 1400 acres he bought near Bordentown. See also **New Spain.**

Forest City

A nickname claimed by Portland, Maine, and Rockford, Illinois.

Forest City of the South, the

A nickname of Savannah, Georgia.

Forest Hills

A shortened form of Forest Hills Tennis Club, in Forest Hills, Queens, New York City, where the U. S. Tennis Association's National Championship, called the U. S. Open, was held annually, until about 1982 when its site was changed to Flushing Meadows, also in Queens.

Forest Lawn

Forest Lawn Memorial Park is a cemetery in the city of Glendale in the Los Angeles metropolitan area. Designed to promote feelings of reverence rather than morbidity in the visitor, its chapels are used for weddings as well as for burials. With its branch parks, Forest Lawn has grown from its original 55 acres to the present 1200. It has gained worldwide fame not only because it is the last resting place of many well-known people, especially Hollywood celebrities, but because its design elements have been widely imitated. It has been the object of perennial interest of writers dealing with American culture and especially with American burial customs, like Aldous Huxley, Jessica Mitford, and Evelyn Waugh.

Formosa

A name given by the Portuguese to an island off the coast of China when they discovered it in 1516; in their language it means 'beautiful.' The island is Taiwan, and it is now so called both officially and generally, but the name *Formosa* remained in quite frequent usage until well into the 1950s and '60s. The state which occupies it is officially known as the Nationalist Republic of China (in contrast with the People's Republic of China on the mainland), which is often abbreviated to Nationalist China.

Fort Dearborn

A U. S. army post that was the first permanent establishment (1803) in the Chicago area. It was named for Henry Dearborn, Secretary of War under President Thomas Jefferson. Around the fort and nearby trading posts, the community grew to the size of a city, despite the hostility of Indians angered by their displacement. On August 15, 1812, at the start of the War of 1812, the Fort Dearborn garrison of soldiers and settlers was ordered to evacuate in order to shrink the military's western perimeter against the British. About two miles south of the fort, the contingent was attacked by a large Indian force; fifty-three men, women, and children were killed and those remaining taken prisoner in what is now known as the Fort Dearborn Massacre. The fort, burned by the Indians the day after the attack, was rebuilt in 1816 and remained functional until 1837. Today, a landmark plaque commemorates the site, at the bend near the mouth of the Chicago River, just west of where it joins Lake Michigan.

Fort Knox

Although there is a military reservation at this locale, in northern Kentucky, southwest of Louisville, it is known chiefly as the repository of all of the gold owned by the United States government.

Fort McHenry

An old fort, now a monument, in the harbor of Baltimore, Maryland. It is remembered as the site of a bombardment by British naval forces on September 14, 1814, in the War of 1812, during which Francis Scott Key wrote the words to *The Star-Spangled Banner*, later set to the tune of an English melody, popular at the time, *To Anacreon in Heaven*. The song was officially adopted as the national anthem by an act of Congress in 1931.

Fortnum & Mason

A small department store in Piccadilly Street, in London. Although clothing and other general items of merchandise are sold there, it is known chiefly for its elaborate food hall, where virtually anything, no matter how exotic, can be obtained with the help of one of the shop assistants, who are attired in morning dress. Its restaurants are also popular, especially at tea time.

42nd Street

A main cross street in New York City, terminating at the Hudson River on the west and the United Nations complex on the east. The part of it usually referred to is between Sixth Avenue (Avenue of the Americas) on the east and Eighth Avenue on the west. In the early days of the 20th century, when it was still "uptown," 42nd Street was the site of many legitimate vaudeville theaters. The Metropolitan Opera stood nearby, at 40th Street between Broadway and Seventh Avenue, before it moved to new quarters (in the mid 1960s) at Lincoln Center. One of the best-known and most popular vaudeville theaters of the time, the New Amsterdam, is on 42nd Street west of Seventh Avenue, though it has long been a motion-picture theater. That the street retained its earlier personality into the 1940s is evidenced by a popular musical of the time, *42nd Street*, revived in the 1980s with great success. Gradually, the area deteriorated, especially during World War II, and became what it is known for today—a disreputable street populated by drunks, pimps, prostitutes, pick-pockets, drug-pushers, conmen, and other of society's dregs; many of the movie houses, which stand, cheek by jowl, along both sides, offer pornographic films, and the shops, where they can be shoehorned in between, cater largely to the same low trade. Nonetheless, it is brilliantly lit by the flashing neon and other signs on store fronts and theater marquees, and is a mecca for young people who find it exciting, if a bit frightening, especially late at night.

47th Street

A block-long area of West 47th Street, between Fifth and Sixth avenues, in New York City, site of the diamond market. See also **Hatton Garden.**

Four Lake City, the

A nickname of Madison, Wisconsin.

Freedom Trail

A marked path, one and a half miles long, which passes many of Boston's most famous historic landmarks along its route from downtown into the North End. It begins and ends at **Faneuil Hall** (*q.v.*), where Bostonians met before the Revolutionary War to protest British "taxation without representation" and unfair trade policies. It passes the site of the Boston Massacre, where British soldiers shot into an angry mob of colonists, killing five of them and wounding scores more; the Old State House which served as the seat of the colonial government; the Old South Meeting House where more fiery speeches inspired the Boston Tea Party; and the Old North Church where the lanterns were hung to warn of the British attack. Among other points of interest along the trail are the site of Benjamin Franklin's birthplace; Paul Revere's home at the time of his midnight ride; the original site of the Boston Latin School, the first public school in the Western Hemisphere, opened in 1635; the Old Granary Burying Grounds, final resting place of Samuel Adams and Paul Revere; the Park Street Church where gunpowder was stored during the War of 1812; and King's Chapel, America's first Unitarian church.

Free-O

The nickname of Freemantle, a seaport in Australia near Perth.

Free State, the

A nickname of Maryland.

Freestone State, the

A former nickname of Connecticut.

Free World, the

A name applied by their inhabitants to those parts of the world in which a Communist or other totalitarian government does not hold sway. In practice it usually refers to the West and to a fluctuating list of Third World countries. See also **Third World**.

French Quarter, the

In the United States, the oldest part of New Orleans, Louisiana, originally founded by Jean Baptiste Le Moyne, Sieur de Bienville, in 1718. It is the area enclosed by Canal and North Rampart streets, Esplanade Avenue, and the Mississippi River. Long a tourist attraction and symbol of the life style of the city, the French Quarter is famous for its Mediterranean architecture, jazz, antique shops, and restaurants, and as a haven for artists and writers. A major landmark is Jackson Square (formerly Place des Armes), adjacent to which are found St. Louis Cathedral, the Cabildo, the Presbytre, and the Pontalba buildings.

French Riviera, the

On the Mediterranean coast of France to the east of Marseilles, *the Riviera*, as it is often simply called, officially stretches from Cannes to the Italian border just beyond Menton; between the two, strung out like pearls along the Corniche, the precipitous coast road, are those playgrounds of the beau monde, Nice, Monte Carlo, Antibes, Cap Ferrat, and Juan-les-Pins. The area was developed as a vacation center by the English aristocracy in the late 19th century (though chiefly not as a summer resort), and ever since the rich and famous have been maintaining its luxurious image. In the postwar years, though, it has come to be viewed by some as staid and "establishment," and further along the coast to the west, St. Raphael and St. Tropez began to encroach on its reputation with the then daring display of topless sunbathers. Most people would now regard this stretch of coastline as part of the Riviera, too. Compare **Italian Riviera**.

Friendly Confines, the

A nickname for Wrigley Field, a baseball park in Chicago.

Frogland

A derogatory nickname for France. French people were originally called *Frogs* or *Froggies* apparently because of their supposed penchant for eating frogs' legs, although in fact in the 17th century these words were applied to the Dutch.

Frogtown

A fairgrounds near Angels Camp, California, the site of an annual frog-jumping contest, the Jumping Frog Jubilee, originally planned to celebrate the paving of the street in downtown Angel Street, supposedly on the spot where Mark Twain's short story, "The Celebrated Jumping Frog of Calaveras County," took place.

Frozen Wilderness, the

A nickname of Alaska.

Furness

A peninsula in Cumbria, in northwest England, just to the southwest of the Lake District. Its main town is Barrow-in-Furness, famous as a shipbuilding center.

Gaiety, the

A burlesque theater, formerly at 46th Street in Times Square, in New York City. It was closed by Mayor Fiorello H. La Guardia (along with other such places of entertainment) in the mid 1930s, but continued as a movie theater. In its heyday, it featured strippers like Ann Corio, Sally Rand, and Gypsy Rose Lee, and, among those who can recall those days, it remains a symbol of the lost opportunities to indulge youthful fantasies.

Gaiety Delicatessen

A large Jewish delicatessen on Seventh Avenue between 53rd and 54th streets, in New York City. Very popular with visitors of every nationality, it offers the typical fare of such restaurants—hot pastrami, corned beef, salami, and other sandwiches on rye bread in which the ingredients are piled so high that it is difficult to see how to bite into them. It has long been a favorite "noshery" of show-business people, and continues to offer kosher dill pickles as a condiment and "celery" tonic for washing it all down.

Galloping Gertie

A nickname of the suspension bridge across the Narrows of Puget Sound at Tacoma, Washington, which, during a high gale in 1940 was seen to buckle and sway violently, tossing vehicles into the waters below. It was so called because the roadbed flexed like a ribbon.

Galloway

A region in the extreme southwest of Scotland, which has given its name to a breed of hardy black cattle. At its tip is the Mull of Galloway, a headland which forms the southernmost point of Scotland.

Gamblers Express

Any mode of transportation for carrying passengers to a casino, racetrack, etc., as the trains or buses between New York City and Atlantic City, New Jersey.

Game-cock State, the

A nickname of South Carolina, so called in reference to the determined fighting the state waged against the abolition of slavery, which led to its being the first state to secede in 1860.

Garden of England, the

A nickname given over the centuries to many of the more picturesquely fertile counties of England, including Worcestershire, but finally bestowed firmly on Kent, which in early summer billows with apple and cherry blossoms.

Garden of France, the

A name often applied to the Touraine, an area of northwestern central France that straddles the Loire River. This is lush agricultural country, justly famous for the excellence of the vegetables and fruit its farmers produce.

Garden of Maine, the

The nickname of Aroostook County.

Garden of the West

A nickname of Illinois and Kansas.

Garden State, the

The official nickname of New Jersey.

Garment District

An area in New York City, one of the busiest places in the world, bounded by Seventh Avenue on the east, Eighth Avenue on the west, and 35th and 40th streets on the south and north. It is a neighborhood of high-rise loft buildings where many of the major women's clothing manufacturers have their factories and showrooms. Down below, the shops along the side streets are sources for buttons, decorations, and all kinds of trimmings used in the garment trade, and the streets are virtually impassable by cars owing to the double-parked trailer trucks, vans, and other vehicles delivering piece goods, hangers, and other supplies, and carting away finished clothing. Seventh Avenue, nicknamed "Fashion Avenue," is a bustle of messengers, workers, salesmen, models, executives, and the ubiquitous wheeled clothes racks used for transporting merchandise to and fro.

Gate City

A nickname claimed by Chattanooga, Tennessee, and Laredo, Texas.

Gate City, the

A nickname of Atlanta, Georgia.

Gateway Arch

A tall, metal arch on the west side of the Mississippi River, at St. Louis, Missouri, designed by Eero Saarinen and symbolizing the city's reputation as the "Gateway to the West." It contains an elevator that enables visitors to ride to the top, 630 feet above the ground, for a view of the surrounding countryside.

Gateway City of the Hills

A nickname of Rapid City, South Dakota.

Gateway of the West, the

A nickname of New York that was acquired during the 19th century when the completion of the Erie Canal connected the Hudson River and Lake Erie.

Gateway State, the

A nickname of Ohio.

Gateway to the South

A nickname of Louisville, Kentucky.

Gatwick Airport

An airport south of London, formerly (before the completion of the M-25 motorway) difficult of access from anywhere but London. It serves many international flights, especially charter flights. See also **Heathrow.**

Gay Nineties, the

A nickname, not conferred till the 1920s, for the last decade of the 19th century, which, in retrospect, seemed so carefree in comparison with the vicissitudes of the first decade of the 20th century, marked by the fall in the stock market in 1905, and of the second decade, marked by the World War. See also **Mauve Decade.**

Gaza Strip, the

A 100-square mile-coastal area at the southeastern corner of the Mediterranean, of disputed ownership. It is almost entirely surrounded by Israel, but was administered by Egypt between 1949 and 1967, when it contained over 200,000 Arab refugees. In the Arab-Israeli war of 1967 it was taken over by Israel. In 1978 an Egyptian-Israeli agreement called for a five-year period of self-government to be followed by a decision about its future status, but to date no arrangement for self-government has been established.

Gehenna of Abominations, the

A former nickname of Chicago.

Gem City of Ohio, the

A nickname of Dayton.

Gem City of the West

A nickname of Quincy, Illinois.

Gem of the Mountains, the

A nickname of Idaho.

Gem State, the

The official nickname of Idaho.

Genesis rock

The nickname for one of the rocks, believed to be more than four billion years old, brought back from the Apollo 15 moonlanding (1971).

gentleman in black velvet, the *or* little gentleman, the

A nickname for the mole that made the hillock that tripped William III's horse, thereby causing the king's death (1702), as used in a Jacobite toast.

Geordieland

A nickname for the Northeast of England. *Geordie* (a diminutive of the name *George*) used to be a local dialect word for a coalminer, and hence is now applied to the inhabitants of this coalmining region. See also **Northeast**.

George Cross Island

Because Malta was a key British naval base in the Mediterranean in World War II, it became a constant target for German attacks, particularly by air. The people of the island put up such a heroic (and successful) resistance to these assaults that in 1942, in a most unusual gesture, Malta itself was awarded the George Cross, a British medal given for great bravery in battle. The nickname *George Cross Island* which it thereby gained is no longer much used, but the Maltese flag still carries a representation of the medal.

George V

A first-class hotel in Paris, always called "the George Sank" by Americans. There are more luxurious accommodations available in Paris, but the *George V* stands out as the mecca of many tourists who can afford it, especially Americans.

German Coast

A nickname for a part of Louisiana, consisting of St. Charles, St. John the Baptist, and St. James parishes, so named because the area was originally settled on both sides of the Mississippi River by Alsatians and Germans between 1719 and 1722. John Law, the perpetrator of the Mississippi Bubble, encouraged this settlement as part of his attempt to colonize Louisiana. The original Côte des Allemands, as it was called in the days of French governance, was 40 miles in length, on both sides of the river, extending about 20 miles north of New Orleans. The area is still marked by some distinctive customs and by the persistence of some German surnames, some of which have been Gallicized.

German Ocean, the

A name used formerly for the North Sea, the sea separating the east coast of Britain from the continent of Europe. It is a direct translation of a term used by the ancient Greek geographer Ptolemy.

Ghirardelli Square

An area in San Francisco around the Ghirardelli Chocolate factory. The factory was restored in the early 1960s, and the entire district bcame a model for urban revitalization, with many restaurants, shopping facilities, etc.

Gib

An informal nickname for Gibraltar, a British a residence (now a museum) built for Francis colony at the southern tip of Spain which guards the entrance to the Mediterranean. It has always been an important naval base, and *Gib* is used particularly in Royal Navy parlance. See also **Rock**.

Gibraltar in the Pacific

A nickname of Hawaii, so called because of the naval base at Pearl Harbor.

Gibraltar of America, the

A nickname of Vicksburg, Mississippi, so called after a fort built by the Spanish on its high banks at the junction of the Mississippi and Yazoo rivers.

Gibraltar of the North

A nickname for the Sveaborg Fortress, in Finland, now named Suomenlinna. Completed in the 1770s, it was bombarded (unsuccessfully) by an Anglo-French fleet in 1855.

Gimbels

Formerly, a large department store in New York City. Its sole branch in the city was at 32nd Street and Sixth Avenue; in the 1960s, a full-scale store was opened at 87th Street and Lexington Avenue to serve the increasing market on the Upper East Side. It was regarded chiefly as a foil for Macy's, with which it waged price wars. Gimbels Basement became proverbial among New Yorkers as a source of bargains. See also **Filene's Basement, Macy's.**

Ginnie Mae

A nickname for the (United States) Government National Mortgage Association (GNMA) and for the mortgage-backed securities issued by that agency. See also **Fannie Mae**.

Ginza, the

A main shopping district in Tokyo, situated in the eastern part of the city, with Harumi Street at its center.

Giotto's Tower

A campanile in Florence, designed by Giotto early in the 14th century as the bell-tower for the cathedral, or Duomo, designed by Brunelleschi and dating from 1420. Its exterior is surfaced with green and white ceramic tiles.

Glamorous Glennis

The nickname for the Bell X-1, an experimental plane, in which Chuck Yeager became the first person to fly faster than the speed of sound. The event took place on October 14, 1947, in Burbank, California. The plane was named after Yeager's wife.

Glastonbury

A town in Somerset, in southwest England. It has many mystical associations especially with Glastonbury Tor and as the burial place of King Arthur; the Holy Grail is said to be buried there, brought by Joseph of Arimathea.

Glencoe

A valley in the southwestern Highlands of Scotland, just to the south of Fort William, which occupies a very special place in Scots history. At the end of the 17th century the new English king, William III, demanded that the Scottish clans swear an oath of allegiance, promising that they would no longer support the dethroned James II. It seems the Macdonalds procrastinated, and the king ordered a terrible retribution; on February 13th, 1692, government troops, accompanied by many Campbell clansmen (traditional enemies of the Macdonalds), cold-bloodedly massacred nearly 40 of the Macdonalds in Glencoe, drove the rest of them into the surrounding mountains, where most died from exposure, and burned down their houses. The incident greatly embittered Scotsmen's feelings toward England, and ever since that day Glencoe has been known as the "Glen of Weeping." The stark beauty and grandeur of its scenery are undeniable, but many would also claim that an air of melancholy pervades it.

Glens, the

A collective name for the craggy valleys of the Highlands of Scotland. Perhaps the most impressive of them is the Great Glen, also known as Glen More, a great geological rift which slices Scotland in two between Inverness and Fort William; it contains a series of lochs, including Loch Ness, and above it towers Ben Nevis, the highest mountain in Britain. Among other well-known glens are Glen Eagles, which gave its name to the Gleneagles Hotel and golf course; Glenfiddich, where a celebrated malt whiskey is produced; and Glengarry, after which a particular sort of Scottish hat was named. See also **Glencoe**.

Glitter Gulch

A nickname for downtown Las Vegas, Nevada, so called because of the brightly lighted, gaudy canyon formed by the high-rise hotels and other buildings.

Gloucester

A town on Cape Ann, on the coast of Massachusetts, formerly a very important fishing village where many of the boats that fished the Grand Banks were berthed. It was on Norman's Woe, a reef off Cape Ann, that the "Wreck of the Hesperus," of Longfellow's poem, took place. It has won its established place in fiction, notably in Rudyard Kipling's *Captains Courageous*; its history and the men lost at sea making it are commemorated in a bronze statue of a fisherman, at the helm of his boat, bearing the inscription from Ps. 107.23:

They that go down to the sea in ships. . . .

God's acre

A nickname for a churchyard.

Golconda

Historically, an ancient city in south central India, to the west of Hyderabad, noted for its fabulous wealth, particularly in diamonds. Conquered in 1687 by the Mogul emperor Aurangzeb, the city and its fortress now lie in ruins; but its name lives on as a synonym for a source of limitless riches.

Gold Coast

A three-block-wide strip of luxury homes and high-rise apartment buildings along **Lake Shore Drive** (*q.v.*) in Chicago, bordering Lake Michigan, on the city's North Side. The area features a number of famous mansions dating from the early 1900s, including the Victorian-style manorhouse on North State Parkway that served for a time as the Playboy Mansion and which is now used for classes and as a dormitory by the School of the Art Institute of Chicago; this four-story, 72-room structure, built between 1903 and 1914, has been renamed Hefner Hall, after *Playboy* editor/publisher Hugh Hefner.

Golden Chersonese, the

A name given in former times to the Malay Peninsula. It arose originally from the line in Milton's *Paradise Lost*: "Thence to Agra and Lahor of great Mogul, down to the golden Chersonese." *Chersonese* is the ancient Greek word meaning 'peninsula,' and in classical times was often applied specifically to the Thracian peninsula, a finger of land to the west of the Hellespont.

Golden City

A nickname of Sacramento, California.

Golden Crescent, the

1. An area around the juncture of the borders of Iran, Afghanistan, and Pakistan, which is a major center for opium production. Its name is based on that of the Golden Triangle, with a sideglance no doubt at the crescent symbol of Islam.

2. An epithet for the coastal area between the **Golden Triangle** (*q.v.*, def. **3**) and Brownsville, Texas, so called because of the rapid and profitable development of the petrochemical industry in the area.

Golden Gate City, the

A nickname of San Francisco, California, so called because both the break in the Coast Range Mountains along which it is located and the strait running through it that connects the Pacific Ocean with San Francisco Bay are called the Golden Gate.

Golden Horn, the

The name given in English to the inlet of the Bosporus around which Istanbul, Turkey, is situated and which forms its harbor; in Turkish it is known as *Haliç*. Its name probably comes partly from its shape—in former times, *horn* was a word often used for the curve of a bay—but may also refer to the rich harvest of fish it has always yielded, cornucopia-like.

Golden Mile, the

A name given to a section of seafront at the vacation resort of Blackpool, in the Northwest of England. There are seven miles of beach there in all, but the Golden Mile itself starts just to the south of Blackpool Tower and bulges with all manner of amusement arcades, seafood stalls, shops, and bingo halls.

Golden State, the

The official nickname of California.

Golden Triangle, the

1. A name given to the triangle of land in Southeast Asia at whose center the borders of Burma, Thailand, and Laos meet, and which is notorious as a source of much of the world's (illicit) opium. It is estimated that between 500 and 700 tons of it were produced there in 1984, most of it in northern Burma, where it is refined into heroin and smuggled into Thailand for export. Compare **Golden Crescent.**

2. An epithet for the triangular section of downtown Pittsburgh, formed by a cross street at the north and the confluence of the Allegheny and Monongahela rivers, where many large companies maintain their executive offices and headquarters.

3. An epithet for a triangular area on the Texas coast, with the cities of Beaumont, Port Arthur, and Orange at the apexes. See also **Golden Crescent, 2.**

Golders Green

An area of northwest London, to the northwest of Hampstead. It is noted for its large proportion of well-to-do middle-class Jewish residents.

Golgotha

1. A nickname for Temple Bar, in the Strand, London, before the 1880s. It was so called because the heads of decapitated traitors and other criminals were once exposed there, impaled on the iron fence spikes or on tall pikestaves.

2. A nickname for the dons' gallery in Great St. Mary's, at Cambridge University. It was so called because the heads of the colleges meet there. [*Golgotha* appears in Latin, Greek, Aramaic, and other languages and goes back to Hebrew *gulgōleth* 'skull.']

Gondwanaland

A name given to the supercontinent believed to have existed in the southern hemisphere over 200 million years ago; it later split up into continents that became Africa, South America, Australia, Antarctica, and India. Compare **Laurasia, Pangaea**.

Goober State, the

A nickname of Georgia, so called because one of its main crops is peanuts.

Gooney Bird

The World War II nickname for the United States twin-engined aircraft, the C-47, known commercially as the DC-3, developed in 1935, so called from its awkward appearance.

Gopher State, the

The official nickname of Minnesota.

Gorbals, the

A district in southeast central Glasgow, Scotland, on the south bank of the Clyde River. In former times it was notorious for its great concentration of slums, which housed the workforce for the city's heavy industry and shipbuilding; but in the latter half of the 20th century the depressing tenements have been gradually cleared away.

Gotham

A nickname of New York City, so named by Washington Irving in *Salmagundi* (1807), in reference to the village in Nottinghamshire, England, whose inhabitants were known for their humor and canniness.

Grand Canyon State, the
The official nickname of Arizona.

Grand Central
Called "Grand Central" or "Grand Central Station" by many, it is properly Grand Central Terminal, for, unlike Pennsylvania Station, it is the New York City *terminus* of the trains that serve it. Before the days of Amtrak and Conrail, it was the main terminal for New York Central trains from the west and from the northeast, including those of the New York, New Haven, and Hartford Railroad, which served commuters from southern Westchester and western Connecticut. It stands at 42nd Street, where it straddles Park Avenue, which divides and runs around it on an elevated roadway before returning to street level to continue north from 46th Street. A radio program of the 1930s, "Grand Central Station [*sic*]," was introduced by an announcer who intoned a description of a train approaching the Terminal, ending with the following words:

"... dives with a roar into the two-and-a-half-mile tunnel that burrows beneath the glitter and swank of Park Avenue and then— [grandly] Grand Central Station, crossroad of a million private lives, giant stage on which are enacted a thousand dramas daily...."

Grand Central Terminal is a magnificent example of Roman style; its main concourse, 120 feet wide and 275 feet long, has a ceiling, 60 to 125 feet above the marble floor, that is painted in pale blue with signs of the zodiac in silvery white. Once a truly grand edifice, it is now dwarfed by high-rise office buildings, especially the Pan Am Building, which loom over it from all directions except the south, where the upper part of its limestone façade and pediment can be viewed from Park Avenue.

Grand Corniche
The main roadway along the Riviera, in the south of France; it winds along the Mediterranean coast, often affording spectacular views as it rises and dips among the Maritime Alps. Its extent is approximately from Cannes, on the west, eastward to Monte Carlo and Menton, at the Italian border.

Grand National, the
A steeplechase horse race run every spring at the Aintree racecourse near Liverpool in northwest England. It is famous for the severity of some of the fences the horses have to jump, particularly one called Beecher's Brook, which regularly claims its share of victims. The race is often familiarly known simply as *the National*.

Grand Strand
A sixty-mile-long stretch of beach between Cherry Grove and Pawleys Island, on the barrier beach of South Carolina. At its center is Myrtle Beach, a popular resort, said to be named for the creeping myrtle (*vinca*

minor) that grows there. There are two amusement parks, the Myrtle Beach and the Grand Strand, as well as vacation homes and other facilities.

Granite City
A nickname of St. Cloud, Minnesota.

Granite City, the
A nickname given to Aberdeen, a city on the northeast coast of Scotland, because of the somewhat austere and spartan aspect of its streets and public buildings, made of the local granite. In the 1970s and '80s, however, it might with more justice be called the "Dallas of the North," since it is the center of Scotland's oil industry.

Granite State, the
The official nickname of New Hampshire.

Granta
The name given locally to the part of the River Cam that flows through Cambridge, England. Compare **Isis**.

Grant's Tomb
A huge mausoleum at Riverside Drive and 122nd Street, in New York City, erected in the 1890s to honor Ulysses S. Grant (1822–85), general of the Union Army in the Civil War and 18th president of the United States (1869–77). His wife is buried there with him. It is the butt of a harmless old joke: for many years, the comedian Groucho Marx, on his television quiz program "You Bet Your Life," in order to avoid allowing a losing contestant to go away empty-handed, would ask "Now, for fifty dollars, Who is buried in Grant's Tomb?"

Grasshopper State, the
A nickname of Kansas.

Grauman's Chinese Theater
The name of a movie theater on Hollywood Boulevard in the Hollywood section of Los Angeles. It was named for the theater entrepreneur Sid(ney) Grauman (1879–1950), who had earlier opened the Million Dollar, Egyptian, and other theaters. Grauman's Chinese Theater opened on May 18, 1927, with Cecil B. de Mille's "King of Kings." In its architectural style, the theater is a flamboyant version of a Chinese temple. It is especially famous for the hand- and footprints of movie stars in the cement pavement in front of the theater. It was renamed Mann's Chinese Theater in the 1970s to reflect its membership in the Mann chain of theaters.

Gravesend

A port on the south side of the Thames, some twenty miles east of London, the first landfall encountered in approaching the estuary from the sea.

Graveyard of the Atlantic, the

A nickname of Cape Hatteras, North Carolina.

Great Britain

See **Britain.**

Great Central State, the

A nickname of North Dakota.

Great Dismal

A nickname of the District of Columbia, attributed to Daniel Webster, probably because when he lived there in the early 19th century the district was poorly lighted and paved and was muddy, damp, and unhealthy.

Greatest Primary Grain Port in the World, the

A former nickname of Chicago.

Great Land

A nickname of Alaska.

Great River City

A nickname of St. Louis, Missouri.

Great South Gate

A nickname of New Orleans, Louisiana.

Great Wen, the

A derogatory nickname (a *wen* is a wart or tumor) applied to London, especially in the 19th century, with reference to the unsightly and unhealthy growth of the metropolis into the surrounding country. The phrase was popularized particularly by the radical writer William Cobbett.

Great White Way

A nickname of Broadway, in New York City, especially the part that passes through Times Square, so called because of the brilliant illumination afforded by the lights of the theater marquees and advertising signs.

Greek Street

A street between Soho Square and Old Compton Street, in London, known mainly for its restaurants. See also **Soho.**

Green Belt

In England, a buffer zone of parkland required to be included in city planning, especially around London, to avoid the uncontrolled spread of residential or commercial building.

Greenham Common

A Royal Air Force station near the village of Greenham in Berkshire, to the west of London, which achieved an unwanted fame in the early 1980s as a base for the deployment of nuclear cruise missiles and, consequently, as the scene of extensive anti-nuclear demonstrations—particularly those undertaken on a permanent basis by an all-female group who became known in the press as the "Greenham Women."

Green Mountain City

A nickname of Montpelier, Vermont.

Green Mountain State, the

The official (and only) nickname of Vermont.

green pound

A nickname for an accounting system set up in 1975 by the European Economic Community to calculate British farm prices.

green room

The name given to the room backstage at a theater (now, also, a television studio) where performers and others gather to await their cues to go onstage. The origin of the term, for which evidence has been found dating to the 17th century, is uncertain, one theory holding it to be a corruption of "scene room."

Green Venice

A name sometimes given to the low-lying area of wetlands on the west coast of France, to the north of la Rochelle; its official designation is the Marais Poitevin 'the Marshes of Poitou.' As the nickname suggests, the whole area is crisscrossed with waterways, many of which are turned into virtual tunnels by the luxuriant vegetation that overgrows them; the main means of transportation there is flat-bottomed boat.

Greenwich Observatory

An astronomical observatory built in 1675 at Greenwich, on the Thames east of London, to the design by Sir Christopher Wren. In 1884, by international agreement, O° longitude was established as passing through it and as the point of reckoning the world time standard, Greenwich Mean Time. Most of the facilities of the observatory have since been transferred (1948–58) to Herstmonceux, a village in Sussex, near Eastbourne.

Greenwich Village

A section of downtown New York City bounded on the east by Washington Square Park and on the north by 12th Street; its other bounds are somewhat vague and changing, but, in general, may be said to be Hudson Street on the west and Houston Street on the south. It is an older part of the city, with many fine private homes—some hundreds of years old—maintained in good condition by their owners. These stand in carefully preserved streets, where the developers who would construct high-rise apartment houses on the valuable property are kept at bay. During the 1920s to '40s, Greenwich Village acquired a reputation as a bohemian neighborhood populated by artists and writers and some students. The rooms and flats were slightly run-down and the rents were cheap. There were many inexpensive restaurants, notably, in the late 1930s and early '40s, Cholmondley's, where a simple meal could be bought for less than a dollar, and nearby The Blue Mill, where a full dinner, with lamb chops, could be purchased for about $1.15. Nightclubs opened there in the later years, among them Nick's, at 10th Street and Seventh Avenue (Sheridan Square), which featured famous jazz musicians, Café Society Downtown, where jazz was also offered, and, especially, The Village Vanguard, which featured young newcomers like The Revuers (with Adolph Green, Betty Comden, and Judy Holliday) as well as Pete Seeger, Leadbelly, and others who popularized folk song singing. This bohemian atmosphere persisted into the 1950s, when increasing property values forced the less wealthy and the artists and writers to seek shelter elsewhere. Most of them moved several blocks to the **East Village** (*q.v.*) and, to distinguish the almost contiguous areas from one another, Greenwich Village, long nicknamed "the Village," became known by its alternate nickname, "the West Village."

Gretna Green

A village at the very southwest tip of Scotland, just across the border from England, which has achieved legendary status as the place to which young couples can elope to get married without their parents' permission. In the old days, all that such couples needed to do was to declare their willingness to marry; the ceremony could then be performed forthwith by any functionary (like the local blacksmith), without the formalities of a license or banns. In practice, though, things have been tightened up over the years. Since 1856 it has been necessary for either the man or the woman to have lived in Scotland for 21 days before the ceremony, and since 1940 marriage by simple declaration has been illegal; whatever village blacksmiths may remain must content themselves with more mundane activities.

Grimethorpe

A mining village in South Yorkshire. Quite apart from the peculiar appositeness of its name, which could almost have been invented by a novelist wishing to encapsulate the soot-flecked drabness of the northern coalfields, it has come to epitomize, through the playing of the now world-famous Grimethorpe Colliery Band, the great tradition of brass bands that is central to the life of northern England.

Grosvenor Square

A large square in Mayfair, in London, identified mainly with the American Embassy, which occupies its western side. Nearby are the Connaught and Claridge's hotels, two of the best (and most expensive) in London.

Ground-hog State, the

A nickname of Mississippi.

Groves of Academe

See **Academy.**

Grub Street

The mythical abode of those writers who eke out a precarious and slender living by churning out articles for newspapers and magazines at so much the yard. Renamed Milton Street in the 1820s, the real Grub Street, in the City of London, was indeed formerly "much inhabited by writers of small histories, dictionaries, and temporary poems" (Dr. Johnson), but they have since moved on. The first reference to it in English literature appears as long ago as the early 17th century, and in 1891 George Gissing wrote a well-known novel, *New Grub Street*, about the grim life of impecunious authors.

Guernica

A town in the Spanish Basque province of Vizcaya, symbol of Basque unity. It was nearly destroyed in 1937 in a bombing raid carried out by the grandGerman Kondor Legion in the service of General Francisco Franco during the Spanish Civil War. The attack, apparently an attempt to demoralize the Basque civilian population loyal to the Republican government, was immortalized by Pablo Picasso in a large mural painting, a nightmarish depiction of the horrors of war. Also, **Guernika.**

Guiana

A large area of northeastern South America, to the north of Brazil. Most of it was colonized by the British, the French, and the Dutch, as an extension of their Caribbean empires, but a large part of it, including the Guiana Highlands, also extends westward into Venezuela. The former British and Dutch possessions are now independent states, known respectively as Guyana and Surinam.

Guinea

A former name for the coastal regions of equatorial West Africa. The south-facing coast, running parallel with the equator between Cape Verde and Cameroon, was known as *Upper Guinea*; the west-facing coast, from Cameroon south to Angola, was *Lower Guinea*. The term survives in several present-day geographical names: Guinea is a republic and former French colony to the west of the Ivory Coast; to the north of it is Guinea-Bissau, formerly Portuguese Guinea; further to the east, below Cameroon, is Equatorial Guinea, formerly Spanish Guinea; and the great bay of the Atlantic Ocean formed by the elbow of West Africa is known as the Gulf of Guinea. The former British guinea, a coin worth 21 shillings, was so called from its having originally been made with gold from Guinea.

Guinea Pig State, the

A nickname of Arkansas, so called because its farmers were willing to try the agricultural experiments suggested by the federal government during the 1930s.

Gulf, the

A gulf is a vast bay, but as a proper name its usage varies around the English-speaking world. In the U. S. it usually means the Gulf of Mexico, from which the **Gulf Stream** (*q.v.*) gets its name; in British English it refers to the Persian Gulf, a large inlet of the sea to the east of the Arabian peninsula; and in Australia, it is the Gulf of Carpentaria, a huge shallow bay in the north of the continent. Accordingly, the term *Gulf States* can refer either to Florida, Alabama, Mississippi, Louisiana, and Texas, the American states that fringe the Gulf of Mexico; or to the oil-producing countries around the Persian Gulf: Iran, Iraq, Saudi Arabia, Kuwait, Bahrain, Qatar, Oman, and the United Arab Emirates.

Gulf City

A nickname of Mobile, Alabama.

Gulf State, the

A nickname of Florida.

Gulf Stream

The name of a major ocean current that forms the northwest edge of a large, clockwise system of currents in the North Atlantic ocean. Benjamin Franklin named it, thinking it began in the Gulf of Mexico, but in fact it originates in the western Caribbean Sea, flows through the Gulf of Mexico and the Florida Straits, northward along the Florida coast to North Carolina, then northeast at Cape Hatteras where it separates, the main part continuing northeastward until it breaks up into eddies east of the Grand Banks off Newfoundland. Its water is 11-18° warmer than the surrounding water, and as a result, the prevailing westerly winds blowing across it provide Norway and the British Isles with much milder winters than any other regions of the same latitude, as evidenced by palm trees growing along the southwest coast of Ireland.

gun that won the west, the
A nickname for the Winchester rifle, one of the first with a magazine, first used in 1856.

Hadrian's Wall
A stone wall, seventy-three miles long, between Carlisle in the west and Wollsend, near Newcastle, in the east, built during the reign of the Roman emperor Hadrian (completed in A.D. 136) at the northern reaches of Roman Britain, to keep the Picts from invading. Large sections of the wall and its stone forts form one of the largest Roman remains in Britain today. Also called **Picts' Wall.**

Haight-Ashbury
A district in downtown San Francisco, in the vicinity of Haight and Ashbury streets. During the 1960s, it was famous as an area populated by hippies and "flower people."

Halles, les
Until 1979 the Paris food market was situated at les Halles—a vibrant place to be in during the hours before dawn. In that year it was moved, much as London's Covent Garden had been, to the outskirts of the city. The famous old market buildings were demolished, but the area surrounding it, on the right bank of the Seine to the northeast of the Louvre, is still known as les Halles. It is being radically redeveloped as a center of entertainment, shopping, and culture, and to the east of the district is the controversial and exhilarating Pompidou Center (known to Parisians as Beaubourg), an arts complex housed in a building of challenging modernity.

Hambledon
A village in Hampshire, southern England, famous as the birthplace of cricket. In fact, the game probably originated centuries before among the shepherds on the South Downs in Sussex, but it was in Hambledon, in the late 18th century, that the legendary village cricket club was founded that took on and beat the best that the rest of England could offer and set the pattern the game was to follow thereafter. In more recent years Hambledon has again been a trendsetter, for it was here in 1952 that Sir Guy Salisbury-Jones planted the vineyard that began the revival of English winemaking. See also **Lord's.**

Hammacher-Schlemmer
A small department store on East 57th Street, in New York City. It is known largely through its mail-order catalogue, which offers some of the oddest and luxurious wares including (from a 1986 catalogue) an automatic vinaigrette mixer ($24.95), an "arboreal" chair ($3750), a lighted electric tie rack ($36.95), a cat's door that can be opened only by an electronic key

worn on your cat's collar ($124.95), an automatic infrared-controlled faucet ($299.50), a cordless electric pot scrubber ($59.95), a two-person hovercraft ($7995), and other esoteric items.

Hampstead

A residential area on high ground to the north of central London. Like many other outlying parts of London, it used to be a village, and it manages to retain the atmosphere of a separate community better than most. It is a fashionable and very expensive part of the capital to live in, and perhaps paradoxically has the reputation of being a socialist stronghold. The socialism is generally of a genteel, Fabian variety, however, rather than red-blooded and revolutionary; "Hampstead intellectual" is a common term of mild abuse applied to those who speculate abstractly on schemes for the betterment of mankind. To the north of the area is Hampstead Heath, one of London's best-known open spaces, which commands fine views over the center of the city.

Hamptons, the

The collective nickname for several towns along the South Shore at the eastern end of Long Island, namely, Bridgehampton, Westhampton, Southampton, and Easthampton, all popular, though expensive, summer colonies where the residents (and investors) let out their houses for the season or a part of it. Easthampton, the farthest east, is the most expensive and the most chic. There are many fine beaches along the Atlantic Ocean, access to which is accorded to residents only.

Hanging Gardens of Babylon

One of the Seven Wonders of the Ancient World, the virtually prehistoric hanging gardens are thought to have been built on terraces formed by the setbacks of a large ziggurat, or step-pyramid, in the ages-old capital of Babylonia, on the Euphrates River.

Hants

The abbreviated name of the county of Hampshire in southern England, often used in speech as well as writing. The county gets its name from the city of Southampton, which was at first, in Anglo-Saxon times, called simply Hamtun, hence the county's original name of Hamtonshire. By the time of the Domesday Book (1086), this had been shortened to Hantshire, from which we get the abbreviation. The full version with a *p* developed later.

Hapsburg lip

The nickname given to the prominent jaw and protrusive lower lip that first appeared with Frederick III, and was later produced ever more markedly through intermarriage, especially among the last Hapsburg kings of

Spain. It is supposed to have been inherited from his mother, the Mazovian princess, Cymbarka.

Hard-case State, the

A nickname of Oregon.

Hardware City

A nickname of New Britain, Connecticut.

Harlem River

The narrow, yet navigable river that separates Manhattan Island from The Bronx, between **Hell Gate** (*q.v.*) and Spuyten Duyvil Creek. See also **East River.**

Harley Street

A street in the West End of London, to the south of Regent's Park, largely the abode of distinguished, or at least expensive, medical consultants, specialists, and psychoanalysts whose fees are not covered by National Health. Anyone who insists on a Harley Street physician or surgeon is likely to be a person who does not worry about the amount charged.

Harringay

A district in north London, the boundaries of which are somewhat unclear. The area just to the north of Finsbury Park is called *Harringay*; its station is called Harringay, and it contains Harringay Stadium, a well-known greyhound racetrack. However, in 1963 a new London borough was created around it, called Haringey, which contains a much larger area than the original Harringay. The new version is a reintroduction of an old spelling, but it has proved hard to remember which name refers to the district and which to the borough.

Harrods

A large department store, in Knightsbridge, London, a renowned mecca for shoppers where, it is claimed, virtually anything in the world can be purchased or ordered, from camels to luxury automobiles.

Harrow

An internationally famous school for boys, founded (1571) at Harrow-on-the-Hill, a suburb west of London. See also **Eton.**

Harry Percy of the Union, the

A nickname of South Carolina, so called to recall the determination of its citizens, in comparison with that of a fiery English soldier who died in a rebellion against Henry IV in the Battle of Shrewsbury (1403).

Harry's American Bar

A bar and restaurant in Paris, frequented for generations by Americans (as well as others) who regard it as a safe haven—a sort of home away from home, especially if they are visiting France for the first time, and where they can be assured of getting the "perfect" martini. For years its advertisements in the *International Herald Tribune* have advised readers to "Just ask the taxi driver to take you to Sank Roo Doe Noo" ('5 rue Daunou').

Harvard Yard

The center of the original Harvard College. This historic, grassy, tree-shaded area is surrounded by libraries, dormitories, and classroom buildings in a variety of architectural styles; George Washington's troops were housed in Massachusetts Hall during the Revolutionary War, and the provincial council met in Harvard Hall. The twelve residential houses for students are modeled after those at Cambridge and Oxford, each with its own dining room, athletic facilities, and library.

Hastings

A town and seaside resort on the coast of Sussex, in southeastern England. It is celebrated as the site of the Battle of Hastings, fought in 1066, when the Norman invaders defeated the Anglo-Saxons; but in fact the battle did not take place at Hastings at all: it was fought 6¾ miles inland, at a place where the village of Battle now stands. Purists often refer to it as the Battle of Senlac, since its actual site was near a stream called Senlac (which means, literally, 'sandy brook').

Hatton Garden

A street in central London that goes from Clerkenwell Road to Holborn Circus, just to the north of Fleet Street. It is lined with jewelers' shops, and has long been celebrated as the center of the London diamond market. Until the mid 17th century the site had been the garden of Ely Place, London residence of the bishops of Ely, which was famous for its roses and fruit.

Hawkeye State, the

The official nickname of Iowa, so called either after a feared Indian chief of that name or after J. G. Edwards, nicknamed "Old Hawkeye," editor of the Burlington *Patriot*, later named the *Hawkeye and Patriot*.

Haymarket, the

1. An old food market area north of Faneuil Hall, in Boston.
2. A broad, short thoroughfare in London, leading from Piccadilly Circus to Pall Mall.

Haymarket Square

The site, on the Near West Side of Chicago, of the May 4, 1886, Haymarket Riot, an incident in which seven policemen and four others were killed and about 70 persons injured by a bomb thrown when police sought to disperse a gathering of some 1500 labor protesters and sympathizers said to have been spurred by a small group of anarchists. Public sentiment, fanned by the establishment press, ran high against the anarchists, despite the sizable amount of support they enjoyed among workers. In what is now considerd to have been a gross miscarriage of justice, eight anarchists were convicted; of these, four were hanged and one, facing a like fate, committed suicide. In 1893, Illinois Governor John Peter Altgeld pardoned the surviving three anarchists on the ground that their trial had been unjust, a decision that hurt his political career. The actual bomb-thrower, who has never been conclusively identified, escaped.

Heart of America, the

A nickname of Kansas City, Missouri.

Heart of Dixie, the

The official nickname of Alabama.

Heart of Georgia, the

A nickname of Macon.

Heart of Midlothian, the

The nickname of the old Edinburgh Tolbooth, or prison, demolishd in 1817. Its fame rests on the novel of the same name, by Sir Walter Scott, in which much of the action is centered on the prison. Midlothian is a former county of Scotland, in which Edinburgh was situated; in 1975 it became merged into the new Lothian region.

Heart of the New Industrial South, the

A nickname of Alabama.

Heathrow

The main airport serving London, which is about 25 miles to the northeast. One of the busiest in the world, Heathrow Airport is in a continuous state of construction and expansion. See also **Gatwick.**

Hell Gate

A strait between Eastchester Bay, leading into the Long Island Sound to the east, and the East and Harlem rivers in New York City, bordered by the boroughs of Queens on the south and The Bronx on the north. Owing to the strong currents and tides, it is a turbulent, dangerous body of water, which is probably why it was so named. A huge fixed railway bridge rises high above its waters, the western reaches of which are traversed by one branch of the Triboro Bridge between Randall's Island and Queens; over its eastern end are the Bronx Whitestone and Throggs Neck bridges, linking The Bronx with Long Island. See also **East River, Harlem River.**

Hell's Kitchen

Formerly, the nickname given to the area, on the West Side of New York City, bounded by 42nd and 57th streets on the south and north and Eighth and Tenth avenues on the east and west. The slum-like nature of the neighborhood created an atmosphere where crime was rampant, giving rise to the epithet. The reputation of the area was such that, in 1936, Richard Rodgers wrote the music for a ballet which he named *Slaughter on Tenth Avenue.* Today, *Hell's Kitchen* is known to real estate people as the Clinton District; De Witt Clinton High School was formerly at Tenth Avenue and 59th Street.

Hell Upon Earth

A description by its inmates of the Confederate prison at Andersonville, Georgia, during the Civil War. A complete lack of shelter and sanitary facilities, a dearth of food and clothing, and the filth of the 16-acre enclosure into which as many as 30,000 prisoners were crowded caused the death of more than 12,000 men. Similar conditions existed in various Union prisons.

Helvetia

The Latin name for Switzerland, originally a Roman province in central Europe in the area of present-day southern Germany and northern and western Switzerland, in ancient times inhabited by the Celtic Helvetii tribe. *Helvetia* is still used on Swiss stamps, avoiding the need to choose among the French, German, Italian, and Romansh versions of the country's name.

Hemp State, the

A nickname of Kentucky.

Henley

A town in Oxfordshire, on the River Thames—its full name is Henley-on-Thames. It is synonymous with rowing, for every July the famous Henley Royal Regatta is held here, in which the best crews in Britain and many from around the world compete. The event began in 1839, and as the 19th century wore on attendance became a mandatory part of the fashionable London society season. It retains a powerful aura of Edwardian high summer, with parasoled girls in frilly dresses and young men sporting straw boaters and colorful blazers.

Herald Square

Today, Herald Square is an unprepossessing area formed by the angular crossing of Broadway and Sixth Avenue, at 34th Street, in New York City.

If it is known for anything, it is that Macy's occupies the western side of it, from 34th to 35th streets. Around the turn of the century, however, before the central commercial focus of the city had moved on up toward Times Square, ten blocks to the north, Herald Square was still a part of the Great White Way, as Broadway is known. That fame is preserved in George M. Cohan's song (1904), "Give My Regards to Broadway," which begins:

> Give my regards to Broadway,
> Remember me to Herald Square.
> Tell all the boys on Forty-Second Street
> That I will soon be there.

Heroic City, the

A nickname of Cartagena, Colombia.

Herring Pond, the

A somewhat dated, humorous nickname for the North Atlantic Ocean, often abbreviated to simply *the Pond*. It is first recorded in the late 17th century.

Hibernia

A name given by the Romans to Ireland. It derives ultimately from the same Gaelic source that yielded Erin, the poetic name for Ireland.

High, the

To all habitués of Oxford, the High Street is familiarly known as *the High*. Among the colleges here are Magdalen, Queen's, Brasenose, St. Edmund Hall, and University College. See also **Broad**.

Highgate

An area in north London, just to the northeast of Hampstead, and like Hampstead on the top of a hill. In character, too, it somewhat resembles Hampstead: it is a high-class and trendy residential area, the resort perhaps of those whose pockets do not quite stretch to the west side of Hampstead Heath. It is famous as the spot where in the 14th-century Dick Whittington thought better of his decision to leave London, and for its cemetery, which houses several luminaries, including Karl Marx.

Highlands, the

A mountainous region in the north of Scotland. Its southern limit is not universally agreed upon. Some see it as starting to the north of the central Lowlands, and thus including the Grampian mountains. In this context, the town of Stirling, to the northeast of Edinburgh, is often known as "the gateway to the Highlands." Alternatively, some would exclude the Grampians, and say that the Highlands start just to the south of the long valley that includes Loch Ness. This view is probably influenced by the fact that the official Highland region more or less corresponds with this area; it was formed in 1975 from the former counties of Caithness, Sutherland, Nairn-shire, and most of Inverness-shire and Ross and Cromarty. This is a remote and spartan land, where scattered crofters eke out a bare living; but it is also famous for the dramatic scenic beauty of its heather-covered hillsides. It remains a bastion of the Scots Gaelic language and culture. Its chief town is Inverness, at the northern end of Loch Ness. See also **Capital of the Highlands.**

Highveld, the

A high flat treeless plateau in the Transvaal, in northeastern South Africa. It is sometimes also known as the **Northern Karoo.**

Hill, the

A nickname for Capitol Hill, a small hill in Washington, D. C., on which stands the Capitol Building in which the Congress holds its sessions. Capitol Hill is used metaphorically to refer to the Congress. See also **Capitoline.**

Hill City

A nickname claimed by Portland, Maine, and Lynchburg, Virginia.

Hilton Head Island

A major resort area in South Carolina, the largest sea island between New Jersey and Florida, situated about thirty miles north of Savannah, Georgia.

Hindustan

A name ultimately derived from *Hind*, the Persian word for India, but for obvious reasons so closely linked with the Hindu religion and the Hindi language that in modern usage it is usually applied to those parts of the Indian subcontinent inhabited by Hindus, in contrast to Muslims, and those parts in which Hindi is the main language. In practice, this means the portion to the north of the Deccan, and more particularly the area around the Ganges.

Hog Butcher for the World

A nickname of Chicago, bestowed by Carl Sandburg in his poem, "Chicago."

Hog & Hominy State, the

A nickname of Tennessee.

Hogtown

A nickname of Toronto, Canada.

Holland

1. A name commonly applied to the Netherlands. Historically it referred to a county of the Holy Roman Empire, which constitutes only a part of the modern Netherlands; now divided into the provinces of North and South Holland, it contains Rotterdam, Amsterdam, and the Hague.

2. In former times, an adminstrative area of Lincolnshire, in eastern England. It was in the southeastern part of the county, based at Boston. Its title in full was the Parts of Holland. Its name is now incorporated into that of a local parliamentary constituency. Compare **Kesteven, Lindsey**.

Hollywood

A section of Los Angeles located between Beverly Hills and downtown Los Angeles. Laid out and named in 1886 by Horace Wilcox, it was incorporated in 1903 and then was annexed by Los Angeles in 1910. The movie business began around 1910, and within a decade the name Hollywood became almost synonymous with American cinema. Since the advent of television, the movie studios have moved elsewhere, and today few actors actually live in Hollywood: but the name still retains its earlier connotations. "Hollywood" and related forms such as "hollywoodish" are universally used to describe individuals or places that are showy, glamorous, or flamboyant (or sometimes cheap and tawdry). Its glitter and brashness have earned Hollywood (and, by extension, all of Los Angeles) the name of "Tinseltown," said to have originated in a derisive remark made by Oscar Levant in the 1940s.

Hollywood and Vine

A reference to the intersection of Hollywood Boulevard and Vine Street in the Hollywood district of Los Angeles. Although it has been called "The Times Square of the West" (a name also applied to Hollywood Boulevard), it is only an intersection of normal size and has no unusual characteristics. There are no significant historical or literary associations, and the adjacent buildings have never been particularly noteworthy. Somehow the intersection of Hollywood and Vine acquired the reputation of being a place where one could see film stars or perhaps a place where celebrities would congregate. It all might have started with a joking reference on a radio comedy show and then been perpetuated despite its falsity. Any sightseers attracted to Hollywood and Vine by this rumor could only be disappointed.

Holy Land, the

1. A name given to the ancient territory of Palestine or sometimes more specifically to Judea. It is first recorded, in its Latin form, *terra sancta*, in the 11th century, and refers to Jesus's birth, life, and death there. It was further reinforced during the Crusades by the presence of the Holy Sepulchre in Jerusalem.

2. In the 19th century, the parish of St. Giles, London, just to the east of Soho, was familiarly known as the Holy Land, from the large number of Irish (Roman Catholic) people who lived there.

Holy Mother of the Russians

An epithet for Moscow, chiefly in the 19th century.

Holy Name Cathedral

The Near North Side seat of the Roman Catholic archdiocese of Chicago, and center of one of the largest of the city's 449 Catholic parishes. The cathedral occupies ground given to the Catholic Church by William B. Ogden and Walter L. Newberry, owners of a large amount of North Side property and advocates of a city-built bridge over the Chicago River at Clark Street to provide easier access to their land from the Loop. It is said that in return for the valuable block along State Street on which Holy Name stands today, bridge proponents were delivered the sizable Catholic vote. Constructed in 1874–75, in place of a church that was burned down in the Great Chicago Fire of 1871, the cathedral has been renovated several times, most recently in 1968–69. Ironically, Holy Name has served as a setting or backdrop for at least two bloody Prohibition-era incidents. Across the street, on November 9, 1924, gangster and flower fancier Dion O'Banion was gunned down—in the flower shop he co-owned—by members of the South Side Al Capone/Johnny Torrio gang. Two years later, the cathedral itself was riddled with machine-gun bullets when O'Banion's successor, Hymie Weiss, and his chauffeur were cut down on the cathedral steps by Capone henchmen.

Home Counties, the

A collective name for counties surrounding and bordering on London; it is not, though, an exact term, and not everyone would agree on which ones are included. By common consent, Surrey is one—indeed, it is perhaps the quintessential home county—and all authorities agree that Essex and Kent can bear the name, as could Middlesex when it existed. Most people wold also include the counties to the north and west of London, Hertfordshire, Buckinghamshire, and Berkshire. The Home Counties have a rather unexciting public image; they are inhabited on the whole by "nice," comfortable, and conformist middle-class people, many of whom commute to London to work, and the area as a whole is more safely buffered against economic stringency than much of the rest of Britain. Compare **Southeast**.

Home of the Cheeseburger, the

A nickname of Denver, Colorado, so called because this sandwich was invented there during the 1930s.

Homesteader's Paradise

A nickname of Palestine, Texas.

Honkers

A nickname for the British colony of Hong Kong, used especially by British people who live and work there or elsewhere in the Far East.

Hoosier State, the

The official nickname of Indiana, so called either in reference to *hoozer* 'hill dweller' or 'highlander,' or to the settlers, who were said to be so inquisitive that they pulled the latchstring of any new house they passed and yelled "Who's here?"

Hornet's Nest, the

A nickname of Charlotte, North Carolina, so called because it was the center of opposition to the Union forces during the Civil War.

Horn of Africa, the

The name given to the vast pointed peninsula of land at the northeastern extremity of Africa, which projects to the south of Arabia. It contains Somalia and the southeastern part of Ethiopia.

Horse Latitudes, the

A name given to two belts around the oceans of the world at about 30° north and south of the equator, characterized by light variable winds and long periods of flat calm. In the days of sail they were best avoided if one wished to make a speedy voyage. It is thought that their name may come from the high death rate of horses carried as cargo in ships that became becalmed there, but many even more bizarre explanations have been offered. See also **Doldrums**.

Hot Water State, the

A nickname of Arkansas, so called in reference to its hot springs.

House, the

A name applied familiarly to several institutions, particularly as a shortened form. Legislative bodies are often so designated; in the U. S., the House of Representatives, and in Britain the House of Lords or, more typically, the House of Commons. If any grave political matter arises in England, it is sure that "questions will be asked in the House." In addition, the London Stock Exchange is informally called the House, as is Christ Church, a college of Oxford University.

House of Burgesses

The first representative legislature in America, formed in 1619, in Jamestown, Virginia, the first meeting of which was called by Governor George

Yeardley. The House of Burgesses met with the governor and his council and this combined lawmaking body was called the General Assembly of Virginia.

House That Ruth Built

A nickname for the Yankee Stadium, a sports arena in the west Bronx, in New York City. The home of the New York Yankees baseball team, it was built during the 1930s when Babe Ruth, the Yankee pitcher whose record for home runs stood for almost forty years, played there and proved a significant enough attraction to ensure the financial success of the team.

Hub City

A nickname of Compton, California, and Brainerd, Minnesota.

Hub of New York City

Columbus Circle at 59th Street where Broadway and Eighth Avenue inter-sect is so-called because distance on all roads is measured from here. See also **Broadway.**

Hub of the Universe, the

A nickname of Boston, Massachusetts.

Hudson River

A river that flows from Lake George, in the Adirondack Mountains, 300 miles south to empty into New York Bay. It was once a great fishery resource, especially for sturgeon and, in the spring, shad; but pollution has destroyed most of the widlife larger than a microbe. It flows along the west side of Manhattan Island, which, a century ago, offered bathing clubs along its shores. At the Tappan Zee, it widens to more than a mile (in the area of the town of Harmon and Bear Mountain State Park), while further south, as it approaches New York City, its western banks rise hundreds of feet in a row of picturesque cliffs, about forty miles in length, called **the Pali-sades** (q.v.).

Hull House

A part of the famous social settlement in Chicago established in 1889 by Jane Addams and Ellen Gates Starr; they, with other reformers, helped pioneer such welfare laws as workmen's compensation and insurance, an eight-hour work law for women, and tenement-house regulations. The spiritual birthplace of the profession of social work, Hull House performed many services for the multi-ethnic Near, or Lower, West Side neighbor-hood in which it stood, while emerging as a national focal point and symbol for most of the liberal causes of the day—particularly women's suffrage and pacifism. The two remaining buildings of the original Hull House complex have been restored and are now national landmarks, while

remnants of the old "settlement style" neighborhood stretch west along
Taylor Street.

Hummer, the

The nickname for the HMMWV, High Mobility Multipurpose Wheeled
Vehicle, a four-wheel-drive diesel-powered vehicle designed for off-road
use.

Huntingdonshire

A former county in the east Midlands of England. In the local government
reorganization of 1974 it became part of Cambridgeshire.

Hyde Park Corner

Being almost rectangular, London's Hyde Park has four corners, but it is
only the southeastern corner (where the park's main entrance is situated)
that has appropriated the name. It is at the confluence of several major
roads, including Knightsbridge, Piccadilly, Park Lane, and Constitution Hill,
and the junction, officially called Wellington Place, is the busiest traffic
center in London; it has been calculated that well over a hundred vehicles
pass there every minute. See also **Speakers' Corner.**

Iberia

The name given by the Romans to the southwestern European peninsula
now occupied by Spain and Portugal; it derives from *Iberus*, the ancient
name for the River Ebro. It remains in fairly common use in the phrase
"Iberian peninsula," a handy means of coupling its two modern states.
Confusingly, Iberia was also in former times a region in southwestern Asia,
to the south of the Caucuses, which corresponded to modern Georgia in
the Soviet Union. See also **Peninsula.**

Icebox of the United States, the

A nickname of International Falls, Minnesota, so called because it is almost
always the coldest city in the country.

"In" and "Out," the

The nickname of the Naval and Military Club, in Piccadilly Street, London,
so called after the signs on the columns that flank the driveway before its
entrance.

Indiana's Gateway City

A nickname of Jeffersonville.

Indian-Appian Way

The nickname of the Maunee and Wabash rivers (in Indiana), so called
because the Indians and fur traders made as extensive use of it as people in

the Roman Empire made of the Appian Way, which ran from Rome to Capua.

Indian summer

The American name for a period of warmer than usual weather in late autumn, usually mid November.

Indies, the

An archaic term that referred to much of the southern and southeastern parts of the Asian continent, including not only India but also Indo-China and the East Indies. The area's fabled wealth was a magnet for 15th- and 16th-century voyagers, but attempts to find a westward route to it got no further than the islands of the Caribbean. Their discoverers were under the misapprehension that they had arrived at their goal, hence the name for the islands that survives to this day: the West Indies.

Indochina

A somewhat ambiguous term, it standardly refers to the mainland of Southeast Asia, a peninsula at the southeast corner of Asia, sandwiched between India and China, that contains Burma, Thailand, Cambodia, Laos, Vietnam, Malaya, and Singapore. However, it also happens to be the collective name the French gave to their colonial possessions in this area: Annam, Cochin China, and Tonkin (now joined together to form Vietnam), as well as Cambodia and Laos. Because of the potential confusion between *Indochina* and *Southeast Asia*—and also perhaps because of the unwelcome taint of colonialism—the term is not heard as much today as formerly. See also **Southeast Asia**.

Industrial Center of the Great South, the

A nickname of Birmingham, Alabama.

Inland Empire, the

A roughly rectangular region of plains, centered on Spokane, Washington, in the Pacific Northwest of the United States, bounded on the west by the Cascade Mountains, on the south by the Blue Mountains, on the east by the Rocky Mountains, and on the north by the Selkirk range. About 200 square miles across, irrigated by the Columbia River, it is an economic region, originally established in the 1880s as an agricultural area where wheat and peas were grown; subsequent development of its mineral and timber resources led to its becoming a rail center. Physically in Washington, Oregon, Idaho, Montana, and Canada (British Columbia), it flourished well into the 20th century. It received its name from a Congregational missionary, George Henry Atkinson, who, in 1848, analyzed its soil and foresaw its great potentials.

Inland Metropolis, the

A nickname of Birmingham, Alabama.

Inner Mongolia

Although it may sound like an informal epithet or a nickname, Inner Mongolia is the shortened form of the officially named Inner Mongolian Autonomous Region, under the control of China. See also **Outer Mongolia.**

Inns of Court and Chancery

The Inns of Court at London are Gray's Inn, Lincoln's Inn, the Inner Temple, and the Middle Temple. The first two became established in the 13th century literally as inns where students of law resided with their masters and read law; they are named for the men who operated them. The latter two were established later, in the early part of the 15th century, and are named for the seat of the Knights Templars, suppressed in 1312, whose premises they later occupied. All were rented from their owners and bore their names. As it later developed, it was unnecessary for all those engaged in legal work—as in the drawing of wills, the transfer of land, and so forth—to be educated in the refinements of law required of those who practised in the courts, and the inns of chancery, severally attached to the inns of court, emerged. In the 16th century, the division was formalized, resulting in the present division between barristers and solicitors, belonging to inns of court and chancery, respectively. In the early 19th century, the system finally broke down after 200 years of decay and was reestablished in 1854 by order of the common law commissioners, with all four inns functioning as a unified educational body. In Ireland, a body, the King's inns, similar to that of the original inns at London, was instituted, but the separation into barristers and solicitors was not brought about there till 1866. In Scotland, the Faculty of Advocates at Edinburgh functions in a like manner. In the 1980s, there is some move afoot to eliminate the distinction between barristers and solicitors, but the outcome is unlikely to be resolved for some years.

Insurance City

A nickname of Hartford, Connecticut.

International City, the

A nickname of Montreal, Canada.

Iodine State, the

A nickname of South Carolina.

Irish Channel

A neighborhood of New Orleans, Louisiana, bounded by St. Joseph and Constance streets, Louisiana Avenue, and the Mississippi river, that had a reputation for rowdy and disorderly behavior, street gangs, and crime, especially in the last quarter of the nineteenth century. Named for the large number of Irish immigrants who settled there beginning in the 1840s, it is still popular with those of Irish extraction.

Irish Free State, the

From 1921 to 1937, the name of the country now known as the Republic of Ireland.

Iron City

A nickname of Pittsburgh, Pennsylvania.

Iron Curtain, the

A name given to the boundary between the communist countries of Eastern Europe and the capitalist countries of the West. It refers in part to the closely guarded physical frontier, which runs along the western edge of East Germany, Czechoslovakia, Hungary, and Yugoslavia; but to a greater extent it suggests the ideological and cultural barrier that impedes the free flow of ideas and people between the two sides and symbolizes the hostility with which the two camps regard each other. States to the east of the dividing line are known as "Iron Curtain countries." The name was popularized by Winston Churchill in his speech at Westminster College, Fulton, Missouri, in March 1946, but he was by no means the first to use it. As a general term for a sinister and impenetrable barrier it has been traced back to the Earl of Munster's journal of 1817, and it is first applied to the Soviet Union and its influence in Ethel Snowden's book *Through Bolshevik Russia* (1920). There are several references to it in 1945–46, and Churchill himself used it before his Fulton Address, in a cable to President Truman in June 1945. Compare **Bamboo Curtain**.

Iron Men of May

In New England folklore, the three days around the last full moon in May, traditionally the last potential frost dates, when plants can be set out without likelihood of their freezing.

Iron Mountain State

A nickname of Missouri.

Iron Ore Capital of the World

A nickname of Hibbing, Minnesota.

Isis

In Oxford and further upstream toward its source, the River Thames is known as the *Isis*. The name is a corruption of *Tamesis*, the Latin for 'Thames.'

Island, the

1. A nickname for the Isle of Wight, a largish island in the Channel south of Portsmouth and Southampton, popular among Britons as a holiday site. Its associations are largely Victorian, for Queen Victoria and Prince Albert often sojourned there. It is known to yachtsmen for **Cowes Week** (*q.v.*), a strenuous program of day-sailing races, and for the Round-the-Isle yacht race, usually an all-day affair but in 1986 won by a trimaran in about four hours. Its main physical feature is **the Needles** (*q.v.*). three tall natural chalk obelisks at the western side of the Island, an easily identified landmark from the sea.

2. A nickname, for New Yorkers and others who are in the region, for Long Island, a hundred-mile-long island east of New York City. South Shore is along the Atlantic Ocean; North Shore forms the southern boundary of the Long Island Sound, with Connecticut on the shore opposite. On its western end are the boroughs of Queens, to the north, and Brooklyn, to the south, both of which are part of New York City. The nickname really refers only to Nassau County, east of New York City, and, east of Nassau, to Suffolk County, which splits, east of Riverhead, around Peconic and Gardiner bays, into the North Fork, which ends at Orient Point, and the South Fork, which ends at Montauk Point. Both of these counties are part of New York State. With the improvement of commuter transportation over the years and the increase in local business and industry, the Island has become a year-round residential region. But its eastern reaches, particularly along the South Shore, were and still are summer resort areas. See also **Fire Island, Hamptons, North Shore, South Shore.**

Isle of Athelney, the

A low hill to the northeast of Taunton, Somerset in the Southwest of England. Its classification as an isle comes from the fact that until comparatively recently the region around it was wetland and marsh, and the hill was the only piece of solid ground for some distance. It owes its fame to King Alfred's taking refuge there from Viking attack in 878.

Isle of Dogs, the

Not an island at all, but a sort of peninsula formed by a loop of the Thames in the East End of London, opposite Greenwich. It is at the heart of London's Dockland, and contains the East and West India Docks and the Millwall Docks. These were finally closed to commercial traffic in 1980, and the area was subsequently developed for light industry and as a center for leisure activities. Its curious name has never been satisfactorily explained, but it probably derived either from a royal kennels in the area in former times or from the fact that dead dogs floating down the Thames used to be washed up on its left bank.

Isle of Ely, the

An enclave of the county of Cambridgeshire in eastern England, in the heart of the Fens. In former times it was a county in its own right, but in 1965 it was merged into Cambridgeshire. Its identity survives as the name for the local parliamentary constituency. Before modern techniques of drainage transformed the landscape, the area around the city of Ely was very much an island surrounded by watery wastes, and the great gothic cathedral still dominates the Fenland skyline.

Isle of Thanet, the

An area at the northeastern corner of Kent, in southeastern England, which contains the seaside vacation resorts of Margate, Ramsgate, and Broadstairs. It is no longer an island at all, but in former times it was completely separated from the mainland by the rivers Stour and Wantsum. Tradition has it that Thanet is where the Saxons first landed in England.

Islington

A residential district in northeast London, to the north of King's Cross. Within living memory it was a rather seedy working-class area, but as West End rents rose, its 18th- and early 19th-century squares and terraces began to seem more desirable to London's up-and-coming young bourgeois, and in the 1970s it became perhaps the archetypal gentrified inner-city suburb.

Italian Riviera, the

The northwest coast of Italy, from the French border to La Spezia. Chief among its holiday resorts is San Remo. See also **French Riviera**.

Italy of America, the

A nickname of Arizona, so called after its mountains and scenic areas.

Jack Benny's Home Town

A nickname of Sheboygan, Wisconsin.

Jack Dempsey's

A former restaurant on Broadway, at the northern end of Times Square, in New York City. Owned and operated by "Jack" (William Harrison) Dempsey, world heavyweight boxing champion from 1919 to 1926, it was for many years a popular meeting-place for sports figures, celebrities, and various Broadway types.

Jackson's of Piccadilly

A specialty shop, formerly in Piccadilly Street, London, near Fortnum & Mason. Long a traditional place to shop for exotic foods, condiments, soaps, perfumes, and colognes, Jackson's gave up its retail business in the early 1980s when it failed to come to terms on a new lease with the owners of its building, leaving its former clientele with little more than an occasional pang of nostalgia.

Jacob's Pillow

A summer school of dance founded by modern dance pioneer Ted Shawn in the mid 1930s, situated in the Berkshire mountains of western Massachusetts, and named after a rock formation that suggested the biblical story. Reflecting the eclectic tastes of its founder, the summer school continues to offer instruction in ethnic dance, modern dance, and ballet and a wide variety of concert dance performances to the public.

Jamdung

A Jamaican nickname for the island of Jamaica. *Dung* represents the local pronunciation of *down*, and the word combines Jamaica with the notion of ordinary Jamaicans being oppressed, or "jammed down," by their political masters.

Japan

The name used in English (and, with variations, in other European languages) for the country known by its inhabitants as Nippon. The immediate source of the word is Malay *Japung*, which in turn comes from Chinese *Jih-pun* 'sunrise, orient.' This seems to be a direct translation of Japanese *Ni-pon*: *ni* 'sun' and *pon* 'origin.' *Nihon* is an alternative version, with the same meaning. See also **Land of the Rising Sun.**

Jarrow

A town on the south bank of the Tyne River, in the Northeast of England; in the latter part of the 20th century it forms virtually a suburb of Newcastle-upon-Tyne. Its name is intimately linked with the famous Jarrow march of the early 1930s; the Great Depression had caused crippling unemployment in the town's shipyards, and many of the workers marched en masse to London to bring their plight to the attention of Parliament. To the present day, Jarrow is synonymous with such so-called "hunger marches."

Jayhawker State, the

A nickname of Kansas, so called after the nickname given to the pillagers and outlaws on both sides at the beginning of the Civil War.

Jeep

A nickname for a small, usually open, four-wheel drive vehicle, capable of carrying five people. It was so named by soldiers in World War II as a shortened form of GP (for "General Purpose") vehicle.

Jericho

A district in the northwest corner of Oxford, through the middle of which runs Jericho Street. Very much on the other side of the tracks from the gothic and classical splendor of academic Oxford, it is a jumble of small residential streets clustering round the large premises of Oxford University Press.

Jermyn Street

A street in St. James's, in the West End of London, linking St. James's Street with Regent Street. It is famous for its small but fashionable shops where many of the accouterments of gentlemanly living may be purchased, notably shirts: Jermyn Street is synonymous with fine shirtmaking.

Jersey Blue State, the

A nickname of New Jersey, so called in reference either to the blue uniforms of its Revolutionary War militia or to its Blue Laws.

Jewel City of California, the

A nickname of San Diego.

Jewel of the Adriatic, the

A nickname of Venice, Italy.

Joburg

An abbreviated name often used for Johannesburg, South Africa's largest city. It is in the northeast, in the Transvaal, and is the country's goldmining center. See also **Rand.**

John Bull

A rather dated personification of the English nation, used in former times to symbolize particularly its stalwartness or its insularity. In pictorial representations he usually appeard as a stout jovial gentleman in early 19th-century costume, embellished with a Union Jack vest. His first recorded appearance is in the satire *The History of John Bull* (1712) by the Scottish writer John Arbuthnot. The Irish dramatist George Bernard Shaw wrote a play dealing with Ireland, entitled *John Bull's Other Island.*

Johnstown

A city in Pennsylvania that has been associated since its founding (1793) with three devastating floods. One, in 1889, killed more than 2000 people; another, in 1936, killed 25 and did $40 million in damage; and in 1977, a third killed 85, with property damage of more than $300 million.

Jolly Roger, the

A nickname for the pirates' black flag with white skull and crossed bones, from *roger*, an obsolete word meaning 'rogue, ram.'

Jumbo State, the

A nickname of Texas, acquired before the admittance of Alaska to the Union (1959) made Texas the second largest state.

Jutland

The mainland part of Denmark (in Danish, *Jylland*), which protrudes northward between the North Sea and the Baltic. Its name preserves that of the Jutes, a Germanic tribe of the European Dark Ages. (The Jutes who invaded England in the 6th century A.D. probably came from a little further west, near the mouth of the Rhine.)

Kangaroo Valley

A name conferred in the 1960s on the Earl's Court area of West London because of the large number of more or less temporary Australian immigrants who live there.

Kansas Bibles

The nickname given to rifles bought with money collected in churches by abolitionists in the northern and eastern states and used to ensure that Kansas would remain without slaves. Also called **Beecher's Bibles**, thought to be named for Henry Ward Beecher, a violently abolitionist preacher.

Karelia

A region of northeastern Europe, to the southwest of the White Sea. It used to belong to Finland, and although it was annexed by the Soviet Union following the Winter War of 1939–40, its Finnish associations are strongly maintained by Sibelius's *Karelia Suite*.

Karoo, the

A name given to various dry tableland areas in South Africa, particularly the *Great Karoo* and further south the *Little Karoo*, both in the southern part of Cape Province. In addition, the Highveld is also sometimes called the *Northern Karoo*. The term is probably derived from Hottentot *garo* 'a desert.'

Kasbah, the

The name for the old native quarter of Algiers, Morocco, fabled as a warren of narrow streets and mysterious passageways that have long provided fiction writers with a setting for eastern intrigue. Also spelled **Casbah.**

Kemp Town

A district of east Brighton, on the south coast of England, named after a local MP, Thomas Kemp, who designed and built it in the 1820s.

Kensington

An area of west London, to the west of Belgravia. It is a fashionable and expensive residential district, similar to but more staid and respectable than its livelier neighbor to the south, Chelsea. The area known as South Kensington, familiarly known as *South Ken*, around the Cromwell and Old Brompton roads, is famous for its museums, including the Natural History and the Victoria and Albert; the site on which they are built was bought with some of the proceeds of the Great Exhibition of 1851, at the instigation of Prince Albert. Further north the area includes the Royal Albert Hall and Kensington Gardens, the latter long famous as a venue where nursemaids of wealthy families take their young charges. See also **Royal Borough**.

Kesteven

In former times, an administrative area of Lincolnshire, in eastern England. It was in the southern part of the county, based at Sleaford. Its title in full was the Parts of Kesteven. Compare **Holland, 2; Lindsey**.

Kew Gardens

The informal name for the Royal Botanic Gardens at Kew, in Richmond upon Thames, a borough west of London. Its origins date back to the 17th century. Today it has an important library, extensive museums and greenhouses, and is noted for the pagoda, a Chinese-style building constructed in the 18th century to a design by Sir William Chambers.

Key City, the

A nickname of Vicksburg, Mississippi, so called because of its strategic location, which made it an important base during the Civil War.

Key of the Great Valley, the

A nickname of New Orleans, Louisiana.

Keystone State of the South Atlantic Seaboard, the

A nickname of South Carolina.

Keystone State, the

The official nickname of Pennsylvania, so called either because its initials were carved into the keystone of the arch of the new Pennsylvania Avenue Bridge when the federal government moved to Washington, D. C., or because Pennsylvania cast the last vote, making unanimous the colonies' decision to issue the Declaration of Independence.

Kilburn

A district of northwest London, to the southwest of Hampstead. In former times it was a rather down-at-heels working-class area, with a large Irish population, but as with so many inner London suburbs, the latter part of the 20th century is seeing a rise in its status.

King's City, the

An epithet for Copenhagen (*Kongens By*).

King's Cross

1. A district in north London, to the east of Regent's Park. The term is now virtually synonymous with King's Cross Station (built in 1852), the large terminus from which trains go to northeast England and eastern Scotland, although it has also achieved a certain notoriety as a red-light district. The area originally got its name from a statue of King George IV which once stood at a nearby crossroads. Before the 1830s it was known as Battlebridge.

2. *King's Cross* is also the name of a district in Sydney, Australia, where the city's prostitutes and ecdysiasts ply their trade.

King's Road

A lengthy London thoroughfare that starts in Belgravia, passes through Sloane Square, and continues southwest through Chelsea to finish in Fulham. Its heyday was probably in the 1960s and early '70s, when it rivaled Carnaby Street as a vital artery of "swinging London." It was the proverbial resort of hippies, and later of punks, and inevitably developed from a mecca of genuine youth culture to a mere tourist attraction. In the 1980s it still abounds in boutiques and smart little bistros, but it has something of the air of a museum exhibit of the '60s, whose outlandishly dressed denizens are liable to ask tourists for money if they wish to photograph them. Compare **Carnaby Street**.

Knightsbridge

An area in the West End of London, to the south of Hyde Park and the west of Belgravia. It takes its name from Knightsbridge, a road that is a westward continuation of Piccadilly. Residentially it is a very exclusive and expensive district, but its fame rests on its stores; highly-priced shops and boutiques abound here, but all are overshadowed by Harrods, the largest department store in Europe, which seems to exert a magnetic attraction on visitors to London.

Kocourkov

A mythical village in Bohemia, the mayor, aldermen, and citizens of which are typified by their foolish behavior. Its proverbial character has been preserved in the idiom, ". . . as in Kocourkov," and variants thereof. See also **Chelm, Gotham, Mistelbach.**

Kodak City

A nickname of Rochester, New York, so called because it is the home of the headquarters of Eastman Kodak.

Kremlin, the

A citadel in Moscow which since the 12th century has been the seat of power and influence in Russia, and latterly in the Soviet Union. In addition to several government offices, it contains the former Imperial palace and three cathedrals, with their familiar bulbous onion domes. The name has come to be synonymous with the Soviet government, and indeed those who study Soviet policy are known as "Kremlin watchers," and their discipline as "Kremlinology." The word itself came into English via German; a transliteration of the actual Russian name would be *Kreml.*

Kurfürstendamm, the

A street running through the center of West Berlin. Now that Unter den Linden has been appropriated by the eastern sector, it is the city's main social artery, combining the roles of New York's Broadway and Fifth Avenue.

La Brea Tar Pits

Pits in Los Angeles, discovered in 1769, where fossilized remains of prehistoric animals have been found, together with evidence of human habitation some 15,000 years ago.

Lady of the Lakes, the

A nickname of Michigan, so called because it is surrounded by four of the Great Lakes: Erie, Huron, Michigan, and Superior.

Lake District, the

An area in Cumbria, in the Northwest of England, renowned for its scenic beauty. As its name suggests, it abounds in lakes, most of which are suffixed -*water* or -*mere*: Derwentwater, Ullswater, Wastwater, and Coniston Water, for example, and Windermere, Thirlmere, and Buttermere. They nestle between hills and mountains that are favorites with walkers and climbers; amongst the peaks is Scafell Pike, the highest mountain in England at 3210 feet. Designated a national park in 1951, it is the largest in England and Wales, covering nearly 900 square miles. Its vogue as a popular holiday destination started as early as the late 18th century, when the sort of wild romantic scenery it offers was fashionable, and its reputation was perhaps established by the poets who came to live in and write about the area in the early 19th century—particularly Wordsworth, Coleridge, and Southey, the so-called "Lake poets." In those days it was often known as Lakeland (a name which survives today mainly as an adjective—as in "Lakeland scenery"), or sometimes as the *Lake Country*, but *Lake*

District has gradually established itself as the usual term. An alternative shorthand name in current usage is **the Lakes**.

Lake Shore Drive

A Chicago thoroughfare bordered on the east by Lake Michigan and on the west by a wide variety of luxurious hotels, private mansions, and high-rise apartment houses, as well as a number of such public facilities as museums, hospitals, and parks. A portion of the Drive forms the eastern border of the Near North Side's "**Gold Coast**" (*q.v.*) area, while its generally faster-than-average traffic flow provides easy access to many lakeside landmarks. See also **McCormick Place, Museum of Science and Industry, Navy Pier.**

Lake State, the

A nickname of Minnesota, reputed to have 10,000 lakes.

Lambeth

An area of central London, on the south bank of the Thames opposite Westminster. It is a working-class residential district, renowned for its Cockney joviality. Its most famous road is perhaps Lambeth Walk, which used to house a well-known street market but is now remembered mainly for a popular song and dance, called the Lambeth Walk, which was all the rage in the 1930s. Lambeth also has close associations with the Church of England: Lambeth Palace is the official London residence of the Archbishop of Canterbury, who can confer honorary "Lambeth degrees" on servants of the Church. The conference of bishops of the Anglican Communion, held every ten years, is called the Lambeth Conference; and the name 'Lambeth' is used metaphorically to refer to the Anglican Church in England. In 1965 the new London borough of Lambeth was created, which includes Brixton and Streatham, taking in a far larger area than the original Lambeth.

Landes, the

A region on the southwest coast of France, to the south of Bordeaux, covering about 5400 square miles. Today it is mostly covered by scrubby pine forest, but in former times it was a marshy area, and the local shepherds' habit of walking about on stilts surprisingly survived its draining. It is one of the main parts of France in which small wild birds, especially ortolans, are shot (or trapped) for the table.

Land of a Million Elephants, the

A translation of Lanxang, an epithet used formerly for Laos, a state in southeast Asia. Elephants were, and indeed still are important to the economy of Laos as work animals, and three of them appear on the national flag.

Land of Cakes
> A nickname of Scotland.

Land of Delight Makers
> A nickname of New Mexico, so called in reference to its influence on the arts and literature.

Land of Enchantment
> A nickname of New Mexico.

Land of Flowers, the
> A nickname of Florida (which means 'flowered' in Spanish).

Land of Gold
> A nickname of California.

Land of Heart's Desire, the
> A nickname of New Mexico.

Land of Hiawatha
> A nickname of the Upper Peninsula of Michigan.

Land of Infinite Variety, the
> A nickname of South Dakota.

Land of Lakes, the
> A nickname of Wisconsin.

Land of Lincoln
> A nickname of Illinois.

Land of Little Rain
> A nickname for the region of California lying "between the high Sierras south from Yosemite—east and south . . . beyond Death Valley and on illimitably into the Mojave Desert," as described by Mary Austin in a series of fourteen sketches (1903).

Land of Milk and Honey, the
> A nickname of Israel.

Land of Opportunity, the
> A nickname of New Mexico and the official nickname of Arkansas.

Land of Plenty, the
> A nickname of South Dakota.

Land of Promise
A nickname of Canaan.

Land of Shining Mountains, the
A nickname of Montana.

Land of Steady Habits, the
A nickname of Connecticut.

Land of the Dakotas, the
A nickname of North Dakota. See **Sioux State.**

Land of the Midnight Sun, the
North of the Arctic Circle, the sun never sets in summer; for more than two months there is continuous daylight. The magic and mystery of this time are reflected in the paradoxical name *Land of the Midnight Sun*, which has been applied to the northern parts of Norway, Sweden, Finland, and the northwest U. S. R.; in particular it is often used as an informal epithet for Lapland. In the U. S. it is sometimes used in reference to Alaska.

Land of the Red People, the
A nickname of Oklahoma, a translation of the state's name.

Land of the Rising Sun, the
Since Japan is regarded as being about as far east as you can go without arriving at the west, it is reasonable that it should be known as the Land of the Rising Sun. The Japanese concur, and their former national flag showed a red sphere, with rays projecting, on a white field.

Land of the Rolling Prairie
A nickname of Iowa.

Land of the Saints, the
A nickname of Utah, so called because the Mormons refer to themselves as Latter-Day Saints.

Land of the Sky, the
A nickname of North Carolina.

Land's End to John o' Groat's House
A phrase indicating the length of Great Britain: Land's End being the granite promontory in Cornwall at the southwestern tip of England, and John o' Groat's house, an octagonal structure owned by a Dutchman, Johan de Groot, which formerly occupied the site in Caithness-shire, Scotland, near the northern extremity of Great Britain.

Lanes, the

An area of narrow winding alleyways in central Brighton, on the south coast of England. They are all that remain of the original 17th-century fishing village that became Brighton, and in the late 20th century are full of antique shops, boutiques, and similar enticements for tourists.

Languedoc

A mainly mountainous area of southern France, between the River Rhone and the foothills of the Pyrenees. It used to be a province in its own right, but is now merged into the region of Languedoc-Roussillon. Its name comes from the language spoken in southern France in the Middle Ages, which used *oc* as the word for "yes," in contrast to the northerly French dialect, where *oïl* was used.

Lantern of England

A nickname for the abbey church of Bath, in southwestern England, so called because of the number and size of its traceried windows.

Lapland

The area in northern Scandinavia occupied by the Lapps. It takes in parts of Finland, Sweden, and Norway, and also includes the Kola Peninsula at the very northwest tip of the Soviet Union. It is mostly above the Arctic Circle. See also **Land of the Midnight Sun.**

Last Capital of the Confederacy

A nickname of Danville, Virginia.

Last Frontier

The official nickname of Alaska.

Latin Quarter (Quartier Latin)

1. An area on the Left Bank of the Paris River Seine, in to the south of the Île de la Cité and immediately to the west of the Boulevard St.-Michel. It is renowned as the hub of Paris's intellectual life, housing as it does Sorbonne University and several other colleges, whose students no doubt do much to perpetuate the area's reputation for bohemian unorthodoxy. It gets its name from the fact that in the Middle Ages the scholars at the educational institutions spoke Latin, the international language of learning at that time. See also **Left Bank.**

2. A part of Old Quebec, so named because it is the site of Laval University.

Laurasia

A name given to the supercontinent believed to have existed in the northern hemisphere over 200 million years ago; it later split up into continents that became Eurasia and North America. Compare **Gondwanaland, Pangaea.**

Law Courts, the

The name commonly used for what are officially called the Royal Courts of Justice, a set of imposing Victorian buildings on the Strand in central London, housing the Supreme Court of Judicature, the main civil court of England and Wales.

LAX

The code used by airlines to designate the city of Los Angeles and the Los Angeles International Airport. The airport now covers an area of 3500 acres and is one of the busiest in the world. The name LAX has grown in popularity worldwide in recent decades, partly because of the growing importance of the airport and perhaps partly because it is one of the few three-letter codes that is an actual word (which might be applied in a derisive manner to Los Angeles). The airport is seen frequently by millions of television and movie viewers all over the world.

Lead State, the

A nickname of Colorado and Missouri.

Left Bank, the

The southern bank of the River Seine in Paris. The term *Left Bank* is used for more than just the riverside, however: it covers a largish hinterland, including Montparnasse, St.-Germain-des-Prés, and St.-Michel. It is the artistic, intellectual district of Paris, with the Latin Quarter at its heart; over the past century most of France's great cultural lions have patronized its famous cafés, such as *les Deux Magots* and *le Dôme*, and despite recent commercialization the area is still the center of Paris's bohemian life. See also **Latin Quarter**.

Leghorn

An antiquated Anglicized name for Livorno, a town in Tuscany on the west coast of Italy. It derives from *Legorno,* the local name in the 16th and 17th centuries, which was replaced by *Livorno* as being closer to the original Latin *Liburnus.* Any continued currency it may have in English is probably owing to its associations with a breed of domestic fowl and with a sort of plaited straw from which hats were once made.

Leicester Square

A square in the West End of London, immediately to the east of Piccadilly Circus. It is regarded as the heart of London's theaterland, and is itself surrounded by large movie theaters. It bustles with life by day and far into the night. In the 18th century it was a favorite venue for duels.

Leon & Eddie's

A popular nightclub during the 1930s and '40s, on 52nd Street, in New York City. It featured many of the swing and jazz singers and musicians of the time and was a favorite oasis of the gossip columnists.

Levant, the

An archaic term for the lands bordering the eastern Mediterranean, what is now Lebanon, Israel, and Syria. *The Levant* originally meant 'the land where the sun rises' (from the French *lever* 'to rise'), and indeed, in the 16th and 17th centuries, the High Levant was used in reference to the Far East. Compare **Orient.**

Liberty Hall

Not a specific place at all but any place where one can do as he pleases. It is usually used in reference to free-wheeling hospitality. [So used by Squire Hardcastle in Oliver Goldsmith's play, *She Stoops to Conquer*]

Liberty Harbor

A nickname for New York harbor acquired during the celebration of the centennial of the Statue of Liberty, in July 1986. The actual centennial occurred in October of that year. See also **Bedloe's Island.**

Lifeline of the Confederacy

A nickname of North Carolina.

Limehouse

A district in the Dockland area of the East End of London. In former times it was a fairly tough and violent neighborhood, and in the 19th century London's Chinatown was situated there, but in the latter part of the 20th century, with the closing down of the docks and the development of the area for light industry and leisure, it is acquiring a better image. A particular present-day association of Limehouse is with the evolution of the Social Democratic Party in the early 1980s; one of its founding fathers lived there, and its formative caucus, of Roy Jenkins, David Owen, Shirley Williams, and William Rodgers, was known as the "Limehouse Four." In the early twentieth century the verb *to limehouse* meant 'to make fiery political speeches'; the usage arose out of a speech given by Lloyd George at a turbulent rally at Limehouse in 1909.

Lindsey

In former times, an administrative area of Lincolnshire, in eastern England. It was in the central and northern parts of the county, based at the city of Lincoln. Its title in full was the Parts of Lindsey. Compare **Holland, 2; Kesteven.**

Lindy's

A restaurant at Broadway and 50th Street, in New York City, frequented by the famous of the world of sports and entertainment, who attracted many Broadway "types" as well as newspaper columnists and feature writers during its heyday, from the 1920s to the 1950s. (Its famous cheesecake is still shipped around the world to those who can't get to the restaurant.) It was immortalized as "Mindy's" in the short stories of Damon Runyon, a journalist who often wrote about the "Broadway Scene."

Lion's Den State, the

A nickname of Tennessee.

Literary Emporium, the

A nickname of Boston, Massachusetts.

Little Britain

A small street in the City of London, to the north of St. Paul's Cathedral, which contained the offices of the lawyer Mr. Jaggers in Dickens's *Great Expectations*. It apparently gets its name from the fact that the Duke of Brittany had a house there. In medieval times Brittany (in northern France) was often known as Little Britain, to distinguish it from Great Britain (England, Scotland, and Wales), the spelling of Britain and Brittany in those days being frequently identical. From the 17th to the 19th centuries it was, along with the nearby Paternoster Row and St. Paul's Churchyard, a major center of the book-publishing business in London.

Little Cuba

A nickname of Miami, Florida, so called in reference to the number of Cuban immigrants living there after the establishment of the Castro regime in Cuba.

Little Dipper

An American name for the constellation Ursa Minor, so called from the outline formed by its stars.

Littlehampton

A seaside resort near Brighton, on the English Channel. It is not particularly noteworthy, but British comedians occasionally refer to it archly as "Little Hampton," "Hampton" being short for "Hampton Wick," which is riming slang for *dick*; a vulgar word for penis.

Little Ida

A nickname of Idaho.

Little Italy

A nickname for a neighborhood, in a large American city, occupied mainly by Italians and those of Italian descent. In New York City it is situated on the East Side, north of Canal Street, between the Bowery on the east and Centre Street on the west. Its main street is Mulberry Street where, once a year, at the Feast of San Gennaro, the patron saint of many who settled there, a gala festival is held, with the carts of peddlers of Italian foods and other native goods lining the crowded ways. Many New Yorkers make an annual visit there to join in the festivities.

Little Rhody

The official nickname of Rhode Island.

Little Siberia

A nickname, translated from the French *La Petite Sibérie*, for the Belgian headquarters of NATO, so called because the personnel from sixteen countries do not mix well and because of its isolated site.

Little Swiss Town

A nickname of Damascus, Virginia.

Little Venice

Just to the north of Paddington station in west London, the Regent's Canal branches off the Grand Union Canal. The attractive canal basin at their junction is always crowded with moored pleasure craft, and the feeling of a watery environment in the heart of a city gives the surrounding desirable residential area its name.

Little Vietnam

A nickname for Tondo Foreshore, in the Philippines, once notorious as the largest slum in southeast Asia, so called because of its violence.

Lizard, the

The southernmost point in Britain, a promontory near the western tip of Cornwall in the Southwest of England. Its name has no connection with reptiles; it comes from the Cornish *lis* 'place' and *ard* 'high.'

Lizard State, the

A nickname of Alabama.

Llanfairpwllgwyngyllgogerychwyrndrobwllllantysiliogogogoch

A village on the island of Anglesey, off the northwest coast of Wales. Its celebrity rests on its name, which at 58 letters is the longest place-name in Britain. It is in fact a somewhat bogus name, and not surprisingly it is very seldom used in practice. It was revived in 1973, when the railway station reopened, so as to make something of a tourist attraction of the station signs, but in ordinary everyday use the place is known as Llanfairpwllgwyngill. The full name means 'St. Mary's church by the pool of the white hazel trees, near the rapid whirlpool, by the red cave of the church of St. Tysilio.'

L. L. Bean

A large, old mail-order company, situated in Freeport, Maine, offering mainly sports clothing and camping equipment of quality construction and fairly priced. Although it originally catered to country-dwellers and sportsmen, its popularity spread during the early 1970s, and its catalogue expanded to include informal wear for men and, later on, women. In that period it acquired a status of its own, and in the 1980s its identifying labels began to appear prominently on the outsides, instead of the insides of its clothing.

Lloyd's

An institution, headquartered in the City of London, whose business is to provide insurance, particularly marine insurance. It consists of about 14,000 members, known as underwriters, who jointly or severally accept liability for the sums insured. In the U. S., where it is usually referred to as Lloyd's of London, the connotation is nearly always of insurance of an unusual nature, as the insuring of a dancer's legs against injury and loss of income. Since its beginnings in the late 17th century, Lloyd's has always gathered and disseminated accurate information relating to the world's shipping, and one of its classifications, *A-1*, meaning that a vessel is in first-class condition, has passed into everyday English, meaning 'excellent.' See also **Lutine bell.**

Loamshire

An imaginary southern English county sometimes used by writers of fiction when they wish to avoid naming a real place. Its associations are distinctly rural and agricultural. Compare **Mummerset.**

Lombard Street

A street in the City of London, leading up to the Bank of England, in which the headquarters of many banks and other financial institutions are situated. It derives its name from the bankers from Lombardy, Italy who set up business in the street from the 13th century onward. In the 16th and 17th centuries, banks and money lender's shops were often known as *lombards*, and indeed *Lombard Street* itself used to be used figuratively to refer to London's banking industry, although the expression now has a rather dated air. Another somewhat outmoded phrase that once enjoyed a considerable vogue is *all Lombard Street to a China orange*, used when making an assertion in the form of a wager, staking something of great monetary value against something worthless (a China orange being just an ordinary orange, originally brought from China); it is first recorded in

1819, but an alternative version, of greater antiquity, is *all Lombard Street to an egg shell.*

London

The amorphous British metropolis spreads ever wider, and spawns new names to keep pace with its expanding size and status. At its heart is the original City of London, now the nation's financial center. But even in medieval times, London was seeping out of its city walls; the districts that were to become known as the East End and the West End began to grow up. By the middle of the 19th century it became clear that though only the City was London in name, a much larger area was London in fact. To recognize this, the County of London was formed in 1888, by taking chunks of the counties of Middlesex, Surrey, and Kent and adding them officially on to the City. Often known by the nickname *the Youngest County*, it was governed by the London County Council. London continued to elbow its way through the suburbs in the 20th century, however, gobbling up most intervening patches of green, so it was not long before a new accommodation had to be made. In 1965, *Greater London* was called into being, which added fresh bits of Surrey and Kent to London County, plus part of Hertfordshire, and totally engulfed Middlesex, which disappeared off the map altogether. The whole vast area covers 620 square miles, and is divided into Inner London (twelve boroughs nearest the center) and Outer London (the rest). British people's concept of what *London* actually means has not really kept in step with official nomenclature. Certainly London is no longer thought of simply as the City, but equally many people find it difficult to think of some of the more outlying boroughs, such as Croydon or Bexley, as being really part of the metropolis. For those who live on its fringes, London is most often known familiarly as *town*, as in "I'm going up to town for the day to do some shopping." See also **Great Wen, Smoke.**

London Bridge

Any of several bridges spanning the Thames river between Borough High Street in Southwark and King William Street in the City of London. The Old London Bridge of nursery-rime fame was built between 1176 and 1209 and was the only crossing of the river at London until the 1740s, when Westminster Bridge was built. In the 1820s the Old Bridge was demolished and replaced by New London Bridge. This in turn was replaced in 1960, but the masonry facing was shipped to the U. S. and it has been re-erected at Lake Havasu City, Arizona, where it is a very popular tourist attraction. It is thought that when the promoters of the project in Arizona bought London Bridge, they were under the impression that they were buying Tower Bridge, which still functions in London.

London Underground

London's subway system. It has nine different lines, most of which do indeed run at varying depths below ground in central London (the Circle line surfaces here and there). Several of the lines extend out into the commuterland of the suburbs, where for the most part they run above ground. Londoners call the system the "Underground" or the "Tube." See also **Drain.**

Lone Star of Civilization, the

A nickname of Santa Fe, New Mexico, so called because for a century after its founding (1609) it was the only town in a million square miles of desert and mountains.

Lone Star State, the

The official nickname of Texas.

Loop, the

Specifically, the structure for the elevated railway, dating from 1897, that forms a loop around two square miles of downtown Chicago, the historic heart of the city; generally, the term refers to this area and its immediate environs. The generally run-down South Loop area has been showing signs of rebirth in recent years, thanks to the development of such areas as "Printer's Row" on South Dearborn Street between Congress Parkway and Polk Street, with its many sturdy old commercial buildings ideal for refurbishing into loft apartments, art galleries, and related business establishments. On South Wabash Avenue, Big Jim Colosimo's Café, now an empty lot, served during Prohibition days as informal headquarters for practitioners of organized crime, whose widespread bootlegging and other illicit activities reaped fortunes for such underworld leaders as Al Capone, Johnny Torrio, and Bugs Moran. Nearby were the notorious Lexington and Metropole hotels much frequented by Capone and his cronies.

Lord's

A cricket ground in St. John's Wood, in northwest central London, to the west of Regent's Park. It was opened by Thomas Lord in 1814 and has since become both the spiritual home and the administrative center of English, and indeed world cricket. It is the headquarters of the International Cricket Conference (cricket's governing body), of the venerable Marylebone Cricket Club, and of Middlesex County Cricket Club. International matches and many important domestic matches are played here each summer. See also **Oval**.

Los Angeles

A large city in southern California, founded by the Spanish in 1781. The original name of the settlement, according to some, was La Reina de los Angeles 'The Queen of the Angels'; according to some modern writers it was Nuestra Señora la Reina de los Angeles de Porciúncula; in the American period (beginning in 1846) the name was shortened to Pueblo de los Angeles (or the 'City of the Angels') and then simply to Los Angeles. The

citizens have long resisted the abbreviation "L. A.," just as San Franciscans
have rejectd "Frisco," but the abbreviation no longer has the opprobrium
that it once had and is now commonly used by a large part of the citizenry.
It is thought that the abbreviation might have been used by people who
were unsure of the pronunciation of the name. For years people debated
whether the letter "g" in Los Angeles should be pronounced like the "g" in
"angle" or in "angel"; Mayor Fletcher Bowron finally decided in favor of the
latter when he appointed a jury of citizens to debate the issue in 1952. Los
Angeles is thought by people in other cities to have an unusual character.
Residents of San Francisco and New York, in particular, like to contrast the
idiosyncrasies of Los Angeles with the virtues of their own cities. Known
throughout the world for the stereotypical descriptions of the city, its
inhabitants, and the "L. A. life-style," "laid-back" and "flaky" are two of the
adjectives most commonly used by outsiders to describe Angelenos. In
1976, Jack Smith, a popular columnist for the *Los Angeles Times*, called Los
Angeles "The Big Orange" by analogy with "The Big Apple" (New York), but
the name has not stuck.

Lost Colony, the

The nickname for the second of the first two American colonies settled by
the British (1585 and 1587) on Roanoke Island off the North Carolina coast,
thirty-three years before the Pilgrims landed at Plymouth Rock. The first
group returned to England, but crewmen of a supply ship which arrived
there three years later found no trace of the second group, only the word
"Croatoan" carved on a tree. Virginia Dare, the first child born to English
parents in America, was among those who vanished. What became of
them has remained a mystery to this day.

Low Countries, the

A somewhat dated collective term applied to the countries occupying the
low-lying shoulder of land that projects into the North Sea at the northwest corner of Europe. It now comprises Belgium, the Netherlands (a
translation of Dutch *Nederland*, which itself means 'low country') and
sometimes Luxembourg; but the origin of the name goes back beyond the
formation of these modern states, and it used to include such regions as
Brabant, Flanders, and Zeeland. See also **Benelux**.

Lower East Side, the

An area of New York City, somewhat vaguely delineated on the north by
14th Street, on the west by Lafayette Street, on the south by Canal Street,
and on the east by the East River (South Street). It is one of the oldest parts
of the city but is best known for its settlement by Jewish immigrants from
the 1870s onward for about fifty years. It was always a poor neighborhood, but many of those who spent their childhood there became famous:
Al Jolson, Fanny Brice, George and Ira Gershwin, Irving Berlin, as well as
others who went on to become well-known writers, judges, teachers,

businessmen, etc. On Second Avenue flourished the Yiddish theater, under the direction of Maurice Schwartz, which starred Molly Picon, among others. Because the sabbath is observed on Saturdays, the area around Delancey Street is open for business as usual on Sundays, and New Yorkers looking for bargains and for ethnic Jewish food often shop then. The Essex Street Market, where one can see block-long rows of kosher salamis hanging above the counters, is also popular. Generally, the Lower East Side is associated with both poverty, reflecting the condition of the immigrants who lived there, and success, exemplified by those who had the talent and resourcefulness to emerge, frequently at the top of their profession. See also **East Side.**

Lowlands, the

A roughly fifty-mile-wide corridor of relatively low ground running east and west across central Scotland between the Southern Uplands and the Highlands. It contains Scotland's major cities of Edinburgh and Glasgow and the valleys of the Forth and Clyde. Culturally distinct from the Highlands, it is where the Scots version of the English language, known as Lallands (Lowlands), is spoken, as contrasted to the Gaelic that still survives further north. See also **Highlands.**

Lumber City

A nickname of Bangor, Maine.

Lumber State, the

A nickname of Maine.

Lutine bell

The ship's bell salvaged from the *Lutine,* a British warship wrecked at sea. It hangs at the offices of **Lloyd's** (*q.v.*) of London and is tolled before announcements of ships lost or long overdue.

Lyons of America

A nickname of Paterson, New Jersey.

M & S

A frequent abbreviation for Marks and Spencer, one of Britain's largest chain stores. Almost as often heard, but more colloquial, is the rhyming *Marks and Sparks.*

MacDowell Colony

A composers' and writers' summer residence, established in Peterborough, New Hampshire, by the widow of Edward Alexander MacDowell (1861–1908), the U. S. composer, as a memorial.

Macy's

Formally, R. H. Macy & Company, a department store at Herald Square (34th Street and Broadway) in New York City. It is the largest such store in the world. During the late 1930s and early '40s, Macy's "feuded" with Gimbels, a nearby store nearly as large, which had the motto, "We will not be undersold," and occasional price wars kept customers racing back and forth between the two to find the best bargains. As a result of competitive advertising and strategic merchandising planning, New Yorkers (at least) added to their speech the query "Does Macy's tell Gimbels?" to identify some piece of information better kept confidential. Gimbels has gone.

Madison Avenue

A north-south avenue in New York City, extending from Madison Square, at the southern end, up into Harlem at the northern. Its blocks between 40th and 57th streets are identified mainly with advertising agencies, many of which have—or once had—their offices there. But the avenue has many high-rise office buildings along it, and there are many other businesses there. The association of Madison Avenue with advertising extended to publicity and other kinds of promotion which, in the minds of the public, in turn became associated with spurious claims made for what often turn out to be specious products and services. Hence, "Madison Avenue" has a pejorative connotation, carrying the idea of insincerity and phoniness. In its application to some of the wilder representations, it is shortened to "Mad Avenue" or "Mad Ave."

Madison Square Garden

The name of three different structures in the recent history of New York City, all arenas for sporting events, circuses, and other such happenings. The original, a converted railroad station, was, aptly enough, at Madison Square; its main claim to fame was its roof garden restaurant, where Harry K. Thaw, in 1906, shot and killed Stanford White, a noted architect and partner in the firm of McKim, Mead, and White, when he found him dining with his showgirl wife, Evelyn Nesbit, a beautiful redhead who was billed in a contemporary extravaganza as "The Girl in the Red Velvet Swing." In 1925, that building was demolished and a new Madison Square Garden, usually called "The Garden" among sports aficionados, was built on Eighth Avenue, at 50th Street. That was torn down and Madison Square Garden moved on to a structure built (1968) over the Pennsylvania Station (at 33rd Street and Seventh Avenue), the former station building having been demolished. In the mid 1980s it was rumored that this venue, too, would soon be vacated in favor of a new site, a few blocks away. Any New Yorkers who may retain any nostalgia for the old "Garden" probably think of the one at 50th Street, where boxing matches and other sports were presented but more likely where one attended the rodeo and, especially, the Ringling Brothers, Barnum & Bailey Circus—"The Greatest Show on Earth."

Maelstrom, the

A powerful current in the Arctic Ocean, to the northwest of Norway. Its tidal race funnels through a restricted channel in the Lofoten Islands, and mariners' tales built its reputation into that of a huge and violent whirlpool that sucked ships into it from miles around. Its name, which comes from a Dutch word meaning 'grinding or whirling stream,' has come to be applied to any threatening whirlpool, or more generally to a confusing and dangerous situation. Edgar Allan Poe wrote a short story about it, "A Descent into the Maelstrom."

Mae West

1. A World War II nickname coined by the Royal Air Forces for an inflatable life vest, so called because the wearer resembled the well-endowed actress.
2. A nickname used in diners for a figure-eight cruller.

Mafeking

A town and important railroad junction in South Africa which sprang to fame during the Boer War when the garrison of British troops which had been besieged there was relieved on 17 May 1900. The so-called "Relief of Mafeking" led to such uproarious rejoicing in Britain that the newspapers of the time coined a new verb, *to maffick* 'to indulge in exultant national celebrations.' The town's subsequent history was uneventful, until in 1980 it was ceded to the newly "independent" bantustan (black enclave) of Bophutatswana; in the process its name reverted to its original form, Mafikeng, which in the Tswana language means 'place of stones.'

Maghreb

An all-embracing term for the northwestern part of Africa, including Algeria, Morocco, Tunisia, and sometimes also Libya. In Arabic it means literally 'the West.'

Magic Valley

A nickname of the Rio Grande Valley, in reference to its abundant production of vegetables and citrus fruits.

Magnificent Mile, the

A Chamber of Commerce phrase for that segment of Michigan Avenue in Chicago on the Near North Side, stretching north from the Loop to Oak Street and featuring generally finer shops, department stores, restaurants, and hotels. Landmarks include the Wrigley Building; Tribune Tower; the old **Water Tower** (*q.v.*); the Water Tower Place shopping complex (the world's tallest reinforced-concrete building); the 100-story John Hancock Center; the **Playboy Building** (*q.v.*); the Drake Hotel; and One Magnificent Mile, a 58-story combination of shops, offices, and condominiums.

Magnolia City

A nickname for Houston, Texas.

Magnolia State, the

The official nickname of Mississippi.

magpie houses

A nickname for the half-timbered Tudor period houses whose black-painted wood and white plaster resemble the coloration of the bird.

Maida Vale

A district in northwest London, to the north of Paddington Station, which takes its name from Maida Vale, a large thoroughfare which runs through it. This in turn commemorates the battle of Maida in Italy (1806) during the Napoleonic Wars. In the late 20th century Maida Vale is an upwardly mobile area, not quite as fashionable as Little Venice to the south, but certainly a better place to live than Kilburn to the north. A suburb of Perth, western Australia, is also called Maida Vale. See also **Little Venice**.

Mainland State

A nickname of Alaska.

Main Line

The suburbs of Philadelphia, associated with wealth and upper-class toniness, served by the *Paoli Local* commuter train, namely, Merion, Narberth, Wynnewood, Ardmore, Haverford, Bryn Mawr, Rosemont, Villanova, Radnor, St. Davids, Wayne, Devon, Berwyn, and Paoli.

Main Street

The central or chief thoroughfare of an American village or town, corresponding, in Britain, to the High Street, though the terms are not used interchangeably. In the United States, Main Street connotes the more important activities going on in a town; it also carries with it the notion of small-town life in general and the pervasive stolidity associated with it. This sense is best reflected in Sinclair Lewis's novel *Main Street* (1920). To some, the term connotes salt-of-the-earth solidity and home-town friendliness. These connotations are absent in the British use of High Street, which is associated chiefly with the street as the focus of commerce: the term *High Street shops* denotes those that are economically important, whose volume of business, attitudes toward economic factors, etc., are reported in the financial news.

Main Street of America, the

A nickname of US 66, the federal highway formerly the most direct route from Chicago to Los Angeles, which passes through some of the most outstanding agricultural and scenic sections of Illinois, Missouri, Oklahoma, New Mexico, Arizona, and California.

Malabar Coast, the

The southwest coast of India, from Cape Comorin, the southern tip of India, northward to the former Portuguese colony of Goa. Compare **Coromandel Coast.**

Malibu

An unincorporated coastal area in Los Angeles County. Its limits are rather indefinite, but it is commonly considered to be the stretch of beach from the Pacific Palisades section of Los Angeles west for about 26 miles along the coast of the Pacific Ocean as far as the Ventura County line. Malibu is an Indian name, and the present spelling first appeared in the name of the Topanga Malibu Sequit land grant in 1805. Malibu has become famous for surfing and for the residences of film stars and other celebrities. The name is thought to have a certain cachet and has been used for a model in the Chevrolet line of automobiles. Malibu includes the Malibu Beach Colony, often known simply as "The Colony," a mile of beach houses belonging mostly to rich people associated with the entertainment world.

Malvinas, Islas

See **Falkland Islands.**

Manchester of America, the

A nickname of Lowell, Massachusetts.

Manhattan

An island, about thirteen miles long and, at its broadest, two and a half miles wide, constituting the main part of one of the five boroughs of New York City, (which includes also Brooklyn (technically, Kings County), The Bronx, Queens, and Staten Island (until 1975 named Richmond). It is the focal point of theater—many say for the entire western hemisphere—the financial world (in the Stock Exchange and Wall Street), of the garment industry, the advertising business, of those who run the large radio and television networks, of music and book publishing, and, probably, of many other businesses in the United States. Geologically consisting of solid rock, it has afforded the opportunity to build tall buildings, called skyscrapers, for which the city is known, and these, crowding along the north-south avenues and side streets, create canyons through which New Yorkers walk and where they sit in cars, taxis, and buses, waiting for the perpetual traffic jams to move. Manhattan has been the inspiration for songwriters and bartenders, one of whom named a cocktail after it. Millions of people work in Manhattan, commuting there via train, subway, bus, car, helicopter, boat, and Hovercraft from a radius as great as one hundred miles. Relatively few of these, however, live there, for, although tradition has it that Peter Minuit purchased the island from the Indians in 1626 for $24-worth of beads and trinkets, it today includes some of the most valuable real estate in the world, and there are not many who can afford either the high rents or the huge prices demanded for cooperative apartments. Yet, it remains one of the most populous cities in the world. It is also one of the busiest and, in many ways, the cultural center of the United States. Its libraries, museums, art galleries, ballet and opera companies, orchestras, and other facilities are so numerous that a person could spend his entire life going from one to another without repeating an exhibition. It is host to millions of American and foreign tourists yearly, and many national associations include it among the cities where they hold conventions. Its commercial exhibition centers draw enormous crowds, not only from the outlying areas, but from among New Yorkers, who are not always as cynical as they seem. Bordered on the east by the East and Harlem rivers and on the west by the Hudson (or North) River, Manhattan is filled with and emptied of people through various railroad and four vehicular tunnels, ferries, more than a dozen bridges (only one across the Hudson), and an aerial tramway (to Roosevelt, formerly Welfare, Island). Its virtual center is occupied by Central Park, almost half a mile wide and about two and a half miles long, which is used for concerts, informal sports and games, strolling, horseback riding, ice- or roller-skating, rowing (on its pond), model sailboat racing (on another pond), and, at night, for mugging those foolish enough to enter its precincts. It also has a zoo with a special children's zoo, where adults are forbidden unless accompanied by a child. Street vendors can be found—indeed, cannot easily be avoided—on many corners throughout the downtown (commercial) areas, selling fruits, nuts, roasted chestnuts, ice cream, gelati, cold drinks and every other conceivable kind of food, as well as all kinds of merchandise. It is, in short, one of the most provocative, exciting places on earth, and it evokes a complex of myriad associations for all those who live and work there, who visit it, and even for those whose only experience with it is vicarious.

Mansion House, the

The official home of the Lord Mayor of London. An imposing classical building erected between 1739 and 1753, it stands to the southwest of the Bank in the City of London, opposite the Bank of England. The word *mansion-house* originally meant any dwelling house, and only gradually came to be applied specifically to official residences—particularly, in early days, to those of high-ranking ecclesiastics.

Marais, the

An area of eastern central Paris, on the right bank of the Seine to the north of the Île de la Cité. It is the oldest part of the city, and retains a powerful flavor of the past, with its narrow winding streets, its elegant 17th-century mansions, and its many museums.

Marches, the

1. A *march* is a boundary, particularly a disputed one—it is connected with the word *mark*. In a British historical context, the Marches are the border areas between England and Wales (or occasionally England and Scotland). In the Middle Ages, the Welsh Marches were a particular security risk for England, and the king appointed "Marcher lords," powerful vassals based in Hereford, Shrewsbury, and Chester, whose duty was to guard the frontier against Welsh incursion.

2. A region of Italy, on the Adriatic coast to the east of Florence, is also known as *the Marches* or, in Italian, *le Marche*.

Mare Nostrum

The name used by the ancient Romans for the Mediterranean Sea. As its literal translation, 'our sea,' suggests, they viewed the whole of the Mediterranean as merely Roman territorial waters, and few were able to challenge that view for long.

Marseillaise of the Unemotional Yankee

A nickname of *The Battle Hymn of the Republic*, written by Julia Ward Howe in 1861, a reference to its use by Yankee soldiers as a camp song during the Civil War.

Marshall Field's

A Chicago department store, more commonly known as Fields. Long considered a local institution, it was established in 1902 at its present site in the city's Loop, after having done business at several other locations. The 12-story edifice occupies an entire block and features 71 acres of floor space, a Tiffany-domed ceiling and a brass-encased, nearly eight-ton clock above the sidewalk at State and Washington that has become a famous Loop landmark. The store's reputation and success have been built on a stringent policy of guaranteeing customer satisfaction, in keeping with Marshall Field's famous admonition to an apparently unhelpful floor manager: "Give the lady what she wants!"

Marylebone

An area of central London to the west of Regent's Park. In the early Middle Ages it was known as Tyburn, for a stream of that name flowed there; but Tyburn's increasing association with the gallows, on the site of what is now Marble Arch, led to its name being changed in the 15th century to Maryburn, after the church of St. Mary which stood nearby and *burn* 'stream, brook.' In the 17th century the name evolved to Marylebone, with the extraneous *le* perhaps being introduced by analogy with St. Mary-le-Bow, a church in the City of London, perhaps influenced by the French *Marie la Bonne*. Since that time the area has been known variously as St. Marylebone or just plain Marylebone: the former London borough, for example, that existed until 1965, was called St. Marylebone, but the local

train station, which is a terminus for certain Western Region services, is
Marylebone. See also **Tyburnia.**

Mason-Dixon Line

Properly called Mason and Dixon's Line, it is the line determined (1763–67)
by two English astronomers, Charles Mason and Jeremiah Dixon, who
were hired to survey the border and thus end the dispute between Pennsylvania and Maryland. It is the east-west boundary dividing Pennsylvania
from Maryland and part of West Virginia, and the north-south boundary
between Maryland and Delaware. Prior to the Civil War, the southern
boundary of Pennsylvania was considered the dividing line between slave
and non-slave states, thus giving rise to the common belief that the line
divides the North and the South. See also **Dixie.**

Mauve Decade, the

A nickname for the 1890s, bestowed by Thomas Beer (1889–1940) in his
book of the same title (1926), in which the decade is viewed as a peaceful,
prosperous, and complacent period in Europe and America. See also **Gay
Nineties.**

Maxim's

A well-known restaurant in Paris, on the Boulevard de la Madeleine. It has
been famous for almost a century as the gathering-place of the wealthy
and elegant, and its rich red and gold rococo decor has been widely
imitated. It is the Maxim's of Sigmund Romberg's operetta *The Student
Prince*, in which it figures in a song which begins:

> I go off to Maxim's,
> Where all the girls are dreams.

Maxwell Street

A colorful Near Southwest Side market area in Chicago that derives its
name from the street that forms its core. Crowded streets, aggressive
sidewalk vendors, and the pungent aromas of food all are elements of its
zesty—but increasingly seedy—ambiance. At its busiest (especially Sundays) the multi-ethnic area is filled with buyers, sellers, and sightseers
making their way among shops, stands, stalls, and pushcarts that offer a
wide variety of merchandise, old and new, and almost all at negotiable
prices.

Mayfair

A fashionable area of the West End of London, bounded on the west by
Park Lane, on the east by Bond Street, on the north by Oxford Street, and
on the south by Piccadilly. It was originally known as Brookfield, but it
came to fame because of the fair held there every May in the 17th and
18th centuries, and the new name gradually evolved. In the 18th century it
was a rather disreputable quarter which saw a good deal of gambling and

drunken debauchery—so much so that the fair was eventually officially suppressed. But as early as 1704 building had begun there, and in the 19th century imposing squares and boulevards began to be laid out, providing town residences for the English aristocracy. Among them are Grosvenor Square, Berkeley Square, South Audley Street, and Curzon Street. A Mayfair address continued throughout the early 20th century to provide the ultimate in cachet, but spiraling costs since World War II have reduced Mayfair's residential importance, and today, while its name retains a very special aura, it is mainly a commercial area, with a sprinkling of luxury hotels.

Mayflower

The name of the ship that brought the first group of Pilgrims from England to America, in 1620, landing them in Massachusetts, traditionally at Plymouth Rock. All American schoolchildren are familiar with the story; it is not till later that they are made aware that there are a number of extant families that trace their forebears to those who sailed on the *Mayflower*. Although some of these are indubitably genuine, it has been said that if all such claims were valid, the *Mayflower* would have to have been as large as the *Queen Elizabeth II*.

McAdoo Tubes

A former nickname for the Hudson and Manhattan Railroad Company tunnels, completed in 1912, connecting New Jersey with Manhattan, so called because it was mainly through the efforts of William Gibbs McAdoo that the financing was secured to build them.

McCormick Place

The world's largest exhibition center, on Lake Shore Drive, in Chicago south of the Loop. Destroyed by fire in 1967, it was rebuilt twice its original size and reopened in January 1971, and has since been still further expanded.

Mecca

A nickname of Salt Lake City, Utah.

Med, the

An informal nickname for the Mediterranean Sea.

Megalopolis

A nickname that has been bestowed on the chain of cities from Boston, Massachusetts, to Washington, D. C., as their suburbs have continued to spread outward till they meet in one long continuum. The name is made up of the Greek elements *megalo-* 'great, large' and *-polis* 'city,' and has been bestowed on very large cities that have grown extensively, like Los Angeles and Tokyo.

Melanesia

A collective term for the islands off the northeast coast of Australia, to the south of Micronesia. Its main constituents are Papua New Guinea, Fiji, New Hebrides, New Caledonia, the Solomon Islands, and the Bismarck Archipelago. The name literally means 'black islands,' and was originally coined because of the dark skins of the inhabitants. See also **Micronesia, Oceania, Polynesia.**

Melting Pot, the

A nickname of New York City, so called because most immigrants to the U. S. entered through this port, many remaining and blending their cultures.

Melton Mowbray

A town in Leicestershire, in the Midlands of England, that has powerful associations with food and with foxhunting. It is the headquarters of the manufacture of Stilton cheese (the village of Stilton itself, where the cheese was first sold, is away to the southeast in Cambridgeshire), and it is famous, too, for its pork pies. But it is also at the heart of the Shires, and the noted Quorn hunt operates in the area. Its most bizarre contribution to the terminology of field sports must be the *Melton pad*, a sort of hernia truss specially made to be worn on horseback. In former times Melton Mowbray was a clothmaking center, and *melton* is a heavy woolen fabric named after it.

Memphis of the American Nile, the

An early nickname of St. Louis, Missouri.

Mercia

A kingdom which occupied large parts of the Midlands of England in Anglo-Saxon times. Its most powerful king was Offa (757–96). In modern times the name has been revived and applied to various administrative areas in the region; the West Mercian police, for example, are responsible for the western Midlands, based at Worcester. See also **Offa's Dyke.**

Merseyside

A metropolitan county above the Mersey River in the Northwest of England, comprising the city of Liverpool and surrounding districts. Its name is associated in the public imagination particularly with the Mersey sound, pop music of the sort played by Gerry and the Pacemakers and similar Liverpool groups in the 1960s; but sadly, in the 1980s, it is coming to be linked increasingly with inner-city decline and social tension, as the once busy docks have fallen silent and unemployment has grown.

Mesopotamia

The name for a land in ancient times that lay between the Tigris and Euphrates rivers; much of this is now in modern Iraq. This fertile area was the center of the Sumerian, Akkadian, Babylonian, and Assyrian civilizations. The term, in Greek, means '(land) between the rivers.' See also **Fertile Crescent**.

Metroland

A name given to a large area of land fanning out from northwest London into the Home Counties. In the early 20th century it was served by the Metropolitan Railway, and the name was coined to publicize the scheme by which the railway company bought up large tracts of countryside on both sides of the line and built houses on them; to their remote rural quietness London office workers could return gratefully each evening. The railroad, now the Metropolitan Line of the London Underground, starts at Baker Street Station, passes through what was once Middlesex, and continues into the depths of Hertfordshire and Buckinghamshire—"beechy Bucks," in the words of John Betjeman, the poet who captured the essence of Metroland so evocatively. The name came still further into prominence with Margot Metroland, a character in several of Evelyn Waugh's novels. It has subsequently been applied more generally to any residential belt surrounding a metropolis.

Metropolis of America, the

A nickname of New York City.

Metropolis of North Texas, the

A nickname of Dallas.

Metropolis of the Magic Valley

A nickname of Brownsville, Texas. See also **Magic Valley.**

Metropolis of the Missouri Valley, the

A nickname of Kansas City, Missouri.

Metropolis of the New South

A nickname of Louisville, Kentucky.

Metropolis of the Northeast, the

A nickname of Bangor, Maine.

Micronesia

A collective term for the islands that comprise the northwestern section of Oceania, to the north of Melanesia, in the South Pacific Ocean. Its main constituents are the Caroline Islands, the Marianas (of which Guam is one), the Marshall Islands, Kiribati (formerly the Gilbert Islands), and Nauru.

The name literally means 'small islands.' See also **Melanesia, Oceania, Polynesia**.

Middle Border, the

A name for an area in the Upper Midwest of the United States, including North and South Dakota and parts of Minnesota, Iowa, Wyoming, and Montana.

Middle East, the

The Middle East, or *Mideast* as it is also called, is a vaguely defined area that has moved considerably westward over the years. When it first came into existence as a concept, it was situated, quite neatly and logically, between the Near East and the Far East, and comprised Iran, Iraq, Afghanistan, India, and Burma. Since then, however, its occidental shift has eaten up most of what was formerly the Near East, and left much of its own former territory without a distinguishing epithet. In the 1980s it covers northeast Africa and much of southwest Asia, and by convention includes Egypt, Saudi Arabia, Syria, Iraq, Israel, Lebanon, Jordan, Yemen, the Gulf States and probably Libya and Iran; many would also include Turkey. With the notable exception of Israel, therefore, the Middle East is made up exclusively of Arab, or at least Islamic states, and is often thought of in a shorthand way as corresponding with the Arab World, excepting, of course, Israel. See also **Far East,** Gulf States under **Gulf, Near East**.

Middle Kingdom, the

The name by which China was known in the West in Renaissance times. It is a translation of a term the Chinese themselves used to describe their empire, believing it to be at the center of the world. See also **Cathay**.

Middle Passage, the

A name given in the days of slavery to the middle section of the Atlantic Ocean. It was the route taken by the slave ships from West Africa to North America and the Caribbean, and was probably originally so called because the voyage formed the central part of the slaves' journey from their homes to the estates and plantations where they were being taken.

Middlesex

A former county in southeast England, to the west of London. It became absorbed into London in 1965, but although it no longer officially exists its ghost has certainly not been laid. Teams known as "Middlesex" continue to play in the English county cricket and rugby competitions, for example, and it is probably true to say that most local residents still regard themselves as living in Middlesex. During its official existence it was one of the Home Counties, and in the early 19th century its beauties inspired the poet Keats; but long before its change of status its little villages and hamlets, such as Harrow-on-the-Hill, Twickenham, Isleworth, and Ruislip, had become merged into the general subtopia of London.

Midgetman

A small, mobile, ground-based, intercontinental ballistic missile, the SICBM, scheduled in 1986 for development by the United States.

Midi, le

The French term for what in English is more usually referred to as the South of France. There is a distinction in usage, however; for while *South of France* conjures up mainly the Riviera, *Midi* embraces the hinterland of Mediterranean France. It has no precise boundaries, but the 45th parallel—45° north—is a traditional northern extremity; to the south of this is a land of warmth and sunshine, a land where the classic ingredients of Midi cuisine reign supreme: olive oil, garlic, and tomatoes. Its range west to east extends from the Spanish border to the Italian, although there is some tendency to favor the term *Midi* for the section to the west of the River Rhone, in contrast to Provence to the east.

Midlands, the

A name applied, somewhat by default, to those areas of England that are not the North, the South, the West, or East Anglia. Since the application of these terms is a little vague, the boundaries of the Midlands themselves are rather loosely drawn; but on the whole it may be said with confidence that the Midlands include Leicestershire, Lincolnshire, Northamptonshire, Oxfordshire, Staffordshire, and Warwickshire. Most people would also include at least the southern parts of Cheshire, Derbyshire, and Nottinghamshire, the northern parts of Buckinghamshire and Bedfordshire, and the western part of Cambridgeshire. Although Shropshire and particularly Hereford and Worcester are often regarded as being in the West, they too are not infrequently counted as being in the Midlands. In addition to this general application, a more specific but now somewhat dated usage links the Midlands with the foxhunting counties of the eastern Midlands, particularly in Leicestershire and Northamptonshire—the Shires, as they are often known. See also **East Midlands, West Midlands**.

Midwest, the,

In the United States, an area encompassing those states in the central and somewhat eastern part of the country, namely, Ohio, Indiana, Illinois, Wisconsin, Minnesota, Iowa, Missouri, Arkansas, and Kentucky. The area has no specific definition and its boundaries depend on the point of view of the speaker. Compare **East, South, West.**

Mile High City, the

A nickname of Denver, Colorado.

Millionaire's Resort
A nickname of Jekyll Island, Georgia.

Milton Keynes
A town in Buckinghamshire, in southern England. Until the 1960s it was a small village, but in 1967 it was officially designated a "new town," and it has since been radically transformed: modern buildings have sprouted enthusiastically, commerce and light industry have moved in, the Open University (which operates via broadcasting) was established there in 1971, and it has become a thriving population center. Many feel, though, that like most man-made towns, it suffers from not having grown organically, and it has become something of a byword for artificiality—typified perhaps by a notorious set of plastic cows placed in a field there to foster an air of rural tranquillity.

Mincing Lane
A street in the City of London that is traditionally the center of the capital's tea and wine trades. Its name has nothing to do with chopping things up small; it comes from a convent of *minchins* (an old word for 'nuns') that used to hold property there.

Mineral City of the South, the
A nickname of Birmingham, Alabama.

Mineral Pocket of the Northeast
A nickname of Cumberland, Rhode Island.

Mining State, the
A nickname of Nevada.

Minneapolis of the West, the
A nickname of Spokane, Washington, so called because of its flour mills.

Minsky's
The shortened name of Minsky Brothers' National Winter Garden, a burlesque theater in lower Manhattan, operated by four brothers, Billy, Herbert, Morton, and Abe Minsky. From its early development in the 1870s, burlesque had provided entertainment—"fun for all the family"—which, while not entirely wholesome fare, was characterized more by vulgarity than by lewdness or lasciviousness, even in the eyes of the New York Society for the Suppression of Vice, an organization founded in 1873 by J. P. Morgan to monitor the art, literature, and theater presented to the people of the city. Burlesque in those days was the humor of dialect comedians, of the raucous slapstick of the comics who beat one another with inflated bladders, of leather-lunged "coon-shouters" and other singers, and of the line of costumed dancers, from which the modern musical-

comedy chorus line developed. It was where the *haut monde* and hoi polloi rubbed elbows with the likes of Robert Benchley, Reginald Marsh, e. e. cummings, and Edmund Wilson. Minsky's headlined shimmy dancers like Mademoiselle Fifi, a twenty-year-old, well-constructed blonde billed as "Mlle. Fifi from Paris, France, former Prima Ballerina Assoluta, Imperial Opera House, St. Petersburg, Russia." She was actually Betty Buzby, daughter of George Buzby, a police officer in Philadelphia's Vice Squad. On the night of April 20, 1925, Mlle. Fifi for the first time removed her clothes on stage and, at the direction of John Sumner, Secretary of the Society for the Suppression of Vice, police swarmed through the theater, arresting dancers, comics, and all the other performers they could lay hands on. Seven weeks later the verdict was returned: the case was dismissed. Yet, partly because of the notoriety of the trial and partly because of subsequent developments in the promotion and staging of burlesque, the form deteriorated into a sordid bump-and-grind striptease exhibition, offering little entertainment and appealing only to the prurient. It suffered a revival during the Depression, when Minsky opened theaters on 42nd Street, but then closed in 1937, when Mayor Fiorello H. La Guardia directed the revocation of licenses and forbade even the use of the name, *burlesque.*

Miracle Mile

A stretch of Wilshire Boulevard in Los Angeles, extending approximately one mile from La Brea Avenue to Fairfax Avenue. The name was applied in the 1930s by a real estate developer, A. W. Ross, in order to promote the commercial possibilities of the Boulevard. The decentralization of Los Angeles' central business district began in the 1920s and development was directed westward along major arteries, Wilshire Boulevard in particular. The Miracle Mile became a great commercial success with the establishment of a number of fashionable stores on the boulevard and the motorization of the shopping public.

Mission City

A nickname of San Antonio, Texas.

Mistelbach

A town in Austria, about 20 miles north of Vienna, which has long been the target of jokes about the silly speech and behavior of its inhabitants. See also **Chelm, Gotham, Kocourkov.**

Mistress of the Seas

A nickname of Great Britain.

moaning Minnie

A World War II soldiers' nickname for a German mortar shell *Minnenwerfer*, later transposed to the air-raid warning sirens.

Mo Bay

A nickname in frequent local use for Montego Bay, a luxurious vacation resort on the north coast of the island of Jamaica, which attracts large numbers of American tourists.

Model City

A nickname of Quincy, Illinois.

Modern Rome

A nickname of Richmond, Virginia.

Mohawk Trail

A road between North Adams and Pittsfield, in northwestern Massachusetts, named for the Mohawk Indians, who once dwelt in the area. Parts of it were undoubtedly used as a "trail" by the early inhabitants, but it is not said to follow a particular historic route as is, say, the **Appalachian Trail** (*q.v.*). Now a scenic highway that winds through the northern parts of the Berkshire Mountains, just south of the Vermont border, the Mohawk Trail is a popular drive for tourists, especially in the autumn, when the variegated foliage of the great variety of trees in the surrounding forests can be appreciated to its best advantage.

Mongolia

The region of central Asia inhabited by the Mongols. In the Middle Ages, when it was known as Tartary, the Mongols' sphere of influence, particularly under Genghis Khan, extended over a vast area, from eastern Europe to the Pacific. But today Mongolia is somewhat more circumscribed. It is divided up between three nations: Inner Mongolia, which is a region of China; Tuva, a republic of the Soviet Union; and the Mongolian People's Republic. The last was a Chinese province, known as Outer Mongolia, from 1691 to 1924; since then it has been an independent state. In the West, Outer Mongolia has long been suggestive of the ultimate in remoteness. See also **Tartary**.

Monitor and *Merrimack*

The first ironclad warships whose battle at Hampton Roads, Virginia in 1862 marked a turning point in naval warfare by focusing attention on the importance of armor-plated ships. The *Monitor* was built of iron as well as being ironclad. The *Merrimack* was originally wood and had been scuttled by Federal troops when they evacuated the Navy yard at Portsmouth, Virginia. The Confederates raised it, covered it with iron plates, and renamed it the *Virginian*, though it is usually known by its original name.

Monkey State, the

A nickname of Tennessee, so called in reference to the bill passed in its House of Representatives (1925) that prohibited the teaching of the theory of evolution in any of its schools supported in whole or in part by public funds and resulted in the Scopes, or Monkey Trial.

Montmartre

A district in northern central Paris famed as an artists' quarter. It is built on a hill—Parisians' nickname for it is *la Botte* 'the hillock'—and the white domes of the Sacre Coeur cathedral on its summit are a well-known Paris landmark. Its bohemian reputation owes more to history than to present-day fact. Most of the artists moved over to the Left Bank before World War I, and the artistic efforts on display today in the Place du Tertre are laid on purely for the benefit of tourists. But despite commercialization Montmartre manages to retain much of its quaint village atmosphere. Nightlife is still a local specialty, too, as it was in the days of Toulouse-Lautrec; Pigalle is here, and the girls continue to can-can in the Moulin Rouge.

Monumental State, the

A nickname of Maryland, a reference to the number and quality of monuments in its largest city, Baltimore.

Monument City

A nickname of Baltimore, Maryland.

Moor, the

A familiar abbreviation for Dartmoor, bleak granite uplands in Devon, southwest England. It is used particularly with reference to Dartmoor prison, at Princetown in the heart of the moor, whose isolated position makes it an ideal place to house long-term or dangerous prisoners.

Mormon City

A nickname of Salt Lake City, Utah.

Mormon State, the

A nickname of Utah.

Morningside

A well-to-do southern suburb of Edinburgh, Scotland, that is celebrated for the supposedly ultra-refined accent of its inhabitants. There is a theory that it was first introduced by the Irish elocutionist Thomas Sheridan, father of the more famous Richard Brinsley Sheridan, the playwright.

mosquito armada

The nickname for the courageous fleet of private boats, from rowboats to pleasure cruisers, that joined the Royal Navy in rescuing British troops from across the English Channel on the beaches at Dunkirk in 1940.

Because of their extraordinary bravery, they were later honored by being allowed to fly the cross of St. George.

Mosquito Coast

An epithet of the coasts of Nicaragua and Honduras, along the Gulf of Mexico.

Mosquito State, the

A nickname of New Jersey.

Moss Bros

A familiar name (pronounced "Moss Bross") for Moss Brothers, a well-known British firm of gentlemen's outfitters that is particularly associated with the hire of formal wear. A classy wedding, with many morning coats and toppers in evidence, is most certainly a Moss Bros affair.

Mother-in-Law of the Navy

A nickname of Norfolk, Virginia, so called because the Norfolk Navy Yard, one of the oldest and most important, is directly opposite it on the Portsmouth side of the Elizabeth River.

Mother of Parliaments, the

A name often applied to the British Parliament at Westminster, as being the assembly on which many other such institutions around the world are based. However, the source of the expression, John Bright's "England is the mother of parliaments" (1865), shows its original application to have been slightly different.

Mother of Presidents

A nickname of Virginia, so called because eight of her native sons became presidents of the United States: George Washington, Thomas Jefferson, James Madison, James Monroe, William Henry Harrison, John Tyler, Zachary Taylor, and Woodrow Wilson. However, Ohio also claims the title, for her seven sons: Ulysses S. Grant; Rutherford B. Hayes, James A. Garfield, Benjamin Harrison, William McKinley, William Howard Taft, and Warren G. Harding. William Henry Harrison was living in Ohio when he became president.

Mother of Rivers, the

A nickname of New Hampshire.

Mother of Southwestern Statesmen, the

A nickname of Tennessee.

Mother of States

A nickname for Virginia, so called because all or part of eight other states were formed from western territory originally claimed by her: Illinois, Indiana, Kentucky, Michigan, Minnesota, Ohio, West Virginia, and Wisconsin.

Mother of the West, the

A nickname of Missouri.

Motown

A nickname of Detroit, Michigan, from "motor town" because it is the center of the automobile industry in the United States. The name came into prominence also because it was used as a trade name for a company (in California) that has published popular musical records and tapes.

Moulin Rouge

Literally, the 'Red Mill,' though why it was so named is shrouded in the mysteries of the 19th century. A theater-nightclub in Paris that, historically, at least, gained its reputation as a place of wild abandon, frequented by the *trottoises* of Pigalle but, especially, by Henri de Toulouse-Lautrec, the painter who made it famous through his posters advertising the establishment and, notoriously, the dancer Jane Avril. It is said to be the place where the can-can was first danced, but there are those who would credit the **Folies Bergère** (*q.v.*) with that accomplishment.

Mound City

A nickname of St. Louis, Missouri, so called after the Indian mound builders who formerly inhabited the site.

Mountain State, the

The official nickname of West Virginia and of Colorado.

Mrs. O'Leary's barn

The structure in which Mrs. O'Leary's cow is said to have kicked over a lantern to start the Great Chicago Fire of October 8–10, 1871. The fire killed more than 250 people, destroyed some $200 million worth of property and left about 100,000—a third of the population—homeless. A long period of dry weather and subsequent tinderbox conditions helped the fire to spread rapidly. Most historians agree that the blaze did, in fact, begin in the O'Leary barn on DeKoven Street, about a mile south and just west of the present Loop area, but whether it was caused by the family cow is not certain, and several other possible causes have been given. (Mrs. O'Leary blamed a careless neighbor known to have entered the barn just before the fire began.) The site is today occupied by the Chicago Fire Academy.

Mud-Cat (*or* -Waddler) State, the

A nickname of Mississippi, so called because of the abundance of catfish in its waters.

Mudtown

A former nickname of Chicago.

Mummerset

An imaginary southwestern English county usually invoked to express spurious rusticity; a country yokel portrayed in a play or book as speaking in an exaggerated West Country fashion, with many outlandish but probably obsolete dialectal expressions, is said to have a "Mummerset accent." The name is a blend of *mummer*, an itinerant entertainer in former times, and *Somerset*, a West Country county. Compare **Loamshire**.

Muscle Shoals Area

This area includes the cities of Florence, Muscle Shoals, Sheffield, and Tuscumbia in northwest Alabama, as well as the nearby surrounding areas. The name came from the Muscle Shoals of the Tennessee river, a former navigational hazard that was eliminated by the building of Wilson Dam. One theory of the origin of the name holds that it comes from the Cherokee word *dagunahi*, meaning 'mussel place'—"muscle" being a variant spelling of *mussel*. A second, but less probable explanation in the local area attributes the name to the fact that negotiating the original shoals required considerable "muscle."

Muscovy

A name applied in former ties to Russia. In strict terms Muscovy was a Russian principality, whose capital was Moscow (from which it derived its name) and which existed between the 13th and the 16th centuries; but with the vagueness of early geography, the name soon spread to the rest of the country.

Museum of Science and Industry

The oldest, largest, and most popular museum of its kind in the United States, located in Jackson Park, on the South Side of Chicago. The museum houses a wide range of technological—often nostalgic—exhibits in a spacious edifice that was erected as the Palace of Fine Arts for the World's Columbian Exposition of 1893. Many of the displays are constructed so as to enable visitors to interact by means of knobs, buttons, and other controls. Attractions include a visitable coal mine, an extensive model-railroad layout, and a German U-boat (U-505) captured intact on June 4, 1944, the first enemy warship captured by the U. S. Navy after the War of 1812. See also **White City**.

Mushroom City

A nickname of San Francisco.

Mushroomopolis

A nickname of Kansas City, Missouri.

Nail City

A nickname of Wheeling, West Virginia.

Namibia

A territory of disputed nomenclature (and ownership) in southwestern Africa, to the north of South Africa. Until 1919 it was a German colony, known as German Southwest Africa. Following World War I it was confiscated, and in 1920 was assigned by the League of' Nations as a trust territory to South Africa, since when it has officially been called South-West Africa. The mandate was canceled by the United Nations in 1966, but South Africa refused to give up the territory. In affirmation of its *de jure* independent status, the UN in 1968 declared its name to be Namibia (the Namib is a desert that occupies its coastal region). However, the situation remains fluid, and, whether as a compromise or for clarity, it is often referred to as South-West Africa-Namibia and is shown on maps as Namibia (South-West Africa).

Naples

A city of proverbial beauty on the west coast of Italy. The saying "See Naples and die" implies that anywhere else in the world would be a visual anticlimax, and indeed Naples' setting, built on hills surrounding the wide Bay of Naples, with Mount Vesuvius nearby, is most striking. There is a possible irony in the aphorism, however, for Naples used to be notorious for its rampant cholera and typhoid.

Narrows, the

A strait, about one mile wide, joining Upper and Lower New York Bays, that separates Staten Island from Brooklyn.

Natchez Trace

The name of a trail between Nashville, Tennessee, and Natchez, Mississippi, important in the early development of those areas.

National, the

See **Grand National.**

Nation's Most Corrupt State

A nickname for Rhode Island at the turn of the century, in reference to the graft and corruption there.

Nation's State, the
A nickname of the District of Columbia.

Nation's Thoroughfare, the
A nickname of Louisville, Kentucky.

Native States, the
A collective term used for those states that were more or less self-governing during the time when Britain ruled India. Also known as the *Indian States and Agencies*, there were no fewer than 562 of them, the largest being Hyderabad, Gwalior, Baroda, Mysore, Cochin, Jammu and Kashmir, Travancor, Sikkim, and Indore. They were ruled by their own rajahs and maharajahas, but a British resident or adviser was always present to provide a guiding hand. After independence in 1947 they were gradually merged into India and Pakistan.

Navel of the Nation, the
A nickname of Kansas, because it lies almost at the geographical center of the 48 contiguous states.

Navy Pier
A Lake Michigan facility, located just north of the Loop in Chicago. Originally known as Municipal Pier, the 3,000-foot-long facility has been eclipsed in recent years by the major port developed at Lake Calumet on the city's Far South Side, some thirteen miles south of the Loop. Nowadays, the city-owned pier is the site of many ethnic and cultural events.

Naze, the
A headland on the north Essex coast, just to the east of Colchester in East Anglia, England. The name, which may be connected with the word *nose*, is also applied to Lindesnes, a promontory at the southern tip of Norway.

Near East, the
A term with a dated air to it, which has generally fallen out of use since World War II. In its earliest use it referred more or less to the western lands of area now known as the Middle East: Libya, Egypt, Arabia, Palestine, Syria, and Turkey. But confusingly, *Near East* also once referred to Turkey, the Levant, and large parts of the Balkans, in southeast Europe: in other words, the Ottoman Empire. However, the Ottoman Empire no longer exists, and *Middle East*, though not as specific, is in far wider use as a geographic reference; if it is used at all today, *Near East* most often refers to Turkey. See also **Asia Minor, Far East, Middle East**.

Near North Side
A diverse, trendy, generally upscale section of Chicago where much of its cultural and professional life is centered. Stretching north and a short way

west from the Loop and the Magnificent Mile, the Near North Side includes the often overlapping Old Town, New Town, Lincoln Park, Lakeview, and Wrigleyville areas. Particularly rich in theaters, specialty shops, and ethnic restaurants, the atmosphere of the area bears a distant but growing likeness to that of Greenwich Village in New York City. See also **Billy Goat Tavern, Biograph Theater, Bughouse Square, Cabrini-Green Public Housing Project, Gold Coast, Holy Name Cathedral, the Magnificent Mile, Navy Pier, New Town, Old Town, Rush Street, Water Tower, Wrigleyville.**

Neasden

A district in northwest London immortalized in the 1960s by the satirical magazine *Private Eye.* Innocent of any fine architecture, historical sites, or literary associations, it is of such resounding dullness that it inspired the *Eye* to adopt it as the archetype of gray suburbia, where even monotony would be exciting. Neasden, **Clapham** (*q.v.*), and **Wigan** (*q.v.*) epitomize what in other times and other cultures appear in the folk literature as **Gotham** (*q.v.*) (with its "Wise Men"), **Kocourkov** (*q.v.*), **Mistelbach** (*q.v.*), and, for eastern Europe, **Chelm** (*q.v.*).

Needles, the

A line of three tall sharp chalk pillars that form the western extremity of the Isle of Wight, off the south coast of England. They protrude from the sea like gleaming teeth, and a lighthouse is situated at their tip to warn shipping. See also **Island, 1.**

Neogaea

In the scientific study of the distribution of animal species around the world, the name given to South and Central America. Compare **Arctogaea, Notogaea.**

Nevada Proving Grounds

The site, in southeast Nevada, of the Atomic Energy Commission's nuclear tests conducted at Yucca Flat and Frenchman Flat in 1951.

New England

The area in the northeastern part of the United States encompassing the states that were the places of early settlement by colonists from England, namely, Maine, New Hampshire, Vermont, Rhode Island, Massachusetts, and Connecticut. See also **East.**

New England of the West, the

A nickname of Minnesota.

New Forest

An area of woodland, with some heath, in southern Hampshire, near Southampton, in England. It has been so called for about 900 years.

Newgate Prison

A prison, built in 1769 in London, that figures occasionally in English literature. It was demolished in 1902, and the **Old Bailey** (*q.v.*) now occupies the site.

Newmarket

A town in Suffolk, just to the northeast of Cambridge, that is synonymous with horseracing in England. The first race took place on Newmarket Heath in 1619, watched enthusiastically by King James I, and the place has gone from strength to strength ever since. Today it is home to the Jockey Club, the governing body of English racing, has many training stables for racehorses, holds a famous annual bloodstock sale which realizes many millions of pounds, and hosts several celebrated races, including the 1000 and 2000 Guineas and the Cesarewich.

New Shoreham

The official though seldom used name for Block Island, Rhode Island.

News of the Screws, the

A facetious nickname for the *News of the World*, a popular British Sunday newspaper that specializes in lurid stories of sexual shenanigans.

New Spain

A nickname of New Jersey. See also **Foreigner State.**

New Sweden

A nickname of Delaware, so called because in 1638 a fort at what is now Wilmington was manned by Swedes and Finns, and for many years thereafter, the peninsula was under Swedish rule.

New Town

A richly diverse area of the Near North Side of Chicago, noted for its nightlife and shopping and as the heart of the city's sizable gay community. It is one of several Near North areas currently undergoing so-called "gentrification," the process in which the well-to-do move in, rehabilitate charming old houses, increase property values, rents, and taxes, and attract new businesses—meanwhile forcing away the poor, who can no longer afford to live there.

New Town, the

In the 18th century, increasing prosperity in Edinburgh, Scotland's capital, provided the impetus to expand and break out of the crowded old city huddled around the castle and to build anew and splendidly. The result was the New Town, an area of magnificent Georgian terraces, squares, and crescents, designed mostly by James Craig, fully befitting the dignity of the Athens of the North. Its southern boundary, and most famous thoroughfare, is Princes Street, which has shops along its northern side but to the south is open to a splendid vista of the Castle Rock.

New World, the

A term applied to the Americas by their European discoverers. It was still a sufficiently live general epithet in the late 19th century for Anton Dvořák to name his Ninth Symphony "From the New World." In the present day, though, its main use is probably in zoological and botanical contexts, with reference to the Western Hemisphere as a whole. Compare **Old World**.

New York of the West, the

A former nickname of Chicago.

Niagara of the East

A nickname of Grand Falls on the St. John River in northeastern Maine.

Nine Elms

An area in southwest London, on the south bank of the Thames, just to the north of Battersea. It contains Battersea Power Station, a famous London landmark with its towering chimneys and monolithic cathedral-like nave; and in 1974 it became the home of London's principal fruit and vegetable market, when the New Covent Garden Market was opened.

NoHo

A nickname given to a neighborhood in mid Manhattan, west of Lafayette Street, east of Sixth Avenue, and, as the name suggests, *no*rth of *Ho*uston (pronounced HOWstin) Street. It is a later development than SoHo (so named because it is *so*uth of *Ho*uston), in somewhat jocular imitation of it. It consists largely of commercial loft buildings in which former office and factory areas have been modernized and fitted out as dwelling places and, occasionally, as studios for the artists who occupy them. Also, **No-Ho.** See also **SoHo.**

no man's land

A piece of disputed territory between opposing armies. The expression gained currency during World War I, when it referred to the areas in France across which German and Allied armies seesawed for many months. As these were totally laid waste in the process, the term acquired the additional notion of 'wasteland,' which it sometimes retains today. According to citations in the *Oxford English Dictionary*, the phrase goes back to the early 14th century, when it referred to a section of barren land, north of London Wall, where executions sometimes took place.

North, the

1. In the broadest terms, the North in Britain is anywhere north of London; for example, the route indicated to "The North" on a road sign takes one up to Scotland. More specifically, the North is northern England, but its southern limit is purely a relative matter; to someone from the South, the North quite possibly includes places like Derby and Nottingham, whereas for a Tynesider Sheffield (which is north of Derby and Nottingham) is distinctly in the Midlands. Traditionally, the Humber River is said to make the boundary between the North and Midlands, but this has the disadvantage of excluding, for example, Manchester and Liverpool, which most Britons would assign to the North. In practice, two factors are probably decisive. First, accent: anyone who speaks a dialect roughly similar to that of Yorkshire or Lancashire is likely to be regarded as a Northerner. And second, industrialization: the stereotyped view of the North is of a continuous vista of factory chimneys, cooling towers, coal mines, and slag heaps (although, in fact, it contains areas of great natural beauty). A general rule of thumb based on these factors would be to say that, starting from the west, the North includes northern Cheshire, probably dips down to take in Derbyshire and Nottinghamshire, and then shades off northeast toward the Humber estuary; anywhere between there and the Scottish border is the North. Culturally and sociologically it is quite distinct from the southern part of the country, which is on the whole wealthier and has a preponderance of middle-class inhabitants. Compare **Midlands, Northeast, Northwest, South**. See also **Tyneside, Watford**.

2. In the United States, those states in the northeastern and north central parts of the country north of the Mason-Dixon line, especially those that sided against the Confederates in the Civil War. See also **South.**

3. In geopolitical terms, *the North* has taken on new connotations in the latter part of the 20th century. As contrasted with the South, it refers basically to the economically advantaged and industrially developed nations of the northern hemisphere—the world's "haves." But since, like East and West, it is not a strictly geographical term, southern-hemisphere countries like Australia are included in the North as well. It was popularized as a concept by the publication in 1980 of the so-called *Brandt Report*, in full *North-South, a program for survival; report of the Independent Commission on International Development.*

North Africa

A term used for Africa north of the Tropic of Cancer. It includes Morocco, Algeria, Tunisia, Libya, and Egypt.

North Britain

A circumlocution for Scotland which enjoyed some popularity from the 17th to the 19th centuries. It first came into regular use after 1707, when Scotland and England united to form Great Britain; according to the *Oxford English Dictionary*, it was still current in the 1880s, albeit "chiefly in postal use." It never succeeded in ousting *Scotland* as the standard name for the country, but its memory is preserved particularly in the famous North British Hotel, on Princes Street in Edinburgh.

North Country, the

Geographically, the North Country in Britain corresponds more or less to the North, but its connotations are markedly different. Whereas *the North* suggests a grimy industrialized landscape, *the North Country* stresses its prelapsarian state, before the Industrial Revolution. It conjures up visions of windblown moors and fells, ruddy-cheeked countrymen and women, good ale and beef, and laconic humor. Compare **Broad Acres**.

Northeast, the

1. The northeastern corner of England, including the counties of Northumberland, Durham, Tyne and Wear, and probably also Cleveland. Although often sweepingly included under the broad category, *the North*, the Northeast is proudly distinct from its southerly neighbor, Yorkshire, which Northeasterners often dismiss, only half in jest, as belonging to the Midlands. The heart of the region is probably Newcastle-upon-Tyne and the surrounding Tyneside, whose inhabitants, the Geordies, have given the Northeast its nickname, Geordieland. Geordie is the name of the dialect they speak, too, a lilting speech which in its pure form can often be impenetrable to outsiders. See also **Geordieland, Jarrow**.
2. In the United States, the District of Columbia and those states generally running northwards along the Atlantic coast to New England, namely, Delaware, Maryland, Pennsylvania, New Jersey, New York, and the New England states.

Northeast Corridor

A general term, encountered chiefly in railroad jargon, referring to the rights of way between New York City and Boston, though, technically, it goes beyond into Maine. With the spread of the northeastern **Megalopolis** (*q.v.*), it has lately been extended southward in concept to include Washington, D. C.

Northeast Kingdom

A nickname for a rural part of northeastern Vermont, comprising Caledonia, Orleans, and Essex counties, thought to have been coined in 1949 by George D. Aiken, former governor and U. S. senator. It has become a useful term to designate the area for socio-political, economic, and planning purposes.

North End

The informal name given to that part of Boston bounded by the **Haymarket** (*q.v.*), the Northeast Expressway, and, on the east, the Atlantic Ocean. Primarily a section settled by Italians that retains its ethnic reputation in its restaurants and food markets, the North End has in recent years become gentrified and its population in the mid 1980s would be said to be homogeneous.

Northland, the

A term applied to the northernmost outposts of many countries and continents. In the past it was used for the top third of Scotland, to the north of Inverness, and in present-day usage it covers both the peninsula that contains Norway and Sweden and the northern fastnesses of Canada. Severnaya Zemlya, a Soviet archipelago in the Arctic ocean, means literally 'North Land.'

North Pole

The northern end of the earth's axis of rotation which, owing to libration, changes slightly; the geographic north pole. It is not the same as the north magnetic pole, which varies as much as one degree in a year and may be 12° away from the geographic pole. The surrounding area is composed entirely of ice floes, which float atop the Arctic Ocean. In fancy, it is a cold, remote place inhabited only by polar bears (who actually live farther south) and by Santa Claus. See also **South Pole.**

North Shore

1. An informal name for the east-west shore of Long Island (see **Island**) that borders on the Long Island Sound, between Sands Point and Orient Point, at the tip of the North Fork. It has many old, picturesque, and wealthy communities, notably Sands Point and Oyster Bay, where millionaires long ago established large estates with impressive mansions. Its shores are configured by many deep-water harbors, as at Oyster Bay, Northport (Lloyds Harbor), and Port Jefferson, which are densely occupied by yacht clubs and marinas. The further east one travels, the sparser the concentration of such facilities, and east of Port Jefferson, the shoreline, with only a few inlets for boats, has remained quite rural. See also **South Shore**.
2. A section north of Boston beginning north of Lynn and extending as far as Portsmouth, New Hampshire, along the Atlantic coast. It is associated in the main with affluent horse-owners of inherited wealth, who pursue sports like fox-hunting and polo. It was settled early and its shore is dotted with shipyards, as those at Marblehead, once known for the building of whalers, in recent years for the design and construction of yachts.

North Side

Multi-ethnic, economically diverse area of Chicago stretching north from the downtown, Loop area to the northern city limits and reaching roughly two miles west from the bordering Lake Michigan; on the west is the city's Northwest Side, which includes some of the oldest middle-class enclaves of Polish, Czechoslovakian, and other European immigrants; on the north, along the lake, is the town of Evanston, home of the main campus of Northwestern University, the Chicago area's first university, founded in 1850. Distinctive North Side areas include the generally upscale Near North Side, the Andersonville section, settled by Swedish immigrants, and the relatively poor, often troubled Uptown area, in the latter part of the 20th century the home of many subsistence-level residents, including sizable numbers of Appalachians, American Indians, and Latinos. Also on the North Side, bordering the lake, is Lincoln Park, with its zoo, beaches, jogging paths, and other facilities, and Graceland Cemetery, the spacious, park-like burial place of such figures as George Pullman, builder of the railroad sleeping-car and of the company town of **Pullman** (*q.v.*), now a section of the city's South Side; Cyrus McCormick, inventor of the harvesting machine; architects Louis Sullivan and Daniel Burnham; meat magnate Philip Armour; merchant Marshall Field; real-estate developer Potter Palmer; and former Illinois governor John Peter Altgeld. On the Far North Side, in the northwest reaches of the city, is O'Hare International Airport, the world's busiest. See also **Aragon Ballrom, Haymarket Square, Near North Side, O'Hare International Airport.**

North Star State, the

A nickname of Minnesota.

Northumbria

In Anglo-Saxon times, an extensive independent kingdom that stretched all the way from the Humber River to the south of modern Yorkshire, to the Firth of Forth in Scotland. In modern usage it is sometimes employed as an alternative name for the county of Northumberland, a much more circumscribed area.

Northwest, the

1. The western half of the North of England, which is comprised of Cumbria and Lancashire, including Manchester and Liverpool.
2. In the United States, those western states that lie toward the north, namely, Montana, Wyoming, Washington, and Oregon. Compare **Pacific Northwest, Southwest, West.**

Northwest Frontier, the

The name given to the boundary between Afghanistan and Kashmir. The region is of considerable strategic importance to India, as it controls the Khyber Pass, and in 1901 it became part of British India; it was subsequently the scene of many tribal incursions, and the British army was called into action there on many occasions. Post-independence, Northwest Frontier Province is now the northernmost region of Pakistan.

Northwest Passage, the

From the late 15th century, a route from the Atlantic to the Pacific was sought around the north of the American continent. This was the fabled Northwest Passage, which baffled and killed so many explorers, from Sebastian Cabot in 1497–98, through Sir Martin Frobisher, Henry Hudson, William Baffin, and George Vancouver, to Sir Robert McClure, who finally discovered it in 1850. Roald Amundsen was actually the first to navigate it, in 1903–05.

Notogaea

In the scientific study of the distribution of animal species around the world, the name given to Australasia. Compare **Arctogaea, Neogaea.**

Notting Hill

An area in northwest central London, to the north of Holland Park. The prominent West Indian community in the western part of the district is responsible for the annual Notting Hill Carnival, which draws large crowds of participants and onlookers from all parts of London. The eastern part, Notting Hill Gate, a wealthier residential area, gets its name from a turnpike gate which once stood there.

Number One, London

The former sobriquet of Apsley House, the London residence of the Duke of Wellington, which is now the Wellington Museum. It is situated at Hyde Park Corner, to the northwest of Buckingham Palace, and was once the westmost house in Piccadilly before the open spaces of Hyde Park and Kensington Gardens.

Number 10

Or, more fully, Number 10 Downing Street, the official London residence of the British prime minister. Since the late 19th century the name has become virtually synonymous with the office of prime minister, or indeed with the British government itself—as in "A Number 10 spokesman said today. . . ." As such, it is often contrasted with "Whitehall," which tends to stress more the administrative, civil-service aspect of government. The house itself is a rather drab, unremarkable affair in a side street off Whitehall, to the south of Trafalgar Square. It was assigned to Britain's first prime minister, Sir Robert Walpole, in 1732 in his official capacity as First Lord of the Treasury, and has been used by holders of that post ever since. (Although in practice this means that it has been the prime minister's house, that term did not become usual before the middle of the 19th century.) Next door, Number 11 is the official home of the Chancellor of the Exchequer.

Nuremberg eggs

The nickname for the egg-shaped silver watches made there since the 16th century.

Nutmeg State, the

A nickname of Connecticut, so called because the settlers were said to be so canny that they could sell wooden nutmegs.

Oberammergau

A village high (elev. 3000 ft.) in the Bavarian Alps where the passion play is performed every ten years (in years evenly divisible by ten). It all began in 1634, when the townspeople put on the passion play in hopes of stopping an epidemic of the Plague, which had killed almost a hundred people in the valley during the Thirty Years' War. The decadal event draws tourists from all parts of the world.

Oceania

A collective term for all the territories of the South Pacific Ocean. It is standardly taken as comprising the island groups of Micronesia, Melanesia, and Polynesia, but very often Australia and New Zealand are included as well, and sometimes also the Malay Archipelago. See also **Australasia**.

Ocean State, the

A nickname of Rhode Island.

Odeon

The proper name of many theaters in the western world. It comes originally from Greek *ōideîon* 'place of song; music hall' via Latin *odeum*, with the same meaning. Thus, it can be seen to be related to *ode*, but, likewise, the ignoring of the Latin form, because of its similarity to *odium* 'hatred,' can easily be understood. Its popularity as a name transcends language barriers: there is an *Odéon* in Paris, for example; in the United States it appeared possibly only slightly less frequently as a movie theater name than *Bijou*, which means 'jewel' in French.

Oder-Neisse Line, the

A line that marks the boundary between Poland and East Germany. It more or less follows the course of the Oder River from Stettin, on the Baltic coast, to the south of Frankfurt, where the Neisse River branches off and continues south to the Czech border at Zittau. Before World War II, large areas to the east of these rivers belonged to Germany, and the line was originally set up in 1945 to separate those parts of Germany that would be under direct Soviet control from those that were to become part of Poland.

Offa's Dyke

A barrier, in the form of an earthwork, built under the direction of Offa, king of **Mercia** (*q.v.*), England, in the 8th century. Its purpose was to create a boundary between the English and the Welsh settlements, from the mouth of the Dee to that of the Wye.

Off Broadway, Off-Off Broadway

"Broadway" in these expressions is taken to refer to the mainstream of American theater, not, necessarily to the name of the street (*q.v.*). In fact, few of the legitimate theaters in New York City are actually situated on Broadway: most are in the side streets in the 40s. At the end of World War II, with the revival of the theater, the costs of staging productions became so great that it was impossible to raise the money to produce any but those that could successfully capture the imaginations of wealthy "angels." Theater rents were high, too, so small theater groups took to staging their productions in more modest settings—often just a hired hall—far from the expensive theater district. During the late 1940s, such theatrical productions, which, because of the quality of the original plays and that of the performers were gaining the attention of reviewers for major periodicals, acquired the generic nickname "off Broadway." In the ensuing years, some of these groups became well established (some as repertory companies), and the theaters where they performed began to acquire a stability which their owners exploited by increasing the rents. In time, a new generation of theatrical hopefuls found the Off-Broadway theaters beyond their reach; undaunted ("The show must go on"?), they found, in the late 1960s, even more modest accommodation and settled into abandoned motion-picture theaters and other such facilities, even if they were available for only a few nights a week. As New Yorkers have proved themselves indefatigable theater buffs, these often primitive venues—sometimes nothing more than a large restaurant closed for business that evening—attracted audiences. This manifestation of thespian perseverance, at two removes from the glitter and gold of Broadway, was dubbed "Off-Off Broadway." It is not to be disparaged, for a number of the plays that began Off-Off Broadway—the term is also used adverbially—became popular enough to be staked to Broadway-scale investments (*Oh! Calcutta!*, for example); and some of the players who were first observed strutting their stuff on dime-sized stages in downtown Manhattan neighborhoods so deserted at night that even the rats went uptown, hit the "big time," as, for example, did Bernadette Peters, who starred in *Dames at Sea* in just such a vest-pocket palace.

Ogaden, the

A high arid plateau in southeastern Ethiopia, bordering on Somalia. Over the years it has seen fierce fighting between government troops and local separatist forces, backed by Somalia, who wish to break away and form their own state.

O'Hare International Airport

Covering 60,000 acres (almost 94 square miles) in the northwest reaches of Chicago and handling some 120,000 travelers a day and the arrival or departure of, on the average, four aircraft every three minutes, Chicago-O'Hare ranks as the world's busiest airport.

Ohio's Jewels

The nickname for a group of seven statues on the grounds of the capitol at Columbus, namely, Ulysses S. Grant, William Tecumseh Sherman, Edwin McMasters Stanton, James A. Garfield, and Rutherford B. Hayes, all native sons, and Philip Henry Sheridan and Salmon Portland Chase, who lived in the state for a time.

Oil Capital of the World, the

A nickname of Tulsa, Oklahoma.

Oil Dorado

A nickname of the vicinity around Titusville in the northwestern part of Pennsylvania where oil was first discovered (1859) in the United States.

Oil State, the

A nickname of Pennsylvania.

Ol' Man River

A nickname for the Mississippi River, from the song written by Jerome Kern and Oscar Hammerstein II in 1927 for the musical *Showboat*.

Old Bailey

Officially, Old Bailey is a street in the City of London—a turning to the left going up Ludgate Hill to St. Paul's. But its name has been transferred to its most famous building, the Central Criminal Court—*the Bailey*, as it is known, affectionately to those who work there, perhaps not so affectionately to those who stand trial there. The street has always had associations with the administration of justice, because the grim Newgate Prison once stood there, and until 1868 it was the scene of public hangings. At the end of the 19th century the prison was demolished and on its site the courthouse was built, with its dome surmounted by the familiar figure of Justice. Here have been conducted most of the celebrated English murder trials of this century, including those of Dr. Crippen, George "Brides in the Bath" Smith, and John Christie.

(Old) Bay State

The official nickname of Massachusetts.

Old Colony State

A nickname of Massachusetts, so called in reference to the area of the state that was part of the original Plymouth Colony and older than the Massachusetts Bay Colony.

Old Dart, the

A dated Australian nickname for England. Its origin is unknown, but it may well be a scornful reference to the broad arrow, a symbol of British government property familiar to those who were transported to Australia as criminals.

Old Dirigo State, the

A nickname of Maine, so called after the state motto, *Dirigo* 'I guide.'

Old Dominion

The official nickname of Virginia, so called because the Colony's acceptance of Charles II of England as their king in 1660 so pleased him that he elevated them to the position of a dominion. In 1663 he quartered the Arms of Virginia on his royal shield, thus ranking them with his four other dominions: England, France, Ireland, and Scotland. The name was adopted in remembrance of Virginia's being the oldest and most faithful of the Stuart settlements in America.

Old Glory

A popular name for the (officially named) Flag of the United States, reputed to have first been used by William Driver, skipper of the brig *Charles Doggert* in 1837. See also **Stars and Bars, Stars and Stripes.**

Old Ironsides

The affectionate nickname for the famous frigate of the United States Navy, *Constitution*, now docked on the Charles River in Boston. She is still in commission and is the oldest warship afloat in any of the world's navies. Built at a Boston shipyard between 1794 and 1797, she is 204 feet long, could carry provisions for 475 crewmen, and has a hull of oak with masts of white pine. She was launched in 1797 but won her nickname during the War of 1812 in a battle against the English warship *Guerrière*, during which a seaman is said to have seen British shot bouncing off her sides and to have exclaimed she had sides of iron. She was ordered destroyed as unseaworthy in 1830 but Oliver Wendell Holmes's poem of the same name, which declaims, "Oh, better that her shattered hulk/Should sink beneath the waves," aroused the public and she was rebuilt and restored to service in 1833. After another rebuilding in 1877 she was finally drydocked in 1897 to be preserved as a memorial. In 1927, American schoolchildren raised money for her reconditioning for a tour of U. S. ports; and in 1931, with the help of additional funds appropriated by Congress, she was once again commissioned. After sailing 22,000 miles, she was at last returned to the Boston Naval Shipyard in 1934, where tourists visit her every year.

Old Kent Road, the

A road in the south London borough of Southwark which holds a key place in the working-class mythology of London. Celebrated particularly in the famous old song "Wot Cher," or "Knocked 'em in the Old Kent Road," it is the main thoroughfare of Bermondsey, Walworth, and Camberwell. In the past it was a noted haunt of Cockney costermongers, street traders who sold fruit and vegetables from barrows. The road is at the beginning of the traditional route from London (starting at the Borough) to Dover, and thence to the Continent. See also **Borough**.

Old Lady of Threadneedle Street, the

A nickname since the late 18th century for the **Bank of England** (*q.v.*), the main entrance of which is in Threadneedle Street in the City of London. It gets its name from the female sculpture above this entrance, although no doubt there is some passing reference, too, to the Bank's staid and respectable status amongst financial institutions. In the early 19th century the English radical William Cobbett denounced the directors of the Bank as "old ladies of Threadneedle Street" for their reactionary policies.

Old Line State, the

The official nickname of Maryland, so called both because in early colonial days the state was the dividing line between the Crown land grants of Lord Baltimore and those of William Penn and because it was the only state with regular troops "of the line."

Old North Church

The popular name for Christ Church, the oldest public building in downtown Boston. From this steeple were hung the lanterns warning of a British attack (the 15th of April, 1775) during the Revolutionary War. The tower contains the first set of church bells in the American colonies, cast in 1744. The spire has been rebuilt three times, most recently in 1955 to its original height of 190 feet.

Old North State

A nickname of North Carolina, acquired after the original colony was divided into North and South Carolina.

Old Quebec (Vieux-Québec)

The name of an area of Quebec, Canada, including Place Royale, the Old Port, and the Latin Quarter, noted for its historical landmarks.

Old Sarum

A site in Wiltshire, in southern England, which was occupied as long ago as the early Iron Age, and in Norman times boasted a castle and a cathedral. However, following a dispute between the military and the ecclesiastical authorities, the latter moved out and in 1220 began to build a new cathedral a few miles further south. The city which grew up around this is now known as Salisbury, and a few ruined walls are all that remain of Old Sarum. It is, however, remembered as being one of the notorious "rotten boroughs," parliamentary constituencies with only a handful of electors, that were swept away by the Reform Act of 1832, and for the so-called "Use of Sarum," the order of divine service used in England, Wales, and Ireland before the Reformation.

Old Town

A once-bustling and still surviving business and residential area on the Near North Side of Chicago, just east of Lincoln Park and Lake Michigan. Old Town, centered on a short stretch of North Wells Street, was a precursor of the nearby, diversely upscale "New Town" area. A boom area in the sixties, replete with quaint buildings, offbeat shops and lively bistros, Old Town in the 1980's is undergoing something of a revival after a spell of seediness. Its many culturally vital attractions include the **Second City** (*q.v.*) cabaret theater and The Old Town School of Folk Music.

Old Vic, the

Originally an affectionate nickname, but now the standard name by which London's Royal Victoria Theatre is known. Situated in the Waterloo area south of the Thames, it achieved its considerable reputation under the guiding hand of Lilian Baylis, who instituted a celebrated seris of Shakespeare there in the first part of the 20th century. It was the first home of the National Theatre Company when it got under way in 1963.

Old World, the

According to a Eurocentric world view, the Old World included those parts of the globe known to exist before the discovery of the Americas. By extension, it has come to mean the whole of the Eastern Hemisphere, and is used particularly in zoological and botanical contexts: Old World monkeys, for example, are different in certain crucial respects from those found in the Americas. Compare **New World**.

Oleander City

A nickname of Galveston, Texas.

Opéra, l'

The somberly imposing Paris Opera House was built in the 1860s, and the quarter surrounding it has since become known as *l'Opéra*. It is the center of the city, to the north of the Louvre, and was largely laid out by the renowned town-planner of Paris, Baron Georges Eugène Haussmann. Its wide boulevards are lined with impressive examples of 19th-century architectural *gravitas*, many of them housing smart and expensive stores.

Orange State, the
A nickname of Florida.

Oranges, the
The towns of Orange, East Orange, West Orange, and South Orange, suburban to Newark, New Jersey.

Orchard City
A nickname of Burlington, Iowa.

Oregon Trail
The longest of the overland routes used in the westward expansion of the U. S., it wound 2000 miles from Independence, Missouri, to Fort Vancouver and the Willamette Valley of Oregon, through prairies and deserts and, most important, across the Rocky Mountains through the South Pass. Explorers and fur traders first traced the Trail; Benjamin Bonneville is credited with taking the first wagon train through the South Pass in the 1830s. Sections of the deeply rutted road cut by wagon wheels can still be seen today.

Orient, the
A concept that has dimension in time as well as space, and perhaps exists more in the mind than on the ground. Certainly the Orient is now more—and less—than the East. Originally it referred to any lands east of the Mediterranean or of Southern Europe, that is to say, "the East" from a Roman point of view, including what we would now call the Near and Middle East. The famous luxury train, *the Orient-Express*, went no further east than Istanbul. In the present day, however, the geographical focus of the Orient has moved further east, to the Far East and Southeast Asia, perhaps shading westward to include India. But it is for its connotations and associations, rather than its exact denotative value, that the term is mainly used now. The term conjures up the mysterious lands on the far edge of the earth that Marco Polo visited, with their unsettlingly inscrutable inhabitants, their fabled wealth in jewels, silks, and spices, and their mystical religions and philosophies. The word *Orient* derives ultimately from the Latin verb *oriri* 'to rise,' with reference to the rising of the sun in the east. In the late 19th century, before usage fixed it firmly on the Far East, it was occasionally used in American English to refer to the whole of the Eastern Hemisphere, or even specifically to Europe. Compare **Far East, Levant, Middle East, Near East.**

Orient-Express

1. A luxurious train that plied between Paris and Giurgin on the Danube, about 45 miles from Bucharest. The service opened on October 4, 1883; at that time passengers bound for Constantinople had to suffer the discomfort of disembarking to take a ferry across the Danube, travel by train to Varna, Bulgaria, on the Black Sea, thence to Constantinople via ship. Subsequently, the Orient-Express underwent many changes of routing and accommodation, and there were the obvious lacunae in service during the 1914–18 and the 1939–45 wars. Its heyday, perhaps, came in the 1920s, when its magnificent cars could cover the Paris-Constantinople run in 56 hours. (Constantinople was not renamed Istanbul till 1930.) It gained a reputation as a conveyance for spies and other agents involved in eastern European intrigue during this period, though the owners wrily point out that the company would soon have gone out of business had they relied solely on such passengers. However, Kings' Messengers and Royal Couriers did travel by it, as well as businessmen, holiday-makers, theatrical touring companies, government officials, and others who could afford it or whose way was paid. In the early days of air travel, the Orient-Express traveled to Athens and Turkey in less time than airplanes, because they then had to make night stopovers. The romance of the train and the many associations evoked by references to the intrigues of its passengers are reflected in the half dozen motion pictures and nineteen books that are at least partially set aboard it, though it must be pointed out that Agatha Christie's book, *Murder on the Orient-Express*, originally bore the title *Murder in the Calais Coach* and was not changed till after several editions. There was even a foxtrot, "Orient-Express," published as sheet music in 1933. Officially the Venice Simplon Orient-Express, the train today enjoys a return to its earlier glory in the completely refurbished lavish cars that cover a complex of routes offering day trips within England and between a number of continental cities. It is possible today to take the train from Victoria Station, London, to Folkestone, transfer to the ferry to Boulogne, and resume the journey (albeit on different carriages) all the way to Venice, leaving before noon and arriving early the following evening. As in the past, the tourists are more likely to outnumber the secret agents—if one can distinguish them among the gentlemen in dinner jackets and ladies in silks and jewels.

2. A proposed supersonic (called "hypersonic") U. S. aircraft, capable of suborbital flight and of flying between Washington, D. C., and Tokyo, a distance of 6769 miles, in two hours.

Orly

The name of one of the airports serving Paris, the other being Charles de Gaulle.

Outer Banks

The name of a chain of barrier islands and beaches, almost 500 miles in length, between Bogue Inlet to the south and the North Carolina-Virginia border to the north. It includes Cape Hatteras and Roanoke Island, the site of the first English colony in the New World. The actual shoreline measures 6250 miles, almost twice that of California.

Outer Mongolia

Sometimes used jocularly to identify a place of great remoteness, Outer Mongolia was the former name of a republic officially named the Mongolian People's Republic. See also **Inner Mongolia.**

Outlaw Country

The brush country in the hills along the Big Sioux River in northwest Iowa and the hills along the Big Sioux River in eastern South Dakota. If the law was after a man on the Iowa side, he would cross the river, over the rapids, into South Dakota; and if the law was after a man on the South Dakota side, he would cross the river into Iowa.

Oval, the

A cricket ground in Lambeth, London, headquarters of the Surrey Cricket Club. See also **Lord's.**

Oval Office

An oval room in the wing of the White House where the President of the United States has his office, often used metonymically for the office of the presidency. See also **1600 Pennsylvania Avenue.**

Over South

An old nickname for the Bay View section of San Francisco.

Oxbridge

A portmanteau word coined for the convenience of referring simultaneously to England's two most ancient and prestigious institutions of higher education, Oxford University and Cambridge University. It can be a neutral term: "Amanda's hoping to get into Oxbridge" (i.e., one or the other); but it can also be somewhat censorious, evoking the privileged status these universities enjoy in Britain, which some feel is not always commensurate with their academic excellence.

Oxford Street

A street in the West End of London, that runs between St. Giles Circus to the east and Marble Arch to the west. It is London's chief shopping street—not as expensive as Bond Street and the rest of Mayfair on its southwestern flanks, but more like an ordinary town's main street, with an accent on clothing stores. Probably its flagship is Selfridges, a huge department store famous around the world; but there are many other large emporiums there, including big branches of Marks and Spencer, C & A, and John Lewis.

Oxon

An abbreviated name for the English county of Oxfordshire, from its Latin name *Oxonia. Oxon.*, from Latin *Oxoniensis* 'of or from Oxford,' is also used for the town and university of Oxford; a graduate would be designated "B.A. *or* B.Sc. Oxon.," for example, and the Bishop of Oxford signs himself "Oxon." The Cambridge equivalent is *Cantab.*, for *Cantabrigiensis*, is used for such designations but not as an abbreviated name for the county of Cambridgeshire.

Oyster State, the

A nickname of Maryland.

Oz

A humorous nickname used by Australians for Australia. It is basically an affectionate term and redolent of the open, unstuffy nature of Australian society. It is short for *Aussie*, which is itself sometimes used for *Australia*, although it more usually means 'an Australian.' Its reference is to the magical place in L. Frank Baum's books, notably, *The Wizard of Oz*. See also **TOTO**.

Ozark (Mountain) State

A nickname of Missouri.

Pacific Northwest, the

In the United States, an area encompassing those western states that border on the Pacific Ocean, namely, Washington and Oregon. In some people's minds, the northernmost parts of California would be included but not Alaska, which is too remote. Compare **Northwest, West.**

Pacific Wonderland, the

A nickname of Oregon.

Paddington

An area in west London, to the north of Hyde Park and the east of Bayswater. It contains some elegant streets, but much less so as it comes within the orbit of Paddington Station, the main London terminus for rail services to the West and Wales. In the very southeast corner of the area is Paddington Green, the original village green of Paddington, remembered particularly in the old ballad about "pretty little Polly Perkins of Paddington Green." A more modern association is with the fictional Paddington

Bear, who was discovered at the station having been sent as a parcel from Peru.

Paddo

An Australian nickname for Paddington, an inner suburb of Sydney, Australia. A hilly area of Victorian terraced houses, it is one of Sydney's trendiest residential districts.

Palace, the

British journalistic shorthand for Buckingham Palace, frequently used as a synonym for the sovereign or the royal household (as in "A Palace spokesman today denied that . . .). See also **Buck House.**

Palatinate, the

Either of two regions in Germany that in medieval times were ruled by the Count Palatine, a nobleman of the Holy Roman Empire who exercised virtually imperial power within his own domain. Both were subsequently absorbed into Bavaria, but in 1946 the Lower Palatinate became part of the new state of Rhineland-Palatinate (in German, *Rheinland-Pfalz*) in southwest Germany. The Upper Palatinate is on the Czech border.

Palatine, the

One of the Seven Hills of ancient Rome. According to legend it was the site of the first human settlement in Rome; Romulus reputedly plowed his first furrow at its foot, marking the foundation of the city. In historical times, the Roman emperors had their palace there, and indeed from the hill's original Latin name, *Palatium*, we get the English word *palace*.

Palestine

A region in the Middle East with a fluctuating history that stretches back to Biblical times. It occupies the territory between the Dead Sea and the shores of the Mediterranean and first appeared as a separate entity under the name *Canaan*. It underwent innumerable changes of rule in pre-Christian times, and its role as the scene of most of the events in the Bible led to its being known in later centuries as the Holy Land. It was ruled by Rome from 63 B.C. onward, passed in due course into the Byzantine Empire, and from 638 to 1918 was under Muslim rule; from 1920 it was controlled by Britain as a mandated territory. It finally became an independent Jewish state in 1948, changing its name in the process from Palestine to Israel. Its former name is however kept vigorously alive by the Arabic inhabitants of the area; part of it was actually retaken into Arab hands in 1949—land west of the River Jordan that was captured back by Israel in 1967—and the establishment of an independent Arab state there is the ongoing aim of the Palestine Liberation Organization.

Palisades, the

The name of the basaltic precipices along the west bank of the Hudson River, extending from Jersey City, New Jersey, to near Piermont, New York.

Pall Mall

A street in the West End of London, between Trafalgar Square and St. James's Palace. It is one of the main thoroughfares of London's **Clubland** (*q.v.*), and contains the premises of several distinguished gentlemen's clubs, including the Athenaeum, the Reform, the Army and Navy, and the Travellers'. Its curious name comes from *paille-maille*, a game similar to croquet, which was played on a course constructed there in the late 17th century.

Palmetto City

A nickname of Charleston, South Carolina.

Palmetto State, the

The official nickname of South Carolina.

Palm Springs

A desert resort city in Riverside County, California. Earlier names were Palmetto Spring, Big Palm Spring, and Agua Caliente; but the name Palm Springs was applied to the post office created in 1890. The community has attracted a wealthy clientele since the 1930s because of its desert climate and its proximity to the Los Angeles metropolitan area to the west. Palm Springs attracts sunseekers in winter, but it also has a fair-sized resident population (1980 population 32,171). It is a mecca for golfers and tennis players. A place of great wealth (but not of flamboyance), it is known worldwide for the affluence of its residents and visitors, particularly celebrities connected with the entertainment industry, and, latterly, retired politicians.

Pamplona

A city in the northeastern Spanish region of Navarre, famous for its annual festival, *Fiesta de San Fermín*, during which bulls are stampeded through the narrow streets and the young men of the city try to outrun them. The picturesque, bacchanalian fiesta figures prominently in Ernest Hemingway's novel, *The Sun Also Rises*.

Pangaea

A name given to the earth's supposed primordial supercontinent that split up over 200 million years ago into Gondwanaland and Laurasia. See **Gondwanaland, Laurasia**.

Panhandle, the

Any area of one of the United States that is somewhat longer and narrower than the rest of the state and is shaped like the handle of a pan, as the western extensions of Florida, Texas, and Oklahoma.

Panhandle State, the

A nickname of West Virginia.

Pantiles, the

A street in the spa town of Tunbridge Wells, Kent, in southeast England. Its elegant Regency arcades were built as a promenade for those who came to take the waters in the 18th and 19th centuries; they now house shops. Its name comes from the flat tiles with which it was originally paved (although a pantile is strictly speaking a curved roofing tile).

Papal States, the

A collective name for the area of central Italy that for a long time was under direct papal rule. It was given to the popes by King Pepin III of the Franks in 754, and remained in their control for more than 1100 years. Most of it was absorbed into the newly united kingdom of Italy in the mid 19th century, although the papacy clung on to Rome itself until 1870 and did not recognize the new state of affairs officially until 1929. The Papal States were also known as the *States of the Church*.

Paper City

A nickname of Holyoke, Massachusetts.

Paper Mill Playhouse

A theater in Millburn, New Jersey, owned and operated for many years by Frank Carrington, who was also the director. Popular among New Yorkers as well as the residents of northern New Jersey, the Paper Mill Playhouse was famous for staging the musicals of Sigmund Romberg, Jerome Kern, Rudolf Friml, Noël Coward, and others—productions like *The Chocolate Soldier, Showboat, The Desert Song, Bittersweet*—many of which were made into movies after successful Broadway runs. The Paper Mill burned down, was rebuilt, then burned down again; last rebuilt in 1982, it is now housed in a modern, fireproof structure where the audience lounges in seats that would have impressed earlier patrons as the height of luxury.

Paradise of New England

A nickname of Salem, Massachusetts.

Paradise of the Pacific, the

A nickname of Hawaii.

Paris of America, the

A nickname of Cincinnati, Ohio and of New Orleans, Louisiana.

Park Avenue

A major north-south street on the East Side, in New York City. It begins officially at 34th Street at the south and runs up into east Harlem at the north. Although it extends southward below 34th Street to 8th Street, that interval is named Park Avenue South, a relatively recent change from Fourth Avenue, its name before some time in the late 1940s. Until the 1950s, for most of its length as far as 96th Street, Park Avenue was characterized by its expensive, luxurious apartment houses and hotels. A broad, double roadway divided by a mall (inaccessible except for viewing at a distance), which is maintained with seasonal floral displays by the Park Avenue Association, it has retained much of its former character except for the area between 40th and 57th streets, which has succumbed for the most part to the encroachments of high-rise office buildings. Yet, even in that interval, the Waldorf-Astoria Hotel, the New York Racquet Club, and a few other buildings have resisted the commercial invasion. For many years associated with great wealth, Park Avenue has remained a place as well as a symbol of luxurious residences. The trains serving Grand Central Terminal, which blocks the entire roadway between 42nd and 43rd streets, run beneath Park Avenue to emerge north of 96th Street onto elevated tracks. Here the neighborhood changes, gradually, at first, because of high-rise (low-rent) housing bordering the roadway, then drastically, as the slums of Harlem are approached and the elevated tracks cross over the Harlem River (at about 135th Street) to go on through the Mott Haven train yard, in The Bronx.

Parkdale

The name of a district in Toronto, Canada, that evokes images of its once tough reputation, despite the increase, in recent years, of middle-class residents.

Parker House, the

A long-established, first-class hotel in Boston, famous mainly for the Parker House roll, a circular roll baked from a round piece of white bread dough folded almost in half.

Park Lane

A road in the West End of London, leading from Marble Arch in the north to Hyde Park Corner in the south. It forms the western boundary of Mayfair and has always been the haunt of the extremely wealthy. In former times it was lined with aristocratic mansions, which commanded a fine view over Hyde Park. The stately homes have since been replaced by stately hotels, such as the Dorchester, the Hilton, and the Grosvenor

House, and the once unspoilt view is now marred by a very busy multi-lane roadway.

Patagonia

In broadest terms, the southernmost part of the South American continent, extending below about 40° and containing the southern parts of Chile and Argentina. In more specific use, the name is applied to the most southerly region of Argentina, to the south of the Colorado River, a rugged desolate plateau that sweeps from the lower slopes of the Andes eastward to the Atlantic.

Paternoster Row

A street in the City of London, just to the north of St. Paul's Cathedral. It gets its name from the makers of paternosters, or rosaries, who in pre-Reformation times traded there. Subsequently, in the 18th and 19th centuries, it became a major center of the publishing business in London, along with the nearby Little Britain and St. Paul's Churchyard. However, much of it was destroyed by incendiary bombs in 1940, and the publishing firms had to move on.

Path of Gold

A nickname of Market Street in San Francisco, so called because it is one of the greatest commercial thoroughfares in the city and is elaborately lit at night.

Peacehaven

A village on the Sussex coast of England, to the east of Brighton. An invented name for an invented place, it was built just after World War I as a piece of speculative development by a local businessman, and has since become synonymous with the sort of bland development, with uniform rows of uninspired bungalows, which covered much of the south coast of England during the interwar years. During World War I, Australian and New Zealand troops were stationed nearby, and hence the area was for a time nicknamed *Anzac-on-Sea*.

peacemaker, the

1. A nickname used during the frontier days of Texas and other western states for a gun, especially the Colt .45 revolver, the use of which settled all difficulties.

2. A nickname bestowed in 1984 by President Ronald Reagan on the M-X missile.

Peach State, the

A nickname of Georgia.

Peak District, the

A hilly area of outstanding scenic beauty in Derbyshire and Staffordshire at the southern tip of the Pennines, the mountain chain that bisects northern England. The whole district now forms a national park, 540 square miles in extent. The northern part, known as the High Peak, or Dark Peak, from the dark millstone grit rock of which it is formed, is an area of stark windblown moorland. Southward it merges into the Low Peak or White Peak, a limestone landscape riddled with caverns and potholes. Until comparatively recently the whole area was known simply as the Peak.

Pearl Harbor

A large U. S. naval base on the island of Oahu, Hawaii. It is notable mainly as the target of the Japanese surprise air attack of December 7, 1941, which drew the United States into World War II. Thousands of naval and military personnel were killed in the attack, both on the naval base and at the nearby Army Air Force base, Hickham Field. The projecting parts of the *USS Arizona*, one of the battleships sunk, now serve as a memorial to those who died aboard her and to the others who perished.

Pearl of the Orient

A nickname of Manila, the Philippines.

Pelican State, the

The official nickname of Louisiana.

Peloponnese, the

The southern part of Greece, a rocky peninsula adjoined onto the northern mainland by the narrow Isthmus of Corinth. In ancient times it contained the cities of Sparta and Corinth.

Peninsula, the

In general terms, a peninsula is a piece of land almost but not completely surrounded by water, but until the late 19th century the word was also used more specifically to refer to the Iberian Peninsula, which contains Spain and Portugal. Today the usage survives only in the *Peninsular War*, the name given to the war fought there from 1808 to 1814 by Spain and Portugal, aided by the British under Wellington, against Napoleon's France.

Peninsula State, the

A nickname of Florida and Michigan.

Pennsylvania of the West, the

A nickname of Missouri.

Pentagon, the

A huge (3.7-million-square-foot) office building, a hollow pentagon in plan, in Alexandria, Virginia, across the Potomac River from Washington, D. C. It serves as the headquarters for the Departments of Defense, Army, Navy, Air Force, and Coast Guard, and its name is used metaphorically to refer to the United States military establishment.

Pentonville

A down-at-heels area of north London, just to the east of King's Cross. It is bounded on the south by Pentonville Road. Its most famous association is with Pentonville Prison, which is in fact over half a mile to the north of the area, in the Caledonian Road. The prison's name is often familiarly abbreviated to "the Ville."

Père Lachaise

A celebrated cemetery in Paris. It was opened in 1804, and its incumbents include Honoré de Balzac, Frédéric Chopin, Gioacchino Rossini, Colette, Edith Piaf, and Oscar Wilde. The site was formerly occupied by a Jesuit religious foundation, which was enlarged by Père Lachaise, confessor of Louis XIV.

Persia

A name associated with southwestern Asia since the 6th century B.C., when the great Persian Empire was founded by Cyrus the Great. It lasted two centuries before it was overthrown by Alexander the Great. In modern times its inhabitants have always known their country as Iran, and this was made official in 1935, but in 1949 the government sanctioned the use of *Persia* as an alternative. Nevertheless, in modern usage *Persia* has a rather dated air, and *Iran* is now the standard term.

petro-dollars

The nickname coined in 1974 for Arab profits from the increased prices demanded by OPEC.

Petticoat Lane

A famous London street market selling clothes and various sorts of household goods. The road it takes place in has since the 1830s been officially called Middlesex Street (just to the east of Liverpool Street Station in the City); but it is still popularly known as Petticoat Lane. In former times, Huguenot silk weavers settled there, and its associations with the clothing trade have continued ever since; from the 17th century onward it was London's chief second-hand clothing market. In the 20th century its range of merchandise has widened, and it has become a popular tourist attraction offering broad slices of Cockney life. It is open on Sunday mornings only.

Phoenix City

A nickname of Chicago, bestowed by Henry Ward Beecher after the recovery from the fire (1871).

Piccadilly Circus

A traffic circle in London, where Piccadilly Street, Upper and Lower Regent streets, and Shaftesbury Avenue meet, similar in tawdriness and character to Times Square in New York City. At its center is an aluminum statue called "Eros," though it is actually of "Christian Charity," erected to honor the Earl of Shaftesbury who was originally responsible for much of the property development of the area.

Picnic City

A nickname of Mobile, Alabama.

Pigalle

An area of Montmartre, northern central Paris, centered on the Place Pigalle. It has a risqué reputation for its titillating cabarets and as a place of assignation with ladies of the night, and, in the 1980s, is known for the sex-shops and strip-joints that line its streets.

Pillars of Hercules, the

A name given in ancient times to two rocks that guard the Straits of Gibraltar, at the entrance to the Mediterranean. They were then called Calpe and Abyla and are now known as Gibraltar (Spain) and Jebel Musa (Morocco). According to legend they were once joined together, but Hercules tore them asunder in order to pass through. They represented to the ancients the western boundary of the known world.

Pilsen

A vital Near Southwest Side neighborhood of Chicago, first U. S. home to successive waves of immigrants—Germans, Irish, Czechoslovakians, Poles, and Latinos. Named in commemoration of one of the principal cities of their homeland by the Bohemian immigrants who played a major role in settling the neighborhood, Pilsen still contains many characteristically sturdy brick cottages dating from the 1860s.

Piltdown man

Named for the village of Piltdown, in southeast England, a collection of fossil bone fragments presented, in 1912, as the authentic remains of a prehistoric hominid. Although the find was somewhat suspect, it was not conclusively proved a hoax till the 1950s, when radiocarbon dating and other evidence showed it to be utterly without merit and, in fact, a deliberate fraud.

Pimlico

An area in central London, on the north bank of the Thames to the south of Victoria. It is quite a fashionble first step on the residential ladder for those whose means cannot yet afford Belgravia. It probably gets its name from a tavern run there many centuries ago by a certain Ben Pimlico. In the mid 19th century it was still mainly open fields, but these gradually became filled in with a maze of streets, and public consciousness of it as an area with a separate identity was probably sealed by the 1948 film *Passport to Pimlico*, a fiction in which the local residents set up their own state, declaring unilateral independence from the United Kingdom.

Pine Tree State, the

The official nickname of Maine.

Piovro

A nickname in Italy for organized crime; *piovro* means 'octopus' in Italian.

Pittsburgh of the South, the

A nickname of Birmingham, Alabama.

Pittsburgh of the West

A nickname of Pueblo, Colorado.

Pitt Street

A major thoroughfare in Sydney, Australia. It is the city's financial center, but in former times was famous for its brothels. A "Pitt Street farmer" is an Australian slang expression for an absentee farm landlord.

Place Royale

A part of Old Quebec known as the "cradle of French civilization in North America," so named because of the statue of Louis XIV erected there.

Plantation State, the

A shortening of the official name of Rhode Island, **Rhode Island and Providence Plantations.**

Playboy Building

An office building, formerly the Palmolive Building, near the John Hancock center in Chicago at the northern end of the Magnificent Mile, on the city's Near North Side. The two-billion-candlepower Lindbergh Beacon atop the building, though unused today, once served as a powerful navigational aid to vessels on Lake Michigan. The building now houses the *Playboy* magazine editorial offices, as well as other businesses and professional offices.

Playground of the Nation, the

A nickname of Minnesota.

Plaza, the

A small, open square bounded by Fifth Avenue on the east, Central Park South (59th Street) on the north, 58th Street on the south, and a service road on the west. It is dominated by the Plaza Hotel, on the west side, and by Bergdorf Goodman, a department store, on the south, which combine to give the area a swanky, dignified air. There is a small fountain at its center which feeds into a circular pond.

Plumb Line Port to Panama

A nickname of Charleston, South Carolina.

Plymouth of the West, the

A nickname of San Diego, California, so called because it was one of the first settlements on the West Coast, founded in 1769 by Father Junípero Serra.

poison pill

A nickname for any measure taken by a company to avoid an unwelcome takeover by another company.

Polar Star State, the

A nickname of Maine.

Polish Corridor, the

A name given to the territory granted to Poland under the terms of the Treaty of Versailles in 1919, in order to give it access to the Baltic Sea just to the west of Gdańsk. It more or less followed the line of the Vistula River and in so doing cut a great swath through what had been German territory, isolating East Prussia from the rest of Germany. This arrangement was naturally not popular with the Germans, and the Polish Corridor was one of Hitler's prime territorial targets. It came firmly back under Polish control after World War II, while East Prussia was divided between Poland and the Soviet Union.

Polynesia

A collective term for the islands that comprise the eastern section of Oceania, in the South Pacific Ocean. Its main constituents are Samoa, Tahiti, Tuvalu (formerly the Ellice Islands), the Marquesas, the Cook Islands, Pitcairn Island, and Easter Island. Hawaii is very often included too. When the name, which means 'many islands,' was coined in the 18th century, it had a very general application to the islands of the South Pacific, including those we now know as Melanesia and Micronesia, and today it is still often used in this looser meaning. Many ethnologists, moreover, would regard New Zealand as part of Polynesia, since its Maori inhabitants are descended from successive waves of Polynesian immigrants. See also **Melanesia, Micronesia, Oceania**.

Pompey

A nickname for Portsmouth, a city on the south coast of England. It is Britain's main naval dockyard, and the name is chiefly used in naval contexts; but it has also come to be applied to the city's soccer team. The first record of its use comes from the late 19th century, but its origin is obscure; certainly it has no discernible connection with the Roman general of the same name. Natives of the city are sometimes referred to as *Pomponians*.

Pool, the

1. A local nickname for Liverpool, a large city and port in northwest England.
2. See **Pool of London**.

Pool of London, the

Or, more simply, the Pool, a name given since at least the 17th century to the two-mile stretch of the Thames between London Bridge and Cuckold's Point, beyond which the river bends abruptly south to enter Limehouse reach. The upstream section is known as the Upper Pool, the downstream as the Lower Pool. It is the farthest upriver that large ships can find sufficient depth, and in the days when central London was a major port, myriad vessels would be berthed alongside the wharves and in the docks on both sides of the river, amid forests of cranes. Working-class areas extend beyond the waterfront warehouses: Wapping and Shadwell to the north, Bermondsey and Rotherhithe to the south. In the 1980s, with the docks no longer active, the Pool has lost the air of bustling activity it had when so much of Britain's imports and exports flowed through it.

Poor Man's Paradise, the

A nickname of San Francisco, so called in reference to its year-round moderate climate and to the abundance of cheap fruits and vegetables.

Porkopolis

A nickname of Chicago, and an earlier nickname claimed by both Cincinnati and Cleveland, Ohio.

Porkopolis of Iowa

A nickname of Burlington.

Porte, the

See **Sublime Porte**.

Portland Place

A wide street in the West End of London, just to the south of Regent's Park. At its southern end is Broadcasting House, headquarters of the British Broadcasting Corporation (BBC). *Portland Place* itself is sometimes used as a synonym for the BBC, particularly those parts of it connected with administration and higher management.

Portobello Road

A street in the Notting Hill area of west London which houses a famous flea market. The days have perhaps gone when genuine bargain antiques could be spotted there among the bric-à-brac, but the market remains a lively place to visit. It is there only on Saturdays; during the rest of the week a general market takes over, with a West Indian flavor appropriate to the immigrant community in the area.

Port o' Missing Men, the

A nickname of San Francisco, so called because a man could easily hide amid the cosmopolitan citizenry or escape aboard one of the many ships in the port.

Port of the Southwest, the

A nickname of Galveston, Texas.

Porton Down

A name which makes British people feel uneasy, for it belongs to the place where research into chemical and bacteriological warfare is carried out in Britain. Situated in Wiltshire, in southern England, it is officially called the Chemical Defense Establishment (CED), and is run by the Ministry of Defence, although much peaceful and medically important work is done on the same site by the Centre for Applied Bacteriology and Research.

Potteries, the

An area around and including Stoke-on-Trent, in Staffordshire, in the northwest Midlands of England, which is the major center of the china and earthenware industry. Clay has been worked and fired for centuries in the *potbanks* (the local word for *pottery*), although the name *Potteries* is not recorded until 1825. See also **Five Towns**.

Power City

A nickname claimed by Rochester, New York, and Keokuk, Iowa.

Prado, the

A large art museum in Madrid, Spain, built between 1787 and 1819. It is known particularly for its fine collection of Spanish masters such as Goya, Velásquez, El Greco, Murillo, Zurbarán, and others. It takes its name from the meadow, or *prado*, that once surrounded it.

Prairie City

A nickname of Bloomington, Illinois.

prairie oyster

A nickname for the testis of a calf, used as food.

Prairie Provinces, the

A name for Alberta, Saskatchewan, and Manitoba, which together comprise about one-fifth of Canada's land area.

prairie schooner

The nickname for a huge canvas-covered wagon, requiring ten mules to pull it, that was used during the second half of the 19th century to carry supplies, merchandise, and food across the western plains to the frontier settlers.

Prairie State, the

The official nickname of Illinois.

Principality, the

A principality is a state ruled by a price or a territory from which a prince takes his title—Monaco, for example. In Britain, however, *the Principality* is always Wales. The Welsh rulers of Wales had been known as princes since the eleventh century; but it was in the 14th century, after Wales had been conquered by England, that Edward III conferred the title of Prince of Wales on his young son Edward, the Black Prince, and the eldest sons of British monarchs have held that title ever since.

Printing House Square

A former square in Blackfriars in the City of London, now disappeared but long famous as the site of the headquarters of *The Times* newspaper. The name is very much still associated with the paper, and when it moved its premises to Grays Inn Road in 1974, its new offices were named New Printing House Square. However, it does not seem to have followed *The Times* in its further move to a site in London's Dockland; there, such was the stringency of the security measures adopted to counter feared incursions by disaffected members of the printers' union that the paper's headquarters were nicknamed "Fortress Wapping."

Promised Land, the

A name used in the Bible for Canaan, an area in the Middle East that corresponds roughly to later Palestine. It refers to the promise given by God to Abraham (Genesis 12:7) that he and his descendents would own the land in perpetuity. It has not worked out quite as straightforwardly as that, and in modern usage the term refers, generally, to any future condition in which one's hopes and aspirations will finally be fulfilled.

Provence

An area of southeastern France, formerly a province in its own right but now a part of the administrative region of Côte d'Azur. It is very much an area with its own separate cultural identity; it has its own language (Provençal) and literary tradition and belongs to the Mediterranean world. In ancient times it came under Roman rule considerably earlier than other parts of France, and was known simply as *(nostra) Provincia* 'our *(or* the) Province'; hence the name Provence.

Province, the

A name sometimes applied to Northern Ireland. It refers back to the territory's origins as part of the ancient Irish province of Ulster, which was partitioned when the Republic of Ireland became independent in 1921. (The other provinces of Ireland are Connacht, Leinster, and Munster.) The use of the designation *province* as an actual name is by no means unprecedented: it gave rise to modern Provence.

Prussia

A former state in northern and central Germany; its German name is *Preussen*. In the 19th century it was the leading and most belligerent power among the German states, with a reputation for truculent militarism fostered by its landowning aristocracy, the Junkers. After World War II, it was divided up between East and West Germany, Poland, and the Soviet Union.

puffing billies

A nickname for the steam engines used on the first railroads in the early 19th century, named for the original Puffing Billy built by William Hedley of Newcastle-upon-Tyne, in 1813.

Puke State, the

A nickname of Missouri, possibly from a corruption of *Pikes*, a word used in California to refer to white migratory workers believed to have come from Pike County, Missouri; or because so many Missourians showed up at the Galena, Illinois, lead mines in 1827 that those already there stated "the state of Missouri has taken a 'puke.'

Pullman

A recently refurbished Far Southeast Side area in Chicago that started life as a "company town" in 1881, known also as Pullman Community or Pullman Village. Sleeping-car inventor and manufacturer George Pullman's belief that the town should turn a 6 percent profit led to the Pullman strike of 1894, after worker-residents suffered cuts in wages but not in rents. The strike ended only after President Grover Cleveland ordered in federal troops. Surviving Pullman landmarks include the ornate, Victorian-style Florence Hotel, Greenstone Church, and the administrative clock tower.

Puritan City
> A nickname of Boston, Massachusetts.

Puritan State, the
> A nickname of Massachusetts.

Quai d'Orsay, the
> A street along the Left Bank of the River Seine in Paris, between the Pont de l'Alma and the Pont de la Concorde. It houses the French Foreign Ministry, and also the National Assembly, and consequently is often used as a name for the Foreign Office.

Quaker City
> A nickname of Philadelphia, Pennsylvania. See also **Quaker City of the West, Quaker State.**

Quaker City of the West
> A nickname of Richmond, Indiana.

Quaker State, the
> A nickname of Pennsylvania, so called in reference to William Penn, a Quaker who originally owned the land and encouraged Quaker settlers.

Quality City
> A nickname of Rochester, New York.

Queen City, the
> A nickname of Toronto.

Queen City of Alabama
> A nickname of Gadsden.

Queen City of Lake Superior
> A nickname of Marquette, Michigan.

Queen City of the Border
> A nickname of Caldwell, Kansas, so called because of its location near the border between Kansas and Oklahoma.

Queen City of the East, the
> A nickname of Bangor, Maine.

Queen City of the Iron Range, the
> A nickname of Virginia, Minnesota.

Queen City of the Lakes
A nickname of Buffalo, New York.

Queen City of the Mountains
A nickname of Knoxville, Tennessee.

Queen City of the Ozarks, the
A nickname of Springfield, Missouri.

Queen City of the Plains, the
A nickname of Denver, Colorado.

Queen City of the South
A nickname of Richmond, Virginia.

Queen City of the West
A nickname of Cincinnati, Ohio.

Queen City of Vermont
A nickname of Burlington.

Queen of Summer Resorts
A nickname of Newport, Rhode Island.

Queen of the Antilles
A former nickname for Cuba.

Queen of the Brazos (River)
A nickname of Waco, Texas.

Queen of the Cow Counties
A former nickname of Los Angeles.

Queen of the Eastern Archipelago
A former nickname for Java.

Queen of the Lakes, the
A former nickname of Chicago.

Queen of the Missions, the
A nickname of Santa Barbara, California.

Queen of the Mississippi Valley
A nickname for St. Louis, Missouri.

Queen of the North

A nickname for Edinburgh.

Queen of the Pacific, the

A nickname of San Francisco.

Queen of the Sea

A former nickname for Tyre.

Queen of the South

A nickname of New Orleans, Louisiana.

Queen on the James (River), the

A nickname of Richmond, Virginia.

Queens

A borough of New York City on Long Island, north of Brooklyn. It has some industrial activity, especially at its western end (Long Island City), but is for the most part residential, being divided, more or less, into neighborhoods named Astoria, Jackson Heights, Forest Hills, Rego Park, Whitestone, Flushing, etc., each with its own character. The residents all agree, though, that they live in Queens, not on "the Island." Its two main east-west thoroughfares are Queens Boulevard and Northern Boulevard. Essentially a bedroom community, many of its residents work in Manhattan. La Guardia Airport is situated in its northwest.

Queen State, the

A nickname of Maryland, so called in honor of Henrietta Maria, Queen of Charles I of England.

Queen Street West

The name for a bohemian area of Toronto, associated with avant-garde artists and their work.

Quirinal, the

One of the Seven Hills of ancient Rome, now known as Monte Cavallo. On it is a palace, *il Quirinale*, formerly occupied by the kings of Italy, and in the early 20th century "the Quirinal" was used as a metaphor for the Italian monarchy and government, especially as contrasted with the Papal authority of the Vatican.

R & A, the

A familiar abbreviation for the Royal and Ancient Golf Club, the governing body of golf in Britain, which is based in St. Andrews, Scotland. It was founded in 1764 as the Society of St. Andrews Golfers, and the royal prefix was added in 1834, with the approval of William IV.

RADA

A familiar name (pronounced RAHda) for the Royal Academy of Dramatic Art, London's most famous drama school which has produced many of the country's most famous actors and actresses since its foundation, in 1904, by Beerbohm Tree.

Radio City Music Hall

A world-famous motion-picture theater at Rockefeller Center, in New York City, known for its family-style entertainment and its spectacular stage shows. Opened in 1932, the theater featured a troupe of thirty-two precision dancers called The Roxyettes: their name was changed to The Rockettes in 1934. Originally a sixteen-member troupe from St. Louis, called the Missouri Rockets, their name was changed to The Rockets, then, when they appeared at the Roxy Theatre in New York City, to the Roxyettes. Renowned for their high kicks, the dancers have performed the "Parade of the Wooden Soldiers" routine at the annual Christmas show since 1934.

Railroad City

A nickname of Indianapolis, Indiana.

Railroad Queen of the State, the

A former nickname of Chicago.

raj, the

The name given to the British rule of India, derived from Hindi *rāj*, which comes from Sanskrit *rājya*, from *rājati* 'he rules.'

Rand, the

A nickname for Witwatersrand, the goldmining center of South Africa. Situated in the Transvaal, in the northeast of the country, its great metropolis is Johannesburg, which sits on top of the richest gold deposits in the world. Although applied to the area in general, in strict terms the Rand refers to the range of rocky hills that dominates the landscape; it is also known as *the Reef*. The full name is best known in association with the local university, founded in 1921.

Rann of Kutch, the

A great salt flat, about 9000 square miles in extent, in the Indian subcontinent, on the border of India and Pakistan, which alters seasonally from marsh to desert and back. Possession of the area was long a matter of contention between the two countries, but in 1968 international arbitration awarded about ten per cent of it to Pakistan.

Rapes

In former times, English counties were subdivided for administrative purposes into what were usually called *hundreds* (see **Chiltern Hundreds**), or in some counties *wapentakes*. A few had an additional, higher tier of local government: in Kent, for example, a group of hundreds was called a *lathe*, while in Sussex they were *rapes*, six in all (the Rape of Hastings, the Rape of Arundel, etc.) The word is not connected with *rape* 'ravage.'

Rebel Capital

A nickname of Philadelphia, used by the British when it became the capital of the thirteen colonies in 1776.

redbrick

A nickname, coined by professor Edgar Allison Peers in 1943, for universities other than Oxford and Cambridge, and especially those built after World War II, which used brick, and later concrete, glass, and steel, rather than the stone of the older universities.

Red China

A nickname for the People's Republic of China, coined with reference to its Communist government. A term commonly encountered in the 1950s and '60s, it subsequently went out of use as relations between the West and China improved and as China seemed to abandon Communism as its official ideology.

Red Planet, the

A name given to the planet Mars, which shines redly in the reflected light of the sun. The redness of its surface is caused by dust and oxidation of rocks.

Red Spot, the

The name given to a vast elliptical mark on the surface of the planet Jupiter, which over the centuries has appeared in various shades of red. It is now thought to be a gigantic swirling hurricane, which could swallow up the Earth a dozen times over, but the reason for its color remains obscure.

Red Square

A great open area in the center of Moscow which serves as the venue for Soviet state ceremonies. It is through Red Square that the tanks and missiles rumble in the May Day and October Revolution parades. Situated below the eastern walls of the Kremlin, it also contains the Lenin Mausoleum (from atop which high officials observe the parades), the state department store, GUM, and the celebrated Cathedral of St. Basil (built 1554–60), an architectural phantasmagoria surmounted by ten onion domes of different colors.

Reeperbahn, the

The main thoroughfare of the red-light district of Hamburg, a city in northern West Germany. It has achieved worldwide renown for the lavishness and explicitness of the sexual goods on display there.

Reform Club, the

A gentlemen's club in Pall Mall, in the West End of London, founded in 1836. It takes its name from the great Reform Act passed in 1832, which radically extended voting rights in England, and its membership from the Liberal Party. Among its claims to fame are Lamb Cutlets Reform, a recipe of the legendary Alexis Soyer, who was chef to the club for a time in the 19th century, and the fact that Phileas Fogg, in Jules Verne's novel *Around the World in Eighty Days* (1873), began and ended his epic journey at the club.

Ren Cen

A nickname for the Renaissance Center, a large area of downtown Detroit that was renovated in the 1970s. It includes hotels, a sports arena, office buildings, and a convention center.

Rhineland, the

The name given to the territory along the banks of the Rhine River as it flows through Germany, from the Dutch border southward through the industrial areas around Düsseldorf, past the cities of Cologne and Bonn, and on into the quintessential Rhineland of beetling wooded crags with fairytale castles on their summits and steep vineyards where some of the world's great white wines are produced.

Rhine of America, the

A nickname of the Hudson River, in New York, a reference to the high, rocky hills and beautiful scenery along its length.

Rialto

A market area in Venice that has become generic for such exchanges and shopping marts in other cities around the world. The familiar expression, "What's new on the Rialto," which New Yorkers use in inquiring about happenings on Broadway, echoes the words of Shylock in *The Merchant of Venice.*

Rice State, the

A nickname of South Carolina.

Richest Hill on Earth, the

A nickname of Butte Hill, Butte, Montana.

Richest Village on Earth, the

A nickname of Hibbing, Minnesota, so called because of the iron ore in the mines under the city.

Ridings, the

Yorkshire is the largest county in England, and for administrative purposes it has always been divided into three parts. Since the reorganization of English local government in 1974 these have been known, rather prosaically, as North Yorkshire, West Yorkshire, and South Yorkshire. Before then, however, they were the Ridings. The North Riding covered the area of the Yorkshire Moors and Dales, from Middlesbrough in the north down as far as Harrogate and York. The West Riding was the great industrial heartland, including the manufacturing towns and cities of Leeds, Bradford, Huddersfield, Doncaster, and Sheffield; it is now divided between West and South Yorkshire. The East Riding, always a rather separate and isolated area, with the fishing port of Hull as its main city, was divided up; part went to North Yorkshire, and part is now Humberside, and no longer officially part of Yorkshire at all, although most true Yorkshiremen would dispute this. There never was a South Riding, incidentally, despite the novel of that name by the Yorkshire writer Winifred Holtby. The word *riding* has nothing to do with *to ride*; it comes from an old Viking word *thrithjungr*, or *thirding* as it might be in modern English, meaning 'a third part.' And although it has gone out of use in Britain, it has been exported. As early as 1675, reference was made to the north and west ridings of Long Island, New York, and it is still applied to administrative and electoral districts in Canada.

Rio Grande Valley

A low-lying, flat region north of the Rio Grande in southeastern Texas, often (locally) shortened to "the Valley."

Rip Van Winkle State, the

A former nickname of North Carolina. [Given without explanation in the *Manual of Useful Information*, C. J. Thomas, 1893.]

Roaring Forties

A region in the southern oceans between 40° and 50° south, where gale-force westerly winds are the rule rather than the exception. The term is sometimes also used for the part of the North Atlantic that is at a similar latitude to the north of the equator.

Roaring Twenties, the

A nickname given to the 1920s, especially in the United States, where the decade was characterized by the fashions associated with the "flappers," young women who wore short skirts, long necklaces, and bobbed hair and who submitted to every dance craze, especially the Charleston; by Prohibition, which bred bootleg whiskey, speakeasies, and gangsters; and by a financial boom that continued till October 1929, when the stock market crashed, bringing about the Great Depression.

Rock, the

An abbreviated name commonly used for the Rock of Gibraltar, a 1300-foot-high limestone outcrop on a peninsula at the southern tip of Spain. Gibraltar was a British colony, and the language spoken by the inhabitants, which is a mixture of Spanish and English, is known as "Rock English." See also **Gib**.

Rock City

A nickname of Nashville, Tennessee.

Rockefeller Center

A complex of high-rise office buildings between 48th and 51st streets, on the south and north, and Fifth and Sixth avenues, on the east and west, funded by John D. Rockefeller and built in the 1930s on a site leased from Columbia University, now owned by Rockefeller Center. The first such complex in the world, it reflected the concern that skyscrapers were creating dark, cavern-like streets, so on its three-block site were built a 66-story skyscraper with 13 smaller buildings with ample space and a plaza between. The use of landscaping, fine-quality materials and artwork, together with the consideration of light, air, and space produced a project that influenced such construction in the rest of the world. Originally, several of the buildings were occupied by large corporations after which the buildings were named, though they did not use the buildings exclusively. Thus, the RCA Building, the tallest, (called "Radio City") was occupied partly by the Radio Corporation of America, the Time-Life Building by the publishers, Time, Incorporated, and so on. (The latter has since moved to another building, across Sixth Avenue, which is not a part of the original complex.) A large area, sunk below street level between 49th and 50th streets, west of Fifth Avenue, contains an ice-skating rink, dominated by a large golden sculpture, called *Prometheus*, by Paul Manship. The complex has a vast underground network, with shops and services, that connects with all of the buildings. Rockefeller Center, limestone-faced in Art Deco style moderne, is a favorite among visitors and natives alike, who enjoy strolling along its flower-bedecked Mall and visiting **Radio City Music Hall** (*q.v.*).

Rocket City

A nickname of Huntsville, Alabama, after Redstone Arsenal, the Marshall Space Flight Center, and several industries related to aerospace.

Rockies, the

The nickname for the Rocky Mountains, the largest mountain system in North America, extending more than 3000 miles from the Yukon Territory in Canada, to north central New Mexico. The highest peaks are in Colorado: Mt. Ebert is the tallest at 14,443 feet, but there are 46 others in the state higher than 14,000 feet. Included in the system are the Sangre de Cristo Range, the Middle, Northern, and Canadian Rockies, and the Mackenzie Range. For most of their length they include the Continental Divide. With the lowest pass through them exceeding 10,000 feet in height, they were a formidable barrier to the westward migration of the 1800s, which made the **Oregon Trail** (*q.v.*) so valuable. Also called the **Backbone of North America, the Backbone of the Continent, Roof of the Continent.**

Rock-ribbed State, the

A nickname of Massachusetts.

Rodeo Drive

A street in Beverly Hills, California, Rodeo Drive is largely residential, but the short stretch between Wilshire and Santa Monica boulevards is one of the richest shopping streets in the world, compared with such places as Fifth and Madison avenues in New York, the Via Condotti in Rome, and the Faubourg Saint-Honoré in Paris. Some of the same high-priced luxury goods would be offered on each of these streets. Rodeo Drive differs from the others in its relative newness: its reputation has been forged largely since 1970. It does not carry much heavy traffic, and so one hears jokes about people double-parking their Rolls-Royces there in order to run into one of the shops to purchase a diamond tiara. Rodeo is pronounced "ro-DAY-o."

Roedean

A private secondary school for girls just to the east of Brighton, on the south coast of England. It is the most famous establishment of its type in the country; it was founded in 1885, and has since become virtually synonymous with girls' "public schools." The image it conjures up is perhaps not altogether positive; the strain of haughtiness and upper-class exclusivity which it suggests is captured in this quote from F. Branston (1977): "a Roedean accent which could have flayed the skin off a waiter."

Roger Williams City

A nickname of Providence, Rhode Island, so called after its founder.

Ronan Point

An apartment block in London's Dockland the celebrated demise of which became a powerful focus of feeling against high-rise building in Britain. In May 1968, after it had been occupied for only two months, a gas explosion in one of its apartments set off a domino-effect chain reaction which led to the collapse of one whole corner of the block, killing three people. Widespread unease about the construction methods and the poor quality of the workmanship and materials used for such buildings (as revealed by later investigation) necessitated considerable rethinking among architects and planners, and the name, Ronan Point, continues to exert a powerful grip on the public imagination as a negative symbol of modern building practices.

Roof Garden of Texas, the

A nickname of Alpine.

Roof of the World, the

A name applied to various lofty locations in central Asia, including Tibet and Mount Everest itself. Its principal application, however, is to the Pamirs, a mountainous plateau 30,000 square miles in area at a basic height of 12–13,000 feet above sea level, situated largely in the Soviet Union at the border with China, Pakistan, and Afghanistan. The term is a direct translation of the local name, *Bam-i-Dunya*.

Roost, the

The name given to a violently powerful current that flows to the north of Scotland, around the Orkney and Shetland Islands, where the Atlantic Ocean and the North Sea meet. The word is of Scandinavian origin.

Rose City

A nickname of Portland, Oregon.

Rosedale

The name of a suburb of Toronto that is associated with affluence and power.

Rotten Row

A road along the south side of Hyde Park, parallel to the Knightsbridge Barracks, from Kensington Gardens to Apsley Gate, in London, long known as a bridle path where people rode and promenaded their horses, especially on Sundays. The origin of its name is unknown, but it might have been a sarcastic reference to the wealthy who frequented the area.

Round Pound

A nickname for the one-pound coin that was issued by the British government in 1984 and, by 1986, had replaced all paper currency of that denomination.

Round Table at the Algonquin

A group of writers who met more or less regularly at the dining room of the Algonquin Hotel, on West 44th Street, in New York City, for "liquid lunches" during the 1920s and '30s. In later years, especially after its disbandment about the beginning of World War II, the group became known for its clever quips and somewhat acid commentary on the contemporary scene. Although the cast changed from time to time, the central figures consisted of Harold Ross, Alexander Woollcott, Robert Benchley, Franklin P. Adams, Deems Taylor, George S. Kaufman, Heywood Broun, Edna Ferber, Oscar Levant, and Dorothy Parker.

Route 128

A broad highway designed to allow traffic to bypass Boston on the south and west. Since the 1970s, a number of computer and high-technology companies have built offices and plants along it (and along the Massachusetts Turnpike, toward the west), which has occasioned the nickname, "Silicon Valley of the East." Local residents are somewhat offended by the pretentious naming of the road to "America's Tech Highway."

Roxbury

A section of Boston occupied predominantly by blacks.

Royal Borough, the

A name sometimes applied to Kensington and Chelsea, a borough in west central London, although in fact three other boroughs in England and Wales are officially royal boroughs as well: Kensington-upon-Thames (London), Windsor (Berkshire), and Caernarvon (North Wales). Royal status was granted to Kensington in 1901 by King Edward VII in honor of Queen Victoria, who was born at Kensington Palace. The boroughs of Kensington and Chelsea were merged in 1965, and they now jointly enjoy the honorific title.

Royal Miles, the

A name given to the road which runs from Edinburgh Castle down to the royal palace of Holyroodhouse, in Edinburgh, Scotland. The official names of the streets of which it is comprised are successively Castle Hill, the Lawnmarket, the High Street, and Canongate.

Rubber Capital of the United States, the

A nickname of Akron, Ohio.

Rugby

A school for boys in Rugby, a town in Warwickshire, England. It is probably best known for having developed the game of rugby football (nicknamed *rugger*), on which American football is modeled, and as the setting for perennially popular books, starting with *Tom Brown's School-days*, (1857) by Thomas Hughes. Its headmaster for many years was Thomas Arnold (1795–1842), father of the author Matthew Arnold and noted educational reformer.

Ruhr, the

A region around the valley of the River Ruhr, a tributary of the Rhine in northwestern West Germany. The center of the country's coalmining and heavy industry, it was the target for severe Allied bombing in World War II.

Rumelia

A name given to the part of the Balkans, in southeastern Europe, that used to belong to the Ottoman Empire. It covered parts of what are now Greece, Yugoslavia, Albania, and Bulgaria. Its inhabitants were known as Rume-liotes.

Runnymede

A meadow on the south bank of the River Thames, about three miles from Windsor, to the west of London. It was there in 1215 that the rebellious English barons finally forced King John to put pen to paper and agree to their demands. The resulting document, the famous Magna Carta, has subsequently been interpreted as being a crucial step in the establishment of certain constitutional liberties for English subjects.

Ruritania

An imaginary central European kingdom invented by the 20th-century English writer Anthony Hope for his novel *The Prisoner of Zenda*. It has since come to symbolize swashbuckling adventure, cloak-and-dagger intrigue, and perhaps chiefly the incongruity of royal pomp and circumstance in the matter-of-fact world of the 20th century.

Rush Street

A Near North Side section of Chicago that takes its name from its main thoroughfare. Long known for its often raucous nightlife, Rush Street still draws tourists, conventioneers, and suburbanites in great numbers, especially on weekend nights.

Russia

In ordinary usage, the name *Russia* is frequently used as a synonym for the Soviet Union, but technically it is only one, albeit the most important, of the constituent republics of the Union of Soviet Socialist Republics. Russia, or in full the *Russian Soviet Federated Socialist Republic*, occupies more than three quarters of the total territory of the Soviet Union, extending from the Baltic in the west to the Pacific in the east, an area of more than 6.5 million square miles. Moscow serves as the capital of both Russia and the

Soviet Union. Until the Revolution of 1917 Russia was a vast empire, ruled by the Czar of all the Russias. See also **Soviet Union**.

Rutland

In the East Midlands of England, a former county which was swallowed up by the neighboring Leicestershire in the local government reorganization of 1974. It was the smallest English county.

Sagebrush State, the

A nickname of Wyoming and of Nevada.

Sagehen State, the

A nickname of Nevada.

Sahel, the

A region west of Chad, in north Africa, to the coast, bordering the southern part of the Sahara desert and comprising eight countries and about 35 million people.

Sailor Town

A nickname of Norfolk, Virginia.

St. Andrews

A town on the east coast of Scotland, to the north of Edinburgh, that is virtually synonymous with golf. Records of the game there go back to the 15th century, and it is still the headquarters of the "R & A," the Royal and Ancient Golf Club, which is the governing body of golf in Britain. There are no fewer than four courses there, including the famous Old Course, on which members of the public may play fora relatively small charge. St. Andrews also houses a venerable university, founded in 1411.

St. James's

A fashionable area of the West End of London, bounded on the north by Piccadilly and on the south by the Mall. St. James's keynote is restrained and discreet elegance, as befits a former residential area inhabited by the aristocracy, rather than the sometimes rather flashy opulence of its near neighbor Mayfair. At its heart is St. James's Street, one of the centers of London's Clubland: scattered anonymously up and down the street are many of the most venerable and exclusive gentlemen's clubs, while nearby all the accoutrements necessary to a gentleman are deferentially purveyed by hatters, bootmakers, wine merchants, gun makers, and cigar merchants. At the foot of St. James's Street is the Tudor St. James's Palace; it was for many years the sovereign's official home in London, until Queen Victoria moved to Buckingham Palace. See also **Court of St. James's, Clubland, Mayfair**.

St. John's Wood

An area in northwest central London, to the west of Regent's Park. Its wide boulevards, elegant villas, and luxurious apartment blocks bespeak a wealthy and respectable population, but in the early years of the 20th century it had the reputation as a quarter where gentlemen might obtain clandestine pleasures.

St. Luke's summer

The English name for a period of warmer than usual weather in October, so called because the feast of St. Luke falls on October 18th.

Salem

A name used in the Old Testament for Jerusalem. In Genesis 14:18 we read "And Melchizedek king of Salem was brought forth bread and wine"; and in Psalm 76:2 "In Salem also is his tabernacle, and his dwelling place is Zion." See also **City of David.**

Sally Army, the

A jocular British nickname for the Salvation Army, a Christian organization founded in 1865 to evangelize and improve the social conditions of the poor.

Salop

In the West Midlands of England, an alternative name for the county of Shropshire. It has always had a certain currency as a sort of abbreviation (compare **Hants, Oxon**), but it received apparently final sanction in 1974, when it was declared to be the official name of the county. However, the local people did not take kindly to being told what to call their county, so they campaigned—successfully—to get the old name back: since 1980 Shropshire has again been Shropshire. The alternative continues in unofficial use, however; many locals refer to the county town of Shrewsbury as "Salop," and former pupils of the local public school are called "Old Slopians."

Salt City

A nickname of Syracuse, New York.

Salt Lake State, the

A nickname of Utah.

Sand Hill State, the

A nickname of Arizona.

Sandhurst

A village in Berkshire, to the southwest of London, the name of which has been virtually taken over by the nearby Royal Military College, an army training college for officer cadets that was built in the early 19th century by prisoners-of-war captured during the Napoleonic Wars.

Sandlapper State, the

A nickname of South Carolina, so called because the poorer settlers, who lived on almost barren sand ridges, were said to have been compelled to eat sand in order to survive.

Sandringham

Officially, Sandringham House, a royal residence in Norfolk, England. It is said to have been the favorite of George VI.

San Fernando Valley

A large, flat-floored valley between the Santa Monica and Santa Susana mountains of southern California. It is usually referred to simply as "The Valley." It differs significantly from the rest of Los Angeles—or so the other Angelenos would have it believed. They make particular reference to the Valley's summer heat, comparative lack of industry, low-density residential areas, and especially to the character of the Valley residents. Jokes about "Valley girls" are legion, with particular reference to their hair and clothing styles, their taste in music, and their unusual (limited) vocabularies.

Santa Fe Trail

A trade route from Fort Leavenworth, Kansas, to Santa Fe, New Mexico, begun in 1821, before transcontinental railroads, by William Becknell, who first brought goods to Santa Fe from Missouri. In 1849 a stagecoach service starting from Independence, Missouri, used the same trail.

Sardi's

A restaurant on 44th Street, west of Broadway, in New York City. It is popular with actors and others connected with the theater and by those who hope to catch a glimpse of a favorite celebrity—as well as by those aspiring to be noticed by a casting director. It is also frequented by newspaper people: the offices of *The New York Times* are around the corner, on 43rd Street. The walls are covered with pictures of show-business celebrities, many inscribed "To Vincent Sardi," the former owner.

Sargasso Sea, the

A two-million-square-mile area of the western Atlantic Ocean, on the Tropic of Cancer and to the east of Florida, characterized by huge floating masses of gulfweed and similar brown seaweeds, which quickly entangle any ship that ventures into them. It harbors many forms of marine life, and is famous as the breeding ground of eels; adult eels from American and European rivers congregate there in the fall to lay their eggs, and the young hatch out and eventually find their way back to their parental rivers. The name comes from *sargasso*, an alternative name for the weed derived from Portuguese *sargaço*.

Sauchiehall Street

A major thoroughfare in northwest central Glasgow, Scotland, and per-haps the city's most famous street. It is noted for its shops, theaters, and cinemas, and is a favorite promenade for the Glaswegian citizenry.

Savile Row

A street in Mayfair, in the West End of London, that runs between and parallel to Bond Street and Regent Street. Its name is virtually synonymous with fine tailoring for gentlemen; any well-dressed man about town will proverbially wear a "Savile Row suit."

Savoy, the

A name still occasionally used for an area of central London between the Strand and the Thames, which in the Middle Ages was the site of the Savoy Palace. From housing princes and nobles it went downhill until in the late 17th century it was a notorious haunt of thieves and ruffians; but in the 20th century it is once again frequented by the rich and fashionable, for the Savoy Hotel is situated there. The hotel, known as "the Savoy," is a luxurious caravanserai built to accommodate quests who attended the Savoy Theatre, venue of the Doyly-Carte productions of the operettas of Gilbert and Sullivan.

Sawdust City

A nickname of Minneapolis, Minnesota.

Scandinavia

A collective term for the countries of northwestern Europe: Denmark, Norway, and Sweden, and usually also Finland and Iceland. The name seems to be related ultimately to *Skane*, the very southern part of Sweden. In more restricted usage it refers to the long narrow peninsula containing Norway and Sweden.

Scandinavian Shield, the

A name for the northernmost parts of Norway, Sweden, and Finland along with the Kola Peninsula (including Murmansk). It is called *Nordkalotten* 'the northern skull-cap' in Norway, Sweden, and Denmark; the Finnish name is *Pohjoiskalotti*.

Scarsdale Syndrome

A feeling of guilt observed by psychologists among upper middle-class people who have moved to expensive suburbs, named for Scarsdale, such a suburb of New York City, in Westchester County.

Schrafft's

A tradename of G. Shattuck Company for its chain of restaurants, in the Northeast, especially in New York City, and its products, chiefly chocolates and ice cream. Formerly, there were many restaurants, which were known for their light meals of superior quality, their soda fountains, and their excellent ice cream and chocolates. Except for a Men's Grill, in the multi-storied restaurant at 45th Street and Fifth Avenue, the atmosphere of the others was rather tea-roomy, giving rise to their identification with "little old ladies," many of whom did, indeed, frequent Schrafft's. The restaurants have disappeared, replaced by the ubiquitous "fast-food" restaurants where lingering over tea with a ham sandwich on toasted cheese bread, were it available, would be strictly discouraged.

Scollay Square

A former square in downtown Boston, replaced entirely by Government Center, with its formal, formidable high-rise office buildings. Till the 1960s, Scollay Square was widely known as the honky-tonk center of eastern New England; dance halls, striptease shows, prostitutes, and those who associate themselves with such activities were well established. Those establishments, their personnel, and their clientele were displaced by the construction of the formal, proper, somewhat sterile Government Center and must now be sought in the **Combat Zone** (*q.v.*).

Scotland Yard

The name popularly applied to the Metropolitan Police (the police force that covers the whole of Greater London except the City), or more particularly to its criminal investigation branch. "Scotland Yard baffled" means that its detectives have so far failed to find any clues, a situation often rectified after someone, detained, has been kind enough to "help the police in their enquiries." More officially, *New Scotland Yard* is a building, in the Victoria area of London, that houses the headquarters of the Met. It takes its name from the street, on the north bank of the Thames near Westminster Bridge, in which the previous headquarters were situated until 1967. Before this again, the police had premises in Great Scotland Yard, a small street off Whitehall, from their foundation in 1829 until 1890. See also **Yard.**

Scylla and Charybdis

Respectively, a rock and a whirlpool which jointly constitute a hazard to shipping in the narrow strait of Messina, which separates Sicily from Italy. In classical mythology they were depicted as sea monsters which devoured ships and drowned sailors. In modern usage, to be "between Scylla and Charybdis" means to be faced with two equally unpleasant situations, of which avoiding one will necessitate facing up to the other; the same notion is often rendered in a less literary manner by "between a rock and a hard place."

Sears Tower

The world's tallest building, at 1454 feet, situated at the southwest corner of the Loop in Chicago. The city's next two tallest buildings—the Standard Oil Building (1136 feet) and the John Hancock Center (1127 feet)—are also among the world's five tallest. See also **Chrysler Building, Empire State Building.**

Second City, the

A nickname for Chicago from the 1890s onward (a comparison with New York City; Chicago is now actually third in U. S. population), "Second City" is also the name of the popular Old Town cabaret theater. Founded in 1959 in a former Chinese laundry, it is known for such alumni as Mike Nichols, Elaine May, Ed Asner, and John Belushi. A sister club, also to be called "Second City," is planned for Los Angeles—the city that recently overtook Chicago as the nation's second most populous.

Senegambia

An area in West Africa bounded to the north by the River Senegal (the northern frontier of the State of Senegal) and to the south by the River Gambia (the main artery of the state of the Gambia, which forms a long narrow enclave in Senegal).

Seven Dials

The junction of several rather run-down roads in the West End of London, just to the east of Soho. In former times the Seven Dials area was a notorious warren of thieves and other disreputable characters, but in the late 20th century it is merely rather seedy. It gets its name from a column with seven clock faces on it which used to stand there.

Seven Hills, the

The hills on which the walls of ancient Rome were built. Their names were the Aventine, Caelian, Capitoline, Esquiline, Palatine, Quirinal, and Viminal.

Seven Seas, the

A collective name, variously explained as being either all the major oceans of the world: North and South Atlantic, North and South Pacific, Indian, Arctic, and Antarctic, or principal seas of navigation and trade: Arabian Sea, Atlantic Ocean, Bay of Bengal, Mediterranean Sea, Persian Gulf, Red Sea, and South China Sea. It is a romantic rather than a strictly geographical term, associated with the days of sail, with pirates and explorers, galleons and windjammers.

Seven Sisters

An epithet applied originally to the Pleiades, a group of stars, and over the years to various groups of seven people or things. In modern usage it is the name of three places in Britain: an area of Tottenham, in northeast

London, which gets its name from the Seven Sisters Road running through it (this in turn was probably named for a group of seven elm trees nearby); a dramatic range of seven chalk cliffs on the south coast of England, to the east of Brighton, which culminates in the 500-feet-high Beachy Head; and a village in West Glamorgan, Wales, the name of which derives from a nearby coal mine that was called "Seven Sisters Colliery" after the seven daughters of its first owner.

Shaftesbury Avenue

A street running northeast from Piccadilly Circus to Charing Cross Road, the focus of the theater district of London. See also **Piccadilly Circus.**

Shambles, the

An area in the city of York, in northern England, which used to be the butchers' quarter, housing slaughterhouses and butchers' shops. Today its narrow street, near the Minster (cathedral), is a major tourist attraction, lined on each side by boutiques and antique shops. The history of the word *shambles* is interesting: it originally meant 'a stool'; then 'a table for displaying goods,' later specifically 'meat'; then 'a meat market'; then 'an abattoir'; then 'a scene of great carnage, such as a battlefield'; and finally today 'a ruination or mess.'

Shangri-La

1. An imaginary land of endless and unblemished happiness, whose fame has spread far beyond the confines of the novel in which it originally appeared. It was thought up by the English writer James Hilton, who set his *Lost Horizon* (1933) in a lamasery in the (totally fictitious) Tibetan valley of Shangri-La, the inhabitants of which never grew old.
2. Because of the imaginary (if not the romantic) nature of the fictional place, its name was adopted in 1942 by President Franklin D. Roosevelt as a code name for the aircraft carrier *Hornet*, from which the bombers were launched on April 18th, under the direction of General James P. Doolittle, for the first World War II air raid on Japanese soil—on Tokyo itself as well as Nagoya and other cities.
3. Because of its remote, possibly utopian attributes, *Shangri-La* was later (1945) applied by President Franklin D. Roosevelt to Camp David, Maryland, to avoid identifying its location, which had been secretly established as a presidential retreat, away from the immediate pressures of Washington and the Oval Office.

Sheba

The biblical name of the ancient kingdom of Saba, situated in the area of modern Yemen, in the southwestern part of the Arabian peninsula. In the years between about 930 and 115 B.C. it was a powerful and wealthy nation, having secured a monopoly of the spice trade in its area. Its most famous denizen was its queen, who visited King Solomon with a most impressive display of riches and pomp—"with a very great train," as the Bible puts it. According to the Koran her actual name was Balkis.

Sheffield of Germany

A former epithet of Solingen, in (modern West) Germany, so called originally because of the high quality of the swords and foils made there and, more recently, its cutlery. The original Sheffield, in England, has long enjoyed a reputation for sword-making, cutlery, and silver plate.

Shepheard's Hotel

Formerly, an important hotel in Cairo, frequented by western visitors, especially the British, during the occupation (1880–1922) and afterward, till it was destroyed by fire in the 1950s. Romantic tales were woven about it as a focus of Middle-East intrigue, but it was probably best known for its bartender, Joe, who served concoctions, in tall glasses, called the Dying Bastard and the Dead Bastard, the latter with slices of cucumber floating in it.

Shepherd Market

A little maze of streets and alleyways in the southwestern corner of Mayfair, just off Piccadilly in the West End of London. It was laid out in 1735 by a certain Edward Shepherd, on part of the site of the original May fair which gave its name to the area as a whole. It is a noted haunt of prostitutes. See also **Mayfair.**

Shepherd's Bush

A residential area of west London, to the west of Kensington. In former times it was a decidedly downmarket district, but with the arrival of the BBC Television Centre in 1960 it went up in the world to a certain extent. The origin of its name is uncertain.

Shires, the

In medieval times in England, a *shire* was synonymous with a *county*, but gradually its use became limited mainly to a combining form for counties (e.g., Hertfordshire, Lancashire, Devonshire). However, the term *the Shires* has had some specialized uses: in the 18th and 19th centuries it seems to have been applied by inhabitants of southeast England to any parts of the country other than their own, as being foreign and outlandish regions; then, from the second half of the 19th century onward, *the Shires* was the foxhunting area of the English east Midlands, particularly Northamptonshire and Leicestershire, which in the season became the private playground of the aristocratic members of the Quorn and the Pytchely, the Fernie, the Cottesmore, and the Belvoir (the names of various hunts); finally, in more recent times *the Shires* or Shire Counties has taken on political connotations: the term *knights of the shires* used to denote landed gentry who represented their counties in Parliament, and from that usage

"Shires" has come to mean the rural areas of England, which can be relied on to return Conservative members to Parliament.

Show Me State, the

The official nickname of Missouri, so called after an expression attributed to one of its former U. S. Representatives, Willard D. Vandiver.

Siam

The former name of Thailand, a kingdom in southeast Asia. It was called Siam until 1939, when its name was officially changed to Thailand; then in 1945 it reverted to Siam, but in 1949 it was changed back again to Thailand, which it has remained ever since.

Siberia

A huge region in north central and northeast Asia, which includes most of the Soviet Union to the east of the Urals. Much of it is desolate and sparsely populated, but the Trans-Siberian railway, built between 1891 and 1916 to link Moscow with Vladivostok on the Pacific coast, has gradually made some economic progress possible. Much of Siberia is north of the Arctic Circle, and it has become almost proverbial for cold desolation; any prolonged period of snow and ice is liable to be dubbed "a Siberian winter." More sinisterly, it has gained a reputation as an area to which Soviet dissidents and traitors are sent to molder in the oblivion of the labor camps and the infamous "salt mines."

Sick Man of Europe

A former nickname for the Turkish empire, bestowed by Kaiser Wilhelm (William II), emperor of Germany (1888–1918). See also **Sick Man of the East.**

Sick Man of the East

A former nickname for the Turkish empire, bestowed by Nicholas II, Czar of Russia (1894– 1917). See also **Sick Man of Europe.**

Silent Service

A nickname for the submarine service in the British, American, and (possibly) certain other navies.

Silicon Glen

A nickname for the central lowland belt of Scotland, roughly between Glasgow and Edinburgh, in which a flourishing microelectronics industry has developed during the 1970s and '80s. American and British computer companies have set up many factories in towns such as Livingston, Cumbernauld, and Glenrothes to produce silicon chips, microcircuits, semiconductors, and so forth. The name is modeled on Silicon Valley, California's microelectronics center, *glen* being the Scots word for 'valley.' See also **Silicon Prairie, Silicon Valley**.

Silicon Prairie

A nickname for an area near Dallas, Texas, so called because of the large number of high-technology and computer companies situated there. See also **Silicon Glen, Silicon Valley.**

Silicon Valley

An area south of San Francisco where companies manufacturing microcomputers built plants during the 1970s, so named after the silicon micro-chip which is at the heart of those devices. Companies engaged in ancillary activities, such as the design of software, soon moved there, too, and Silicon Valley became known for its modern buildings, in a park-like setting, occupied by phenomenally successful firms employing some of the highest-paid computer specialists in the world, "boy wonders," many of whom were under thirty. With the decline of popularity of microcomputers, owing partly to saturation of the market, partly to their loss of novelty, and, to a greater extent, to the entrance into the market of huge companies like IBM, the successes of many of the companies were turned to failures. See also **Silicon Glen, Silicon Prairie.**

Silver City

A nickname of Memphis, Tennessee.

Silver City by the Sea

A nickname of Aberdeen, Scotland.

Silver State, the

A former nickname of Colorado and the official nickname of Nevada.

Simpson's (in the Strand)

A very old restaurant in the Strand, in London, known for its beef, especially its roast beef, which is carved at the table from a huge joint on an elaborate trolley.

Simpson's of Piccadilly

A department store in Piccadilly Street, in London, specializing mainly in conservative men's clothing, shirts, and other accoutrements of attire. The rear of the store faces **Jermyn Street** (*q.v.*).

Sind

A region in southeast Pakistan, centered on the lower reaches of the Indus River. Its greatest claim to fame is that it gave rise to perhaps the most celebrated pun ever made on a place-name: in 1843 British forces under

Sir Charles Napier conquered the area; his message back to London was the single word *peccavi*, which is Latin for 'I have sinned.'

Sioux State, the

A nickname of North Dakota, so called because it was the home of the Sioux Indians who called themselves *Dakotas* 'allies.'

Six Counties, the

A name sometimes given to Northern Ireland, which is made up of the counties of Armagh, Antrim, Down, Derry, Fermanagh, and Tyrone.

1600 Pennsylvania Avenue

The street address of the White House, official residence of the President of the United States, often used metonymically for the office of the presidency. See also **Oval Office.**

Skevington's daughter

An instrument of torture invented by Sir W. Skevington, Lieutenant of the Tower of London in the reign of Henry VIII (1509–47). It consisted of a broad hoop of iron which so compressed the body that blood was forced from the nose and ears and sometimes from the hands and feet. Also called **scavenger's daughter.**

Skid Row

The name for an area in a city where vagrants gather. It is also used metaphorically and, converted to a verb, appears as *hit the skids*, in reference to someone who is down-and-out. The origin of *skid row* is uncertain, one popular theory proposing it was named for a street that (in the 1850s) ran up and down a steep hill in Seattle, Washington, that had a lumbermill at the bottom. Logs delivered at the top of the street were skidded down to the mill. As the street along which this was done scarcely allowed for a high grade of businesses or residences, it was characterized by the presence of run-down saloons, shabby hotels, and cheap restaurants, which today characterize the areas frequented by those on their uppers.

Slab City

A former nickname of Chicago. Also, **Slab Town.**

Slave Coast, the

A term sometimes used in the 18th and 19th centuries for the coast of West Africa between eastern Ghana and eastern Nigeria. Names of this type, referring to a major local product, are quite common in this area—Ghana was known as the Gold Coast in colonial days, and next door to it is a state still called the Ivory Coast. In former times slaves, destined for the Americas, were West Africa's leading export.

slider

A nickname for the hamburgers sold by the U. S. chain, White Tower, a two-ounce square patty of ground meat cooked by steam, in its bun, in a bed of onions. Also called **belly buster, gut bomb.**

Sloane Square

An unremarkable-looking square in the heart of London's Belgravia, but one that is the spiritual home of a curious breed of young person first noted by amateur anthropologists in the late 1970s—"Sloane Ranger" (or "Sloane", for short). These sons and daughters of wealthy establishment families introduced reactionary chic, which made it fashionable to wear sensible tweedy clothes that in the 1960s and '70s would have seemed very stuffy. Their usual haunts are Belgravia, Chelsea, and Knightsbridge, although they often decamp to country houses at the weekends.

Slough

A town in Buckinghamshire, to the west of London. Partly no doubt because of its unprepossessing name, with its suggestions of mire and despondency, Slough has an unenviable and not altogether deserved reputation as being the epitome of drab and brain-numbing subtopia, full of uniform streets and occupied by people with uniform tastes and attitudes. It is forever associated with these lines of John Betjeman:

> Come, friendly bombs, and fall on Slough
> It isn't fit for humans now,
> There isn't grass to graze a cow
> Swarm over, Death!

Smithfield

An open area (named for *Smith's field*) in what, at the time, was north of the City of London. There, on every Friday, unless it happened to be a solemn festival, was held "a great market for horses, whither earls, barons, knights, and citizens repaired, to see and to purchase." William Fitz-Stephen, a Canterbury monk, in *Descriptio Nobilissimae Civitatis Londini* (1174), wrote "merchants brought their wares from every nation under Heaven. The Arabian sent his gold; the Sabaeans, spice and frankincense; the Scythians, armour; Babylon, its oil; Egypt, precious stones; India, purple vestments; Norway and Russia, furs, sables, and ambergris; and Gaul, its wines."

Smoke, the

In the days before clean-air legislation, when soot was a major component of the urban atmosphere, large metropolises came to be known, particularly to those in the provinces, as *the Smoke*, or *the Big Smoke*. More specifically, London is *the Smoke* to Britishers, while in Australia the nickname is usually applied to Melbourne or Sydney.

Smoky City

A nickname of Pittsburgh, Pennsylvania.

Snowdonia

A mountainous area of northwest Wales which takes its name from Mount Snowdon, at 3560 feet the highest mountain in Britain south of Scotland. Five mountain ranges and the many lakes make this a region of spectacular scenic beauty, and most of it—about 850 square miles—is a national park. In extent it coincides fairly closely with the ancient realm and modern county of Gwynedd.

Sodom and Gomorrah

1. The names of cities destroyed because of their depravity and wickedness. [Gen. 19:24 ff]
2. A nickname for Stockholm, used among the people in Gothenburg, who consider that city a wicked place.

Sodom of India

A former nickname of Hyderabad, so called because of the beauty of the country and the depravity of its inhabitants. [Brewer's *Reader's Handbook*]

SoHo

A nickname for a neighborhood in mid Manhattan, west of Lafayette Street, east of Sixth Avenue, north of Canal Street, and, as the name suggests, *so*uth of *Ho*uston (pronounced HOWstin) Street. It was developed beginning in the 1960s by artists and others who were attracted by the large former manufacturing lofts, which had fallen into disuse. Several of the more enterprising (and somewhat wealthier) among them bought the smaller buildings and with ingenuity and paint, converted the lofts into studios and living space. Gradually a community sprang up that included galleries exhibiting the paintings and sculpture of SoHo inhabitants and of others. With the passing years, though SoHo has gained in its reputation for panache, its cachet has diminished as the properties increased in value and attracted more and more yuppies (Young Upwardly-mobile Professionals). Also, **So-Ho.** See also **NoHo.**

Soho

A district in the West End of London, to the east of Mayfair and to the north of Trafalgar Square. It has had a rather checkered history. As its small and congested streets, clustered around Soho Square, suggest, it has never been the most fashionable part of the West End. Since the 17th century it has attracted large numbers of immigrants—from France, Italy, Greece, and elsewhere. The cosmopolitan atmosphere that this fostered survives to this day, as is evident from the diversity of foreign restaurants and food shops. Soho's reputation has always remained rather *louche*. In the immediate postwar years it was the haunt of the avant-garde arty set.

It had always, too, been a noted center for prostitution, and in the 1960s and '70s the strip clubs, sex cinemas and shops, peep shows, and any other lucrative form of sleazy entertainment grew apace. In the 1980s, a concerted effort has been made to discourage such establishments, and the area acquired, through the increased property values, an "establishment" tone. The area is now rejuvenated as a place for nightlife, with its wine bars, bistros, and exotic restaurants—notably Chinese, for there is now a considerable Chinese community in Soho. Compare **SoHo.**

Soke of Peterborough, the

A former administrative area of the county of Northamptonshire in the East Midlands of England, which lost its separate identity in 1965. In medieval times a *soke* was a district under the jurisdiction of a local court.

Solent, the

The name given to the strait that separates the Isle of Wight from the southern coast of England, familiar, at least in former times, to passengers in the great transatlantic liners that passed along it on their way to or from the port of Southampton. At its widest it is about four miles across.

Solid City

A nickname of St. Louis, Missouri.

Somerset House

A building in the Strand, in London, formerly housing the National Records Office, more recently occupied by the Courtauld Institute of Art. It was built in 1776 on the site of an unfinished 16th-century palace.

Somers Town

An area of north London just to the west of King's Cross Station. In former times it had the reputation of being a very poor district, and in the early years of its existence many penniless refugees from the French Revolution came to live there.

Sooner State, the

The official nickname of Oklahoma, so called in reference to those who sneaked in ahead of the gun fired to signal that the territory was opened for settlement.

Sound, the

The English name for the busy strait that separates Zealand, the main island of Denmark, from Sweden and joins the Kattegat with the Baltic. At its narrowest point, where Sweden's Helsingborg faces Denmark's Helsingör (the Elsinore of *Hamlet*), it is only three miles across. Further south on opposite coasts are Copenhagen and Malmö. The waterway's Danish name is Öresund.

South, the

1. In the United States, generally an area comprising those states south of the Mason-Dixon Line, namely, Virginia, Kentucky, Arkansas, North and South Carolina, Tennessee, Georgia, Alabama, Mississippi, and Louisiana. Although Florida is, physically, in *the South*, only its northern part is usually considered as being a part of the cultural, social, and economic community associated with the other states mentioned. Compare **Deep South.**

2. In broadest terms, the South of England includes any parts of the country that are not the North, the Midlands, or East Anglia. In practice, however, the Southwest is often excluded too (the phrase "the South and Southwest" is often used), and in this narrower sense the South comprises the core of London and the Southeast, plus Hampshire, the eastern parts of Dorset and Wiltshire, all of Berkshire, and the southerly parts of Oxfordshire. Its reputation is as the Southeast's: economically, as well as climatically, it is the most favored part of Britain, and it is often looked at askance by Northerners, who regard the stereotypical Southerner as effete and aloof.

3. Geopolitically, *the South*, in Britain, has taken on new connotations in the latter part of the 20th century. As contrasted with the North, it refers basically to the economically underprivileged and industrially underdeveloped nations of the southern hemisphere—the world's "have-nots." It was popularized as a concept by the publication in 1980 of the so-called *Brandt Report*, in full *North-South, a program for survival; report of the Independent Commission on International Development.*

South American Alps

A nickname for that part of the Andes Mountains between Chile and Argentina, so called because members of the jet set go to ski resorts such as Portillo after the end of the European season.

South Bank, the

A stretch of the Thames embankment in London just across the river from the Houses of Parliament, from the northern end of County Hall to Waterloo Bridge. The large site was used for the Festival of Britain in 1951, and subsequently has been developed as a national center for the arts. The Royal Festival Hall led the way in 1951, and this has been followed successively by a motion-picture theater, further concert halls, the Hayward Art Gallery, and the National Theatre. From a strict geographical point of view, the South Bank is for the most part the east bank of the Thames.

Southeast, the

The southeastern corner of England, centered on London. In extent it is similar to the Home Counties, plus the capital, but as well as Surrey, Kent, and Essex, it includes Sussex, and usually excludes the western half of

Berkshire and the most northerly parts of Hertfordshire and Buckingham-shire. The large concentration of middle-class professional people who live there, many of them close to places of work in London, makes the South-east the wealthiest and most economically privileged part of Britain; levels of unemployment, for example, are usually significantly lower here than in other areas of the country. Compare **South, 2**.

Southeast Asia

A region consisting of a large bulge of land at the southeastern corner of Asia and of the islands to the south and east of it (the Malay Archipelago). It contains the states of Burma, Thailand, Cambodia, Laos, Vietnam, Malay-sia, Singapore, Indonesia, Brunei, and the Philippines. See also **Indochina**.

Southern Gateway to New England

A nickname of Providence, Rhode Island.

Southern Uplands, the

A hilly region, including the Lowther, Moorfoot, and Lammermuir hills, that covers much of the southern part of Scotland, between the Borders and the Lowlands. See also **Highlands**.

Southie

An area of the south side of Boston, occupied predominantly by people of Irish descent and associated with South Boston High School. Its residents retain strong ties with Northern Ireland and express their sympathies with the militant pro-Catholic factions there, which are bent on separating the country from British rule, by supporting the Sinn Fein and the Irish Republican Army (I.R.A.), both financially and politically, especially by thwarting legislation in the United States directed at the extradition of those who are wanted by the police for their alleged involvement in bombings, shootings, and other acts of violence against British personnel and property.

South of France, the

A term applied to the Mediterranean area of France—it embraces the southern coast stretching westward from the Riviera past Marseilles to the Spanish border, and the hinterland of Provence and Languedoc. It is a land of sun and wine, garlic and olive oil, and a popular vacation area for Europeans. Indeed for most English-speakers the South of France means above all the Côte d'Azur (in contrast to the Midi, the French term it usually translates, which embraces the inland areas to a far greater de-gree). The name retains the whiff of glamour and wealth that first attached itself to it in the 19th century when the titled English disported themselves on their yachts at Monte Carlo and Nice, occasionally venturing ashore for a turn at the casino tables. Latterly, resorts such as Cannes and St. Tropez have outstripped them in chic, adding still further to the sybaritic image of the South of France. Compare **Midi.**

South Pole

The southern end of the earth's axis of rotation which, owing to libration, changes slightly; the geographic south pole. It is situated on the continent of Antarctica, a large land mass, explored only superficially, where several nations maintain bases for research. Unlike the North Pole, it is inhabited, along its shores, by penguins and other birds and by a variety of other sea life. See also **North Pole.**

South Seas, the

A term that can broadly refer to any of the oceans south of the equator, but in practice is usually used today for the South Pacific. In the wider context, "the southern oceans" is the usual term nowadays. In former times, *South Seas* was the standard, neutral name for the area—the famous financial crash of 1720, for example, known as the *South Sea Bubble*, involved a company that traded with the Southern Hemisphere—but in modern usage it has more romantic connotations. The "South Sea Islands," in particular, evoke images of snow-white beaches, grass-skirted maidens, and carefree living in an ideal climate, largely as a result of the novels of Charles Nordoff and James Norman Hall and of idyllic motion pictures made in the 1930s.

South Shore, the

A local designation for the southern shores of Long Island, east of New York City.

South Side

A large area south of the Loop in Chicago and reaching roughly two miles west from bordering Lake Michigan. The major part of the South Side, lying due south of the Loop and reaching east along the southeastern curve of the lake, is the home of most of the city's large black population, with many industrial and poor residential areas, punctuated by such enclaves as the Hyde Park area, in which the University of Chicago is situated. Lake Calumet—some thirteen miles south of the Loop, on the city's Far South Side—is an important port for commercial shipping. On the Far Southeast Side is the historic **Pullman** (*q.v.*) area. The South Side also includes Jackson Park, Washington Park, and the Midway Plaisance (commonly known as, simply, "the Midway") connecting the two. Among its attractions are the **Museum of Science and Industry** (*q.v.*), Chinatown, Comiskey Park (home of the Chicago White Sox baseball club) and such well-known bastions of blues and soul music as the Checkerboard Lounge. A former South Side landmark, the Union Stockyards, was the famous—and, to some observers, infamous—nexus of the nation's meatpacking business. Nearby are the multi-ethnic, historically important

Bridgeport and Back of the Yards neighborhoods; Bridgeport, a favored area of Irish immigrants, is especially noted as the home of four successive Chicago mayors, spanning forty-six years (1933–79): Ed Kelly, Martin Kennelly, Richard J. Daley, and Michael Bilandic. See also **McCormick Place, Pilsen, Stagg Field, Union Stockyards, West Side, 2.**

Southwest, the

1. In the United States, an area encompassing the western states of Colorado, Utah, Nevada, Arizona, New Mexico, and Texas. Compare **West.**
2. The southwestern extremity of England, including the counties of Cornwall, Devon, and Somerset, and usually also western Dorset. It forms the southern and western section of the West Country. Compare **West, 2**.

Soviet Russia

A (post-Czarist) synonym for Russia, and used similarly to mean either the Soviet Union or, more strictly, the Russian Soviet Federated Socialist Republic. See also **Russia, Soviet Union.**

Soviet Union, the

A useful shorthand term usually used in preference to the officially correct but long-winded Union of Soviet Socialist Republics, or U. S. S. R. It is, in area, the largest country in the world, extending from the Polish and Romanian border in the west across most of northern Asia to the Pacific in the east, and covering one seventh of the world's total land surface, more than 8.5 million square miles. It is a federal state consisting of fifteen individual republics, the largest of which is Russia. *Soviet* is the Russian word for a governing council, a system of which, from the local level up to the Supreme Soviet, was put in place throughout the land following the Revolution of 1917. See also **Russia**.

Spaghetti Junction

A nickname given to any major road interchange of bewildering complexity, especially that at Gravelly Hill in north Birmingham, in the West Midlands of England.

Spanish Harlem

A general name given to those sections of Harlem, in New York City, where poorer Puerto Rican families settled upon moving to the mainland of the United States. An enormous influx of Puerto Ricans began to move to New York City, beginning in the late 1930s and early 1940s, largely at the instigation of Vito Marcantonio, a United States Congressman who invited them to move into the district he represented. As Puerto Rico is a commonwealth associated with the United States, its citizens may travel and settle freely anywhere in the U. S. As most of those who settled in New York City were indigent, they readily qualified for welfare (then called relief), the meagre support of which left them still better off than if they had remained in Puerto Rico. Ironically, the district represented by Marcantonio included not only these poorest sections of the city but the upper reaches of Fifth and Park avenues, as well; but these were relatively sparsely settled, especially in contrast to the overcrowded conditions of the Harlem slums, and, with the residents of Spanish Harlem to vote him into office, term after term, the wealthier residents found themselves vastly outnumbered in their attempts to vote him out of office. It was in those days that there originated the term "Silk Stocking District" in reference to the area occupied by Marcantonio's wealthy constituents. By the 1970s, as these Puerto Ricans began to assimilate and to move out of their confining ghetto, the term "Spanish Harlem" began to refer more to the Spanish-speaking population of Harlem than to any well-defined area. See also **East Side, Fifth Avenue, Harlem, Park Avenue, Upper East Side.**

Spanish Main, the

Originally, the Spanish Mainland—that is to say, the Spanish colonies on the northern coast of South America from the 16th century onward. In later use, however, the Spanish Main came to mean the stretch of sea offshore: the southern Caribbean, through which Spanish treasure galleons sailed for Europe with their freight of gold. Such seas were the natural habitat of predatory buccaneers and freebooters in the 17th and 18th centuries; ever since, the Spanish Main has been used as the setting of adventure yarns about pirates.

Spanish State, the

A nickname of New Mexico.

Speakers' Corner

The northeast corner of Hyde Park, London, near Marble Arch, which was moved to its present location from its former site as an entrance to the Palace Gardens and Buckingham Palace. Speakers' Corner is where those who wish to regale listeners on any of a variety of subjects are seen and heard, holding forth from soapboxes or other makeshift platforms. See also **Hyde Park Corner.**

Spice Islands, the

A term used since at least the 17th century for islands in the East from which spice was imported, but usually applied more specifically in past times to a group of islands between Sulawesi (Celebes) and Papua New Guinea, in the East Indies. In the 16th and 17th centuries they were at the focus of a fierce contest for the monopoly of the spice trade between Portugal, Spain, and Holland, in which the Dutch prevailed. In later years they were known as the Moluccas, and since 1949 they have been part of the republic of Indonesia, of which they form the Maluku province.

Spindle City

A nickname of Lowell, Massachusetts, and of Cohoes, New York, so called because of the numerous textile mills situated there.

Square Mile, the

A nickname given to the City of London, particularly with reference to its status as a financial center. Its precise area is in fact 675 acres, just over one square mile.

Squatter State, the

A nickname of Kansas, so called in reference to the many settlers rushed into the territory by both pro- and antislavery groups just before the Civil War.

Stagg Field

An athletic facility, birthplace of the Atomic Age, which began in Chicago on December 2, 1942, when Enrico Fermi and University of Chicago scientists, working on the "Manhattan Project," achieved the first self-sustaining nuclear chain reaction. The research was conducted in a converted old squash court under a stadium grandstand; the site is now marked by a sculpture by Henry Moore.

Stamboul

An archaic form of the Turkish name for the city previously known by its Greek name, Constantinople, and in more modern times as Istanbul. It is perhaps best remembered from the title of Graham Greene's novel, *Stamboul Train*, which concerns events on the Orient-Express to the then Turkish capital.

Stannaries, the

In the Middle Ages, tin was mined and smelted extensively on Dartmoor, in western Devon and eastern Cornwall, southwestern England. The mining area became known as *the Stannaries* (from Latin *stannum*, 'tin'), and in its heyday was virtually a self-governing enclave; the tinners had their own courts ("stannary courts") with very wide jurisdiction, and their own parliament, which met in the open air on Crockern Tor from 1304 to 1749. The whole legal apparatus was abolished in 1896, but tin continues to be mined in Cornwall when prices on the world market warrant.

Star Chamber

The name of an apartment in the Palace of Westminster, in London, where the King's Council dispensed justice in medieval times. It was named for the stars that decorated its blue ceiling. During the reign of the Stuarts, the Court of Star Chamber, its successor, dispensed such arbitrary and ruthless justice that "star-chamber proceedings" came to be associated with injustice. The Court was abolished in 1641.

Star City

A nickname of Lafayette, Indiana, and a former nickname of Chicago.

Stars and Bars

A nickname for the flag of the Confederate states during the Civil War, consisting of two horizontal red bars on white, and a circle of eleven white stars on a field of blue. See also **Old Glory, Stars and Stripes.**

Stars and Stripes

A nickname for the (officially named) Flag of the United States, first used in 1897 by John Philip Sousa for his march, "Stars and Stripes Forever." It was next used for a U. S. army newspaper published in France during World War I, then again during World War II when an army publication for soldiers was so named.

Star Wars

The nickname for the Strategic Defense Initiative, a United States plan of the 1980s for placing into fixed orbit in space over the earth weapons capable of detecting and destroying missiles launched against the U. S.

Stealth

A nickname for the Advanced Technology Bomber, a United States military aircraft, the existence of which is denied by officials, designed to make its presence difficult to detect by ordinary means such as radar and other sensory devices.

Steel State, the

A nickname of Pennsylvania.

Stoke Mandeville

A village to the southeast of Aylesbury, in Buckinghamshire, northwest of London. Its name has become virtually synonymous with that of its world-famous hospital for paraplegics, whose regime of active therapy culminates in the Stoke Mandeville Games, a sort of mini-Olympics.

Stork Club

For almost three decades, till his death in the 1960s, Sherman Billingsley operated the Stork Club, on 53rd Street between Fifth and Madison avenues, in New York City. During those years it became a focal point of the night life of the city, catering to celebrities and café society alike, while the goings-on and gossip were reported by the columnists Walter Winchell, "Cholly Knickerbocker," Leonard Lyons, Ed Sullivan, Dorothy Kilgallen, and others.

Storyville

Attempts to limit the spread of prostitution in New Orleans, Louisiana, were culminated in 1897 when the City Council passed a municipal ordinance establishing a red-light district where those practices would be tolerated. The limits of this district, called Storyville after Alderman Sidney Story, the sponsor of the ordinance, were the blocks of the city contained within Customhouse (later renamed Iberville), Robertson, St. Louis, and Basin streets. In its heyday a flourish of about 2000 strumpets in about 230 houses plied their profession there, the brothels ranging from sparsely furnished cribs to opulent parlor houses. New Orleans jazz had many of its roots in Storyville, and the neighborhood served as a tawdry tourist attraction. It was already in considerable decline when it was closed in 1917 under pressure from the Navy Department.

Strawberry Fields

A Salvation Army orphanage in Liverpool, in the Northwest of England, immortalized in the Beatles song of the same name, which they first recorded in 1967.

Strawberry Hill

A fine home in Twickenham, near Richmond-upon-Thames, west of London, once the seat of Horace Walpole.

Street, the

1. A nickname for Wall Street.
2. A nickname for any area or circumstance where news may be exchanged, rumors heard, etc. "What do you hear on the Street?" usually means 'What rumors are about? What's the latest news?' It usually refers to goings-on in a particular trade, profession, or industry.

Strip, the

1. The section of highway in Las Vegas, Nevada, that is lined with hotels, gambling casinos, and other places of entertainment.
2. The name of the downtown area of Toronto, that is the focus of amusement and entertainment, somewhat parallel in connotation to Times Square in New York City or the Sunset Strip in Los Angeles.
3. See **Sunset Boulevard.**

Stub-toe State, the

A nickname of Montana, so called after the steep slopes of its mountains.

Subcontinent, the

In modern usage, a word used for the vast triangular peninsula at the south of the Asian landmass, containing the states of India, Pakistan, Bangladesh, Sri Lanka, Nepal, and Bhutan. In more general terms, a subcontinent is any large subdivision of a continent, with some sort of separate character of its own, and indeed up until the beginning of the 20th century the word was used specifically to refer not to India but to South Africa.

Sublime Porte, the

The name given to the government and court of the former Ottoman Empire. A French term, it is a direct translation of the Turkish *Baba Ali* 'imperial [*literally* high] gate'; this probably refers ultimately to the entrance to the sultan's tent, where in ancient times audiences were held. The term was often abbreviated to simply *the Porte*, and in the 17th and 18th centuries was commonly mistaken as a reference to Constantinople as a sea port.

subtopia

A word coined by British architect journalist Ian Nairn in the 1950s for suburban housing estates, the owners of which devote many hours each day to making the best of their small plots.

Sucker State, the

A nickname of Illinois, so called either because the local miners went to the mines in the spring and returned in the fall, as the suckers (fish) did in the rivers, or because, in the early days of settlement, the prairie water was usually to be found only in crawfish holes and had to be sucked up by means of reeds, which the people called "suckers."

Sudan, the

A name given to the vast sweep of the African continent that lies south of the Sahara desert and north of the tropical rain forests. From the 4th century onward it was the seat of the powerful and vigorous Sudanic civilization, a Negro culture the leading states of which were Ghana, Hausa, Kanem, and Songhai. It declined as Islam began to filter southward in the Middle Ages, and had disappeared by the 19th century; but the memory of its name is preserved in the modern state at its eastern extremity, which is the largest country in Africa.

Sudetenland, the

An area along the northwestern border of Czechoslovakia, occupied by two mountain ranges: the Erzgebirge on the frontier with East Germany, and the Sudeten Mountains on the frontier with Poland. It achieved an unwanted celebrity in 1938 when Adolf Hitler's annexation of the area to Germany, using as a pretext its having, historically, been inhabited by German-speaking people, became one of the factors leading up to World War II. In 1945 it was returned to Czechoslovakia, and most of the German-speaking population was expelled.

Sugar Hill

A vaguely circumscribed neighborhood in north Harlem, in New York City. On a high promontory, at about 135th Street and St. Nicholas Avenue, overlooking the areas to the east—the Harlem River and The Bronx beyond—it was a residential section where the wealthier blacks lived. It was so named because those who resided there had the "sugar" to afford it.

Sugar State, the

A nickname of Louisiana.

Summit City

A nickname of Akron, Ohio.

Sunbelt

A geographical area of the southern United States that includes those states, particularly Florida, Arizona, and New Mexico, that have relatively milder weather than the rest of the country all year round and tend to attract retired people and those who prefer subtropical to temperate climates.

Sunflower State, the

The official nickname of Kansas.

Sunset Boulevard

An east-west road, approximately thirty miles long, running from downtown Los Angeles to the Pacific Ocean. Commercial structures dominate the eastern half of Sunset Boulevard (east of Beverly Hills), residential structures the western half (Beverly Hills, Bel Air, Westwood, Brentwood, and Pacific Palisades). The images of Sunset Boulevard held by outsiders are those provoked by the commercial stretches, especially the Sunset Strip, often known simply as "The Strip," the section of the Boulevard between Beverly Hills and Fairfax Avenue. The Strip is an area of restaurants, nightclubs, boutiques, and garish billboards. Schwab's Drugstore still exists, but the Garden of Allah Hotel (1927–1959) is no more. Those who know the area mostly through its fictional representations will think of Billy Wilder's movie, *Sunset Boulevard*, (1950), when the name is mentioned.

Sunset State (*or* Land)

A nickname of Arizona.

Sunset State, the

A nickname of Oregon.

Sunshine City

A nickname of St. Petersburg, Florida.

Sunshine State

A nickname arrogated by Florida, New Mexico, and South Dakota in their efforts to merchandise their climates.

Surrey

A county in southern England, immediately to the south and southwest of London. It is one of the Home Counties, and is often regarded slightingly as possessing quintessential Home County characteristics: a comfortable plasticized commuterland with respectable villas and neatly mown lawns interspersed with patches of mild scenery that have been allowed to remain undeveloped.

Swamp State, the

A nickname of South Carolina.

Swiss Cottage

A small, fairly trendy area of northwest London, to the north of St. John's Wood. Its curious name comes from a pub there, built in the style of a Swiss chalet. Originally called the Swiss Tavern, it was put up in 1803–4, and its name was subsequently changed to the Swiss Cottage. When a London Underground station was opened there in the late 19th century it was called Swiss Cottage, and the name spread thence to the district. The pub is still there, although it has passed through several metamorphoses since its original construction.

Switzerland of America, the

A nickname claimed by Colorado, Maine, New Hampshire, New Jersey, and West Virginia.

Swone-one

British Sloane Ranger slang (pronounced SWUN-WUN) for the Battersea area of London, whose designation as a postal district is SW11. See also **Sloane Square.**

Sycamore City

A nickname of Terre Haute, Indiana.

T, the

The local nickname for the train system serving urban and suburban Boston; Boston Transport.

Table Mountain

The name of a flat-topped mountain, more than 3600 feet high, that dominates the area of Cape Town, South Africa. Its *table cloth* appears occasionally—a flat-topped white cloud that seems to hang halfway down over its sheer face.

Tarheel State, the

The official nickname of North Carolina, originally a derisive nickname given by Mississippians to a brigade of North Carolinians who failed to hold their position during a battle in the Civil War.

Tartary

A vast sweep of central Asia occupied in the Middle Ages by the Tartars, a fierce Mongoloid people. Under Genghis Khan the Tartar empire extended from eastern Europe as far eastward as the shores of the Pacific; in 1552, it was conquered and subdued by the Russians. See also **Mongolia**.

Telford

A new town in Shropshire, England. It was so designated in 1963 for development purposes, but it is associated with the industrial revolution and is the site of the famed Iron Bridge.

Temple, the

An area of central London between Fleet Street and the Thames. In early medieval times it was occupied by the buildings of the Knights Templars, but their order was suppressed in 1312, and since the mid 14th century the site has been given over to the law. In modern usage, *the Temple* refers first and foremost to the buildings of the two Inns of Court (societies of lawyers) known as the Inner and Middle Temples. As a term for the area in general, it was reinforced by the naming of the local London Underground station as "Temple."

Terrapin State, the

A nickname of Maryland.

Territories, The

The collective name for the Yukon Territory and the Northwest Territories, which together cover about one third of Canada's land area. They consist chiefly of forest-covered mountains, with the rest of the region being frozen most of the year, and are very rich in mineral deposits.

Territory, the

A colloquial abbreviation by which the Northern Territory is known in Australia. It is an administrative area (rather than a fully fledged state) in northern central Australia which, apart from its tropical coastal strip, is a semiarid wilderness. See also **Center**.

Texas Tea

A nickname for oil and natural gas.

Thames Valley, the

The low-lying country in southern England through which the River Thames flows, particularly the upper reaches of it, to the west of London, in the counties of Berkshire and Oxfordshire. It is a gentle and peaceful landscape, with still many unspoiled stretches of river, and several charming towns and villages, such as Henley and Marlow. Its chief centers of population are Maidenhead, Reading, and Oxford. Its name is used in certain official designations: the local police force, for example, is known as the Thames Valley police.

Third Avenue

In the late 19th and early 20th centuries, when elevated "subways" were being built along various north-south thoroughfares in New York City to improve transportation for those who were beginning to populate the outlying sections of the city, little heed was paid to the effects these continuous steel bridges would have on the avenues below. One of the typical results was to create a dark and dingy atmosphere beneath them through which sunlight barely penetrated; another was to create a maze of steel pilings that proved a hazard to traffic. Because of the noise and dirt of the steam locomotives, not replaced by electric trains (which made almost as much noise) till many years later, the once-broad boulevards on which the elevated train systems (called "els") were set lost much of their property value and became, above the inevitable retail establishments below, slums. In general, this situation was not relieved till the 1950s, when the last of those in downtown Manhattan was demolished. Third Avenue was one of the first to be burdened by an "el," and it came, over the ensuing years, to epitomize the worst sort of neighborhood along its entire length, with disreputable bars, seedy hotels, flophouses, and lunch counters; the only area that fared worse was Tenth Avenue (see **Hell's Kitchen**). Finally, upon the removal of the elevated structure in the 1950s, Third Avenue began gradually to recover: retail shops moved in, new apartment houses were built above 60th and below 40th streets, and, in between, posh modern office buildings rose above the din of the street traffic below.

Third World, the

On the view that the capitalist and communist blocs represent the two major ideological Establishments, the countries outside these two political camps have taken to themselves—or been given—the label *Third World*, at once an affirmation of separate (and nonaligned) status and an admission of the pecking order. In general it is taken to include most of the countries of Africa, Asia, and South America, but there are, of course, crucial exceptions to this broad classification, such as Japan and South Africa. *Third World* is increasingly a synonym for 'economically undeveloped; poor.'

Thirteen Original Colonies

The earliest areas in North America settled by English colonists during the seventeenth and eighteenth centuries, called colonies till 1776, after which they became states of the United States of America, namely, New Hampshire, Massachusetts, Rhode Island, Connecticut, New York, New Jersey, Pennsylvania, Delaware, Maryland, Virginia, North Carolina, South Carolina, and Georgia.

Thorney Island

An unpromising dreary tract of silt that was the germ in the Dark Ages of the area of London now known as Westminster. According to tradition a church was first built on this island in the Thames in 616, and the original Westminster Abbey was founded in 750. Since then the abbey has gone through several metamorphoses into the magnificent Gothic structure of today, and Thorney Island has long since merged into the mainland of the north bank of the Thames.

Throgmorton Street

A street in the financial heart of the City of London. Often abbreviated familiarly to Throg Street, it has come to be used as a shorthand term for London's stockmarket dealings; the Stock Exchange is at the corner of Throgmorton and Threadneedle streets.

Thule

A name given in ancient times to an island or piece of land six days' sailing to the north of Britain. It is not clear precisely what it refers to—Shetland and a part of Norway have been put forward—but its general signification was the northern limit of the known world, as its frequent epithet, *ultima Thule*, suggests. In modern usage, Thule is a U. S. airforce base in northwest Greenland.

Thunderer, the

A nickname of *The Times* [London], coined in the 19th century when its editorial columns inveighed powerfully against the misdeeds of governments and scourged errant ministers. It is in allusion to a passage in an article by Captain Edward Sterling, its editor, who wrote, "We thundered forth the other day an article on the subject of social and political reform." In many people's eyes the right to the sobriquet was forfeited in the 20th century, when the newspaper became much more the organ of the Establishment. See also **Turnabout.**

Tidal Basin

A large pond, in Washington, D. C., an inlet of the Potomac River, in front of the Jefferson Memorial. During late March—early April each year, it is an attraction to visitors who come to view the blooming of hundreds of cherry trees, a gift of the Japanese government in 1912.

Tidewater Virginia

The name given to one of the five main land regions of the state of Virginia. The other four are Appalachian Plateau; Appalachian Ridge and Valley Region; Blue Ridge; and Piedmont. Each has its own distinctive dialect. Also called the Atlantic Coastal Plain, the term is applied to the lowland coastal section extending as far west from the Atlantic Ocean and Chesapeake Bay as its rivers are affected by the tides. It is divided into three peninsulas by the James, Potomac, and Rappahannock rivers, and includes the Virginia portion of the Delmarva peninsula. It was the first part settled by colonists.

Tierra del Fuego

The name of an archipelago at the southern tip of South America, separated from the continent by the Strait of Magellan. It is composed of the main island, also called Tierra del Fuego, and smaller ones, which include Desolation, Clarence, Dawson, and others. Divided politically between Argentina and Chile, it was discovered by Magellan in 1520. The name, which means 'Land of Fire' in Spanish, does not refer to the climate, which is raw, cold, windy, and snowy for much of the year, but rather to the scores of Indian camp fires the explorers could see at night.

Tiffany's

Properly, "Tiffany and Company," this New York City landmark, at 57th Street and Fifth Avenue, long ago entered the language as a symbol of the wealth and elegance associated with diamond necklaces and tiaras, bracelets, and brooches. On an international scale, it vies for prominence with Van Cleef and Arpels, across Fifth Avenue, and with Cartier, farther down Fifth Avenue, at 54th Street. But to New Yorkers, Tiffany's epitomizes the finest in precious gems, an image that was contributed to by Truman Capote's short story, "Breakfast at Tiffany's," later made into a film.

Timbuktu

A town in the republic of Mali, West Africa, near the Niger River. Its name evidently has a bizarre sound to Western ears, since in the past it has often been used to suggest any imprecisely located town or city that seems improbably remote or exotic. This comic verse attributed to Bishop Wilberforce (1805–73) betrays a lack of exact geographical knowledge:

> If I were a cassowary
> On the plains of Timbuctoo,
> I would eat a missionary,
> Cassock, band, and hymn-book too.

tin Lizzie

The affectionate nickname for the first mass-produced car, the "model T," 15 million of which were produced by Henry Ford between 1908 and 1927.

Tin Pan Alley

A term used both in Britain and the U. S. for the haunt of popular song writers and music publishers. In New York City, where the term was coined in the early 1900s, referring specifically to an area at Broadway and West 28th Street, then the center of the popular music industry. In Britain the nickname has traditionally been applied to Denmark Street, a small alleyway just off the Charing Cross Road in London, but in recent years Old Compton Street, a couple of hundred yards to the southwest in Soho proper, has taken over the mantle. In New York City, as businesses moved uptown, so did Tin Pan Alley, and for several decades its focus has been at 1650 Broadway (at 50th Street) and in the Brill Building.

Tintagel

Properly, Tintagel Head, a promontory on the west coast of Cornwall, England, site of Tintagel Castle, now a ruin, the legendary birthplace of King Arthur.

Tire City of the United States, the

A nickname of Akron, Ohio.

Tivoli Gardens

A large park, in central Copenhagen, containing restaurants, amusement areas, horticultural gardens, and, at night, attractive lighting.

Tobacco Capital of the World, the

A nickname of Durham, North Carolina.

Tobacco State, the

A nickname of Kentucky.

Toddling Town, That

A nickname of Chicago derived from the lyrics of the song, "Chicago" (1922) by Fred Fisher.

Tolpuddle

A village in Dorset, in southern England, famous for the so-called "Tolpuddle Martyrs," a group of farm workers sentenced to be transported to Tasmania in 1834 for setting up an early form of labor union to resist wage cuts. The name is actually something of a bowdlerization: it is derived from the local river, the Piddle, and other villages in the area, such as Piddletrenthide and Piddlehinton, retain the original form.

Tommy (Atkins)

A nickname for British soldiers, equivalent to G. I. Joe in the U. S., used by Rudyard Kipling in his "Barrack Room Ballads" (1892):

O it's Tommy this, an' Tommy that, an' 'Tommy go away';
But it's 'Thank you, Mr. Atkins,' when the band begins to play.

Tommy gun

A World War II nickname for the Thompson sub-machine gun.

Toothpick State, the

A nickname of Arkansas, so called because it was held that the early settlers used their bowie knives as toothpicks. See also **Bowie State.**

Top End, the

An informal Australian name for the extreme north of Australia, which lies well inside the tropics.

Torquay

A seaside resort in Devonshire, England, on the English Channel. It is considered comparatively expensive and is frequented mainly by upper middle-class visitors, especially the elderly. As a sardonic jingle has it, "Dover for the continent, Torquay for the incontinent." See also **Bourne-mouth.**

TOTO

The nickname for the Totable Tornado Observatory, at the National Severe Storms Laboratory, Norman, Oklahoma, so called both as an acronym and after Dorothy's dog in *The Wizard of Oz*, by Frank L. Baum. See also **Oz**.

Tower, the

Any reference to "the Tower" in Britain will be instantly recognized as signifying the Tower of London, the famous fortress on the north bank of the Thames. In modern usage, of course, a tower is a relatively lofty structure, not, like the Tower of London, a castle spread over a wide site; but it seems that the Tower as a whole took its name from the White Tower, the tall Norman keep which formed its original nucleus. Aside from its reputation as a prison through the centuries, the Tower also serves as the repository for the royal treasure or *regalia*, closely guarded by the Yeomen Warders, and still dominates the Thamesside scene.

Tower Bridge

A lift bridge across the Thames near the Tower of London. It has a lofty tower at each end, but derives its name from **the Tower** (*q.v.*). Much to the amusement of Londoners (and others in the know), it is thought that the Americans who bought and transported to Arizona what was designated as **London Bridge** (*q.v.*), a rather ordinary structure, thought that they were buying the Tower Bridge, which is much more picturesque and figures often as a symbol of London and of England.

Tower Hamlets
A new London borough formed in 1965 by combining the former East End boroughs of Bethnal Green, Poplar, and Stepney. In feudal times these three boroughs, or *hamlets* as they then were, belonged to the Tower of London.

Town That Moved Overnight, the
A nickname of Hibbing, Minnesota, so called because after it had grown to considerable size, it was moved to provide access to the huge beds of iron ore beneath it.

Toxteth
An underprivileged area of Liverpool that achieved an unwelcome notoriety in the early 1980s as the scene of inner-city unrest and rioting. In an attempt to defuse the negative connotations of the name, many locals tend to refer to the area by its postal designation, Liverpool 8.

Track, the
The name of the red-light district in Toronto.

Trail of Tears
The name given, figuratively, to those wilderness roads over which the members of the Five Civilized Tribes (Choctaw, Chickasaw, Cherokee, Creek, and Seminole) traveled to Indian Territory (later Oklahoma) under terms of the Indian Removal Act (1830).

Trans-Jordan
A name (literally "across the (river) Jordan") given to the territory now occupied by the kingdom of Jordan, when it was administered by the British under a League of Nations mandate between World Wars I and II.

Transylvania
A region in northern Romania, bounded to the south and east by the Carpathian Mountains. Until 1918 it belonged to Hungary. Its remote forests and valleys provide a fitting setting for chilling stories of vampires, and its reputation for eeriness has become fixed in the public imagination since the publication of Bram Stoker's *Dracula* (1897).

Treasure State of the Rockies, the
A nickname of Colorado.

Treasure State, the
The official nickname of Montana.

Tree Planter's State, the

A nickname of Nebraska.

Tribeca

A relatively new section at the West Side of New York City, an acronym from "the *triangle below Canal Street."* It is one of several areas reclaimed for residential use by the renovation of dilapidated commercial loft buildings. (See also **NoHo, SoHo.**) Most of its residents are energetic younger people, particularly writers and artists.

Tri-Cities

A collective name applied to the three cities of Florence, Sheffield, and Tuscumbia, located in Lauderdale and Colbert counties in extreme northwest Alabama. Since the later incorporation of Muscle Shoals into this area, the term *Quad Cities* is now often used.

Trimountain City

A nickname of Boston, Massachusetts, so called because it was founded (1630) on three hills: Fort's Hill on the east, Copp's on the north, and Beacon on the west.

Triple-headed Monster

A disparaging name for the Constitution of the United States, used by those states that opposed its ratification. It refers to the three branches of government: the legislative, judicial, and executive.

Trossachs, the

An area of great natural beauty to the north of Glasgow, in western Scotland. Its lochs and wooded valleys inspired the pen of Sir Walter Scott, and his loving descriptions in *Lady of the Lake* and *Rob Roy* made it a tourist attraction in the early 19th century—a status it has retained ever since.

Trucial States, the

A collective name formerly used for seven emirates on the Arabian coast of the Persian Gulf in the days when together they formed a British protectorate. Also known as Trucial Oman or the Trucial Coast, they became fully independent in 1971, since when they have been called the United Arab Emirates; they are Abu Dhabi, Dubai, Sharjah, Ajman, Umm al Quaiwain, Ras el Khaimah, and Fujairah. In former times piracy and sea warfare were rife in this part of the Gulf (the area used to be known as the *Pirate Coast*), but in 1835 the truculent local sheikhs, at the inducement of the British government, signed a truce promising to end their maritime hostilities; the name Trucial States derived from this truce.

Tunbridge Wells

A town in Kent, southeast England, the full name of which is Royal Tunbridge Wells. It is one of only two towns in England (the other is Royal Leamington Spa) allowed to use this prefix, granted in honor of visits by Queen Victoria. It is a staid middle-class residential town, populated in the public imgination by reactionaries and stuffed shirts; anyone composing a parody of an angry letter to the newspapers complaining about the moral degeneracy of modern times will standardly sign it "Disgusted, Tunbridge Wells."

Turnabout, the

A former nickname of *The Times* [London], in allusion to the changes toward the political attitudes it espoused; it was not consistently either Whig or Tory. See also **Thunderer.**

Turpentine State, the

A nickname of North Carolina.

Tussaud's Waxworks Museum, Madame

An attraction housed in a building in Marylebone Road, London, that consists mainly of waxen figures, both historical and contemporary, executed with amazing skill. Most are merely on exhibition, but some are placed in appropriate and vividly reconstructed historical settings. The figures are so life-like that visitors are sometimes deceived into believing that one of the guards, purposely remaining immobile for some minutes, is one of the exhibits. Madame Tussaud was a Frenchwoman who, it is said, created waxen images as memento mori of royalty from death masks obtained after they had visited the guillotine during the French Revolution. She took her collection to London, where she established the museum; today, greatly expanded, it proves one of the most interesting and popular drawing-cards in London, for residents and tourists alike.

"21" Club

Formally, "Jack and Charlie's 21 Club," this hangout of the rich and famous on 52nd Street, west of Fifth Avenue, started as a speakeasy, during Prohibition. With Repeal, it opened its doors legitimately and has, ever since, been a more or less exclusive luncheon and dining place for executives of the publishing and entertainment worlds where the occasional member of "high society" can still be seen. As in the cast of that erstwhile cafe society mecca, the Stork Club, the comings and goings of those who came and went in "stretch" limousines, whose chauffeurs chatted outside the wrought-iron railings, were reported by the gossip columnists of the New York newspapers and syndicated press services. Its brownstone staircase, with wrought-iron banister, is decorated with "jockey hitching-post" figures which are painted in the stable colors of the 21 Club's patrons.

Twickenham

A part of Richmond-upon-Thames, in greater London. It is associated with rugby football, and the headquarters of the English Rugby Football Union are situated there.

Twin Sisters, the

A reference to North and South Dakota.

twopenny tube

A former nickname of Central London Railway (underground).

Tyburnia

A nickname given in the 19th century to a residential area in the West End of London, to the north of Hyde Park. The gallows humor of its derivation may account for its going out of use: until 1783, Tyburn (where Marble Arch now stands) was the site of public executions in London.

Tyneside

A name given to the industrialized conurbation that sprawls on both sides of the Tyne River, in the Northeast of England, from South Shields and Tynemouth on the coast inland to Newcastle-upon-Tyne. Geographically it is the focus of the metropolitan county of Tyne and Wear; culturally it is the heart of Geordieland. Its trade is predominantly shipbuilding.

Uncle Sam

A cartoon figure recognized in 1961 by Congress as the national symbol of the United States, but in use since the 1830s, when Seba Smith, a humorous political essayist, was cartooned as Uncle Sam, and Dan Rice, a clown during the 1800s, popularized the costume decorated with stars and stripes. The name was first used as an unfriendly nickname for the United States government during the War of 1812, and first appeared in print in a newspaper in Troy, New York, in 1813; by 1816 it had become so popular that a book was written about *The Adventures of Uncle Sam*. It is thought to have derived from the initials *U.S.* stamped on barrels of salt meat by Samuel Wilson, an army meat inspector and provisioner. See also **Brother Jonathan.**

Uncle Sam's Crib

A nickname of the U. S. Treasury.

Uncle Sam's Pocket Handkerchief

A nickname of Delaware, so called because of its size.

underground railroad

The nickname for any secret system used to help people escape to safe territory. It originated during the Civil War in the U. S. when abolitionists set up "stations, junctions," and "conductors" to help fugitive slaves get to the North or Canada. During World War II allied servicemen caught or shot down behind enemy lines were aided by Europeans in this manner, and during the 1980s groups have used the same sort of system to bring those seeking political asylum into the U. S. from Central America, with the name being applied in each case.

Union Jack, the

A nickname for the national flag of the United Kingdom of Great Britain and Ireland, properly used only when the small form, the "jack," is flown, as at the tip of a vessel's bowsprit. The jack is never flown on shore, and the nickname is never used for the large flag. The reference is to the union of the cross of St. George with the diagonal crosses of Saint Andrew and Saint Patrick, patron saints of England, Scotland, and Ireland.

Union Station

One of the last major railroad stations in Chicago, completed in 1925, and today the center of all Amtrak travel into and out of the city. A recent renovation has restored some of the station's former splendor, but it is still only a ghost of its former glamorous self, when movie stars all seemed to make a point of arriving there on Santa Fe's "Super Chief," from Los Angeles, New York Central's "Twentieth-Century Limited" or Pennsylvania's "Broadway Limited," the latter two providing overnight runs between Chicago and New York.

Union Stockyards

A former complex of slaughterhouses and meatpackers in Chicago, now the site, on the city's South Side, of a range of light industries. Once the heart of the nation's meatpacking industry, the Union Stockyards were opened in 1865 and thrived for nearly 100 years before being made obsolete by the rise of a system of regional slaughterhouses. In its heyday, the odoriferous, often unsanitary complex, the employees of which were cruelly exploited, was the target of reform-minded writers like Upton Sinclair, whose novel, *The Jungle*, aroused public indignation and led to improved conditions.

United Kingdom, the

In full, the United Kingdom of Great Britain and Northern Ireland, the official name of the British state since 1922, when the rest of Ireland became independent. The term had been used long before that, however: in the 18th century it referred to the union of Scotland with England and Wales in 1707; and in 1801 its scope was enlarged to include Ireland, which in that year entered into the union. See also **Britain, England**.

University City

A nickname of Cambridge, Massachusetts.

Unter den Linden

A street in East Berlin. In the days when a united Berlin was the capital of all Germany, this was its main social artery, leading from the Tiergarten to the Royal Palace and lined with department stores, luxurious hotels, foreign embassies—and, of course, the lime trees that gave it its name.

Upper East Side, the

Generally, the area in New York City bounded by Fifth Avenue on the west, the East River on the east, and 59th and 96th streets on the south and north. It is, especially at its eastern and western extremes, characterized by luxurious town houses and expensive cooperative apartments and by the people who can afford such accommodation. See also **East Side, Lower East Side.**

uptown

In some cities of the United States, the residential areas and neighborhoods, away from the downtown, commercial areas. See also **downtown.**

U. S. S. R., the

The Union of Soviet Socialist Republics. See **Soviet Union.**.

V & A

The colloquial name for the Victoria and Albert, a museum in South Kensington in West London which houses Britain's national collection of the applied and decorative arts.

Valentine State, the

A nickname of Arizona, so called in reference to 14 February 1912, the date of its entry into the Union.

Valley of the Sun, the

A nickname of metropolitan Phoenix, Arizona.

Valleys, the

In South Wales a series of parallel rivers drain southward from the foothills of the Brecon Beacons toward the Bristol Channel. On their way the Taff, the Rhymney, the Ebbw, and others flow through slate-gray hills dotted with small mining villages. These are the Valleys, which are central to the modern mythology of Wales. In the 19th and early 20th centuries they were at the heart of Britain's industrial might, pouring out coal from the mines and steel from the foundries, and they were cradles of Methodism and Radicalism. Today, with the steelworks closed and the mines in decline, their former glories have passed, but names like Merthry Tydfil, Ebbw Vale, Rhondda, Treorchy, and Tredegar still retain their powerful associations.

Van Diemen's Land

The original name of Tasmania, an island off the southeast corner of Australia. It was bestowed by the island's Dutch discoverer Abel Tasman in 1642 in honor of his patron. It became a British settlement in 1803, and many of Britain's less desirable criminals were transported there; as a result, when this form of punishment was abolished in the mid 19th century, its name was changed to *Tasmania*, since its old name had such unfortunate associations.

Vauxhall

An area (pronounced "voxhall") of south central London, on the south bank of the Thames opposite Westminster. It is a largely working-class residential district, but is famous for the Vauxhall Gardens, a public park and pleasure ground that flourished there from 1661 to 1859.

Venice of the East

An epithet for Bangkok, Thailand.

Venice of the North

A title often conferred on Amsterdam, in the Netherlands, because of its extensive system of canals and 290 bridges, but also claimed by Stockholm, Sweden, another watery city.

Venice of the West

An epithet for Glasgow.

Vichy

A town in central France associated with water and collaboration. A place of natural alkaline springs, its vogue as a spa was started in 1861 by Napoleon III, who was much addicted to taking the waters; since then Vichy has spread around the world in bottled form. Less congenial are the memories evoked by the French government set up there under Marshal Henri Pétain in 1940 as a virtual puppet of the German occupiers; the words *Vichy France* leave an unpleasant taste in the mouths of the French who lived through those less than glorious years in their nation's history.

Victoria

An area in southwest central London, to the north of Pimlico and the east of Belgravia. It takes its name from the large railroad terminus there that serves the south of England and boat trains to the Continent; it was opened in 1860 and named in honor of Queen Victoria.

Ville, the

See **Pentonville.**

Vinland

The name given to the coastal region of eastern North America visited by Leif Ericson and other Vikings around the year 1000. It was brought to wider fame in 1957 with the discovery of the so-called Vinland Map, an apparently early-15th-century representation of the area the validity of which is in doubt.

Violet-crowned City, the

A nickname for Athens, Greece, so referred to by the poet Pindar and the playwright Aristophanes because of its association with the Muses, the Graces, and the goddess Aphrodite.

Volunteer State, the

The official nickname of Tennessee, so called in reference to the 30,000 men who volunteered at one time (1847) to fight in the Mexican War.

Wailing Wall, the

A length of high stone wall in Jerusalem which is said to have been part of the ancient temple of Herod, reputedly on the site of, and containing some of the stones of the original temple of Solomon. It is greatly venerated in Judaism and has become a shrine and center of pilgrimage. In former times Jews would gather there to lament the diaspora (hence its name), but since Jerusalem was fully absorbed into Israel in 1967 such lamentation has not been so appropriate, and one is now officially encouraged to refer to the wall as the Western Wall.

Walden Pond

A pond at Concord, Massachusetts, made famous through the philosophical writings of Henry David Thoreau (1817–62), especially *Walden, or Life in the Woods* (1854). Although Thoreau lived at Walden Pond for only about two years, its associations remain fixed in the minds of modern readers with peace, solitude, and the love of nature.

Wall Street

A short, narrow street in downtown Manhattan. It is the site of the New York Stock Exchange; at its north end stands the United States Subtreasury Building. The surrounding multistory office buildings are occupied largely by brokers' and bankers' offices. The financial center of the United States and for much of the rest of the world—notwithstanding similar centers in London and elsewhere—*Wall Street* has become the worldwide metaphor for finance and big business.

Wardour Street

A street in Soho, in the West End of London, which has come to be synonymous with the British movie industry from the large number of film companies that have had their offices there over the years. In the 19th century, however, it abounded in fake antique furniture shops, and in 1888 the designer and poet William Morris coined the term "Wardour Street English" for the sort of pseudo-medieval poetic diction that was enjoying a certain vogue among versifiers at that time.

Warren Street

A street west of Tottenham Court Road, near Euston Road, in the West End of London, known for its dealers in second-hand cars.

Wash, the

A large shallow rectangular inlet of the North Sea on the east coast of England, at the point where the bulge of East Anglia meets the coast of Lincolnshire. The Fenland rivers Nene, Great Ouse, and Welland drain into it. Originally, and up until the 18th century, the Wash was known as *the Washes*; this referred to sandbars which were repeatedly washed by the ebbing and flowing tide, and at low tide formed paths that could be used to ford the inlet.

Waterloo

An area in central London, on the southern bank of the Thames just to the rear of the South Bank arts complex. The name celebrates the Duke of Wellington's victory over Napoleon at Waterloo, Belgium, in 1815, and was originally used for Waterloo Bridge; this was opened in 1817, replacing the old Strand Bridge. It was then adopted for the new railroad terminus opened at the southern end of the bridge in 1848, and since has come to be used for the surrounding district. As the capital's main train station serving the southern and southwestern suburbs and Surrey, Waterloo is perhaps more closely associated than any other with the commuter treadmill. See also **Bakerloo**.

Water Tower

A distinctive Chicago landmark, on the city's Near North Side, along the Magnificent Mile. Along with its nearby pumping station, the gothic, castle-like tower survived the Great Chicago Fire of 1871, the only two structures in the area to do so. Today the tower serves as a public information center, and the pumping station houses a free, multimedia promotional view of the city.

Water Wonderland, the

A nickname of Michigan.

Watford

A town in Hertfordshire, just to the northwest of London. As a place it is unremarkable, although it cannot be said quite to rival Slough as the epitome of dull suburbia. It is of considerable geographical importance in modern British folklore, however, for it is often viewed by Southerners as marking the northern limit of civilized life; anywhere "north of Watford" being deemed provincial and boorish. Those who take this view are unlikely to make any clear distinction between the **Midlands** (*q.v.*) and the actual **North** (*q.v.*).

Watts

A residential area in south-central Los Angeles known especially for the riots that occurred there in a six-day period in August 1965. Occupying an area of about 2½ square miles, Watts was not considered a particularly depressed area or potential trouble spot until the riots, which started with a minor incident but which accelerated rapidly and resulted in 34 deaths and 1032 injuries, as well as great property damage. Watts gained instant national recognition, and its name is invoked whenever troubles arise in black ghettos, not just in Los Angeles but in the United States generally.

Weald, the

A band of hilly sandstone country across the center of Sussex and Kent in southeastern England, separating the chalky North and South Downs. The word *weald*, cognate with German *Wald*, meant 'forest' in Anglo-Saxon times, and today sufficient wooded areas survive to give one an idea of the former extent of the woodlands here. In the Middle Ages an iron-smelting and forging industry throve in the Weald, and in the days of wooden ships much of the timber to build the British navy came from Wealden oaks.

Webfoot State, the

A nickname of Oregon, so called in reference to its wet winter climate.

Weimar

A city in the southwestern part of (modern East) Germany. In the late 18th and early 19th centuries, during the reign of the Grand Duke Charles Augustus, it was perhaps Germany's leading cultural center. Goethe, Germany's chief literary and intellectual lion, held court there, and it was also home to Schiller, Herder, and Wieland. In 1919, the constitution under which Germany was to be governed after World War I was drawn up and adopted there, and the political system that held sway until Hitler took over in 1933 was known as the *Weimar Republic*.

Wembley Stadium

A sports arena west of London, in the borough of Brent; it is the British national soccer stadium, accommodating more than 80,000 spectators.

Wessex

A region in the southern part of England that has varied widely in size, status, and character over the centuries. Its origins go back to the late 5th century, when the West Saxons settled and founded their kingdom in the upper Thames Valley. It gradually extended its territory to the south and west, and in the 9th century, under Alfred the Great, it was the dominant English kingdom. It disappeared with the Norman Conquest, but its name was revived in the late 19th century by the English novelist Thomas Hardy for the area in which many of his stories were set; it refers principally to Dorset, but also includes parts of the surrounding counties of Hampshire and Wiltshire. To such an extent has the name caught on that it has returned to official use for certain administrative purposes: the local area of the National Health Service, for example, is known as the *Wessex Region*.

West, the

1. The world divides itself into East and West along a wavering boundary. Where it is drawn is a purely relative matter. In geographical terms the Western Hemisphere is North and South America, and the Eastern Hemisphere takes all the rest; but the situation is not so straightforward. In ancient and medieval times, *the West* referred to the Western Roman, or later the Holy Roman Empire, as contrasted with the Eastern, or Byzantine Empire and areas further east. This sowed the seeds of our modern view of the West, which from a cultural point of view may be taken as anywhere north of the Mediterranean and west of the Black Sea—in other words, all of Europe (with the exception of the eastern parts of European Russia) and North America. To the south is Africa, which does not enter the East/West equation, but, like the East, lies outside the Christian tradition that is the historical and cultural hallmark of the West. However, the geographical logic of this has been destroyed by the ideological wrangling of the late 20th century. Now, *the East* or Eastern bloc are those nations, including much of Europe, under Soviet influence, while *the West* includes territories of the Eastern Hemisphere such as Japan and Australia, which share the capitalist ethos of much of Europe and North America.

2. In Britain, *the West* is not as established a concept as, say, the **North** (*q.v.*). When it is used, usually in such contexts as "Wales and the West," it generally includes not just the **West Country** (*q.v.*), but also rather more northerly western counties such as Herefordshire, Worcestershire, and Shropshire. As far as any official distinction is made, for example on road signs, "the West" refers to the area focused on Bristol, including particularly Avon and Gloucestershire, as contrasted with the Southwest.

3. In the United States, the part of the country called *the West* depends on the point of view of the individual and where he resides. Saul Steinberg, a well-known artist, once produced a cover illustration (for *The New Yorker* magazine) that depicted a "New Yorker's view of the United States," in which the world stopped, essentially, at the Hudson River, with the rest of the country shown as wasteland except for a small collection of buildings in the middle distance (Chicago) and some glitter on the west coast (Hollywood), accurately reflecting the view of chauvinistic residents of New York City, especially of Manhattan. More generally, though, people in America consider *the West* as including the states west of the Missouri River as far as Kansas City (North and South Dakota and Nebraska), then southward to include Kansas, Oklahoma, and Texas. See also **Deep South, East, Far West, Midwest, Northwest, Pacific Northwest, South, 1.**

West Bank, the

The name given to the territory to the west of the Jordan River and the Dead Sea which until 1967 belonged to Jordan, but in that year was annexed by Israel.

West Country, the

The southwestern part of England, which includes the counties of Cornwall, Devon, Somerset, Avon, Gloucestershire, and the western parts of Dorset and Wiltshire. It covers territory otherwise known as the West and the Southwest, but the term *West Country* is used particularly if one wishes to stress the rural aspects of the area: it is redolent of the gentle rolling hills and sheltered valleys of Devon and Somerset, of ruddy countrymen and -women, with their characteristic West Country burr, and of the agricultural products of the region: West Country cider, cheeses, butter, and cream.

West End, the

The western part of central London, north of the Thames. It is almost more of a concept than a district that can be accurately delimited on a map. If the City stands for the earnest accumulation of money and the East End is London's working-class area, the West End is the place to come for a good time—or to live, if one can afford it. The heart of the West End, a rectangle bounded by Oxford Street, Regent Street, the Strand, and Kingsway, is London's theaterland; Londoners going "up West" for a show or a meal will make for this area. Its northwest corner contains the more risqué entertainments of **Soho** (*q.v.*). Beyond this spreads the commercial quarter of the West End, from the large department stores of **Oxford Street** (*q.v.*) and Regent Street to, further south, the more exclusive retail establishments and posh hotels of **Mayfair** (*q.v.*), **Piccadilly** (*q.v.*), and **St. James's** (*q.v.*). And finally come the fashionable residential areas at the western extremity of the West End: **Belgravia** (*q.v.*).

Western Desert, the

A portion of the Libyan desert that lies in western and central Egypt. It is associated particularly with the extensive fighting there between the Allies and the Axis powers in World War II. Its name contrasts it with the Eastern Desert, which lies between the Nile River and the Red Sea. It should not be confused with the Western Sahara, which is in southern Morocco and northwest Mauretania.

Western Isles, the

A name given to the Hebrides, a collection of over 500 islands off the west coast of Scotland. They fall into two groups. Those nearer the mainland, including Skye, Jura, and Islay, are the Inner Hebrides. Further west, beyond a channel known as the Minch, are the Outer Hebrides, including Harris and Lewis, North and South Uist, and Benbecula. The latter were formally reconstituted in 1975 into a region of Scotland, officially known as the *Western Isles*.

Western Ocean, the

A name used in former times for the Atlantic Ocean, reflecting a Eurocentric geography in which the ocean was indeed to the west of the then known civilized world.

West Midlands, the

A metropolitan county in the middle of England, created in 1974. It is centered on and largely made up of Birmingham, England's second largest city, but also includes the Black Country to the northwest and Coventry to the southeast. It is one of the great industrial heartlands of England, specializing particularly in engineering and the manufacture of motor vehicles. Less specifically, the term *West Midlands* is also used to refer to the western part of the Midlands, including also Shropshire, Herefordshire, Worcestershire, Warwickshire, and western Staffordshire, but because of possible confusion with the new county name this is not officially encouraged. See also **Midlands.**

Westminster

An area of central London immediately to the west of the City of London. In 1900 it was made a city in its own right, and in 1965 large areas of St. Marylebone and Paddington in the north and west were joined on to it to make the new borough of the City of Westminster. However, its nucleus, and the part which most people think of as Westminster, remains the area to the west and south of St. James's Park, centered on Parliament Square, Westminster Abbey, and the Palace of Westminster. The Palace contains the House of Commons and the House of Lords, and over the years Westminster has become synonymous with the British parliament.

Westmorland

In the Northwest of England, a former county between Cumberland to the north and Lancashire to the south. In the local government reorganization of 1974 it became part of Cumbria. The name survives in the town of *Appleby-in-Westmorland*.

West Point

A town in New York on the bluffs overlooking the Hudson River about fifty miles north of New York City. It is the site of the U. S. Military Academy, established by Congress in 1802.

West Point of the Air, the

A nickname of San Antonio, Texas, so called because Randolph Field is there and a number of large military airfields are nearby.

West Side

1. To New Yorkers, the West Side represents something of a comedown when considered in contrast to the East Side. In fact, although the rents are lower on the West Side and the cooperative apartments, with some exceptions, are less expensive than those on the East Side, much of the area, especially along Central Park West (between 59th and 90th streets) and Riverside Drive (from 72nd Street northward), is far more attractive than most of the East Side: the views of Central Park from Central Park West are comparable to those from Fifth Avenue, and the extended vistas of the Hudson River from the apartments along Riverside Drive are in every way more scenic than those of the East River, with its views of the factory buildings in Queens. Yet, despite the presence of well-known luxury apartments houses, like the Century, Majestic, and **Dakota** (*q.v.*) on Central Park West and the Chatsworth at 72nd Street west of Riverside Drive, of Lincoln Center for the Performing Arts, at Lincoln Square (65th Street and Broadway), and of the fine old private brownstone and limestone private houses along the side streets, the West Side seems unable to rid itself of the stigma of being somewhat déclassé. Its population is more homogeneous than that of the East Side, with more younger people able to afford to live there, but, as in all areas in New York City, there are some neighborhoods it is wiser to avoid for the sake of safety, especially at night. Above 90th Street, along Central Park West, the section begins to deteriorate slightly, then markedly beyond the end of Central Park, at Cathedral Parkway (110th Street). But to the west, along Morningside Drive, Amsterdam Avenue, Broadway, and Riverside Drive, this narrow corridor improves till one goes north of Columbia University, which owns much of the property in its neighborhood and makes a valiant effort to keep up its standards. There are some fine old apartment houses along Riverside Drive and Claremont Avenue (which extends from 116th to 124th streets, between Riverside Drive and Broadway), and local landmarks in the neighborhood are **Grant's Tomb** (*q.v.*), International House (occupied by foreign students), and Riverside Church. This section and points north are commonly referred to as the "Upper West Side," especially north of 135th Street to Washington Heights, the name for the area between about 155th (site of the Museum of the American Indian) and 168th streets (site of the Columbia Presbyterian Medical Center, usually called just "The Medical Center"). From 155th Street north, to the tip of Manhattan, the area is dominated by the George Washington Bridge, at 178th Street, a double-decker suspension bridge, opened in the mid 1930s, that spans the Hudson River to New Jersey. When the bridge was first opened, there was a restaurant atop its east tower, reached by an elevator, and for many years, north of the bridge on the New Jersey side, was a swanky nightclub, Bill Marden's (later Bill Miller's) Riviera. North of the bridge, in Manhattan, is the Fort Tryon section, named for Fort Tryon Park, which is the site of the Cloisters, a museum, officially part of the Metropolitan Museum of Art (at 83rd Street and Fifth Avenue), that houses one of the finest collections of medieval art in the world. It was endowed by John D. Rockefeller, Jr., who went so far as to buy all the land along the Palisades on the opposite New Jersey shore just to preserve the view. At the foot of the east tower of the bridge stands a small lighthouse, once a navigational beacon to warn ships of the projecting rocky prominence there. No longer needed and long disused, it was to be demolished, but, owing to public outcry, it has survived because it commemorates a popular children's story, "The Little Red Lighthouse." See also **Broadway, East Side.**

2. A vast area of Chicago, made up of many culturally distinct neighborhoods, with large industrial areas and including Columbus, Douglas, Garfield, Humboldt, and Marquette Parks. For more than 100 years, various poor or middle-class West Side neighborhoods have served as the new home for successive waves of Poles, Germans, Irish, Italians, Greeks, Scandinavians, Czechs, Lithuanians, Ukrainians, blacks, and Latinos, who occasionally blended in but more often retained their ethnic (and a measure of linguistic) independence. Milwaukee Avenue, running diagonally from the city's downtown Loop area to well beyond the northwestern city limits, is one of the West Side's most important, and most colorful thoroughfares, with many small shops, offices, and restaurants; it constitutes, for much of its length, a vital nexus for the city's large Polish and other Eastern European immigrant communities. On the Near Northwest Side are the Wicker Park and Noble Square neighborhoods, originally settled by Germans, Poles, and other Europeans, and now predominantly Puerto Rican. Bordering the Loop on the west and southwest is the Near, or Lower West Side, including historic **Haymarket Square** (*q.v.*) and, along a short stretch of Halsted Street, the Greek Town enclave, which once served as home for Greek immigrants, many of whom have since moved to New Greek Town, on the city's Northwest Side. Nearby, to the south, are **Hull House** (*q.v.*) and the adjoining Taylor Street area, heart of one of the oldest Italian settlements (much of which was recently razed to make room for the Chicago Circle campus of the University of Illinois. Also in this vicinity is the site of **Mrs. O'Leary's barn** (*q.v.*) where the Great Chicago Fire is believed to have started. Further south are the colorful **Maxwell Street** (*q.v.*) market area and the **Pilsen** (*q.v.*) neighborhood. Among Southwest Side features are Marquette Park; the upscale Beverly Hills-Morgan Park area; and Midway Airport. The hard-core West Side, reaching west some four miles from the Loop and including the gang-plagued

Humboldt Park area, is a gritty mixture of industrial plants and retail outlets, interspersed with various residential subsections. See also **O'Hare International Airport.**

Wheat State, the
A nickname of Minnesota.

Where Mexico Meets Uncle Sam
A nickname of Brownsville, Texas, so called because it is situated on the border between the two countries.

Whitechapel
A district of the **East End** (*q.v.*) of London, immediately to the east of the Tower of London. In the 19th century it had a bad name as an area of slums to be avoided. The more sinister aspects of its reputation were fueled by the lurid and notorious "Whitechapel murders" of 1888, in which Jack the Ripper killed and mutilated five local prostitutes. Until well into the 20th century it was to a considerable extent a Jewish quarter, many having settled there after fleeing persecution in Russia in the 1880s. In the latter part of the 20th century they have been largely replaced by immigrants from the Indian subcontinent.

White City
1. The lakefront city-within-a-city, on the South Side of Chicago, that served as the site of the World's Columbian Exposition of 1893, held to celebrate the 400th anniversary of Christopher Columbus' discovery of the Americas. Among the attractions were the first Ferris wheel—the 260-foot tall, steel-and-iron invention of George Washington Gale Ferris—and a cluster of classical palaces, each containing exhibits denoting man's progress in industry and art. Although most of White City is mere memory now, some prized legacies remain, namely the Palace of Fine Arts (now the **Museum of Science and Industry** (*q.v.*)), Jackson Park and the University of Chicago's Midway Plaisance.
2. An epithet for Helsinki. [A translation of *Den vita staden.*]

White Cliffs, the
The rolling hills of the North Downs of Kent are cut off abruptly by the English Channel. At the point where they meet, ranks of high chalk cliffs stretch out to both sides of Dover, a harbor town at the southeast tip of England. Their distant shimmer of white ascending the horizon is the first glimpse many a traveler from the Continent gets of England, and the "White Cliffs of Dover" have become a potent symbol of hoped-for homecoming for English people abroad.

Whitefriars

Another name for the **Alsatia** (*q.v.*) area of London in medieval and early modern times, a district near the Thames inhabited by criminals and the like. It got its name from the Carmelite monastery on Fleet Street, founded in 1241; Carmelites were known as white friars, from the color of their habits.

Whitehall

A street in Westminster, in central London, linking Parliament Square with Trafalgar Square. As well as the Horse Guards, with its mounted troopers of the Household Cavalry outside, and the Banqueting Hall—virtually all that remain of Henry VIII's royal palace of Whitehall—it contains numerous government buildings, including the Treasury, the Foreign Office, and the Ministry of Defence. Downing Street leads off it, on the right-hand side going south. Its name has become synonymous with the British government, particularly the executive side of government—ministers and civil servants—as contrasted with the legislators who inhabit Westminster.

white man's burden

An epithet for Britain's responsibility for her empire, probably coined in the late 19th century.

White Man's Grave, the

A nickname for West Africa in the days of European colonial expansion. The tropical forests of Nigeria and the Guinea coast harbor diseases and noxious insects to which European settlers frequently fell victim.

White Mountain State, the

A nickname of New Hampshire.

White Otter Castle

A large edifice with a four-story tower, built single-handedly of logs by Jimmy McOuat in 1914. Situated on remote White Otter Lake, in Canada, it is a symbol of pioneer days on the northwestern Ontario frontier.

Wickedest City on Earth, the

An 1870s nickname of Chicago.

Wigan

A town near Manchester, England. Situated in a coal-mining area, Wigan is associated in the minds of the British with the ordinary man-in-the-street, a typically unthinking person representative of the unthinking masses. Music-hall comedians are wont to refer to performances at "Wigan Pier," and that apocryphal place is retained in the title of a book, *The Road to Wigan Pier*, by George Orwell.

Wilderness City

A nickname of the District of Columbia, attributed to Mrs. John Adams who lived there from 1797–1801, when it was still sparsely settled and surrounded by woods.

Wild West, the

The western frontier of the United States before the areas and territories gained statehood. It is an indefinite concept that shifted with the westward expansion during the last two thirds of the nineteenth century and is associated with the legends and traditions of pioneers, outlaws, cowboys, gunslingers, dancehall queens, gambling casinos, and other fixtures of the "untamed" frontier, chiefly as depicted in novels, films, and other fictional media.

Wilhelmstrasse, the

A street in central Berlin in which many German government offices were situated until the end of World War II. The most notable and formidable of these was the Foreign Ministry, and it eventually took unofficial possession of the street's name, in much the same way as the French Foreign Ministry has come to be known as the **Quai d'Orsay** (*q.v.*).

Wimbledon

A middle-class residential suburb to the southwest of London that has become famous around the world for the lawn tennis championships held there every summer at the All-England Club.

Wimpole Street

A road in the West End of London, just to the west of Harley Street. Its fame rests on the mid-19th-century occupants of No. 50, the Barrett family. A daughter of the house, Elizabeth, had fallen in love with the famous poet Robert Browning, but her tyrannical father had forbidden the match; their subsequent elopement is perhaps the most celebrated in English literary history.

Windmill Theatre, the

A theater in Great Windmill Street, near Piccadilly Circus, in London, built as a movie theater in 1910, and later converted into a small—326-seat—theater in 1931. During the 1930s it became famous for burlesque, particularly for the Windmill Girls who posed in the nude (entirely legal provided that they did not move), and for comedians like Harry Secombe and Tony Hancock, who got their starts there. During World War II, and, especially, the Blitz, the *Windmill* gained fame for continuing its shows through everything, and Londoners felt affection for it because it stuck to its motto, "We Never Close." From 1964 till 1981, it changed roles several times, first to become a motion picture theater, then again as a theater showing risqué comedy and, later, a nude review. It finally did close and is now a restaurant.

Windscale

A nuclear reprocessing plant on the coast of Cumbria in the Northwest of England which since 1952 has been producing plutonium. Both for its role in the manufacture of nuclear weapons, and because it was the first atomic plant in Britain to suffer an accidental leak, its name has become powerfully linked with the negative aspects of nuclear energy. In 1981 its owners, British Nuclear Fuels, changed its name to Sellafield, after two nearby hamlets, High and Low Sellafield. But if they thought this move would magically transform the plant's public image, they were to be disappointed; it continues to be widely known, particularly by its detractors, by its old name.

Windy City

A famous nickname for Chicago, now taken as literal (though several other large cities are windier), but originally referring to its blustering self-confidence. Credit for the name is generally given to *New York Sun* newspaper editor Charles A. Dana, who used it to characterize Chicago as an upstart for presuming to contend with New York and other cities for the honor of hosting the World's Columbian Exposition of 1893. In an editorial designed to nurture the egos of his readers, Dana advised them to ignore the "nonsensical claims of that windy city. Its people could not hold a world's fair even if they won it." Windy or not, Chicago managed to convince Congress that it was the place for the fair, and held it successfully.

Wirral, the

A large oblong peninsula that separates the estuaries of the rivers Mersey and Dee in northwestern England. Its northeastern shore, across the river from Liverpool, is largely given over to the port and shipbuilding facilities of places like Birkenhead and Ellesmere Port, but the sandy beaches have encouraged some vacation resorts to spring up, too, such as New Brighton.

Wolds, the

A line of rolling chalk hills in Humberside (formerly Yorkshire), northern England, which in places rise to 800 feet above sea level. Stone Age and Bronze Age burial mounds are a characteristic feature of the area. The hills continue further south, where they are known as the *Lincolnshire Wolds*, but the name *Wolds* on its own is generally taken as referring to the more northerly section. The word *wold* meant 'forest' in Anglo-Saxon times (the *Weald* comes from it), but interestingly, as Britain's forests began to be cut down in medieval times, particularly in upland areas, it gradually came to mean 'open hilly ground.' Today it only survives in proper names, such as *Cotswolds*, and the *Wolds*.

Wolverine State, the
The official nickname of Michigan.

Wonder State, the
A nickname of Arkansas.

woolsack, the
A nickname, also used metonymically, for the seat of the Lord Chancellor when presiding over the House of Lords, a reference to the original seat in the 1300s during the reign of Edward III being made of four bound sacks of wool which symbolized its importance in the English economy.

Woolwich
A town on the south side of the Thames, east of Greenwich and London, known chiefly as the site of a major arsenal where, in the 19th century, Congreve rockets and other arms were manufactured. At its shipyards, where the *Nelson* was launched, there were extensive facilities including a ropewalk, an anchor forge, etc. Woolwich is also known as a terminus for a Thames ferry.

Workshop of the Nation, the
A nickname of New Jersey.

World's Egg Basket, the
A nickname of Petaluma, California.

World's Workshop, the
A nickname of Pittsburgh, Pennsylvania.

Wormwood Scrubs
A large open space in west London, to the north of Shepherd's Bush. Its fame rests on the prison of the same name, situated at its southwestern corner, which is often known familiarly as *the Scrubs*.

Wrigleyville
A Near North Side neighborhood in Chicago, immediately surrounding Wrigley Field, home of the Chicago Cubs baseball team, the only major-league park without lights for night games. The planned installation of lights at Wrigley Field by the Cubs' parent Tribune Company has spurred controversy in the area, with influential groups like C.U.B.S. (Citizens United for Baseball in Sunshine) contesting the issue with those who contend that lights are the only way to keep the team from seeking a new home elsewhere.

Yankee Land of the South, the
A nickname of Georgia.

Yankee State, the

A nickname of Ohio, so called because it was settled primarily by people from New England.

Yard, the

A common abbreviation of Scotland Yard, the London Police or its head-quarters. It is used particularly in newspapers: "Yard called in to help local force," a headline might read. In the days of heroic detectives, both real and fictional, particularly successful sleuths were often granted the epithet "of the Yard": "Fabian of the Yard," for example, had a vogue in crime fiction for a while. See also **Scotland Yard**.

Yellowhammer State, the

A nickname of Alabama, so called because of the yellowish tinge of the home-dyed gray uniforms worn by the Confederate soldiers.

yellow peril, the

An old name, formerly used by those who feared the domination or destruction of western civilization by Asiatics, owing to their great numbers.

Yerevan

The capital of the Armenian Soviet Socialist Republic. Its radio station is the butt of jokes behind the Iron Curtain, which take the form of Queries and Answers. For example:

Q: Comrades, the other day I was walking in a
forest and saw that the entire ground was covered
with ants. How do you explain this?
A: Comrade, under the leadership of the
Party, Soviet industry has achieved numerous
momentous successes; however, prophylactics and
contraceptive pills for ants are not scheduled for
development till the next Five-Year Plan.

Ypres

A Flemish town in western Belgium, near the French border. It has been trampled in the mud and blood of several military campaigns down the centuries, and in World War I three battles were fought over it at terrible cost. Its name was all too familiar to Allied soldiers, but the English-speaking ones could never quite manage its pronunciation, and it became known to that generation as "Wipers."

Zenith City of the Unsalted Seas

A nickname of Duluth, Minnesota, so called because of its location on the Great Lakes.

Zululand

An area on the east coast of South Africa that is the homeland of the Zulu people. At just over 10,000 square miles, it is much reduced from the huge territory, covering the present-day Transvaal and Natal, which they controlled at the height of their power in the 19th century. It corresponds in area more or less to the official Zulu bantustan, Kwazulu.

Index

Index

A

Alexandra Palace: Ally Pally
Alexandria, Virginia: Pentagon, the
Alexius I: Alexiad, the
Alfred, King: Isle of Athelney, the
Alfred the Great: Wessex
Algeria: Barbary Coast, the; Maghreb;
  North Africa
Algiers: Kasbah, the
Algonquin Hotel: Round Table at the Algon-
  quin
Alhambra, The: Alhambra
Alicante: Costa Blanca
Alice Springs: Ayers Rock; Center, the
Alice, the: Alice Springs
Allegheny Mountains: Appalachian Moun-
  tains
Allegheny River: Golden Triangle, the, 2
All-England Club: Wimbledon
all Lombard Street to a China orange: Lom-
  bard Street
all Lombard Street to an egg shell: Lombard
  Street
Alonzo, Mateo: Christ of the Andes
alpha Tauri: Aldebaran
Alpine, Texas: Roof Garden of Texas
Alps: Bernese Oberland, the
Alps, the: Brenner Pass
Alsace: Alsatia
Alsatia: Whitefriars
Altgeld, John Peter: Haymarket Square;
  North Side
Amazon basin: Amazonia
Amazon River: Amazonia
America: Mauve Decade, the; *Mayflower*
America: America's Cup
American Embassy: Eisenhower Platz; Gros-
  venor Square
American Indian, Museum of: West Side, 1
American Locomotive Company: City That
  Lights and Hauls the World
Americans: Brother Jonathan
American Stock Exchange: Big Board, the
Americas: New World, the
"America's Tech Highway": Route 128
Ames, Ohio: Coonskin Library
Amsterdam: Diamond City; Holland, 1; Ven-
  ice of the North
Amsterdam Avenue: Broadway, 1; West
  Side, 1
Amtrak: Grand Central; Union Station
Amundsen, Roald: Northwest Passage, the
Anatolia: Asia Minor
Andersonville: North Side
Andersonville, Georgia: Hell Upon Earth
Andes Mountains: South American Alps

Angels Camp, California: Frogtown
Anglesey: Llanfairpwllgwyngillgoger-
  ychwyrndroblllantysiliogogogoch
Anglican Church: Lambeth
Anglo-Saxons: Hastings
Angola: Guinea
Angostura bitters: Angostura
Ankara: Angora
Annam: Indochina
Anna of the Five Towns: Five Towns, the
Anne, Queen: Ascot
Anniston, Alabama: City of Churches, the
Antarctica: dinosaur of darkness;
  Gondwanaland; South Pole
Antarctic Ocean: Seven Seas, the
Antibes: French Riviera, the
Antrim: Six Counties, the
Anzac-on-Sea: Peacehaven
Aphrodite: violet-crowned city, the
Apollo: City of the Sun
Apollo 15 moonlanding: Genesis rock
Appalachian Mountains: Appalachia; Blue
  Ridge Mountains, the; Cumberland Gap
Appalachian Plateau: Tidewater Virginia
Appalachian Ridge and Valley Region: Tide-
  water Virginia
Appalachian Trail: Mohawk Trail
Appian Way: Indian-Appian Way
Applied Bacteriology and Research, Centre
  for: Porton Down
Apsley Gate: Rotten Row
Apsley House: Number One, London
Arabia: Horn of Africa, the; Near East, the
Arabia Deserta: Arabia
Arabian peninsula: Empty Quarter, the;
  Gulf, the; Sheba
Arabian Sea: Seven Seas, the
Arab-Israeli war: Gaza Strip, the
Arab states: Middle East, the
Arab World: Middle East, the
Araby: Arabia
Arbuthnot, John: John Bull
Arcadia: Arcadia
Arcady: Arcadia
Arc de Triomphe: Champs-Élysées, the
Archbishop of Canterbury: Lambeth
Archway Road: Archway
Arctic Circle: Far North, the; Land of the
  Midnight Sun, the; Lapland; Siberia
Arctic icecap: Far North, the
Arctic Ocean: Maelstrom, the; North Pole;
  Seven Seas, the
Arden Shakespeare: Arden
Ardmore: Main Line

Argentina: Christ of the Andes; Falkland Is-
lands, the; Patagonia; South American
Alps; Tierra del Fuego
Aristophanes: violet-crowned city, the
Arizona: Apache State; Aztec State; Baby
State; Copper State; Grand Canyon
State; Italy of America; London Bridge;
Sand Hill State; Southwest, the, 1; Sun-
belt; Sunset State (*or* Land); Tower
Bridge; Valentine State; Valley of the
Sun, the
Arizona, USS: Pearl Harbor
Arkansas: Bear State; Bible Belt; Bowie
State; City of Roses; Diamond State;
Guinea Pig State; Hot Water State;
Land of Opportunity; Midwest, the, 1;
South, the, 1; Toothpick State; Wonder
State
Armagh: Six Counties, the
Armenian Soviet Socialist Republic: Yerevan
Armentières: Flanders
Armour, Philip: North Side
Army and Navy Club: Pall Mall
Arnold, Matthew: City of Dreaming Spires;
Rugby
Arnold, Thomas: Rugby
Aroostook County: Garden of Maine
Around the World in Eighty Days: Reform
Club, the
Arrow collars and shirts: Collar City
arsenal: Woolwich
Art Deco: Chrysler Building; Clock at the
Astor, Biltmore
Arthur, King: Glastonbury; Tintagel
artists' quarter: Chelsea 1
Arundel, Rape of: Rapes
ascot: Ascot
Ascot Heath: Ascot
Ashbury Street: Haight-Ashbury
Asia: Anatolia; Arabia; Arctogaea; Asia Mi-
nor; Black Death, the; East, the, 2;
Eurasia; Far East, the; Indochina; Little
Vietnam; Middle East, the; Mongolia;
Persia; Roof of the World, the; Siberia;
Southeast Asia; Soviet Union, the; Sub-
continent, the; Tartary; Third World,
the
Asia Minor: Anatolia
Asner, Ed: Second City
Assyria: Fertile Crescent, the; Mesopotamia
Astor Hotel: Clock at the Astor, Biltmore
Astoria: Queens
Aswan: Abu Simbel
Aswan Dam: Abu Simbel
As You Like It: Arden

Athena: Erechtheum
Athenaeum Club: Pall Mall
Athenaeum, the: Clubland, 1
Athens: Academy, the; Agora, the; Erech-
theum; Orient-Express; violet-crowned
city, the
Athens of the North: New Town, the
Atkinson, Dr.: Camberley
Atkinson, George Henry: Inland Empire, the
Atlanta: Dogwood City; Gate City
Atlantic Avenue: Cobble Hill
Atlantic City: Boardwalk; Gamblers Express
Atlantic Coastal Plain: Delmarva Peninsula;
Tidewater Virginia
Atlantic Inter-Coastal Waterway: Dismal
Swamp, the
Atlantic Ocean: Atlantic States; Atlantis;
Bermuda Triangle, the; Canary Islands;
Delmarva Peninsula; Guinea; Hamp-
tons, the; Middle Passage, the; North
End; Northwest Passage, the; Roost,
the; Sargasso Sea, the; Seven Seas, the;
Tidewater Virginia; Western Ocean,
the
Atomic Age: Staff Field
Atomic Energy Commission: Nevada Prov-
ing Grounds
atomic plant: Windscale
Atomic Weapons Research Establishment:
Aldermaston
Aurangzeb: Golconda
Aussie: Oz
Austin, Mary: Land of Little Rain
Austin, Texas: City of the Violet Crown
Australasia: Notogaea
Australia: Alice Springs; Antipodes, the; Ap-
ple Isle, the; Ashes, the; Australasia;
Ayers Rock; Bananaland; Bondi Beach;
Botany Bay; Center, the; Coat Hanger,
the; East, the, 2; Free-O; Gondwana-
land; Gulf, the; King's Cross, 2; Maida
Vale; Melanesia; North, the, 3; Oceania;
Old Dart, the; Oz; Paddo; Pitt Street;
Smoke, the; Territory, the; Top End,
the; Van Diemen's Land; West, the, 1
Australia II: America's Cup
Austria: Brenner Pass; Mistelbach
Austro-Hungarian empire: Balkans, the
Avalon: Camelot, 1
Aventine: Seven Hills, the
Avenue B: East Village, the
'Avenue of the Americas': 42nd Street
Avon: West Country, the; West, the, 2
Avril, Jane: Moulin Rouge
Aylesbury: Stoke Mandeville

B

Babylon: Fertile Crescent, the; Mesopotamia
Babylonia: Hanging Gardens of Babylon
Back of the Yards: South Side
Baffin, William: Northwest Passage, the
Bahrein: Arabia; Gulf, the
Bailey, the: Old Bailey
Baker, Josephine: Folies Bergère
Baker Street: Bakerloo
"Baker Street irregulars": Baker Street
Baker Street Station: Metroland
Balkan peninsula: Balkans, the
"Balkan problem": Balkans, the
Balkans: Near East, the; Rumelia
Balkis: Sheba
ballet: Covent Garden
Balliol College: Broad, the
Baltic Sea: Baltic States; Jutland; Oder-
    Neisse Line, the; Polish Corridor, the;
    Russia; Sound, the
Baltimore: Fort McHenry; Monumental
    State; Monument City
Baltimore, Lord: Old Line State
Balzac, Honoré de: Père Lachaise
banana benders: Bananaland
Bananalander: Bananaland
Bangkok: Venice of the East
Bangladesh: Subcontinent, the
Bangor: Lumber City; Metropolis of the
    Northeast; Queen City of the East
Bank: Bank of England, the; Mansion
    House, the
Bank of England: Bank, the; City, the; Lom-
    bard Street; Mansion House, the; Old
    Lady of Threadneedle Street, the
Bank station: Drain, the
Banqueting Hall: Whitehall
Bantam work: Coromandel Coast, the
barbarian: Barbary Coast, the
Barbary States: Barbary Coast, the
Barbican Centre: Barbican, the
Barbizon: Fontainebleau
Barcelona: Costa Brava, the
Barchester: Barset
bargain basement: Filene's Basement
Baroda: Native States, the
Barrett, Elizabeth: Wimpole Street
Barrett, Richard: Wimpole Street
Barrie, Sir James: Adelphi, the
Barrow-in-Furness: Furness
Barsetshire: Barset
Baseball Hall of Fame: Birthplace of Baseball
Basin Street: Storyville
Basque: Guernica

Bath: Acemannes burh; Lantern of England
Battersea: Nine Elms; Swone-one
Battersea Dogs' Home: Battersea
Battersea Power Station: Battersea; Nine
    Elms
Battle: Hastings
Battlebridge: King's Cross, 1
Battle Bridge Road: Battlebridge
Battle Creek: Breakfast Food City
Battle Creek Sanitarium: Breakfast Food
    City
Battle Hymn of the Republic, The:
    Marseillaise of the Unemotional Yankee
Baum, Frank L.: TOTO
Bavaria: Bayreuth; Palatinate, the
Bavarian Alps: Oberammergau
Baylis, Lilian: Old Vic, the
Bay of Bengal: Seven Seas, the
Bay of Naples: Naples
Bayswater: Paddington
Bay View: Over South
BBC: Ally Pally; Auntie; Beeb, the; Portland
    Place; See also *British Broadcasting Cor-
    poration* in Index.
BBC Television Centre: Shepherd's Bush
Beachy Head: Seven Sisters
Beacon Hill: Trimountain City
Beale, Miss: Cheltenham
Bear Gardens: Bankside
Bear Mountain State Park: Hudson River
Beatles, the: Abbey Road; Strawberry Fields
Beaubourg: Halles, les
Beaumont: Golden Triangle, the, 3
Becknell, William: Santa Fe Trail
Bedfordshire: Midlands, the
Bedloe, Isaac: Bedloe's Island
"bed-sitter-land": Bayswater
Beecher, Henry Ward: Kansas Bibles; Phoe-
    nix City
Beecher's Brook: Grand National, the
Beekman Street: Tribeca
beer: Burton upon Trent
Beer, Thomas: Mauve Decade, the
Begin, Menachem: Camp David
Bel Air: Sunset Boulevard
Belbenoit, René: Devil's Island
Belgium: accidental war, the; Benelux;
    Cockpit of Europe, the; European Eco-
    nomic Community, the; Flanders; Little
    Siberia; Low Countries, the; Waterloo;
    Ypres
Belgrave: Belgravia
Belgravia: Kensington; King's Road; Knights-
    bridge; Pimlico; Sloane Square; Victo-
    ria; West End, the

Boodle's: Clubland, 1
Book of the Mormons: Deseret State
book publishing: Little Britain; Manhattan
booksellers' shops: Fleet Street
boom: Roaring Twenties, the
Booth, John Wilkes: Ford's Theater
bootleg whiskey: Roaring Twenties, the
boots: Chelsea 1
Bophutatswana: Mafeking
Bordeaux: Landes, the
Border Ballads: Border, the
Borders: Southern Uplands, the
Borneo: East Indies, the
Borough High Street: Borough, the; London
    Bridge
Borough, the: Old Kent Road, the
Bosnia: Balkans, the
Bosporus: Anatolia
Bosporus Sea: Golden Horn, the
Boston: Athens of America; Back Bay; Bay
    Horse; Beacon Hill; Beantown; Boston
    Post Road; Bunker Hill; City of Kind
    Hearts; Classic City; Combat Zone; Co-
    ney Island of Boston; Coonskin Library;
    Cradle of Liberty; Durgin Park; Faneuil
    Hall; Filene's Basement; Freedom Trail;
    Haymarket, the, 1; Holland, 2; Hub of
    the Universe; Literary Emporium, the;
    Megalopolis; Northeast Corridor; North
    End; North Shore, 2; Old North
    Church; Parker House, the; Puritan
    City; Route 128; Roxbury; Scollay
    Square; Southie; Trimountain City; T,
    the
Boston Latin School: Freedom Trail
Boston Massacre: Freedom Trail
Boston Public Library: Back Bay
Boston Red Sox: Back Bay
Boston Tea Party: Freedom Trail
Boston Transport: T, the
Boswell, James: Athens of the North, the
Boulevard St. Germain: Deux Magots, les
"Bouwerie": Bowery, the
Bow: East End
Bow Bells: Bow
Bow Church: Bow
Bowery bums: Bowery, the
Bowery, the: Five Points; Little Italy
Bowie, James: Alamo, the
Bowling Green: Broadway, 1
Bowron, Fletcher: Los Angeles
Bow Street Magistrates' Court: Bow Street
"Bow Street Runners": Bow Street
Boylston Street: Combat Zone
Bozeman, John M.: Bozeman Trail

Brabant: Low Countries, the
Bradford: Broad Acres, the; Ridings, the
Brahmins: Back Bay
Brainerd, Minnesota: Hub City
Brandt Report: North, the, 3; South, the, 3
Branston, F.: Roedean
Brasenose College: High, the
Brazil: Amazonia; Copacabana, 1; Guiana
"Breakfast at Tiffany's": Tiffany's
Breasted, James H.: Fertile Crescent, the
Brecon Beacons: Valleys, the
Breed's Hill: Bunker Hill
Brentwood: Sunset Boulevard
brewing: Burton upon Trent
Brice, Fanny: Lower East Side
Bridewell: B, the
Bridgehampton: Hamptons, the
Bridgeport: South Side
Bright, John: Mother of Parliaments, the
Brighton: Bognor Regis; Costa del Sol; Costa
    Geriatrica, the; Dr. Brighton; Kemp
    Town; Lanes, the; Littlehampton;
    Peacehaven; Roedean; Seven Sisters
Brighton Albion: Albion
Brill Building: Tin Pan Alley
Bristol: West, the, 2
Bristol Channel: Valleys, the
Britain: Blighty; Border, the; Brum; Dales,
    the; East Indies, the; England; German
    Ocean, the; Hadrian's Wall; Henley;
    House, the; Lizard, the; M & S; North,
    the, 1; Number 10; Snowdonia; Thule;
    Tin Pan Alley; Valleys, the
Britain, Battle of: Coventry
Britain, Festival of: Battersea
British Broadcasting Corporation: Auntie;
    Beeb, the; See also *BBC* in Index.
British Caledonian: Caledonia
British Columbia: Inland Empire, the
British India: Northwest Frontier, the
British Isles: Channel, the; Continent; Gulf
    Stream
British Museum: Bloomsbury
Brittany: Little Britain
Brittany, Duke of: Little Britain
Brixton: Lambeth
Brixton Prison: Brixton
broad arrow: Old Dart, the
Broadcasting House: Portland Place
Broadstairs: Isle of Thanet, the
Broad Street: Broad, the
Broadway: Birdland; Columbus Circle; Great
    White Way; Herald Square; Hub of
    New York City; Jack Dempsey's;
    Lindy's; Sardi's; West Side, 1

"Broadway Limited": Union Station
Brody, Steve: Brooklyn Bridge
Bronx, The: Broadway, 1; Brooklyn; Feath-
erbed Lane; Harlem River; Hell Gate;
House that Ruth Built; Manhattan; Park
Avenue; Sugar Hill
Bronx Whitestone Bridge: Hell Gate
Bronze Age: Wolds, the
Brookfield: Mayfair
Brookline: Back Bay
Brooklyn: Brooklyn Bridge; City of
Churches, the; Cobble Hill; Dormitory
of New York; East River; Island, the, 2;
Manhattan; Narrows, the; Queens
Brooklyn Bridge: Brooklyn; Foley Square;
Lower East Side
Brooklyn Dodgers: Brooklyn
Brooklyn Heights: Brooklyn; Cobble Hill
Brooklyn-Queens Expressway: Cobble Hill
Broun, Heywood: Round Table at the Al-
gonquin
Browning, Robert: Wimpole Street
Brownsville: Metropolis of the Magic Valley;
Where Mexico Meets Uncle Sam
Brownsville, Texas: Golden Crescent, the, 2
Brummagem: Brum
Brummies: Brum
Brunei: Southeast Asia
Brunelleschi: Giotto's Tower
Bryn Mawr: Main Line
bubonic plague: Black Death, the
Buccellati: Fifth Avenue
Bucharest: Orient-Express
Buckingham and Chandos, Duke of: Buck
House
Buckingham House: Buck House
Buckingham Palace: Buck House; Number
One, London; Palace, the; Speakers'
Corner; St. James's
Buckinghamshire: Chiltern Hundreds, the;
Home Counties, the; Metroland; Mid-
lands, the; Milton Keynes; Slough;
Southeast, the; Stoke Mandeville
Buddhism: Forbidden City, the
Buffalo: Bison City; City of Flour; Queen
City of the Lakes
"Bugger Bognor!": Bognor Regis
Bulgaria: Balkans, the; Rumelia
Bull Durham: Bull City
buns: Chelsea, 1
burlesque: Minsky's
Burlington: Porkopolis of Iowa; Queen City
of Vermont
Burlington, Iowa: Orchard City
Burlington Arcade: Burlington House

Burlington Gardens: Burlington House
Burma: Burma Road, the; Golden Triangle,
the, 1; Indochina; Middle East, the;
Southeast Asia
Burnham: Chiltern Hundreds, the
Burnham, Daniel: North Side
Burslem: Five Towns, the
Bursley: Five Towns, the
business, big: Wall Street
Butte Hill: Richest Hill on Earth
Butte, Montana: City that is a Mile High and
a Mile Deep; Richest Hill on Earth
Buttermere: Lake District, the
Buzby, Betty: Minsky's
Byron, George, Lord: Bridge of Sighs, 1
Byron, Lord: Albany
Byzantine Empire: West, the, 1

C

C-47: Gooney Bird
C & A: Oxford Street
Cabildo, the: French Quarter, the
Cabot, Sebastian: Northwest Passage, the
"Cabrini-Green": Cabrini-Green Public Hous-
ing Project
Cadbury's: Bourneville
Caerleon: Camelot, 1
Caernarvon: Royal Borough, the
Café Society Downtown: Greenwich Village
Cairo, Illinois: Egypt
Cairy: Shepheard's Hotel
Caithness: Highlands, the
Caithness-shire: Land's End to John o'
Groat's House
Calais: Chunnel, the
Calcutta: Black Hole (of Calcutta)
Caldwell, Kansas: Queen City of the Border
Caledonia County: Northeast Kingdom
Caledonian Canal: Caledonia
Caledonian Market: Bermondsey Market
Caledonian Road: Caledonian Market;
Pentonville
calf's testis: prairie oyster
Calgary, Alberta: Foothill City
California: Beverly Hills; Boystown; Bur-
bank; City of Flowers and Sunshine;
City of One Hundred Hills; Crown City
of the Valley; Disneyland; Donner Pass;
El Dorado State; Far West, the; Golden
Gate City; Golden State; Land of Gold;
Land of Little Rain; Mushroom City;
Pacific Northwest, the; Palm Springs;
Plymouth of the West; Poor Man's Par-
adise; Port o' Missing Men; Queen of

the Cow Counties; Queen of the Missions; Queen of the Pacific; Rodeo Drive; San Fernando Valley; Silicon Glen; Watts

Calpe: Pillars of Hercules, the

Calumet, Lake: South Side

Camberley: Bagshot

Camberwell: Old Kent Road, the

Cambodia: Indochina; Southeast Asia

Cambrian Mountains: Cambria

Cambrian Period: Cambria

Cambridge: Backs, the; Granta; Newmarket

Cambridge, Massachusetts: University City

Cambridgeshire: East Anglia; Fens, the; Huntingdonshire; Isle of Ely, the; Melton Mowbray; Midlands, the; Oxon

Cambridge Town: Camberley

Cambridge University: Bridge of Sighs, 3; Golgotha, 2; Oxbridge

Camden: Camden Town

Camden Lock: Camden Town

Camden Passage: Camden Town

Camelford: Camelot, 1

Cameroon: Guinea

Campbell: Glencoe

Camp David: Shangri-La, 3

Camp David Accords: Camp David

Cam River: Backs, the; Granta

Canaan: Land of Promise; Promised Land, the

Canaan: Palestine

Canada: Acadia; Atlantic Provinces, the; Bay Street; D.S.N.C.O.; dust bowl, the; Far North, the; Foothill City; Hogtown; Inland Empire, the; International City, the; Northland, the; Old Quebec (Vieux-Québec); Parkdale; Place Royale; Prairie Provinces, the; Queen City, the; Queen Street West; Ridings, the; Rosedale; Strip, the, 2; Territories, the; Track, the; White Otter Castle

Canadian Rockies: Rockies, the

Canal Street: Avenue of the Americas; Bowery, the; Chinatown, 1; French Quarter, the; Little Italy; Tribeca

can-can: Moulin Rouge

Cannes: French Riviera, the; Grand Corniche; South of France, the

Canning, George: Albany

Canning Town: East End

Canongate: Royal Miles, the

Cantab.: Oxon

Canterbury pilgrims: Borough, the

Canton Street: Chinatown, 2

Cape Ann: Gloucester

Cape Breton Island: Acadia

Cape Cod: Cape, the

Cape Cod Bay: Cape, the

Cape Comorin: Malabar Coast, the

Cape Hatteras: Graveyard of the Atlantic; Gulf Stream

Cape La Nao: Costa Blanca

Cape Province: Karoo, the

Cape Town: Table Mountain

Cape Verde: Guinea

Cap Ferrat: French Riviera, the

capitalist countries: Iron Curtain, the

Capitol: Capitoline, the

Capitol Building: Hill, the

Capitol Hill: Hill, the

Capitoline: Seven Hills, the

Capitol, the: Broadway, 1

Capone, Al: Holy Name; Loop, the

Capote, Truman: Tiffany's

Captain Kidd: *Adventure*

Captains Courageous: Gloucester

Cardiff: Coal Metropolis of the World

Caribbean: Spanish Main, the

Caribbean Sea: Middle Passage, the

Carlisle: Hadrian's Wall

Carlton, the: Clubland, 1

Carlyle, Thomas: Athens of the North, the

Carmelite monastery: Whitefriars

Carnaby Street: King's Road

Caroline Islands: Micronesia

Carpathian Mountains: Transylvania

Carrington, Frank: Paper Mill Playhouse

Carroll, Harry: Blue Ridge Mountains, the

Cartagena: Costa Blanca

Cartagena, Colombia: blue-light district; Heroic City

Carter, Jimmy: Camp David

Cartier: Fifth Avenue; Tiffany's

Cascade Mountains: Inland Empire, the

Castle Hill: Royal Miles, the

Castle Rock: New Town, the

Cathay Pacific: Cathay

Cathedral: Holy Name

Cathedral Parkway: West Side, 1

Catskill Mountains: Appalachian Mountains; Borscht Circuit

CED: Porton Down

Cedar Rapids, Iowa: Cereal City

Celebes: East Indies, the; Spice Islands, the

"Celebrated Jumping Frog of Calaveras County, The": Frogtown

Cellini, Benvenuto: Fontainebleau

cemetery: Forest Lawn

Central America: banana republic; Neogaea

Central Criminal Court: Old Bailey

Centralia: Center, the

Central Park: Columbus Circle; Fifth Avenue; Manhattan; West Side, 1

Central Park South: Plaza, The

Central Park West: Broadway, 1; Columbus Circle; Dakota, the, 2; West Side, 1

Centre Street: Bridge of Sighs, 2; Chinatown, 1; Little Italy

Century, the: West Side, 1

Cephissus: Academy, the

Cesarwich: Newmarket

Chad: Sahel, the

chalk cliffs: Seven Sisters

Chalk Farm Road: Camden Lock

Chamberlain, W. J.: Amen Corner

Chambers, William: Kew Gardens

Champlain, Lake: Clinton's ditch

Champs Élysées: Faubourg St. Honoré, Rue du

Chancellor of the Exchequer: Number 10

"Change at Crewe": Crewe

Charing: Charing Cross

Charing Cross Road: Charing Cross; Shaftesbury Avenue; Tin Pan Alley

Charing Cross Underground station: Embankment, the

Charles Augustus, Grand Duke: Weimar

Charlesbourg-Ouest: D.S.N.C.O.

Charles I: Charing Cross; Queen State

Charles II: Old Dominion

Charles River: Bunker Hill

Charleston: Roaring Twenties, the

Charleston, South Carolina: America's Most Historic City; City of Secession; Earthquake City; Palmetto City; Plumb Line Port to Panama

Charlestown: Bunker Hill

Charlotte, North Carolina: Hornet's Nest

Charlotte Street: Fitzrovia

Charlottetown, Prince Edward Island: Birthplace of Canada

Charrière, Henri: Devil's Island

Charus of Lindus: Colossus of Rhodes

Chase, Salmon Portland: Ohio's Jewels

Chatham: Cape, the

Chatsworth, the: West Side, 1

Chattanooga: Gate City

Chattanooga, Battle of: Battle above *or* in the Clouds

Chaucer: Borough, the

Checkerboard Lounge: South Side

Cheddar Gorge: Cheddar

Chelm: Neasden

Chelsea: Battersea; Earl's Court; Fitzrovia; Kensington; King's Road; Royal Borough, the; Sloane Square

Chelsea Arts Club Ball: Chelsea, 1

Chelsea Embankment: Embankment, the

Chelsea Hotel: Chelsea, 2

Chelsea Pensioners: Chelsea, 1

Chelsea Royal Hospital: Chelsea, 1

Cheltenham Ladies' College: Cheltenham

Chemical Defense Establishment: Porton Down

Cherokee: Trail of Tears

Cherry Grove: Fire Island; Grand Strand

Chesapeake Bay: Delmarva Peninsula; Tidewater Virginia

Cheshire: Crewe; Midlands, the; North, the, 1

Chester: Marches, the, 1

Cheviot Hills: Backbone of England, the

Cheyne Walk: Chelsea, 1

Chiang Kai-shek: Burma Road, the

Chicago: Aragon Ballroom; Atchison, Topeka, & Santa Fe; Big Town; Billy Goat Tavern; Biograph Theater; Bughouse Square; Cabrini-Green Public Housing Project; City of Churches, the; Congregation of Spires, a; Empire State Building; Financial Capital of the Midwest, the; Fort Dearborn; Gehenna of Abominations, the; Gold Coast; Greatest Primary Grain Port in the World, the; Haymarket Square; Hog Butcher for the World; Holy Name; Hull House; Lake Shore Drive; Loop, the; Magnificent Mile, the; Marshall Field's; Maxwell Street; McCormick Place; Mudtown; Museum of Science and Industry; Navy Pier; Near North Side; New Town; New York of the West, the; North Side; O'Hare International Airport; Old Town; Phoenix City; Pilsen; Playboy Building; Porkopolis; Pullman; Queen of the Lakes, the; Railroad Queen of the State, the; Rush Street; Sears Tower; Second City, the; Slab City; South Side; Staff Field; Star City; Toddling Town, That; Union Station; Union Stockyards; Water Tower; West Side; West, the, 3; White City, 1; Wickedest City on Earth, the; Wrigleyville

"Chicago": Hog Butcher for the World; Toddling Town, That

Chicago Circle: West Side, 2

Chicago Cubs: Wrigleyville

Chicago Fire Academy: Mrs. O'Leary's Barn
Chicago, University of: South Side; Staff
     Field
Chicago White Sox: South Side
Chickasaw: Trail of Tears
Chickasaw County, Mississippi: Egypt Land
Chihuahua, Mexico: Camino Real, el
Childe Harold's Pilgrimage: Bridge of
     Sighs, 1
Chile: Christ of the Andes; Patagonia; South
     American Alps; Tierra del Fuego
Chiltern Hundreds, Stewardship of: Chil-
     tern Hundreds, the
China: Burma Road, the; Cathay; Celestial
     Empire, the; Coromandel Coast, the;
     Far East, the; Forbidden City, the; For-
     mosa; Indochina; Inner Mongolia; Mid-
     dle Kingdom, the; Mongolia; Red China;
     Roof of the World, the
China, Nationalist: Formosa
China, Nationalist Republic of: Formosa
China, People's Republic of,: Formosa; Red
     China
Chinatown: Foley Square; Limehouse; South
     Side
Chinese: Soho
Chisholm, Jesse: Chisholm Trail
chocolate: Bourneville
Chocolate Soldier, The: Paper Mill Playhouse
Choctaw: Trail of Tears
Chomondley's: Greenwich Village
Chopin, Frédéric: Père Lachaise
Christ Church: House, the; Old North
     Church
"Christian Charity": Piccadilly Circus
Christie, Agatha: Orient-Express
Christie, John: Old Bailey
Chrysler Building: Empire State Building
Chungking: Burma Road, the
Churchill, Winston: Camp David; Iron Cur-
     tain, the
Church of England: Lambeth
churchyard: God's acre
Cimon: Academy, the
Cincinnati: Conservative Cincinnati; Paris of
     America; Porkopolis; Queen City of the
     West
Circle Line: London Underground
citadel, Roman: Capitoline, the
"City gent": City, the
City Hall: Foley Square
City of New York, Museum of: Fifth Ave-
     nue
"City of the Angels": Los Angeles
City Road: Angel, the

Ciudad Bolívar: Angostura
Clapham: Neasden
Clapham Junction: Clapham
Clapham Sect: Clapham
Clare College: Backs, the
Claremont Avenue: West Side, 1
Clarence Island: Tierra del Fuego
Claridge's Hotel: Grosvenor Square
Cleopatra's Needle: Embankment, the
Clerkenwell Road: Hatton Garden
Cleveland: Northeast, the, 1; Porkopolis
Cleveland, Grover: Pullman
Caelian: Seven Hills, the
clink, in the: Clink Street
Clinton, De Witt: Clinton's ditch
clock tower: Pullman
Cloisters, the: West Side, 1
Club: Newmarket
Clubland: Athenaeum, the; Pall Mall; St.
     James's
Clubland circuit: Clubland, 2
Cluett, Peabody Company: Collar City
Clumber Park: Dukeries, the
Clydebank: Clydeside
Clyde, River: Clydeside; Gorbals, the; Low-
     lands, the
coal: Dusky Diamonds
coal mine: Seven Sisters
coalmining: Ruhr, the
Cobbett, William: Great Wen, the; Old Lady
     of Threadneedle Street, the
Cochin: Native States, the
Cochin China: Indochina
Cockney: Lambeth; Old Kent Road, the; Pet-
     ticoat Lane
Cockneys: East End
codfish: Cape Cod turkey
Cohan, George M.: Broadway, 1; Herald
     Square
Cohoes, New York: Spindle City
Colbert County: Tri-Cities
Colchester: Naze, the
Coleridge, Samuel Taylor: Lake District, the
Colesberg Hill: Big Hole, the
Colesberg Kopje: Big Hole, the
Colette: Père Lachaise
Coliseum: Columbus Circle
Coliseum, New York: Broadway, 1
Cologne: Rhineland, the
"Colony, The": Malibu
Colorado: Buffalo Plains State; Centennial
     State; Convention City; Home of the
     Cheeseburger; Lead State; Mile High
     City; Mountain State; Queen City of the
     Plains; Silver State; Southwest, the, 1;

Switzerland of America; Treasure State
of the Rockies
Colosseum: Domus Aurea
Columbia Presbyterian Medical Center:
West Side, 1
Columbia River: Inland Empire, the
Columbia University: Bloomingdale's; Broad-
way, 1; Rockefeller Center
Columbus: Ohio's Jewels
Columbus, Christopher: Columbus Circle
Columbus Avenue: Broadway, 1
Columbus Circle: Broadway, 1; Hub of New
York City
Columbus Park: West Side, 2
Comden, Betty: Greenwich Village
Comiskey Park: South Side
"Committee of 100": Aldermaston
Common Market: European Economic Com-
munity, the
Communist bloc: East, the, 2
Communist China: Bamboo Curtain, the
communist countries: Iron Curtain, the
"Community, the": European Economic
Community, the
Comnena, Anna: Alexiad, the
Comnenus: Alexiad, the
Compton, California: Hub City
Concord, Massachusetts: Walden Pond
Coney Island: Brooklyn
Confederate flag: Stars and Bars
Confederate prison: Hell Upon Earth
Confederate States: City of Five Flags
Congress: Hill, the
Congress Parkway: Loop, the
Congress (U. S.): Capitoline, the
Congreve rockets: Woolwich
Coniston Water: Lake District, the
Connacht: Province, the
Connaught Hotel: Grosvenor Square
Connecticut: Blue Law State; Brother
Jonathan; Brownstone State; Charter
Oak City; City of Elms; Constitution
State; East, the, 1; Freestone State;
Grand Central; Hardware City; Insur-
ance City; Island, the, 2; Land of
Steady Habits; New England; Nutmeg
State; Thirteen Original Colonies
Conrail: Grand Central
Conservative: Shires, the
Conservative Party: Carlton Club, the
Constable, John: Constable Country
Constance Street: Irish Channel
Constantinople: Orient-Express; Stamboul;
Sublime Porte, the
Constitution: Old Ironsides

Constitution Hill: Hyde Park Corner
Contemporary Art, Institute of: Back Bay
Continental Congress: Birthplace of Ameri-
can Liberty
Continental Divide: Rockies, the
Convent Garden: Covent Garden
Cook, Captain James: Botany Bay
Cook Islands: Polynesia
Cooperstown, New York: Birthplace of
Baseball
Copenhagen: Christiana; King's City; Sound,
the; Tivoli Gardens
Copley Square: Back Bay
Copp's Hill: Trimountain City
Corinth: Peloponnese, the
Corinth, Gulf of: Aetolia
Corinth, Isthmus of: Peloponnese, the
Corio, Ann: Gaiety, the
Cornhill: Bank, the
Corniche: French Riviera, the
Cornwall: Cornish Riviera, the; Land's End
to John o' Groat's House; Lizard, the;
Southwest, the, 2; Stannaries, the;
Tintagel; West Country, the
Costa Blanca: Costa Brava, the
Costa Brava: Blackpool
Costa del Sol: Blackpool; Costa Blanca; Costa
Brava, the
Côte d'Azur: Provence; South of France, the
Côte des Allemands: German Coast
Cotswolds: Wolds, the
Cottesmore: Shires, the
County Hall: South Bank, the
Courrèges: Faubourg St. Honoré, Rue du
Courtauld Institute of Art: Somerset House
Court of Star Chamber: Star Chamber
Court Street: Cobble Hill
Covent Garden: Bow Street; Halles, les
Coventry: West Midlands, the
Coventry Gaol: Coventry
Coward, Noël: Paper Mill Playhouse
Cowes Week: Island, the, 1
Cradle of Liberty: Faneuil Hall
Craig, James: New Town, the
Creek: Trail of Tears
Cretan colony: Atlantis
cricket: Hambledon
cricket ground: Lord's
criminal: Bellevue
Crippen, Dr.: Old Bailey
Critias: Atlantis
Croatia: Balkans, the
"Croatoan": Lost Colony, the
Crockern Tor: Stannaries, the
Crockett, Davy: Alamo, the

Crofton: Devils Nest
Cromwell: Coventry
Cromwell Road: Kensington
Croydon: London
Cuba: Queen of the Antilles
C.U.B.S.: Wrigleyville
Cuckold's Point: Pool of London, the
cuckoo clocks: Black Forest, the
Cumberland: Westmorland
Cumberland, Rhode Island: Mineral Pocket of the Northeast
Cumberland Mountains: Appalachian Mountains
Cumbernauld: Silicon Glen
Cumbria: Cumberland; Furness; Lake District, the; Northwest, the, 1; Westmorland; Windscale
cummings, e. e.: Minsky's
Curtiss, Glenn Hammond: Cradle of Aviation
Curzon Street: Mayfair
Customhouse Street: Storyville
Cutler's Company: Elephant and Castle
cutlery: Sheffield of Germany
Cymbarka: Hapsburg lip
Cymry: Cambria
Cyrus the Great: Persia
Czechoslovakia: Bohemia; Iron Curtain, the; Sudetenland, the

D

Dakota, the: West Side, 1
Dales: Broad Acres, the; Ridings, the
Daley, Richard J.: South Side
Dallas: Big D; Big Tex; City of Homes; Dallas Book Depository; Metropolis of North Texas; Silicon Prairie
"Dallas of the North": Granite City, the
Damascus, Virginia: Little Swiss Town
Dames at Sea: Off Broadway, Off-Off Broadway
Dana, Charles A.: Windy City
Danube River: Orient-Express
Danville, Virginia: Last Capital of the Confederacy
Dare, Virginia: Lost Colony, the
Dark Peak: Peak District, the
Dartmoor: Moor, the; Stannaries, the
David, King: City of David, the
Davies, Marion: Dakota, the, 2
Davis Park: Fire Island
Dawson Creek, British Columbia: Alcan Highway
Dawson Island: Tierra del Fuego

Dawson Springs, Kentucky: City of Health
Dayton: Gem City of Ohio
Dayton, Ohio: Birthplace of Aviation
DC-3: Gooney Bird
Dead Bastard: Shepheard's Hotel
Dead Heart of Australia, The: Center, the
Dead Sea: Palestine; West Bank, the
Dean, Penny: Channel, the
Dearborn, Henry: Fort Dearborn
Death Valley: Land of Little Rain
Deccan: Hindustan
Declaration of Independence: Birthplace of American Liberty; Keystone State
Dedham Vale: Constable Country
Dee River: Offa's Dyke; Wirral, the
Defence, Ministry of: Whitehall
de Gaulle, Charles: Orly
DeKoven Street: Mrs. O'Leary's Barn
Delancey Street: Lower East Side
Delaware: Atlantic States; Blue Hen State; Chemical Capital of the World; Delmarva Peninsula; Diamond State; First State; Mason-Dixon Line; New Sweden; Northeast, the, 2; Thirteen Original Colonies; Uncle Sam's Pocket Handkerchief
Delmarva peninsula: Tidewater Virginia
Demetrius I: Colossus of Rhodes
de Mille, Cecil B.: Grauman's Chinese Theater
Dempsey, William Harrison "Jack": Jack Dempsey's
Denmark: Christiana; European Economic Community, the; Jutland; King's City; Scandinavia; Scandinavian Shield, the; Sound, the; Tivoli Gardens
Denmark Street: Tin Pan Alley
Denver: Convention City; Home of the Cheeseburger; Mile High City; Queen City of the Plains
Den vita staden: White City, 2
Derby: Epsom; North, the, 1
Derbyshire: Midlands, the; North, the, 1; Peak District, the
Derry: Six Counties, the
Derwentwater: Lake District, the
Desborough: Chiltern Hundreds, the
Descent into the Maelstrom, A: Maelstrom, the
Desert Song, The: Paper Mill Playhouse
Desolation Island: Tierra del Fuego
Detroit: Automobile Capital of the World; Dynamic City; Motown; Ren Cen
Deux Magots, les: Left Bank, the

Devon: Cornish Riviera, the; Main Line; Moor, the; Southwest, the, 2; Stannaries, the; West Country, the
Devon Riviera: Cornish Riviera, the
Devonshire: Dartmoor; Shires, the; Torquay
Devonshire Place: Baker Street
diamond market: 47th Street; Hatton Garden
Dickens, Charles: Little Britain
Dillinger, John: Biograph Theater
District of Columbia: Capital City; Capital of Houses without Streets; City of Magnificent Distances; City of Receptions; East, the, 1; Executive City; Federal City; Great Dismal; Nation's State; Wilderness City
Dix, John A.: Albany Regency
Dixieland: Dixie
Dixon, Jeremiah: Dixie; Mason-Dixon Line
Dockland: Chinatown, 2; Isle of Dogs, the; Limehouse; Printing House Square; Ronan Point
Dodge City, Kansas: Boot Hill
Doges' Palace: Bridge of Sighs, 1
dog pound: Battersea
Dogs, Isle of: Billingsgate; Dockland
Dog Star: dog days
dollar: baloney dollar
Dôme, le: Left Bank, the
Domesday Book: Hants
Dominicans: Blackfriars
Donald Duck: Disneyland
Doncaster: Ridings, the
Donner, George and Jacob: Donner Pass
Doolittle, Gen. James P.: Shangri-La, 2
Dorchester: Park Lane
Doré, Gustave: East End
Doris: Aetolia
Dorset: South, the, 2; Southwest, the, 2; Tolpuddle; Wessex; West Country, the
Doubleday, Abner: Birthplace of Baseball
Douglas Park: West Side, 2
Dover: Cinque Ports, the; Old Kent Road, the; White Cliffs, the
Dover, Straits of: Dover
Down: Six Counties, the
Downing Street: Whitehall
Doyle, Arthur Conan: Baker Street
Dracula: Transylvania
Drake Hotel: Magnificent Mile, the
Drennan, William: Emerald Isle, the
Dreyfus, Alfred: Devil's Island
Driver, William: Old Glory
drought: dust bowl, the
Drury Lane Theatre: Drury Lane

Dry Guillotine: Devil's Island
Dubai: Trucial States, the
Duberger: D.S.N.C.O.
Dudley: Black Country, the
Duffy Square: Broadway, 1
Duluth, Minnesota: Zenith City of the Unsalted Seas
Dung: Jamdung
Dunhill: Fifth Avenue
Dunkirk: mosquito armada
Duomo: Giotto's Tower
Durham: Northeast, the, 1
Durham, North Carolina: Bull City; Tobacco Capital of the World
Düsseldorf: Rhineland, the
Dutch: Frogland
Dvořák, Anton: New World, the
Dying Bastard: Shepheard's Hotel

E

Earl of Munster: Iron Curtain, the
Earl's Court: Bayswater; Kangaroo Valley
Earl's Court Exhibition: Earl's Court
earthenware industry: Potteries, the
East, the: North, the, 3; Orient, the; Spice Islands, the; West, the, 1
East African Community: East Africa
East and West India Docks: Dockland
East Anglia: Broads, the; Constable Country; Midlands, the; Naze, the; South, the, 2; Wash, the
East Bergholt: Constable Country
East Berlin: Berlin Wall, the; Unter den Linden
Eastbourne: Beachy Head; Costa Geriatrica, the
Eastchester Bay: Hell Gate
East End: Bow; City, the; Isle of Dogs, the; Limehouse; London; Tower Hamlets; West End, the; Whitechapel
East Enders: Dockland
Easter Island: Polynesia
Eastern bloc: East, the, 2; West, the, 1
Eastern Desert: Western Desert, the
Eastern Europe: Iron Curtain, the
Eastern Hemisphere: Old World, the; Orient, the; West, the, 1
East European Communism: Bamboo Curtain, the
East Germany: Berlin Wall, the; Iron Curtain, the; Oder-Neisse Line, the; Prussia; Sudetenland, the; Weimar
Easthampton: Hamptons, the
East India: East Indies, the

East India companies: Coromandel Coast, the

East India Company: East Indies, the

East India Docks: Isle of Dogs, the

East Indies: Indies, the; Spice Islands, the

East Midlands: Rutland; Soke of Peterborough, the

East Midlands Airport: Lincolnshire

East Orange: Oranges, the

East Prussia: Polish Corridor, the

East Riding: Ridings, the

East River: Brooklyn; Brooklyn Bridge; East Side; Hell Gate; Lower East Side; Manhattan; West Side, 1

East Side: Clock at the Astor, Biltmore; Little Italy; Park Avenue; West Side, 1

"East-West talks": East, the, 2

Ebbets Field: Brooklyn

Ebbw River: Valleys, the

Ebbw Vale: Valleys, the

Ebro River: Iberia

Eclogues: Arcadia

Edinburgh: Athens of the North, the; Auld Reekie; Firth of Forth Bridge; Heart of Midlothian, the; Highlands, the; Inns of Court and Chancery; Lowlands, the; Morningside; New Town, the; North Britain; Queen of the North; Royal Miles, the; Silicon Glen; St. Andrews

Edinburgh Castle: Royal Miles, the

Edinburgh Tolbooth: Heart of Midlothian, the

Edward I: Charing Cross

Edward III: Principality, the; woolsack, the

Edwards, J. G.: Hawkeye State

Edward, the Black Prince: Principality, the

Edward VII, King: Royal Borough, the

EEC: European Economic Community, the

Egypt: Gaza Strip, the; Middle East, the; Near East, the; North Africa; Western Desert, the

Egyptian: Barbary Coast, the

Egyptian Theater: Grauman's Chinese Theater

Eiffel Tower: Blackpool

Eighth Avenue: Broadway, 1; Chelsea, 2; Columbus Circle; 42nd Street; Garment District; Hub of New York City; Madison Square Garden

Eisenhower, Dwight D.: Camp David; Eisenhower Platz

Eleanor Cross: Charing Cross

Elephant and Castle: Bakerloo

El Greco: Prado, the

Ellesmere Port: Wirral, the

Ellice Islands: Polynesia

El Salvador: Casa Oscar Romero

Ely: Isle of Ely, the

Ely, bishops of: Hatton Garden

Ely Place: Hatton Garden

Élysée Palace: Champs Élysées, the

Embankment: Charing Cross

Embankment Station: Embankment, the

Empire State Building: Chrysler Building

"Empty State Building": Empire State Building

England: Acemannes burh; Albion; Ashes, the; Avebury; Backbone of England, the; Banbury Cross; Beachy Head; Black Country, the; Black Friday, 2; Blackpool; Bognor Regis; Bournemouth; Bourneville; Bridge of Sighs, 4; Broad Acres, the; Broads, the; Bullrng, the; Burton upon Trent; Camberley; Camelot, 1; Cheltenham; Cinque Ports, the; Cornish Riviera, the; Costa Geriatrica, the; Cottonopolis; Coventry; Cowes Week; Crewe; Cumberland; Dartmoor; Dorset; Dover; East Anglia; East Midlands, the; Epsom; Etruria; Fens, the; Flixborough; Furness; Garden of England, the; Geordieland; Glastonbury; Golden Mile, the; Granta; Green Belt; Gretna Green; Hambledon; Hants; Hastings; Holland, 2; Huntingdonshire; Isle of Athelney, the; Isle of Ely, the; Isle of Thanet, the; Jarrow; John Bull; Kemp Town; Kesteven; Lake District, the; Land's End to John o' Groat's House; Lanes, the; Lantern of England; Law Courts, the; Lindsey; Little Britain; Lizard, the; Loamshire; Marches, the, 1; *Mayflower*; Melton Mowbray; Mercia; Merseyside; Middlesex; Midlands, the; Milton Keynes; Moor, the; Mother of Parliaments, the; Mummerset; Naze, the; Needles, the; New Forest; Newmarket; North Britain; Northeast, the, 1; North, the, 1; Northwest, the, 1; Offa's Dyke; Old Dart, the; Old Dominion; Old Sarum; Oxbridge; Pantiles, the; Peacehaven; Peak District, the; Piltdown man; Pompey; Pool, the, 1; Porton Down; Potteries, the; Principality, the; Ridings, the; Roedean; Royal Borough, the; Rugby; Rutland; Salop; Sandringham; Seven Sisters; Shambles, the; Shires, the; Soke of Peterborough, the; Solent, the; Southeast,

the; Southwest, the, 2; Spaghetti Junction; Stannaries, the; Strawberry Fields; Surrey; Telford; Thames Valley, the; Tintagel; Tolpuddle; Torquay; Tower Bridge; Tunbridge Wells; Tyneside; United Kingdom, the; Wash, the; Weald, the; Wessex; West Country, the; West Midlands, the; Westmorland; White Cliffs, the; Wigan; Windscale; Wirral, the; Wolds, the; woolsack, the
English Channel: Channel, the; Chunnel, the; Dover; Eddystone Light; Island, the, 1; White Cliffs, the
English Midlands: Arden
English Rugby Football Union: Twickenham
Enigma: Coventry
Epirus: Aetolia
Epsom Downs: Epsom
Epsom salts: Epsom
Equatorial Guinea: Guinea
Ericson, Leif: Vinland
Erie Canal: Clinton's ditch; Gateway of the West
Erie, Lake: Clinton's ditch
Erin: Hibernia
"Eros": Piccadilly Circus
Erzgebirge: Sudetenland, the
Esplanade Avenue: French Quarter, the
Esquiline: Seven Hills, the
Essex: Constable Country; East Anglia; Home Counties, the; Naze, the; Southeast, the
Essex County: Northeast Kingdom
Essex Street Market: Lower East Side
Estonia: Baltic States
Ethiopia: Abyssinia; Horn of Africa, the; Ogaden, the
Et in Arcadia ego: Arcadia
Euphrates River: Fertile Crescent, the; Hanging Gardens of Babylon; Mesopotamia
Eurasia: Far North, the; Laurasia
Euromarket: European Economic Community, the
Europe: Anatolia; Arctogaea; Balkans; Black Death, the; Channel, the; Continent; Eurasia; Flanders; German Ocean, the; Low Countries, the; Mauve Decade, the; West, the, 1
European Economic Community: Continent; green pound
Evangeline: Acadia
Evanston: North Side
Everglades: Alligator Alley
executions, public: Tyburnia

F

"Fabian of the Yard": Yard, the
Faculty of Advocates: Inns of Court and Chancery
Fairbanks, Alaska: Alcan Highway
Fairfax Avenue: Miracle Mile; Sunset Boulevard
Falmouth: Cornish Riviera, the
Faneuil Hall: Durgin Park; Freedom Trail; Haymarket, the
Far East: East, the, 2; Honkers; Levant, the; Middle East, the; Orient, the
Faribault, Minnesota: Athens of the Northwest
Far North Side: North Side
Far Southeast Side: Pullman; South Side
Far South Side: Navy Pier; South Side
"Fashion Avenue": Garment District
fashion industry: Carnaby Street
Faubourg Saint-Honoré: Rodeo Drive
Fayetteville: Athens of Arkansas
Federal National Mortgage Association: Fannie Mae
Federal Republic of Germany: Berlin Wall, the
Fenland: Isle of Ely, the
Fenland River: Wash, the
Fens: Isle of Ely, the
Fenway Park: Back Bay
Ferber, Edna: Round Table at the Algonquin
Fergus Falls, Minnesota: City Beautiful in the Land o' Lakes
Fermanagh: Six Counties, the
Fermi, Enrico: Staff Field
Fernie: Shires, the
Ferris, George Washington: White City, 1
Ferris wheel: White City, 1
Festival of Britain: South Bank, the
Festival Theater: Bayreuth
Field, Marshall: North Side
Field's: Marshall Field's
Fiesta de San Fermín: Pamplona
Fifth Avenue: Chelsea, 2; "21" Club; East Side; Empire State Building; Plaza, the; Rockefeller Center; Rodeo Drive; Spanish Harlem; Stork Club; Tiffany's
Fifth Avenue Hotel: Amen Corner
figure-eight cruller: Mae West, 2
Fiji: Australasia; Melanesia
film studio: Ealing
financial center: Bay Street; City, the; Wall Street
financial panic: Black Friday, 2

Fine Arts, Museum of: Back Bay
Finland: Country of the Thousand Lakes;
    Gibraltar of the North; Karelia; Land of
    the Midnight Sun, the; Lapland; Scandi-
    navia; Scandinavian Shield, the
Finsbury Park: Harringay
Fire Island Pines: Fire Island
Fire of 1666: Bedlam
Firth of Forth: Northumbria
Fisher, Fred: Toddling Town, That
Fisk, James: Black Friday, 3
Fitzroy Square: Fitzrovia
Fitzroy Tavern: Fitzrovia
Fitz-Stephen, William: Smithfield
Five Civilized Tribes: Trail of Tears
Five Points Gang: Five Points
Flag of the United States: Old Glory; Stars
    and Stripes
Flanders: Low Countries, the
Flanders poppy: Flanders
"flappers": Roaring Twenties, the
Flatbush: Brooklyn
Flatford: Constable Country
"Flatford Mill": Constable Country
Fleet Street: Alsatia; Blackfriars; Chancery
    Lane; Hatton Garden; Temple, the;
    Whitefriars
flintlock musket: brown Bess
floods: Johnstown
Florence: City of Lilies, the; Marches,
    the, 2; Muscle Shoals Area; Tri-Cities
Florence Hotel: Pullman
Florence, Italy: Giotto's Tower
Florida: Alligator Alley; Alligator State;
    American Nile, the; America's Oldest
    City; Atlantic States; Boston Post Road;
    Chicago of the South; City of Opportu-
    nities; Everglade State; Fontainebleau
    Hotel; Gulf State; Gulf, the; Land of
    Flowers; Little Cuba; Orange State;
    Panhandle, the; Peninsula State; South,
    the, 1; Sunbelt; Sunshine City; Sun-
    shine State
"flower people": Haight-Ashbury
Flushing: Queens
Flushing Meadows: Forest Hills
flying bombs: doodlebugs
FNMA: Fannie Mae
Fogg, Phileas: Reform Club, the
Foley Square: Chinatown, 1
Folkestone: Chunnel, the
Fontainebleau Palace: Fontainebleau Hotel
food market: Halles, les
Ford, Henry: tin Lizzie
foreign embassies: Embassy Row

Foreign Ministry, French: Wilhelmstrasse,
    the
Foreign Ministry, German: Wilhelmstrasse,
    the
Foreign Office: Whitehall
Forest Hills: Queens
Forest Hills Tennis Club: Forest Hills
Forster, E. M.: Bloomsbury
Fort Dearborn massacre: Fort Dearborn
Forth, River: Lowlands, the
Fort Laramie, Wyoming: Bozeman Trail
Fort Leavenworth, Kansas: Santa Fe Trail
Fort Myers, Florida: City of Palms
Fortnum & Mason: Jackson's of Piccadilly
Fort's Hill: Trimountain City
Fort Smith, Arkansas: Chisholm Trail
Fort Towson, Indian Territory: Chisholm
    Trail
Fort Tryon Park: West Side, 1
Fort Vancouver: Oregon Trail
Fort William: Black Hole (of Calcutta); Glen-
    coe; Glens, the
42nd Street: 42nd Street
"Fountainblue": Fontainebleau Hotel
Fourth Avenue: Park Avenue
foxhunting: Melton Mowbray
France: Camargue, the; City of Five Flags;
    City of Light, the; Cockpit of Europe,
    the; Côte d'Azur; European Economic
    Community, the; Flanders; Fontaine-
    bleau; French Riviera, the; Frogland;
    Grand Corniche; Green Venice; Landes,
    the; Languedoc; Little Britain; no man's
    land; Old Dominion; Peninsula, the;
    Provence; South of France, the; Vichy
Francis I: Fontainebleau; Fontainebleau Ho-
    tel
Franco, Francisco: Guernica
Frankfurt: Oder-Neisse Line, the
Franklin, Benjamin: Freedom Trail; Gulf
    Stream
Franz Ferdinand, Archduke: accidental war,
    the
Frederick III: Hapsburg lip
Fredericksburg, Virginia: America's Most
    Historic City; Boyhood Home of George
    Washington
Frederick the Great of Prussia: Bayreuth
Freemantle: Free-O
Freeport, Maine: L. L. Bean
French Foreign Office: Quai d'Orsay, the
French Guiana: Devil's Island
French Lick Springs, Indiana: Carlsbad of
    America
Frenchman Flat: Nevada Proving Grounds

French National Assembly: Quai d'Orsay, the
French Riviera: Cornish Riviera, the; Côte d'Azur
Friedrichstrasse: Checkpoint Charlie
friendliness: Main Street
Friml, Rudolf: Paper Mill Playhouse
"Frisco": Los Angeles
Frobisher, Sir Martin: Northwest Passage, the
"From the New World": New World, the
frost dates: Iron Men of May
Fry, Roger: Bloomsbury
Fuengirola: Costa del Sol
Fujairah: Trucial States, the
Fulham: King's Road
Funfair: Battersea
"fun for all the family": Minsky's

G

Gadsden: Queen City of Alabama
Gaiety Theatre: Broadway, 1
Galena, Illinois: Crescent City of the Northwest
Galloway, Mull of: Galloway
Galveston: Oleander City; Port of the Southwest
Gambia: Senegambia
Gambia River: Senegambia
Ganges River: Hindustan
gangsters: Roaring Twenties, the
"Garden, the": Madison Square Garden
Garden, the: Covent Garden
Gardiner Bay: Island, the, 2
Garfield, James A.: Mother of Presidents; Ohio's Jewels
Garfield Park: West Side, 2
Garment District: Barbican, the; Fashion Avenue
garment industry: Manhattan
Garnett, David: Bloomsbury
garo: Karoo, the
Garrick, David: Adelphi, the
"gateway to the Highlands, the": Highlands, the
"Gateway to the West": Cumberland Gap; Gateway Arch
gay: Boystown
Gdańsk: Polish Corridor, the
General Electric: City That Lights and Hauls the World
Genghis Khan: Mongolia; Tartary
Geordieland: Northeast, the, 1; Tyneside
Geordies: Northeast, the, 1

George, David Lloyd: Limehouse
George, Lake: Hudson River
George III: Buck House
George IV: Brighton; King's Cross, 1
George V: Bognor Regis
George VI: Sandringham
George Cross, the: George Cross Island
George Washington Bridge: West Side, 1
Georgia: Atlantic States; Blue Ridge Mountains, the; Buzzard State; Cracker State; Deep South, the; Dogwood City; Empire State of the South; Gate City; Goober State; Iberia; Peach State; South, the, 1; Thirteen Original Colonies; Yankee Land of the South
German Democratic Republic: Berlin Wall, the
German Southwest Africa: Namibia
Germany: accidental war, the; Cockpit of Europe, the; East Indies, the; Oder-Neisse Line, the; Palatinate, the; Polish Corridor, the; Rhineland, the; Sheffield of Germany; Sudetenland, the; Unter den Linden; Weimar
Gerrard Street: Chinatown, 2
Gerry and the Pacemakers: Merseyside
Gershwin, George and Ira: Lower East Side
Gervais: blackthorn winter
Ghana: Slave Coast, the; Sudan, the
Gibraltar: Costa del Sol; Gib; Pillars of Hercules, the; Rock, the
G. I. Joe: Tommy (Atkins)
Gilbert Islands: Micronesia
Gillespie, Dizzy: Birdland
Gimbels: Filene's Basement; Macy's
Gimbels Basement: Gimbels
"Girl in the Red Velvet Swing, The": Madison Square Garden
Gissing, George: Grub Street
Giurgin: Orient-Express
"Give My Regards to Broadway": Herald Square
Gladstone, W. E.: Albany
Glasgow: Clydeside; Gorbals, the; Lowlands, the; Sauchiehall Street; Silicon Glen; Trossachs, the; Venice of the West
Glastonbury Tow: Glastonbury
Glencoe, Massacre of: Glencoe
Glendale: Forest Lawn
Glen Eagles: Glens, the
Glenfiddich: Glens, the
Glengarry: Glens, the
Glen More: Glens, the
"Glen of Weeping": Glencoe

Glenrothes: Silicon Glen
Globe theater: Bankside
Gloucestershire: Cheltenham; West Country, the; West, the, 2
GNMA: Ginnie Mae
Goa: Malabar Coast, the
Godiva, Lady: Coventry
Goethe, Johann von: Weimar
Gold Coast: Cabrini-Green Public Housing Project; Lake Shore Drive; Slave Coast, the
"Golden House": Domus Aurea
Golden Mile: Blackpool
Golden Triangle: Golden Crescent, the, 2
goldmining: Joburg; Rand, the
Goldsmith, Oliver: Liberty Hall
golf: R & A, the; St. Andrews
Gómez, Arturo: Big Mac, the
Gomez Object: Big Mac, the
Gondwanaland: Pangaea
gone for a Burton: Burton upon Trent
Gordon Square: Bloomsbury
Gotham: Neasden
Gould, Jay: Black Friday, 3
Government Center: Scollay Square
Government National Mortgage Association: Ginnie Mae
Goya, Francisco de: Prado, the
GP: Jeep
Graceland Cemetery: North Side
Graces: violet-crowned city, the
Grampian Mountains: Highlands, the
Granada: Alhambra
Grand Banks: Atlantic Provinces, the
Grand Central: East Side
"Grand Central Station": Grand Central
Grand Central Terminal: Grand Central; Park Avenue
Grand Falls, Maine: Niagara of the East
Grand Union Canal: Little Venice
Grant, Duncan: Bloomsbury
Grant's Tomb: West Side, 1
Grant, Ulysses S.: Grant's Tomb; Mother of Presidents; Ohio's Jewels
Grauman, Sidney: Grauman's Chinese Theater
Gravelly Hill: Spaghetti Junction
Gray's Inn: Inns of Court and Chancery
Gray's Inn Road: Printing House Square
Great Britain: Britain; Cambria; City of Five Flags; England; Land's End to John o' Groat's House; Little Britain; Mistress of the Seas; North Britain
Great British Seaside Holiday: Bognor Regis

Great Chicago Fire: Holy Name; Mrs. O'Leary's Barn; Water Tower; West Side
Great Depression: Empire State Building; Jarrow; Roaring Twenties, the
Great Dismal Swamp National Wildlife Refuge: Dismal Swamp, the
Greater London: Britain; London
"Greatest Show on Earth, The": Madison Square Garden
Great Exhibition of 1851: Crystal Palace; Kensington
Great Expectations: Little Britain
Great Glen: Glens, the
Great Karoo: Karoo, the
Great Lakes: Lady of the Lakes
Great Ouse River: Fens, the; Wash, the
Great Sandy Desert: Empty Quarter, the
Great Scotland Yard: Scotland Yard
Great South Bay: Fire Island
Great South Beach: Fire Island
Great St. Mary's: Golgotha, 2
Great Valley: Appalachian Mountains
Great White Way: Herald Square
Great Windmill Street: Windmill Theatre, the
Greece: Aetolia; Arcadia; Balkans, the; Cradle of Civilization; European Economic Community, the; Peloponnese, the; Rumelia; violet-crowned city, the
Greek Town: West Side
Green, Adolph: Greenwich Village
Greene, Graham: Stamboul
"Greenham Women": Greenham Common
Greenland: Far North, the
Green Mountains: Appalachian Mountains
Greenock: Clydeside
Greenstone Church: Pullman
Greenwich: Isle of Dogs, the
Greenwich Mean Time: Greenwich Observatory
Greenwich Village: Near North Side
Gregory, J. W.: Center, the
greyhound racetrack: Harringay
Grimethorpe Collier Band: Grimethorpe
Grosvenor: Belgravia
Grosvenor House: Park Lane
Grosvenor Square: Berkeley Square; Eisenhower Platz; Mayfair
"groupers": Fire Island
Guam: Micronesia
Gucci: Fifth Avenue
Guerrière: Old Ironsides
Guggenheim Museum: Fifth Avenue
Guiana Highlands: Guiana

Guinea: Guinea; White Man's Grave, the
Guinea-Bissau: Guinea
Guinea, Gulf of: Guinea
Guinness, Alec: Ealing
Gulf of Carpentaria: Gulf, the
Gulf of Mexico: Gulf, the; Mosquito Coast
Gulf States, the: Gulf, the; Middle East, the
Gulf Stream: Gulf, the
Gulf & Western building: Columbus Circle
GUM: Red Square
gun: big Bertha; peacemaker, the, 1
gunfights: Boot Hill
Gunga Din: Aldershot
Guyana: Guiana
Gwalior: Native States, the
Gwynedd: Snowdonia

H

Hadrian: Hadrian's Wall
Hadrian's Wall: England
Hague, the: Holland, 1
half-timbered houses: magpie houses
Haliç: Golden Horn, the
Hall, Sir Benjamin: Big Ben
Halsted Street: West Side
Hamburg: Reeperbahn, the
Hamlet: Sound, the
Hammerstein II, Oscar: Ol' Man River
Hammondsport, New York: Cradle of Aviation
Hampshire: Aldershot; Bournemouth; Camelot, 1; Hambledon; Hants; New Forest; South, the, 2; Wessex
Hampstead: Caledonian Market; Camden Town; Golders Green; Highgate; Kilburn
Hampstead Heath: Archway; Hampstead; Highgate
"Hampstead intellectual": Hampstead
Hampton Roads, Virginia: *Monitor* and *Merrimack*
Hamtonshire: Hants
Hamtun: Hants
Hanbridge: Five Towns, the
Hancock, Tony: Windmill Theatre, the
Hanford, Washington: First Atomic City
Hanley: Five Towns, the
Hannibal, Missouri: Bluff City
Hantshire: Hants
Hapsburg empire: Bohemia
Hardcastle, Squire: Liberty Hall
Harding, Warren G.: Mother of Presidents
Hardy, Thomas: Adelphi, the; Dorset; Wessex

Haringey: Harringay
Harlem: Broadway, 1; Fifth Avenue; Madison Avenue; Park Avenue; Spanish Harlem; Sugar Hill
Harlem River: Broadway, 1; Featherbed Lane; Hell Gate; Manhattan; Park Avenue; Sugar Hill
Harley Street: Baker Street; Wimpole Street
Harmon: Hudson River
Harringay Stadium: Harringay
Harris and Lewis: Western Isles, the
Harrison, Benjamin: Mother of Presidents
Harrison, William Henry: Mother of Presidents
Harrods: Knightsbridge
Harrogate: Ridings, the
Harrow-on-the-Hill: Harrow; Middlesex
Hartford: Charter Oak City; Insurance City
Hartford College: Bridge of Sighs, 4
Hartford, Huntington: Columbus Circle
Harumi Street: Ginza, the
Harvard College: Harvard Yard
Harvard Hall: Harvard Yard
Hasidic Jews: Brooklyn
Hastings: Cinque Ports, the
Hastings, Battle of: Hastings
Hastings, Rape of: Rapes
Hatteras, Cape: Outer Banks
Hausa: Sudan, the
Hausmann, Baron Georges Eugène: Opéra, l'
haute couture: Faubourg St. Honoré, Rue du
Haverford: Main Line
Hawaii: Aloha State; Banzai Pipeline; Gibraltar of the Pacific; Paradise of the Pacific; Pearl Harbor; Polynesia
Hayes, Rutherford B.: Mother of Presidents; Ohio's Jewels
Haymarket Riot: Haymarket Square
Haymarket Square: West Side
Haymarket, the: North End
"Haywain, The": Constable Country
Hayward Art Gallery: South Bank, the
Hearst, William Randolph: Dakota, the, 2
heavy industry: Ruhr, the
Hebrew: Fertile Crescent, the
Hebrides Islands: Western Isles, the
Hefner Hall: Gold Coast
Hefner, Hugh: Gold Coast
Height of Land: Continental Divide, the
Helios: Colossus of Rhodes
Hellespont, the: Golden Chersonese, the
Hell Gate: East River; Harlem River
Helsingborg: Sound, the
Helsingör: Sound, the

Helsinki, Finland: White City, 2
Hemingway, Ernest: Pamplona
Henley: Thames Valley, the
Henley-on-Thames: Henley
Henley Royal Regatta: Henley
Henrietta Maria, Queen: Queen State
Henry IV: Harry Percy of the Union
Henry VIII: Skevington's daughter; White-
    hall
Henry VIII: Blackfriars
Herald Square: Broadway, 1; Macy's
Herder, Johann von: Weimar
Hereford: Marches, the, 1; Midlands, the
Herefordshire: West Midlands, the; West,
    the, 2
Herod, temple of: Wailing Wall, the
heroin: Golden Triangle, the, 1
Herstmonceux: Greenwich Observatory
Hertfordshire: Home Counties, the; London;
    Metroland; Shires, the; Southeast, the;
    Watford
Herzegovina: Balkans, the
Hibbing, Minnesota: Iron Ore Capital of the
    World; Richest Village on Earth; Town
    That Moved Overnight
Hickham Field: Pearl Harbor
High, the: Broad, the
High Holborn: Drury Lane
Highlands: Capital of the Highlands, the;
    Glencoe; Glens, the; Lowlands, the
High Levant, the: Levant, the
High Mobility Multipurpose Wheeled Vehi-
    cle: Hummer, the
High Peak: Peak District, the
high-rise public housing complex: Cabrini-
    Green Public Housing Project
High Sellafield: Windscale
High Street: High, the; Main Street; Royal
    Miles, the
high street of Mayfair: Bond Street
Highveld: Karoo, the
Hilton: Park Lane
Hilton, James: Shangri-La, 1
Hindenburg disaster: Empire State Building
Hindi: Hindustan
Hindu: Hindustan
Hipparchus: Academy, the
hippies: Haight-Ashbury; King's Road
Hispanic: Barrio, the
Hitler, Adolf: Polish Corridor, the; Sudeten-
    land, the; Weimar
HMMWV: Hummer, the
Holborn: Camden Town; Chancery Lane
Holborn Circus: Hatton Garden
Holland: Spice Islands, the

Holland Park: Notting Hill
Holliday, Judy: Greenwich Village
Hollywood: Beverly Hills; Broadway, 1;
    Grauman's Chinese Theater; Hollywood
    and Vine; West, the, 3
Hollywood Boulevard: Grauman's Chinese
    Theater; Hollywood and Vine
Holmes, Oliver Wendell: Old Ironsides
Holmes, Sherlock: Baker Street
Holtby, Winifred: Ridings, the
Holy Grail: Glastonbury
Holy Land: Palestine
Holyoke, Massachusetts: Paper City
Holy Roman Empire: Holland, 1; Palatinate,
    the; West, the, 1
Holyroodhouse: Royal Miles, the
Holy Sepulchre: Holy Land, the, 1
Home Counties: Metroland; Middlesex;
    Southeast, the; Surrey
homosexuals: Boystown; Castro, the; Fire Is-
    land
Honduras: Mosquito Coast
Hong Kong: Cathay; Honkers
honky-tonk: Broadway, 2
Hooker, Thomas: Constitution State
hoozer: Hoosier State
Hope, Anthony: Ruritania
Hore-Belisha, Leslie: Belisha beacon
Hornet: Shangri-La, 2
Horse Guards: Whitehall
horseracing: Newmarket
Hot Springs, Arkansas: Baden-Baden of
    America
Household Cavalry: Whitehall
House of Commons: Westminster
House of Lords: House, the; Westminster
House of Representatives: House, the
Houston: Magnolia City
Houston, General Sam: Alamo, the
Houston Street: East Village, the; Green-
    wich Village; NoHo
Hove Albion: Albion
Howard, Eddy: Aragon Ballroom
Howe, Julia Ward: Marseillaise of the
    Unemotional Yankee
Huddersfield: Broad Acres, the; Ridings, the
Hudson, Henry: Northwest Passage, the
Hudson River: Clinton's ditch; Forty-Second
    Street; Gateway of the West; Manhat-
    tan; Palisades, the; Rhine of America;
    West Point; West Side, 1; West, the, 3
Hudson River Valley: Appalachian Moun-
    tains
Hudson Street: Greenwich Village
Hughes, Thomas: Rugby

Hull: Ridings, the
Hull House: West Side
Humber estuary: North, the, 1
Humber River: North, the, 1; Northumbria
Humberside: Ridings, the; Wolds, the
Humboldt Park: West Side
Hume, David: Athens of the North, the
hundreds: Chiltern Hundreds, the; Rapes
Hungary: Iron Curtain, the; Transylvania
"hunger marches": Jarrow
Huntsville, Alabama: Rocket City
Hyannisport: Cape, the
Hyde Park: Belgravia; Crystal Palace; Hyde
    Park Corner; Knightsbridge; Number
    One, London; Paddington; Park Lane;
    Rotten Row; South Side; Speakers' Cor-
    ner; Tyburnia
Hyde Park Corner: Number One, London;
    Park Lane
Hyderabad: Golconda; Native States, the;
    Sodom of India
"hypersonic" aircraft: Orient-Express
Hythe: Cinque Ports, the

I

Iberian Peninsula: Peninsula, the
Iberian peninsula: Iberia
Iberville Street: Storyville
Iceland: Scandinavia
"ice saints": blackthorn winter
Idaho: Bozeman Trail; Gem of the Moun-
    tains; Gem State; Inland Empire, the;
    Little Ida
Idlewild: Brooklyn
Île de la Cité: Latin Quarter, the, 1; Marais,
    the
Îles du Salut: Devil's Island
"I'll be seeing you": Abyssinia
Illinois: Corn State; Egypt; Garden of the
    West; Land of Lincoln; Midwest, the;
    Mother of States; Prairie State; Sucker
    State
Illinois, University of: West Side
Imperial City: Forbidden City, the
Imperial Valley, California: America's Great
    Winter Garden
Imperial War Museum: Bedlam
In Darkest Africa: Dark Continent, the
Independence Hall: Birthplace of American
    Liberty
Independence, Missouri: Oregon Trail;
    Santa Fe Trail
India: Bhopal; Black Hole (of Calcutta);
    Blighty; Ceylon; Coromandel Coast, the;

Deccan, the; East, the, 2; Eurasia; Far
    East, the; Golconda; Gondwanaland;
    Hindustan; Indies, the; Indochina; Mal-
    abar Coast, the; Middle East, the; Na-
    tive States, the; Northwest Frontier,
    the; Orient, the; raj, the; Rann of
    Kutch, the; Subcontinent, the
Indiana: Hoosier State; Midwest, the;
    Mother of States; Railroad City
Indianapolis: Railroad City
Indian Ocean: Seven Seas, the
Indian Removal Act: Trail of Tears
Indian States and Agencies: Native States,
    the
Indian Territory: Trail of Tears
Indies, the: East Indies, the
Indo-China: Far East, the; Farther India; In-
    dies, the
Indonesia: East Indies, the; Southeast Asia;
    Spice Islands, the
Indore: Native States, the
Indus River: Sind
Inner City: Forbidden City, the
Inner Hebrides: Western Isles, the
Inner Mongolia: Mongolia
Inner Mongolian Autonomous Region: Inner
    Mongolia
Inner Temple: Inns of Court and Chancery;
    Temple, the
Innsbruck, Austria: Brenner Pass
Inns of Court: Chancery Lane; Temple, the
insanity: Bellevue
Interlaken: Bernese Oberland, the
International Cricket Conference: Lord's
International Falls, Minnesota: Icebox of the
    United States
International Herald Tribune: Harry's Ameri-
    can Bar
International House: West Side, 1
Inverness: Capital of the Highlands, the;
    Glens, the; Highlands, the; Northland,
    the
Inverness-shire: Highlands, the
Iowa: Corn State; Hawkeye State; Land of
    the Rolling Prairie; Middle Border, the;
    Midwest, the; Outlaw Country
Ipanema: Copacabana, 1
Iran: Golden Crescent, the, 1; Gulf, the;
    Middle East, the; Persia
Iraq: Gulf, the; Mesopotamia; Middle East,
    the
Ireland: Britain; Emerald Isle, the; Erin; Eu-
    ropean Economic Community, the; Hi-
    bernia; Inns of Court and Chancery;
    Old Dominion; United Kingdom, the

Ireland, Northern: Southie
Ireland, Republic of: Eire; Irish Free State,
    the; Province, the
Irish Free State: Eire
Irish Republican Army: Southie
Iron Bridge: Telford
Iron Curtain: Bamboo Curtain, the; Yerevan
Iron Curtain countries: Iron Curtain, the
Irving, Washington: Alhambra; Gotham
Islam: Golden Crescent, the, 1; Sudan, the
Islamic states: Middle East, the
Islas Malvinas: Falkland Islands, the
Islay: Western Isles, the
Isleworth: Middlesex
Islington: Camden Town
Islington High Street: Angel, the
Israel: Gaza Strip, the; Land of Milk and
    Honey; Levant, the; Middle East, the;
    Palestine; West Bank, the
Istanbul: Golden Horn, the; Orient, the; Ori-
    ent-Express; Stamboul
Italian Riviera: Cornish Riviera, the
Italy: Brenner Pass; Bride of the Sea; Bridge
    of Sighs, 1; Campagna, the; City of Lil-
    ies, the; City of the Seven Hills, the;
    Etruria; European Economic Commu-
    nity, the; Italian Riviera, the; Jewel of
    the Adriatic, the; Leghorn; Marches,
    the, 2; Naples; Papal States, the; Pi-
    ovro; Rialto; Scylla and Charybdis;
    Seven Hills, the
Ivory Coast: Guinea; Slave Coast, the

J

jack: Union Jack, the
Jack and Charlie's 21 Club: "21" Club
Jackson Heights: Queens
Jackson, Mississippi: Chimneyville
Jackson Park: Museum of Science and In-
    dustry; South Side; White City, 1
Jackson Square: French Quarter, the
Jack the Ripper: Whitechapel
Jaggers, Mr.: Little Britain
Jamaica: Cockpit Country, the; Jamdung;
    Mo Bay
James I: Addled Parliament; Newmarket
James II: Charter Oak City; Glencoe
James River: Tidewater Virginia
Jamestown, Virginia: House of Burgesses
jammed down: Jamdung
Jammu and Kashmir: Native States, the
Japan: East, the, 2; Far East, the; Land of
    the Rising Sun, the; Third World, the;
    Tidal Basin; West, the, 1

Japung: Japan
Jarrow march: Jarrow
Java: Coromandel Coast, the; East Indies,
    the; Queen of the Eastern Archipelago
Jefferson Memorial: Tidal Basin
Jefferson, Thomas: Billingsgate; Fort Dear-
    born; Mother of Presidents
Jeffersonville: Indiana's Gateway City
Jehovah: Adonai
Jekyll Island, Georgia: Millionaire's Resort
Jenkins, Roy: Limehouse
Jericho Street: Jericho
Jermyn Street: Simpson's of Piccadilly
Jerome Avenue: Featherbed Lane
Jersey City: Palisades, the
Jerusalem: City of David, the; Holy Land,
    the, 1; Salem; Wailing Wall, the
Jih-pun: Japan
Johannesburg: Joburg; Rand, the
John, Augustus: Chelsea, 1; Fitzrovia
John Bull's Other Island: John Bull
John Hancock Center: Magnificent Mile,
    the; Playboy Building; Sears Tower
John Hancock Tower: Back Bay
John, King: Runnymede
John Lewis: Oxford Street
John o' Groat's house: Land's End to John
    o' Groat's House
Johnson, Dr.: Grub Street
Jolson, Al: Lower East Side
Jones, Inigo: Covent Garden
Jordan: Middle East, the; Trans-Jordan;
    West Bank, the
Jordan River: West Bank, the
Joseph of Arimathea: Glastonbury
Juan-les-Pins: French Riviera, the
Jubilee Market: Covent Garden
Judaism: Wailing Wall, the
Judea: Holy Land, the, 1
Jugoslavia: Dalmatia
Juilliard School: Broadway, 1
Jumping Frog Jubilee: Frogtown
Jungle, The: Union Stockyards
Junkers: Prussia
Jupiter: Capitoline, the; Red Spot, the
Jura: Western Isles, the
Jutes: Jutland
Jylland: Jutland

K

Kalamazoo: Celery City
Kampuchea, People's Republic of: Cambodia
Kanal, der: Channel, the
Kanem: Sudan, the

Kangaroo Valley: Earl's Court
Kansas: Battleground of Freedom; Bleeding Kansas; Central State; Cyclone State; Garden of the West; Grasshopper State; Jayhawker State; Kansas Bibles; Navel of the Nation; Queen City of the Border; Squatter State; Sunflower State; West, the, 3
Kansas City: West, the, 3
Kansas City, Missouri: Heart of America; Metropolis of the Missouri Valley; Mushroomopolis
Kansas-Nebraska Bill: Battleground of Freedom
Kansas Pacific Railroad: Chisholm Trail
Karelia Suite: Karelia
Kashmir: Northwest Frontier, the
Kattegat Strait: Sound, the
Kaufman, George S.: Round Table at the Algonquin
Keats, John: Middlesex
Keller, Helen: City of Kind Hearts
Kelly, Ed: South Side
Kemp, Thomas: Kemp Town
Kennedy, Edward: Chappaquiddick
Kennedy, Jacqueline: Camelot, 2
Kennedy, John F.: Camelot, 2; Chappaquiddick; Dallas Book Depository
Kennedy, John F. Airport: Brooklyn
Kennedy, Robert F.: Chappaquiddick
Kennelly, Martin: South Side
Kensington: Chelsea, 1; Shepherd's Bush
Kensington and Chelsea: Royal Borough, the
Kensington Gardens: Bayswater; Kensington; Number One, London; Rotten Row
Kensington Palace: Royal Borough, the
Kensington-upon-Thames: Royal Borough, the
Kent: Dover; Garden of England, the; Home Counties, the; Isle of Thanet, the; London; Pantiles, the; Rapes; Southeast, the; Tunbridge Wells; Weald, the; White Cliffs, the
Kentucky: Appalachia; Bear State; Bible Belt; Bluegrass State; City of Beautiful Churches; Commonwealth; Convention City; Corn-cracker State; Dark and Bloody Ground State; Fort Knox; Gateway to the South; Hemp State; Metropolis of the New South; Midwest, the; Mother of States; Nation's Thoroughfare; South, the, 1; Tobacco State
Kenya: East Africa
Keokuk, Iowa: Kodak City

Kern, Jerome: Ol' Man River; Paper Mill Playhouse
Key: Kew Gardens
Key, Francis Scott: Fort McHenry
Keynes, John Maynard: Bloomsbury
Key West: Boston Post Road
Khmer Republic: Cambodia
Khrushchev, Nikita S.: Camp David
Khyber Pass: Northwest Frontier, the
Kilburn: Maida Vale
Kilgallen, Dorothy: Stork Club
Kimberley, South Africa: Big Hole, the
kimberlite: Big Hole, the
King Arthur: Camelot, 1
King George V Docks: Dockland
King Kong: Empire State Building
King of Kings: Grauman's Chinese Theater
King's Chapel: Freedom Trail
King's College: Backs, the
Kings County: Brooklyn; Manhattan
King's Cross: Battlebridge; Islington; Pentonville
King's Cross Station: Battlebridge; King's Cross, 1; Somers Town
King's inns: Inns of Court and Chancery
King's Road: Chelsea, 1
Kingsway: West End, the
King, Wayne: Aragon Ballroom
King William Street: London Bridge
Kipling, Rudyard: Gloucester
Kiribati: Micronesia
"Knickerbocker, Cholly": Stork Club
Knightsbridge: Harrods; Hyde Park Corner; Sloane Square; West End, the
Knightsbridge Barracks: Rotten Row
knights of the shires: Shires, the
Knights Templars: Inns of Court and Chancery; Temple, the
"Knocked 'em in the Old Kent Road": Old Kent Road, the
Knoxville: Queen City of the Mountains
Knype: Five Towns, the
Kokomo, Indiana: City of Firsts
Kola Peninsula: Lapland; Scandinavian Shield, the
Kongens By: King's City
Kopechne, Mary Jo: Chappaquiddick
Korea: Far East, the
Kreml: Kremlin, the
Kremlin: Red Square
"Kremlinology": Kremlin, the
"Kremlin watchers": Kremlin, the
Krishna River: Coromandel Coast, the
Krupp, Friedrich Alfred: big Bertha
Kuwait: Gulf, the

Kwazulu: Zululand

L

"L. A.": Los Angeles
la Botte: Montmartre
La Brea Avenue: Miracle Mile
"Lady in Red": Biograph Theater
Lady of the Lake: Trossachs, the
Lafayette, Indiana: Star City
Lafayette Street: Lower East Side; NoHo;
   SoHo
La Guardia Airport: Queens
La Guardia, Fiorello H.: Broadway, 1; Gai-
   ety, the; Minsky's
Lake Country: Lake District, the
Lake District: Furness
Lake Erie: Gateway of the West; Lady of
   the Lakes
Lake Havasu City: London Bridge
Lake Huron: Lady of the Lakes
Lakeland: Lake District, the
Lake Michigan: Lady of the Lakes
"Lake poets": Lake District, the
Lake Pontchartrain: Florida Parishes
Lakes, the: Lake District, the
Lake Shore Drive: Gold Coast; McCormick
   Place
Lake Superior: Lady of the Lakes
Lakeview: Near North Side
Lallands: Lowlands, the
Lamb Cutlets Reform: Reform Club, the
Lambeth: Bedlam; Brixton; Oval, the
Lambeth Conference: Lambeth
"Lambeth degrees": Lambeth
Lambeth Palace: Lambeth
Lambeth Walk: Lambeth
Lammermuir hills: Southern Uplands, the
Lancashire: Blackpool; Cottonopolis; North,
   the, 1; Northwest, the, 1; Shires, the;
   Westmorland
'Land of Fire': Tierra del Fuego
Land of Look Behind: Cockpit Country, the
Languedoc: South of France, the
Languedoc-Roussillon: Languedoc
Lanvin: Faubourg St. Honoré, Rue du
Lanxang: Land of a Million Elephants, the
Laos: Golden Triangle, the, 1; Indochina;
   Land of a Million Elephants, the;
   Southeast Asia
Lapland: Land of the Midnight Sun, the
Lapps: Lapland
Laredo, Texas: Gate City
La Rochelle: Green Venice
Lashio: Burma Road, the

La Spezia: Italian Riviera, the
Last Chronicle of Barset, The: Barset
Las Vegas, Nevada: Glitter Gulch; Strip,
   the, 1
lathe: Rapes
Latin Quarter: Left Bank, the; Old Quebec
   (Vieux-Québec)
Latter-Day Saints: Land of the Saints
Latvia: Baltic States
Lauderdale County: Tri-Cities
"Laugh-In": Burbank
Laurasia: Pangaea
Laval University: Latin Quarter, the, 2
Law Courts: Chancery Lane
Law, John: German Coast
Lawnmarket: Royal Miles, the
lawn tennis championships: Wimbledon
Lawrence: Bleeding Kansas
Law Society: Chancery Lane
lawyers: Chancery Lane
Leadbelly: Greenwich Village
Lear, Edward: Coromandel Coast, the
Leavenworth, Kansas: Cottonwood City
Lebanon: Levant, the; Middle East, the
Leeds: Broad Acres, the; Dales, the; Ridings,
   the
Lee, Gypsy Rose: Gaiety, the
Left Bank: Deux Magots, les; Latin Quarter,
   the, 1; Montmartre; Quai d'Orsay, the
Leicestershire: Belgravia; Lincolnshire; Mel-
   ton Mowbray; Midlands, the; Rutland;
   Shires, the
Leinster: Province, the
Le Moyne, Jean Baptiste: French Quarter,
   the
Lenin Mausoleum: Red Square
Lennon, John: Dakota, the, 2
Leofric: Coventry
lesbian: Boystown
Les Saules: D.S.N.C.O.
Levant, Oscar: Hollywood; Round Table at
   the Algonquin
Levant, the: Near East, the
Lever House: East Side
Lewis, Sinclair: Main Street
Lewis, Wyndham: Fitzrovia
Lexington: Athens of Virginia; Birthplace of
   American Liberty
Lexington Avenue: Chrysler Building
Lexington Commons: Birthplace of Ameri-
   can Liberty
Lexington Hotel: Loop, the
Lexington, Kentucky: Athens of the West;
   Belle City of the Bluegrass Regions;
   Bluegrass Capital

Lhasa: Forbidden City, the
Liberty Island: Bedloe's Island
Liberty of the Clink, the: Clink Street
Libya: Maghreb; Middle East, the; Near
   East, the; North Africa
Libyan desert: Western Desert, the
life vest: Mae West, 1
lighthouse: West Side, 1
Limehouse: Bow; Chinatown, 2; East End;
   Pool of London, the
"Limehouse Four": Limehouse
Lincoln: Lindsey
Lincoln, Abraham: Ford's Theater
Lincoln Center: Broadway, 1; Forty-Second
   Street
Lincoln Center for the Performing Arts:
   West Side, 1
Lincoln Park: Near North Side; North Side;
   Old Town
Lincolnshire: Fens, the; Flixborough; Hol-
   land, 2; Kesteven; Lindsey; Midlands,
   the; Wash, the
Lincolnshire Wolds: Wolds, the
Lincoln's Inn: Chancery Lane; Inns of Court
   and Chancery
Lincoln Square: Broadway, 1; West Side, 1
Lindbergh, Charles A: Bourget, le
Lindesnes: Naze, the
Lithuania: Baltic States
Little Britain: Paternoster Row
Little Karoo: Karoo, the
"Little Red Lighthouse, The": West Side, 1
Little Rock: City of Roses
Little Venice: Maida Vale
Liverpool: Merseyside; North, the, 1; North-
   west, the, 1; Pool, the, 1; Strawberry
   Fields; Toxteth; Wirral, the
Liverpool Street Station: Petticoat Lane
Livingston: Silicon Glen
Livorno: Leghorn
Llanfairpwllgwyngill:
   Llanfairpwllgwyngillgogerychwyrn-
   drobllllantysiliogogogoch
Lloret de Mar: Costa Brava, the
Lloyd's of London: City, the; Lloyd's
Lloyds Harbor: North Shore, 1
Loch Ness: Glens, the; Highlands, the
Locris: Aetolia
Lofoten Islands: Maelstrom, the
Loire River: Garden of France, the
Lombards: Lombard Street
Lombard Street: Bank, the
Lombardy: Lombard Street

London: Abbey Road; Adelphi, the; Albany;
   Aldermaston; Aldershot; Ally Pally; An-
   gel, the; Archway; Army & Navy
   Stores; Ascot; Ashes, the; Athenaeum,
   the; Bagshot; Baker Street; Bankside;
   Battersea; Battlebridge; Bayswater; Bel-
   gravia; Berkeley Square; Big Ben; Bil-
   lingsgate; Blackfriars; Black Friday, 1;
   Blackwall Tunnel; Bloomsbury; Bond
   Street; Borough, the; Bow; Bow Street;
   Bray; Brixton; B, the; Buck House; Bur-
   lington House; Caledonian Market;
   Camden Lock; Camden Town; Carey
   Street; Carlton Club, the; Carnaby
   Street; Centre Point; Chancery Lane;
   Charing Cross; Chelsea, 1; Chiltern
   Hundreds, the; Chinatown, 2; City, the;
   Clapham; Clink Street; Clubland, 1;
   Covent Garden; Crystal Palace; Dock-
   land; Downing Street; Drury Lane; Eal-
   ing; Earl's Court; East End; Eisenhower
   Platz; Elephant and Castle; Embank-
   ment, the; Eton; Fitzrovia; Fortnum &
   Mason; Gatwick Airport; Golders
   Green; Golgotha, 1; Gravesend; Great
   Wen, the; Greek Street; Green Belt;
   Greenwich Observatory; Grosvenor
   Square; Halles, les; Hampstead; Harley
   Street; Harringay; Harrods; Harrow;
   Hatton Garden; Heathrow; Henley;
   Highgate; Holy Land, the, 2; Home
   Counties, the; Hyde Park Corner; "In"
   and "Out," the; Isle of Dogs, the; Isling-
   ton; Jackson's of Piccadilly; Jermyn
   Street; Kangaroo Valley; Kensington;
   Kew Gardens; Kilburn; King's Cross, 1;
   King's Road; Knightsbridge; Lambeth;
   Law Courts, the; Leicester Square;
   Limehouse; Little Venice; Lord's; Maida
   Vale; Marylebone; Mayfair; Metroland;
   Middlesex; Neasden; Newgate Prison;
   Nine Elms; North, the, 1; Notting Hill;
   Number 10; Number One, London; Old
   Kent Road, the; Old Vic, the; Orient-Ex-
   press; Oval, the; Oxford Street; Pad-
   dington; Pall Mall; Park Lane;
   Paternoster Row; Pentonville; Petticoat
   Lane; Piccadilly Circus; Pimlico; Pool of
   London, the; Portland Place; Portobello
   Road; RADA; Reform Club, the; Ronan
   Point; Rotten Row; Royal Borough, the;
   Runnymede; Sandhurst; Savile Row; Sa-
   voy, the; Scotland Yard; Seven Dials;
   Seven Sisters; Shaftesbury Avenue;
   Shepherd Market; Shepherd's Bush;

Simpson's (in the Strand); Simpson's of Piccadilly; Sloane Square; Slough; Smoke, the; Soho; Somerset House; Somers Town; South Bank, the; Southeast, the; Speakers' Corner; Star Chamber; St. James's; St. John's Wood; Stoke Mandeville; Strawberry Hill; Surrey; Swiss Cottage; Swone-one; Temple, the; Thames Valley, the; Thorney Island; Thunderer, the; Tin Pan Alley; Tower Hamlets; Turnabout, the; Tussaud's Waxworks Museum, Madam; Twickenham; Tyburnia; V & A, the; Vauxhall; Victoria; Wardour Street; Warren Street; Waterloo; Watford; Wembley Stadium; West End, the; Westminster; Whitechapel; Whitefriars; Whitehall; Wimbledon; Wimpole Street; Windmill Theatre, the; Woolwich; Yard, the

London Bridge: Borough, the; Clink Street; Elephant and Castle; Pool of London, the; Tower Bridge

London, center of: Charing Cross

London, City of: Bank of England, the; Bank, the; Barbican, the; Bart's; Bedlam; Billingsgate; Blackfriars; Bow; City, the; Derry; Dockland; Drain, the; Fleet Street; Grub Street; Little Britain; Lloyd's; Lombard Street; London; London Bridge; Mansion House, the; Marylebone; Mincing Lane; Old Bailey; Old Lady of Threadneedle Street, the; Paternoster Row; Petticoat Lane; Printing House Square; Smithfield; Square Mile, the; Throgmorton Street; West End, the; Westminster

London County Council: London

London, County of: London

Londonderry: Derry

London Dock: Dockland

London Docklands Development Corporation: Dockland

London, Inner: London

London Labour and the London Poor: East End

London, Lord Mayor of: Bank, the; Mansion House, the

London, Outer: London

London Stock Exchange: House, the

London, Tower of: Billingsgate; Chinatown, 2; Dockland; East End; Tower Hamlets; Tower, the; Whitechapel

London Underground: Archway; Bakerloo; Drain, the; Metroland; Temple, the

London University: Bloomsbury

London Wall: no man's land

Longfellow, Henry Wadsworth: Acadia; Gloucester

Long Island: Brooklyn; Brooklyn Bridge; East River; Fire Island; Hamptons, the; Hell Gate; Island, the, 2; Narrows, the; Queens; Ridings, the

Long Island City: Queens

Long Island Sound: Hell Gate; Island, the, 2; North Shore, 1

Longshaw: Five Towns, the

Longton Potteries, the: Five Towns, the

Looe: Cornish Riviera, the

Lookout Mountain: Battle above *or* in the Clouds

Loomis, R. S.: Camelot, 1

Loop: Billy Goat Tavern; Holy Name; Magnificent Mile, the; Marshall Field's; McCormick Place; Mrs. O'Leary's Barn; Navy Pier; Near North Side; North Side; Sears Tower; South Side; West Side

López de Santa Ana, Antonio: Alamo, the

Lord Chancellor: woolsack, the

Lord Mayor: City, the

Lord's Cricket Ground: Ashes, the

Lord, Thomas: Lord's

Los Angeles: Beverly Hills; Burbank; City of Flowers and Sunshine; Forest Lawn; Grauman's Chinese Theater; Hollywood; Hollywood and Vine; La Brea Tar Pits; LAX; Malibu; Megalopolis; Miracle Mile; Queen of the Cow Counties; San Fernando Valley; Second City; Strip, the, 2; Sunset Boulevard; Watts

Los Angeles International Airport: LAX

Los Angeles Times: Los Angeles

Lost Horizon: Shangri-La, 1

Lothian: Heart of Midlothian, the

Louisiana: Alligator State; Child of the Mississippi; Creole State; Crescent City; Deep South, the; Florida Parishes; French Quarter, the; German Coast; Great South Gate; Gulf, the; Irish Channel; Key of the Great Valley; Paris of America; Pelican State; Queen of the South; South, the, 1; Storyville; Sugar State

Louisiana Avenue: Irish Channel

Louisville: City of Beautiful Churches; Convention City; Fort Knox; Gateway to the South; Metropolis of the New South; Nation's Thoroughfare

Louisville, Kentucky: City of Homes
Louis XIV: Père Lachaise
Louvre, the: Halles, les; Opéra, l'
Lowell, Massachusetts: Manchester of
    America; Spindle City
Lower East Side: Five Points
Lower East Side, the: East Village, the
Lower Guinea: Guinea
Lower Palatinate: Palatinate, the
Lower Pool: Pool of London, the
Lower Regent Street: Piccadilly Circus
Lower Thames River Street: Billingsgate
Lower West Side: Hull House; West Side
Lowlands: Highlands, the; Lowlands, the;
    Southern Uplands, the
Low Peak: Peak District, the
Low Sellafield: Windscale
Lowther hills: Southern Uplands, the
Ludgate Circus: Fleet Street
Ludgate Hill: Old Bailey
lunatic asylum: Bloomingdale's
Luxembourg: Benelux; European Economic
    Community, the; Low Countries, the
Lynchburg, Virginia: Hill City
Lynn: North Shore, 2
Lynn, Massachusetts: City of Soles
Lyons, Leonard: Stork Club

M

Macaulay, Thomas: Albany
MacDonald, Ballard: Blue Ridge Mountains,
    the
Macdonalds: Glencoe
MacDowell, Edward Alexander: MacDowell
    Colony
Macedon: Colossus of Rhodes
Macedonia: Balkans, the
Mackenzie Range: Rockies, the
Macon: Heart of Georgia
Macy's: Broadway, 1; Filene's Basement;
    Gimbels; Herald Square
"Mad Avenue": Madison Avenue
Madeleine, Boulevard de la: Maxim's
Mademoiselle Fifi: Minsky's
Madhya Pradesh: Bhopal
Madison: Four Lake City
Madison Avenue: Clock at the Astor,
    Biltmore; Rodeo Drive; Stork Club
Madison, James: Mother of Presidents
Madison Square: Broadway, 1; Madison Av-
    enue
Madrid: Prado, the
Mafiking: Mafeking
Magdalen College: High, the

Magellan: Tierra del Fuego
Magellan, Strait of: Tierra del Fuego
Magna Carta: Runnymede
Magnificent Mile, the: Near North Side;
    Playboy Building; Water Tower
Maida: Maida Vale
Maidenhead: Thames Valley, the
Maine: Border State; Boston Post Road;
    Down East; Down East State; East,
    the, 1; Lumber City; Lumber State;
    Metropolis of the Northeast; New Eng-
    land; Northeast Corridor; Old Dirigo
    State; Pine Tree State; Polar Star State;
    Queen City of the East; Switzerland of
    America
Main Street: Boston Post Road
"Main Street": Camino Real, el
Main Street: Main Street
Majestic, the: West Side, 1
Majorca: Costa Brava, the
Málaga: Costa del Sol
Malaya: Indochina
Malay Archipelago: East Indies, the; Far
    East, the; Oceania; Southeast Asia
Malay Peninsula: Golden Chersonese, the
Malaysia: East Indies, the; Southeast Asia
Mali: Timbuktu
Malibu Beach Colony: Malibu
Mall, the: St. James's
Malmö: Sound, the
Malory, Sir Thomas: Camelot, 1
Malta: George Cross Island
Maluku: Spice Islands, the
Mamertus: blackthorn winter
Manche, la: Channel, the
Manchester: Cottonopolis; North, the, 1;
    Northwest, the, 1; Wigan
Mandalay: Burma Road, the
Manhattan: Broadway, 1; Brooklyn; Brook-
    lyn Bridge; brownstone; Dormitory of
    New York; East River; East Side; Har-
    lem River; Hudson River; McAdoo
    Tubes; NoHo; Off Broadway, Off-Off
    Broadway; Queens; SoHo; Third Ave-
    nue; Wall Street; West, the, 3; See also
    New York City in the Index.
Manhattan Island: Bedloe's Island
"Manhattan Project": Staff Field
Manila: Pearl of the Orient
man-in-the-street: Wigan
Manitoba: Prairie Provinces, the
Mann's Chinese Theater: Grauman's Chi-
    nese Theater
"man on the Clapham omnibus": Clapham
Manship, Paul: Rockefeller Center

Mansion House: Bank, the
mansion-house: Mansion House, the
Maori: Polynesia
Marais Poitevin: Green Venice
Marbella: Costa del Sol
Marble Arch: Marylebone; Oxford Street;
    Park Lane; Speakers' Corner; Tyburnia
Marblehead: North Shore, 2
Marcantonio, Vito: Spanish Harlem
Marches, Welsh: Marches, the, 1
Marcy, William L.: Albany Regency
Margate: Isle of Thanet, the
Marguery, the: East Side
Marianas Islands: Micronesia
Maritime Provinces: Atlantic Provinces, the
Market Street: Path of Gold
Marks and Sparks: M & S
Marks and Spencer: Baker Street; M & S;
    Oxford Street
Marlborough, Duke of: Blenheim Palace
Marlow: Thames Valley, the
Maroons: Cockpit Country, the
Marquesas: Polynesia
Marquette, Michigan: Queen City of Lake
    Superior
Marquette Park: West Side
Mars: Red Planet, the
Marseilles: Côte d'Azur; French Riviera, the;
    South of France, the
Marshall Islands: Micronesia
Marshall Space Flight Center: Rocket City
Marsh, Reginald: Minsky's
Martha's Vineyard: Chappaquiddick
Marx, Groucho: Grant's Tomb
Marx, Karl: Highgate
Maryburn: Marylebone
Maryland: Atlantic States; Camp David;
    Cockade State; Delmarva Peninsula; Di-
    amond State; Dixie; Fort McHenry;
    Free State; Mason-Dixon Line; Monu-
    mental State; Monument City; North-
    east, the, 2; Old Line State; Oyster
    State; Queen State; Shangri-La, 3; Ter-
    rapin State; Thirteen Original Colonies
Marylebone Cricket Club: Lord's
Marylebone Road: Tussaud's Waxworks
    Museum, Madam
Mason, Charles: Dixie; Mason-Dixon Line
Mason-Dixon line: North, the, 2; South,
    the, 1
Massachusetts: Athens of America; Baked
    Bean State; Bay Horse; Beantown;
    Birthplace of American Liberty; Boston
    Post Road; Cape, the; Chappaquiddick;

City of Kind Hearts; Classic City; Com-
    monwealth; Cradle of Liberty; East,
    the, 1; Gloucester; Hub of the Uni-
    verse; Jacob's Pillow; Literary Empo-
    rium, the; *Mayflower*; Megalopolis;
    Mohawk Trail; New England; (Old) Bay
    State; Old Colony State; Puritan City;
    Puritan State; Rock-ribbed State; Thir-
    teen Original Colonies; Trimountain
    City
Massachusetts Avenue: Embassy Row
Massachusetts Bay Colony: Old Colony State
Massachusetts Hall: Harvard Yard
Massachusetts Turnpike: Route 128
Maunee River: Indian-Appian Way
Mauretania: Western Desert, the
Maxwell Street: West Side, 2
May, Elaine: Second City
Mayfair: Belgravia; Berkeley Square; Gros-
    venor Square; Park Lane; Savile Row;
    Shepherd Market; Soho; St. James's;
    West End, the
Mayhew, Henry: East End
McAdoo, William Gibbs: McAdoo Tubes
McClure, Sir Robert: Northwest Passage,
    the
McCormick, Cyrus: North Side
McKim, Mead, and White: Madison Square
    Garden
McKinley, William: Mother of Presidents
McOuat, Jimmy: White Otter Castle
"Medical Center, the": West Side, 1
Mediterranean coast: Grand Corniche
Mediterranean Sea: Anatolia; Costa Blanca;
    Costa Brava, the; Costa del Sol; Costa
    Smeralda; Côte d'Azur; Fertile Cres-
    cent, the; French Riviera, the; George
    Cross Island; Gib; Levant, the; Mare
    Nostrum; Med, the; Orient, the; Pales-
    tine; Pillars of Hercules, the; Seven
    Seas, the; South of France, the; West,
    the, 1
megalopolis: Northeast Corridor
Melanesia: Australasia; Micronesia; Oceania;
    Polynesia
Melbourne: Smoke, the
Melbourne House: Albany
melton: Melton Mowbray
Melton pad: Melton Mowbray
Memphis: Bluff City; Commercial Metropolis
    of Western Tennessee; Silver City
Mendoza, Argentina: Christ of the Andes
Menton: French Riviera, the; Grand Cor-
    niche
Mercia: East Anglia

Mercia, king of: Offa's Dyke
Merion: Main Line
Mersey River: Merseyside; Wirral, the
Mersey sound: Merseyside
Merthry Tydfil: Valleys, the
Mesopotamia: Babylon
Messina, Strait of: Scylla and Charybdis
Metroland, Margot: Metroland
Metropole Hotel: Loop, the
Metropolitan Line: Metroland
Metropolitan Museum of Art: Fifth Avenue;
     West Side, 1
Metropolitan Opera: Forty-Second Street
Metropolitan Opera House: Broadway, 1
Metropolitan Police: Scotland Yard
Metropolitan Railway: Metroland
Met, the: Scotland Yard
Mexican War: Volunteer State
Mexico: Big Bend
Miami: Alligator Alley; City of Opportuni-
     ties; Little Cuba
Miami Beach: Fontainebleau Hotel
Michigan: Automobile Capital of the World;
     Auto State; Breakfast Food City; Celery
     City; Dynamic City; Lady of the Lakes;
     Mother of States; Motown; Peninsula
     State; Water Wonderland; Wolverine
     State
Michigan Avenue: Magnificent Mile, the
Michigan, Lake: Aragon Ballroom; Gold
     Coast; Lake Shore Drive; Navy Pier;
     North Side; Old Town; South Side
Mickey Mouse: Disneyland
Micronesia: Australasia; Melanesia; Oceania;
     Polynesia
Middle Atlantic States: Atlantic States
Middle East: Arabia; East, the, 2; Far East,
     the; Near East, the; Orient, the; Pales-
     tine; Promised Land, the
Middle Rockies: Rockies, the
Middlesbrough: Ridings, the
Middlesex: Home Counties, the; London;
     Metroland
Middlesex County Cricket Club: Lord's
Middlesex Street: Petticoat Lane
Middle Temple: Inns of Court and Chan-
     cery; Temple, the
Mideast: Middle East, the
Midi, the: South of France, the
Midlands: Five Towns, the; Huntingdon-
     shire; Melton Mowbray; Mercia; North,
     the, 1; Northeast, the, 1; Potteries, the;
     Shires, the; South, the, 2; Watford
Midlands, the: East Midlands, the

Midlothian: Border, the; Heart of Midlo-
     thian, the
"Midway, the": South Side
Midway Airport: West Side
Midway Plaisance: South Side; White
     City, 1
Mies van der Rohe, Ludwig: East Side
Mile End: East End
Millburn, New Jersey: Paper Mill Playhouse
Million Dollar Theater: Grauman's Chinese
     Theater
Millwall: East End
Millwall Docks: Dockland; Isle of Dogs, the
Miltiades: Academy, the
Milton, John: Golden Chersonese, the
Milton Street: Grub Street
Milwaukee: Blonde Beauty of the Lakes;
     Cream City; Deutsch-Athens
Milwaukee Avenue: West Side
minchins: Mincing Lane
Minch, the: Western Isles, the
"Mindy's": Lindy's
Ming Street: Chinatown, 2
Minneapolis: City of Flour; Sawdust City
Minnenwerfer: moaning Minnie
Minnesota: Bread and Butter State; Bread
     Basket of the World; City of Flour; Go-
     pher State; Lake State; Middle Border,
     the; Midwest, the; Mother of States;
     New England of the West; North Star
     State; Playground of the Nation; Wheat
     State
Minoan colony: Atlantis
Minsky, Billy, Herbert, Morton, and Abe:
     Minsky's
Minsky Brothers' National Winter Garden:
     Minsky's
Minster: Shambles, the
Minuit, Peter: Manhattan
Minute Men: Birthplace of American Lib-
     erty
Mississippi: Alligator State; Bayou State;
     Bluff City; Border Eagle State; Deep
     South, the; Ground-hog State; Gulf, the;
     Magnolia State; Mud-Cat (*or* -Waddler)
     State; South, the, 1
Mississippi Bubble: German Coast
Mississippi River: Backbone of the Confed-
     eracy; Child of the Mississippi; Cres-
     cent City; dust bowl, the; Florida
     Parishes; French Quarter, the; German
     Coast; Gibraltar of America; Irish
     Channel; Ol' Man River
Missouri: Bullion State; Gateway Arch;
     Great River City; Iron Mountain State;

Lead State; Memphis of the American Nile; Midwest, the; Mother of the West; Mound City; Ozark (Mountain) State; Pennsylvania of the West; Puke State; Show Me State; Solid City

Missouri River: Devils Nest; West, the, 3

Missouri Rockets: Radio City Music Hall

Mobile: City of Five Flags; Gulf City; Picnic City

model T: tin Lizzie

Mojave Desert: Land of Little Rain

Moldavia: Balkans, the

Moldavian Soviet Socialist Republic: Bessarabia

mole: gentleman in black velvet, the

Moluccas: Spice Islands, the

Monaco: Principality, the

Mongolian People's Republic: Mongolia; Outer Mongolia

Mongols: Mongolia

Monongahela River: Golden Triangle, the, 2

Monopoly: Boardwalk

Monroe, James: Mother of Presidents

Mons: Cockpit of Europe, the

Montana: Big Sky Country; Bonanza State; Bozeman Trail; Inland Empire, the; Land of Shining Mountains; Middle Border, the; Northwest, the, 2; Stubtoe State; Treasure State

Montauk Point: Island, the, 2

Monte Carlo: French Riviera, the; Grand Corniche; South of France, the

Monte Cavallo: Quirinal, the

Montego Bay: Mo Bay

Montenegro: Balkans, the

Montgomery, Alabama: Cradle of the Confederacy

Montmartre: Pigalle

Montparnasse: Left Bank, the

Montpelier, Vermont: Green Mountain City

Montreal: International City, the

Moore, Henry: Staff Field

Moorfoot hills: Southern Uplands, the

Moran, Bugs: Loop, the

Morgan, J. P.: Minsky's

Moriches Bay: Fire Island

Moriches Inlet: Fire Island

Mormons: Land of the Saints

Morningside Drive: West Side, 1

Morocco: Barbary Coast, the; Kasbah, the; Maghreb; North Africa; Pillars of Hercules, the; Western Desert, the

Morris, William: Wardour Street

Moscow: Holy Mother of the Russians; Kremlin, the; Muscovy; Red Square; Russia; Siberia

Moses, Robert: Fire Island

Moss Brothers: Moss Bros

"motor town": Motown

Mott Haven: Park Avenue

Moulin Rouge: Montmartre

Mount Ebert: Rockies, the

Mount Etna: Atlantis

Mount Everest: Roof of the World, the

Mount Hacho: Pillars of Hercules, the

Mount Helicon: Aganippides, the

Mount Katahdin, Maine: Appalachian Trail, the

Mount Snowdon: Snowdonia

Mount Vesuvius: Naples

movie industry: Wardour Street

Mrs. O'Leary's barn: West Side, 2

Mt. Eden Avenue: Featherbed Lane

Muhammad: Al Borak

Mulberry Street: Little Italy

Municipal Pier: Navy Pier

Munster: Province, the

Murder in the Calais Coach: Orient-Express

Murder on the Orient-Express: Orient-Express

Murillo, Bartolomé: Prado, the

Murmansk: Scandinavian Shield, the

Muscle Shoals: Muscle Shoals Area; Tri-Cities

Muses: Aganippides, the; violet-crowned city, the

music publishing: Manhattan

Muslims: Hindustan

M-X missile: peacemaker, the, 2

Myrtle Beach: Grand Strand

Mysore: Native States, the

N

Nairn, Ian: subtopia

Nairnshire: Highlands, the

Namib: Namibia

Napier, Sir Charles: Sind

Napoleon: Peninsula, the; Waterloo

Napoleonic Wars: Maida Vale

Narberth: Main Line

Narmada River: Deccan, the

Nashville: Athens of the South; Dimple of the Universe; Rock City

Nashville, Tennessee: Natchez Trace

Nassau County: Island, the, 2

Natal: Zululand

Natchez: Bluff City

Natchez, Mississippi: Natchez Trace
National, the: Grand National, the
National Health Service: East Anglia; Wessex
National Theatre: South Bank, the
National Theatre Company: Old Vic, the
NATO: Little Siberia
natural gas: Texas Tea
Natural Histories: Albion
Natural History, Museum of: Kensington
Nauru: Micronesia
Naval and Military Club: "In" and "Out," the
Navarre: Pamplona
Neal, John: Brother Jonathan
Near East: East, the, 2; Far East, the; Middle East, the; Orient, the
Near North Side: Biograph Theater; Bughouse Square; Cabrini-Green Public Housing Project; Holy Name; Lake Shore Drive; Magnificent Mile, the; New Town; North Side; Old Town; Playboy Building; Rush Street; Water Tower; Wrigleyville
Near Northwest Side: West Side
Near Southwest Side: Maxwell Street; Pilsen
Near West Side: Haymarket Square; Hull House; West Side
Nebraska: Antelope State; Bad Lands, the; Blackwater State; Bug-eating State; Cornhuskers State; Devils Nest; Tree Planter's State; West, the, 3
Needles, the: Island, the, 1
Neisse River: Oder-Neisse Line, the
Nelson: Woolwich
Nene River: Fens, the; Wash, the
Nepal: Subcontinent, the
Nero: Domus Aurea
Nesbit, Evelyn: Madison Square Garden
Netherlands: Benelux; Diamond City; East Indies, the; European Economic Community, the; Flanders; Holland, 1; Low Countries, the; Venice of the North
Neufchâtel: D.S.N.C.O.
Nevada: Battle-born State; Far West, the; Glitter Gulch; Mining State; Sagebrush State; Sagehen State; Silver State; Southwest, the, 1
New Amsterdam: Bowery, the; Broadway, 1; 42nd Street
Newark, New Jersey: Oranges, the
Newberry, Walter L.: Holy Name
New Bond Street: Bond Street
New Brighton: Wirral, the
New Britain: Hardware City
New Brunswick: Atlantic Provinces, the

New Caledonia: Melanesia
Newcastle: Hadrian's Wall
Newcastle, Duke of: Dukeries, the
Newcastle-upon-Tyne: Jarrow; Northeast, the, 1; Tyneside
New Covent Garden Market: Nine Elms
New England: Atlantic States; blue laws; Boston Post Road; Brother Jonathan; Cape, the; Iron Men of May; Yankee State
New England Conservatory of Music: Back Bay
New England states: Northeast, the, 2
New England Thruway: Boston Post Road
Newfoundland: Atlantic Provinces, the
Newgate Prison: Old Bailey
New Greek Town: West Side
New Grub Street: Grub Street
New Hampshire: Appalachian Mountains; East, the, 1; Granite State; Mother of Rivers; New England; Switzerland of America; Thirteen Original Colonies; White Mountain State
New Haven: City of Elms
New Haven, Connecticut: blue laws
New Hebrides: Melanesia
New Jersey: Atlantic States; Boardwalk; Camden and Amboy State; Clam State; Cockpit of the Revolution; East, the, 1; Foreigner State; Gamblers Express; Garden State; Jersey Blue State; Lyons of America; McAdoo Tubes; Mosquito State; New Spain; Northeast, the, 2; Palisades, the; Switzerland of America; Thirteen Original Colonies; West Side, 1; Workshop of the Nation
New London Bridge: London Bridge
Newmarket Heath: Newmarket
New Mexico: Cactus State; Land of Delight Makers; Land of Enchantment; Land of Heart's Desire; Land of Opportunity; Rockies, the; Southwest, the, 1; Spanish State; Sunbelt; Sunshine State
New Orleans: Crescent City; French Quarter, the; German Coast; Great South Gate; Irish Channel; Key of the Great Valley; Paris of America; Queen of the South; Storyville
Newport, Rhode Island: America's Cup; Capital of Vacationland; City by the Sea; Queen of Summer Resorts
New Printing House Square: Printing House Square
New Scotland Yard: Scotland Yard

News of the World: News of the Screws, the

New South Wales: Bondi Beach

newspaper industry: Fleet Street

New Town: Athens of the North, the; Near North Side

"New Town": Old Town

New York: Albany Regency; Appalachian Mountains; Aqueduct City; Atlantic States; Bison City; Black Friday, 3; Bourget, le; Brother Jonathan; City of Churches, the; City of Flour; City That Lights and Hauls the World; Clinton's ditch; Convention City; Dormitory of New York; East, the, 1; Empire State; Excelsior State; Featherbed Lane; Fire Island; Gateway of the West; Island, the, 2; Los Angeles; Northeast, the, 2; Queen City of the Lakes; Rhine of America; Rodeo Drive; Thirteen Original Colonies; West Point

New York Bay: Hudson River; Narrows, the

New York Central: Grand Central

New York City: Abercrombie & Fitch; Avenue of the Americas; Bellevue; Big Apple; Birdland; Bloomie's; Bloomingdale's; Boston Post Road; Bridge of Sighs, 2; Broadway, 1; Brooklyn; Brooklyn Bridge; Brooks Brothers; brownstone; Capital of the World; Chelsea, 2; Chinatown, 1; Chrysler Building; City of Towers; Clock at the Astor, Biltmore; Columbus Circle; Dakota, 2; East Side; East Village, the; Empire City; Empire State Building; Fashion Avenue; Fifth Avenue; Filene's Basement; Fire Island; Five Points; Foley Square; Forest Hills; 42nd Street; 47th Street; Gaiety, the; Gaiety Delicatessen; Gamblers Express; Garment District; Gimbels; Gotham; Great White Way; Greenwich Village; Hammacher-Schlemmer; Hell Gate; Herald Square; House that Ruth Built; Hudson River; Island, the, 2; Jack Dempsey's; Leon & Eddie's; Lindy's; Little Italy; Lower East Side; Macy's; Madison Avenue; Madison Square Garden; Manhattan; Melting Pot; Metropolis of America; Near North Side; Northeast Corridor; Park Avenue; Plaza, the; Queens; Radio City Music Hall; Sardi's; Schrafft's; Spanish Harlem; Stork Club; Strip, the, 2; Sugar Hill; Tiffany's; Tin Pan Alley; Tribeca; West

Side, 1; West, the, 3; See also *Manhattan* in the Index.

New York City Ballet: Broadway, 1

New York City Opera: Broadway, 1

New York City Visitors Center: Columbus Circle

New Yorker, The: West, the, 3

New York harbor: Liberty Harbor

New York, New Haven, and Hartford Railroad: Grand Central

New York Racquet Club: Park Avenue

New York Society for the Suppression of Vice: Minsky's

New York Stock Exchange: Big Board, the; Wall Street

New York Times, the: Sardi's

New York Yacht Club: America's Cup

New York Yankees baseball team: House that Ruth Built

New Zealand: Antipodes, the; Australasia; East, the, 2; Oceania; Polynesia

Nicaragua: Mosquito Coast

Nice: French Riviera, the; South of France, the

Nicholas II: Sick Man of the East

Nichols, Mike: Second City

Nick's: Greenwich Village

Nidderdale: Dales, the

Nigeria: Slave Coast, the; White Man's Grave, the

Niger River: Timbuktu

Nihon: Japan

Nile River: Abu Simbel; Western Desert, the

Nilgiri hills: Deccan, the

Nine Elms: Covent Garden

Nine, the: European Economic Community, the

Ninth Avenue: Broadway, 1

Niobrara: Devils Nest

Nippon: Japan

Noble Square: West Side

non-slave states: Mason-Dixon Line

Nordkalotten: Scandinavian Shield, the

Norfolk: East Anglia; Fens, the; Sandringham

Norfolk Broads: Broads, the

Norfolk Navy Yard: Mother-in-law of the Navy

Norfolk, Virginia: Mother-in-law of the Navy; Sailor Town

Norman: Hastings

Norman Conquest: Wessex

Norman, Oklahoma: TOTO

Norman's Woe: Gloucester

North: Midlands, the; North Country, the; Northwest, the, 1; South, the, 2; Watford

North, the: Clubland, 2; Mason-Dixon Line; Northeast, the, 1; South, the, 3; West, the, 2

North Adams: Mohawk Trail

North Africa: Black Death, the

North America: Arctogaea; Laurasia; Middle Passage, the; Vinland; West, the, 1

Northamptonshire: Lincolnshire; Midlands, the; Shires, the; Soke of Peterborough, the

North Atlantic: Roaring Forties

North Atlantic Ocean: Herring Pond, the; Seven Seas, the

North Britain: Britain

North British Hotel: North Britain

North Carolina: Atlantic States; Dismal Swamp, the; Graveyard of the Atlantic; Land of the Sky; Lifeline of the Confederacy; Lost Colony, the; Old North State; Outer Banks; Rip Van Winkle State; South, the, 1; Tarheel State; Thirteen Original Colonies; Turpentine State

North Dakota: Flickertail State; Great Central State; Land of the Dakotas; Middle Border, the; Sioux State; Twin Sisters; West, the, 3

North Downs: Weald, the; White Cliffs, the

Northeast: Geordieland; Jarrow

Northeast Expressway: North End

Northern Boulevard: Queens

Northern England: Clubland, 2

northern hemisphere: North, the, 3

Northern Ireland: Derry; Province, the; Six Counties, the

Northern Karoo: Highveld, the; Karoo, the

Northern Rockies: Rockies, the

Northern Territory: Alice Springs; Ayers Rock; Territory, the

North Fork: Island, the, 2; North Shore, 1

North Holland: Holland, 1

North of the Border: Border, the

"north of Watford": Watford

North Pacific Ocean: Seven Seas, the

Northport: North Shore, 1

North Rampart Street: French Quarter, the

North Riding: Ridings, the

North River: Manhattan

North Sea: Dales, the; Fens, the; Firth of Forth Bridge; German Ocean, the; Jutland; Low Countries, the; Roost, the; Wash, the

North Shore: Island, the, 2

North Side: Aragon Ballroom; Gold Coast

North-South, a program for survival: South, the, 3

North-South, a program for survival; report of the Independent Commission on International Development: North, the, 3

North Uist: Western Isles, the

Northumberland: Northeast, the, 1; Northumbria

North Wales: Royal Borough, the

North Wells Street: Old Town

Northwest, the: Crewe; Cumberland; Golden Mile, the; Lake District, the; Merseyside; Strawberry Fields; Westmorland; Windscale

Northwestern University: North Side

Northwest Frontier Province: Northwest Frontier, the

Northwest Side: North Side; West Side, 2

Northwest Territories: Territories, the

North York Moors: Broad Acres, the

North Yorkshire: Ridings, the

Norway: Gulf Stream; Land of the Midnight Sun, the; Lapland; Maelstrom, the; Naze, the; Northland, the; Scandinavia; Scandinavian Shield, the; Thule

Notre Dame Mountains: Appalachian Mountains

Nottingham: Lincolnshire; North, the, 1

Nottinghamshire: Dukeries, the; Lincolnshire; Midlands, the; North, the, 1

Nottinghamshire, England: Gotham

Notting Hill: Portobello Road

Notting Hill Carnival: Notting Hill

Notting Hill Gate: Notting Hill

Nova Scotia: Atlantic Provinces, the

Nubia: Abu Simbel

nuclear cruise missiles: Greenham Common

nuclear weapons: Windscale

Nuestra Señora la Reina de los Angeles de Porciúncula: Los Angeles

Number 11: Downing Street; Number 10

Number 10 Downing Street: Number 10

O

Oahu: Pearl Harbor

Oak Street: Magnificent Mile, the

O'Banion, Dion: Holy Name

oc: Languedoc

Ocean Bay Park: Fire Island

Ocean Beach: Fire Island

Oceania: Australasia; Micronesia; Polynesia

oceans: Doldrums, the; Horse Latitudes, the; Roaring Forties

Oder River: Oder-Neisse Line, the

Offa, King: Mercia

Ogden, William B.: Holy Name

O'Hare International Airport: North Side

Oh! Calcutta!: Off Broadway, Off-Off Broadway

Ohio: America's Little Switzerland; Buckeye State; Conservative Cincinnati; Gateway State; Midwest, the; Mother of Presidents; Mother of States; Paris of America; Porkopolis; Queen City of the West; Rubber Capital of the United States; Summit City; Tire City of the United States; Yankee State

oil: Black Gold; Texas Tea

oïl: Languedoc

Okeechobee, Florida: Chicago of the South

Oklahoma: Bible Belt; Boomer State; Chisholm Trail; Lane of the Red People; Panhandle, the; Queen City of the Border; Sooner State; Trail of Tears; West, the, 3

Old Bailey: Newgate Prison

Old Bond Street: Bond Street

Old Brompton Road: Kensington

"Old Bullion": Bullion State

Old Compton Street: Greek Street; Tin Pan Alley

Old Course: St. Andrews

Old Granary Burying Grounds: Freedom Trail

"Old Hawkeye": Hawkeye State

Old London Bridge: London Bridge

Old North Church: Freedom Trail

Old Port: Old Quebec (Vieux-Québec)

Old Quebec: Latin Quarter, the, 2; Place Royale

"Old Slopians": Salop

Old South Meeting House: Freedom Trail

Old State House: Freedom Trail

Old Town: Near North Side; Second City

Old Town School of Folk Music: Old Town

O'Leary's barn, Mrs.: West Side

O'Leary's cow, Mrs.: Mrs. O'Leary's Barn

Oman: Arabia; Gulf, the

One Magnificent Mile: Magnificent Mile, the

Ontario: White Otter Castle

Ootacamund: Deccan, the

OPEC: petro-dollars

Open University: Milton Keynes

opera: Covent Garden

opium: Golden Crescent, the, 1; Golden Triangle, the, 1

Orange: Golden Triangle, the, 3; Oranges, the

Oregon: Beaver State; Far West, the; Hardcase State; Inland Empire, the; Northwest, the, 2; Oregon Trail; Pacific Northwest, the; Pacific Wonderland; Sunset State; Webfoot State

Oregon Trail: Rockies, the

Öresund: Sound, the

Orient, the: East, the, 2; Levant, the

Oriental Street: Chinatown, 2

Orient-Express: Orient, the; Stamboul

Orient Point: Island, the, 2; North Shore, 1

Orkney Island: Roost, the

Orlando, Florida: Disneyland

Orleans County: Northeast Kingdom

ortolans: Landes, the

Orwell, George: Wigan

Oswald, Lee Harvey: Dallas Book Depository

Otto I of Bavaria: Disneyland

Ottoman Empire: Bessarabia; Near East, the; Rumelia; Sublime Porte, the

Our American Cousin: dundrearies

'our sea': Mare Nostrum

Outer City: Forbidden City, the

Outer Hebrides: Western Isles, the

Outer Mongolia: Mongolia

Overend and Gurney: Black Friday, 2

Ovid: Eternal City, the

Owen, David: Limehouse

Oxford: Bridge of Sighs, 4; Broad, the; City of Dreaming Spires; High, the; Isis; Jericho; Thames Valley, the

Oxfordshire: Banbury Cross; Chiltern Hundreds, the; Henley; Midlands, the; Oxon; South, the, 2; Thames Valley, the

Oxford Street: Baker Street; Bloomsbury; Bond Street; Centre Point; Fitzrovia; Mayfair; West End, the

Oxford University: Bodleian Library; House, the; Oxbridge

Oyster Bay: North Shore, 1

P

Pacific Northwest: Inland Empire, the

Pacific Ocean: Australasia; Northwest Passage, the; Pacific Northwest, the; Russia; Soviet Union, the

Pacific Palisades: Malibu; Sunset Boulevard

Paddington: Bayswater; Little Venice; Paddo; Westminster

Paddington Bear: Paddington

Pepin III, King of the Franks: Papal States, the
"perfidious Albion": Albion
Persian Empire: Persia
Persian Gulf: Arabia; Fertile Crescent, the; Gulf, the; Seven Seas, the; Trucial States, the
Perth, Western Australia: America's Cup; Free-O; Maida Vale
Pétain, Marshal Henri: Vichy
Petaluma, California: World's Egg Basket
Peterborough, New Hampshire: MacDowell Colony
Peters, Bernadette: Off Broadway, Off-Off Broadway
Petersburg, Virginia: Cockade City
petroleum shortage: double nickel
Philadelphia: Birthplace of American Liberty; City of Brotherly Love, the; Main Line; Quaker City; Rebel Capital
Philippines: Little Vietnam; Pearl of the Orient
Philippines, the: East Indies, the; Southeast Asia
Phoenicia: Fertile Crescent, the
Phoenix: Valley of the Sun, the
"Physiognomical Haircutting": Columbus Circle
Piaf, Édith: Père Lachaise
Picasso, Pablo: Guernica
Piccadilly: Albany; Bond Street; Hyde Park Corner; Knightsbridge; Mayfair; Number One, London; Shepherd Market; St. James's; West End, the
Piccadilly Circus: Leicester Square; Shaftesbury Avenue; Windmill Theatre, the
Piccadilly Street: Burlington House; Fortnum & Mason; "In" and "Out," the; Jackson's of Piccadilly; Piccadilly Circus; Simpson's of Piccadilly
Picon, Molly: Lower East Side
Picts: Hadrian's Wall
Piddle: Tolpuddle
Piddlehinton: Tolpuddle
Piddletrenthide: Tolpuddle
Piedmont Region: Blue Ridge Mountains, the; Tidewater Virginia
Piermont, New York: Palisades, the
Pigalle: Montmartre; Moulin Rouge
pig's foot: Cincinnati oyster
Pilgrims: *Mayflower*
Pillars of Hercules: Atlantis
Pilsen: West Side, 2
Piltdown: Piltdown man
Pimlico: Victoria

Pimlico, Ben: Pimlico
Pindar: violet-crowned city, the
"Pines, the": Fire Island
"Pirate Coast": Trucial States, the
pirates: Spanish Main, the
pirates' black flag: Jolly Roger
Pisco Elqui, Chile: Big Mac, the
Pitcairn Island: Polynesia
Pittsburgh: Birmingham of America; City of Steel; Golden Triangle, the, 2; Iron City; Smoky City; World's Workshop
Pittsfield: Mohawk Trail
"Pitt Street farmer": Pitt Street
Place de la Concorde: Champs Élysées, the
Place des Armes: French Quarter, the
Place du Tertre: Montmartre
'place of stones': Mafeking
Place Royale: Old Quebec (Vieux-Québec)
Plague: Oberammergau
Plaistow: East End
Plato: Academy, the; Atlantis
Playboy: Gold Coast; Playboy Building
Playboy Building: Magnificent Mile, the
Playboy Mansion: Gold Coast
Plaza Hotel: Fifth Avenue; Plaza, the
Plaza, the: Fifth Avenue
Pleiades: Seven Sisters
Pliny: Albion
PLO: Palestine
plutonium: Windscale
Plymouth: Eddystone Light
Plymouth Colony: Old Colony State
Plymouth Rock: *Mayflower*
Poe, Edgar Allen: Maelstrom, the
Pohjoiskalotti: Scandinavian Shield, the
Point Calimere: Coromandel Coast, the
Point o' Woods: Fire Island
Poland: Oder-Neisse Line, the; Prussia; Soviet Union, the; Sudetenland, the
Polk Street: Loop, the
"Polly Perkins of Paddington Green": Paddington
Polo, Marco: Cathay; Orient, the
Polo Lounge: Beverly Hills Hotel
Pol Pot regime: Cambodia
Polynesia: Australasia; Oceania
Pompidou Center: Halles, les
Pomponians: Pompey
"Pond, the": Herring Pond, the
Pontalba buildings: French Quarter, the
Pont de la Concorde: Quai d'Orsay, the
Pont de l'Alma: Quai d'Orsay, the
Poplar: East End; Tower Hamlets
popular music: Tin Pan Alley
porcelain: Chelsea, 1

Port Arthur: Golden Triangle, the, 3
Portillo: South American Alps
Port Jackson: Botany Bay
Port Jefferson: North Shore, 1
Portland, Maine: Beautiful City by the Sea; Forest City; Hill City
Portland, Oregon: City of Roses; Rose City
Porto Cervo: Costa Smeralda
Portsmouth: Island, the, 1; Pompey
Portsmouth, New Hampshire: North Shore, 2
Portugal: European Economic Community, the; Iberia; Peninsula, the; Spice Islands, the
Portuguese Guinea: Guinea
potbanks: Potteries, the
Potomac River: Pentagon, the; Tidal Basin; Tidewater Virginia
Potteries: Etruria
Poultry: Bank, the
Pratt's: Clubland, 1
prehistoric reptile: dinosaur of darkness
Presbytre, the: French Quarter, the
Prescott, Arizona: Cowboy Capital
presidential retreat: Shangri-La, 3
Preussen: Prussia
Prime Minister (Britain): Downing Street; Number 10
Prince Edward Island: Atlantic Provinces, the
Princes Street: New Town, the; North Britain
Princetown: Moor, the
"Printer's Row": Loop, the
prison: Moor, the; Wormwood Scrubs
Prisoner of Zenda, the: Ruritania
Private Eye: Neasden
Prohibition: "21" Club; Roaring Twenties, the
Prometheus: Rockefeller Center
pro-slavery partisans: Bleeding Kansas
Prospect Park: Brooklyn
Provençal: Provence
Provence: Midi, the; Province, the; South of France, the
Providence, Rhode Island: Beehive of Industry; Roger Williams City; Southern Gateway to New England
Provincetown: Cape, the
Prudential Center: Back Bay
Prudential Tower Office: Back Bay
Ptolemy: German Ocean, the
"Public Enemy Number One": Biograph Theater
Public Garden: Back Bay

"public schools": Roedean
publishing: Paternoster Row
Pueblo, Colorado: Pittsburg of the West
Pueblo de los Angeles: Los Angeles
Puerto Rican: Barrio, the; Spanish Harlem
Puerto Rico: Commonwealth
Puget Sound: Galloping Gertie
Pullman: South Side
Pullman, George: North Side; Pullman
Pullman, Illinois: City of Brick
Pullman Community: Pullman
Pullman Village: Pullman
punks: King's Road
Puritans: blue laws
Pyrenees Mountains: Languedoc

Q

Qatar: Arabia; Gulf, the
Quad Cities: Tri-Cities
Quai d'Orsay: Wilhelmstrasse, the
Quakers: Brother Jonathan
Quantrill, William: Bleeding Kansas
quasars: Big Mac, the
Quebec: D.S.N.C.O.; Old Quebec (Vieux-Québec)
Quebec, Canada: Appalachian Mountains
'Queen of the Angels': Los Angeles
Queens: Brooklyn; East River; Forest Hills; Hell Gate; Island, the, 2; Manhattan; West Side, 1
Queens Boulevard: Queens
Queen's Camel: Camelot, 1
Queen's College: Backs, the; High, the
Queensland: Bananaland
Quincy, Illinois: Gem City of the West; Model City
Quirinal: Seven Hills, the
Quirinale, il: Quirinal, the
Quorn and the Pytchely: Shires, the
Quorn hunt: Melton Mowbray

R

Racine: Belle City (of the Lakes)
"Radio City": Rockefeller Center
Radio Corporation of America: Rockefeller Center
radio networks: Manhattan
Radnor: Main Line
Raffles: Albany
Raleigh, North Carolina: City of Oaks
Ramillies: Cockpit of Europe, the
Ramses II: Abu Simbel
Ramsgate: Isle of Thanet, the

Rand, Sally: Gaiety, the
Randall's Island: Hell Gate
Randolph Field: West Point of the Air
rapes: Rapes
Rapid City, South Dakota: Denver of South
    Dakota; Gateway City of the Hills
Rappahannock River: Tidewater Virginia
Ras el Khaimah: Trucial States, the
Rastafarians: Babylon
RCA Building: Rockefeller Center
Reading: Thames Valley, the
Record Office: Chancery Lane
Red Center: Center, the
red-light district: blue-light district;
    Reeperbahn, the; Storyville; Track, the
Red Sea: Arabia; Seven Seas, the; Western
    Desert, the
Reef, the: Rand, the
Reform, the: Clubland, 1
Reform Act: Reform Club, the
Reform Act of 1832: Old Sarum
Reformation: Babylon
Reform Club: Pall Mall
Regent's Canal: Camden Lock; Camden
    Town; Little Venice
Regent's Park: Baker Street; Camden Town;
    Harley Street; King's Cross, 1; Lord's;
    Marylebone; Portland Place; St. John's
    Wood
Regent Street: Carnaby Street; Jermyn
    Street; Savile Row; West End, the
Rego Park: Queens
Reina de los Angeles, la: Los Angeles
Relief of Mafeking: Mafeking
"Remember the Alamo": Alamo, the
remoteness: Mongolia; Timbuktu
Renaissance Center: Ren Cen
Repeal: "21" Club
Revere, Massachusetts: Coney Island of Bos-
    ton
Revere, Paul: Freedom Trail
Revolutionary War: Blue Hen State; Faneuil
    Hall; Harvard Yard
Rhineland-Palatinate: Palatinate, the
Rhine River: Black Forest, the; Rhineland,
    the; Ruhr, the
Rhode Island: Cape, the; East, the, 1; Little
    Rhody; Nation's Most Corrupt State;
    New England; Ocean State; Plantation
    State; Thirteen Original Colonies
Rhodes: City of the Sun; Colossus of Rhodes
Rhondda: Valleys, the
Rhone River: Camargue, the; Languedoc;
    Midi, the
Rhymney River: Valleys, the

Rialto Bridge: Bridge of Sighs, 4
Rice, Dan: Uncle Sam
Richmond: Manhattan
Richmond, Indiana: Quaker City of the
    West
Richmond, Virginia: Modern Rome; Queen
    City of the South; Queen on the James
    (River)
Richmond-upon-Thames: Kew Gardens;
    Strawberry Hill; Twickenham
Ridge-and-Valley Province: Appalachian
    Mountains
Ring, the: Bayreuth
Ringling Brothers, Barnum & Bailey Circus:
    Madison Square Garden
Rio de Janeiro: Copacabana, 1
Rio Grande: Big Bend
Rio Grande Valley: Magic Valley
Riverhead: Island, the, 2
River House: East Side
Riverside Church: West Side, 1
Riverside Drive: Grant's Tomb; West
    Side, 1
Riviera, Bill Miller's: West Side, 1
Riviera, le: French Riviera, the; Grand Cor-
    niche; Midi, the; South of France, the
Rivoli, the: Broadway, 1
Road to Wigan Pier, the: Wigan
Roanoke Island: Lost Colony, the; Outer
    Banks
Robertson Street: Storyville
Rob Roy: Trossachs, the
Rochester, New York: Aqueduct City; City
    Built by Hands; Kodak City; Quality
    City
Rockefeller, John D.: Rockefeller Center
Rockefeller, Jr., John D.: West Side, 1
Rockefeller Center: Radio City Music Hall
"Rock English": Rock, the
Rockets, the: Radio City Music Hall
Rockettes, the: Radio City Music Hall
Rockford, Illinois: Forest City
Rocky Mountains: Continental Divide, the;
    dust bowl, the; Inland Empire, the; Or-
    egon Trail; Rockies, the
Rodgers, Richard: Hell's Kitchen
Rodgers, William: Limehouse
Roebling, John A.: Brooklyn Bridge
Roebling, William A.: Brooklyn Bridge
Romania: Bessarabia; Soviet Union, the;
    Transylvania
Romberg, Sigmund: Maxim's; Paper Mill
    Playhouse
Rome: Campagna, the; Capitoline, the; City
    of the Seven Hills, the; Domus Aurea;

Rome: Campagna, the; Capitoline, the; City
   of the Seven Hills, the; Domus Aurea;
   Eternal City, the; Palatine, the; Papal
   States, the; Quirinal, the; Rodeo Drive;
   Seven Hills, the
Romney: Cinque Ports, the
Romulus: Palatine, the
Roosevelt, Franklin Delano: Camp David;
   Shangri-La, 3
Roosevelt Island: Manhattan
Rose, Billy: Copacabana, 2
Rosemont: Main Line
Ross and Cromarty: Highlands, the
Ross, A. W.: Miracle Mile
Rossetti, Dante Gabriel: Chelsea, 1
Ross, Harold: Round Table at the Algonquin
Rossini, Gioacchino: Père Lachaise
Rotherhithe: Pool of London, the
"rotten boroughs": Old Sarum
Rotterdam: Holland, 1
Round-the-Isle yacht race: Island, the, 1
Rowan and Martin: Burbank
Rowlandson, Thomas: Adelphi, the
Roxburgh: Border, the
Roxyettes, the: Radio City Music Hall
Roxy Theatre: Radio City Music Hall
Royal Academy (of Arts): Burlington House
Royal Academy of Dramatic Art: RADA
Royal Albert Docks: Dockland
Royal Albert Hall: Kensington
Royal and Ancient Golf Club: R & A, the;
   St. Andrews
Royal Ascot: Ascot
Royal Botanic Gardens: Kew Gardens
Royal Courts of Justice: Law Courts, the
Royal Docks: Dockland
Royal Enclosure: Ascot
Royal Exchange: Bank, the
Royal Festival Hall: South Bank, the
Royal Leamington Spa: Tunbridge Wells
Royal Military Academy: Bagshot;
   Camberley
Royal Military College: Sandhurst
Royal Opera House: Covent Garden
Royal Palace: Unter den Linden
'Royal Road, the': Camino Real, el
Royal Society: Burlington House
Royal Tunbridge Wells: Tunbridge Wells
Royal Victoria Docks: Dockland
Royal Victoria Theatre: Old Vic, the
Royal Yacht Squadron: Cowes Week
Rub' al Khali: Empty Quarter, the
rugby football: Rugby; Twickenham
Ruhr River: Ruhr, the
Ruislip: Middlesex

Rumania: Balkans, the
Rumeliotes: Rumelia
rumors: Street, the, 2
Runyon, Damon: Lindy's
Russia: Kremlin, the; Muscovy; Soviet
   Union, the
Russian Empire: Balkans, the
Russians: Tartary
Russian Soviet Federated Socialist Republic:
   Russia; Soviet Russia
Russias, Czar of all the: Russia
Ruth, Babe: House that Ruth Built
Rye, England: Cinque Ports, the
Rye, New York: Border Town

S

Saarinen, Eero: Gateway Arch
Saba: Sheba
Sackville Street: Albany
Sacramento, California: Golden City
Sacre Coeur: Montmartre
Sadat, Anwar el-: Camp David
Sage, Anna: Biograph Theater
Sahara desert: Sudan, the
St. Andrews: R & A, the
St. Augustine: America's Oldest City
St. Bartholomew's Church: Park Avenue
St. Bartholomew's Hospital: Bart's
St. Bartholomew's Medical School: Bart's
St. Basil's Cathedral: Red Square
St. Charles Parish: German Coast
St. Cloud, Minnesota: Granite City
St. Davids: Main Line
St. Edmund Hall: High, the
St.-Germain-des-Prés: Left Bank, the
St. Giles: Holy Land, the, 2
St. Giles Circus: Oxford Street
St. James Parish: German Coast
St. James's: Clubland, 1; Jermyn Street;
   West End, the
St. James's Palace: Pall Mall; St. James's
St. James's Park: Westminster
St. James's Street: St. James's
St. John's College: Backs, the; Bridge of
   Sighs, 3
St. John's River: American Nile, the
St. John's Wood: Abbey Road; Lord's; Swiss
   Cottage
St. John the Baptist Parish: German Coast
St. Joseph Street: Irish Channel
St. Katherine's Dock: Dockland
St. Laurent, Yves: Faubourg St. Honoré,
   Rue du

St. Louis: Gateway Arch; Great River City; Memphis of the American Nile; Mound City; Queen of the Mississippi Valley; Solid City

St. Louis Cathedral: French Quarter, the

St. Louis Street: Storyville

St. Marylebone: Marylebone; Westminster

St. Mary-le-bow: Bow; Marylebone

St. Mary of Bethlehem: Bedlam

St.-Michel: Left Bank, the

St.-Michel, Boulevard: Latin Quarter, the, 1

St. Nicholas Avenue: Sugar Hill

St. Paul's Cathedral: Bankside; Barbican, the; Little Britain; Old Bailey; Paternoster Row

St. Paul's Churchyard: Little Britain; Paternoster Row

St. Petersburg: Sunshine City

St. Raphael: French Riviera, the

St. Tropez: French Riviera, the; South of France, the

Saks Fifth Avenue: Fifth Avenue

Salem, Massachusetts: City of Peace; City of Witches; Paradise of New England

Salisbury: Old Sarum

Salisbury-Jones, Sir Guy: Hambledon

Salmagundi: Gotham

Salop: Telford

salsa bands: Aragon Ballroom

Saltaire: Fire Island

Salt Lake City: City of the Saints; Mecca; Mormon City

Salvation Army: Bowery, the; Sally Army, the; Strawberry Fields

Samoa: Polynesia

San Angelo, Texas: City of the Angel

San Antonio: Alamo City; Alamo, the; Cradle of Texas Liberty; Mission City; West Point of the Air

San Antonio,Texas: Chisholm Trail

San Benito, Texas: Casa Oscar Romero

Sandburg, Carl: Hog Butcher for the World

Sandhurst: Camberley

San Diego: Birthplace of California; Jewel City of California; Plymouth of the West

Sands Point: North Shore, 1

Sandwich: Cinque Ports, the

San Fernando Valley: Burbank

San Francisco: Alcatraz; Broadway, 2; Castro, the; Chinatown, 1; City of One Hundred Hills; Embarcadero; Fisherman's Wharf; Ghirardelli Square; Golden Gate City; Haight-Ashbury; Los Angeles; Mushroom City; Over South;

Path of Gold; Poor Man's Paradise; Port o' Missing Men; Queen of the Pacific; Silicon Valley

San Gennaro, Feast of: Little Italy

Sangre de Cristo Range: Rockies, the

San Jacinto: Alamo, the

"Sank Roo Doe Noo": Harry's American Bar

San Remo: Italian Riviera, the

Santa Barbara: Queen of the Missions

Santa Claus: North Pole

Santa Fe, New Mexico: Camino Real, el; Lone Star of Civilization; Santa Fe Trail

Santa Fe Trail: Atchison, Topeka, & Santa Fe

Santa Monica Mountain: San Fernando Valley

Santa Susana Mountain: San Fernando Valley

Santiago, Chile: Christ of the Andes

Santorini: Atlantis

Saracens: Barbary Coast, the

Sarajevo: accidental war, the

Sardinia: Costa Smeralda

Sargent, John Singer: Chelsea, 1

Saskatchewan: Prairie Provinces, the

Saturnine Hill: Capitoline, the

Saudia Arabia: Gulf, the

Saudi Arabia: Arabia; Middle East, the

Savage, the: Clubland, 1

Savannah, Georgia: Forest City of the South; Hilton Head Island

Savoy Hotel: Savoy, the

Savoy Palace: Savoy, the

Saxons: Broads, the; Isle of Thanet, the

Scafell Pike: Lake District, the

Scandinavia: Far North, the; Lapland

Schenectady: City That Lights and Hauls the World

Schiller, Johann von: Weimar

School of the Art Institute of Chicago: Gold Coast

Schwab's Drugstore: Sunset Boulevard

Schwartz, Maurice: Lower East Side

Schwarzwald: Black Forest, the

Science and Industry, Museum of: South Side; White City, 1

Scotland: Athens of the North, the; Auld Reekie; Backbone of England, the; Balmoral Castle; Border, the; Britain; Caledonia; Capital of the Highlands, the; Clydeside; England; Firth of Forth Bridge; Glencoe; Glens, the; Gorbals, the; Granite City, the; Gretna Green; Heart of Midlothian, the; Highlands, the; Inns of Court and Chancery; Land

of Cakes; Land's End to John o' Groat's
House; Little Britain; Lowlands, the;
Marches, the, 1; Morningside; New
Town, the; North Britain; Northland,
the; Northumbria; Old Dominion; R &
A, the; Roost, the; Royal Miles, the;
Sauchiehall Street; Silicon Glen; Silver
City by the Sea; Southern Uplands, the;
St. Andrews; Trossachs, the; United
Kingdom, the; Western Isles, the
Scotland Yard: Yard, the
Scots Gaelic: Highlands, the
Scott, Sir Walter: Athens of the North, the;
Border, the; Heart of Midlothian, the;
Trossachs, the
Scranton, Pennsylvania: City of Black
Diamonds
"Scrubs, the": Wormwood Scrubs
Scunthorpe: Flixborough
Seagram Building: East Side
Sears Tower: Empire State Building
Seattle, Washington: Skid Row
Seaview: Fire Island
Secombe, Harry: Windmill Theatre, the
Second Avenue: East Village, the; Lower
East Side
Second City: Old Town
Seeger, Pete: Greenwich Village
"See Naples and die": Naples
Seine River: Halles, les; Latin Quarter,
the, 1; Left Bank, the; Marais, the;
Quai d'Orsay, the
Selfridges: Oxford Street
Selkirk: Border, the
Selkirk Range: Inland Empire, the
Seminole: Trail of Tears
send to Coventry: Coventry
Senegal: Senegambia
Senegal River: Senegambia
Senlac, Battle of: Hastings
sent to Botany Bay: Botany Bay
Serbia: Balkans, the
Serendip: Ceylon
serendipity: Ceylon
Serra, Father Junípero: Plymouth of the
West
Serra, José Correa da: City of Magnificent
Distances
Seven Hills: Capitoline, the; Palatine, the;
Quirinal, the
"Seven Sisters Colliery": Seven Sisters
Seven Sisters Road: Seven Sisters
Seventh Avenue: Fashion Avenue; 42nd
Street; Gaiety Delicatessen; Garment
District

seventh heaven: Al Borak
Seven Wonders of the Ancient World:
Hanging Gardens of Babylon
Seven Wonders of the World: Colossus of
Rhodes
Severn: Arden
Severnaya Zemlya: Northland, the
sexual fulfillment: Diddy wa Diddy
Shadwell: Pool of London, the
Shaftesbury Avenue: Piccadilly Circus
Shakespeare, William: Arabia; Arden; Black-
friars
Shangri-La: Camp David
Sharjah: Trucial States, the
Shaw, George Bernard: John Bull
Shawn, Ted: Jacob's Pillow
Sheboygan, Wisconsin: Evergreen City; Jack
Benny's Home Town
Sheffield: Broad Acres, the; Muscle Shoals
Area; North, the, 1; Tri-Cities
Sheldonian Theatre: Broad, the
Shenandoah Valley: Blue Ridge Mountains,
the
Shepherd, Edward: Shepherd Market
Shepherd's Bush: Wormwood Scrubs
Sheridan, Philip Henry: Ohio's Jewels
Sheridan, Richard Brinsley: Morningside
Sheridan, Thomas: Morningside
Sheridan Square: Greenwich Village
Sherman, William Tecumseh: Ohio's Jewels
Sherwood Forest: Dukeries, the
She Stoops to Conquer: Liberty Hall
Shetland: Thule
Shetland Island: Roost, the
shipbuilding: Clydeside; Furness
Shires, the: Melton Mowbray; Midlands, the
shirtmaking: Jermyn Street
shopping: Oxford Street
Shoreditch: East End
"shot heard round the world": Birthplace of
American Liberty
Showboat: Ol' Man River; Paper Mill Play-
house
Shrewsbury: Marches, the, 1; Salop
Shropshire: Midlands, the; Salop; Telford;
West Midlands, the; West, the, 2
Sianis, Sam: Billy Goat Tavern
Sibelius, Jean: Karelia
Siberia: Far East, the
Siberia: Dakota, 1
SICBM: Midgetman
Sicily: Scylla and Charybdis
Sidney, Sir Philip: Arcadia
Sierra Mountains: Land of Little Rain
Sierra Nevada Mountains: Donner Pass

Sikkim: Native States, the
Silicon Valley: Silicon Glen
"Silicon Valley of the East": Route 128
"Silk Stocking District": East Side; Spanish
   Harlem
Sim, Alastair: Ealing
Sinatra, Frank: Broadway, 1
Sinclair, Upton: Union Stockyards
Singapore: Indochina; Southeast Asia
Sinn Fein: Southie
Sioux Indians: Bozeman Trail
Sirius: dog days; Dog Star
"sisters of the Bank": Bankside
Sixth Avenue: Avenue of the Americas;
   Chelsea, 2; 42nd Street; Gimbels; Her-
   ald Square; NoHo; Rockefeller Center;
   SoHo
"Six, the": European Economic Community,
   the
Skevington, Sir W.: Skevington's daughter
Skye: Western Isles, the
skyscrapers: Chrysler Building; Empire
   State Building; Manhattan
slaughterhouses: Shambles, the
Slaughter on Tenth Avenue: Hell's Kitchen
slavery: Middle Passage, the
slaves, fugitive: underground railroad
slave ships: Middle Passage, the
slave states: Mason-Dixon Line
Sleaford: Kesteven
"Sloane": Sloane Square
Sloane Ranger: Sloane Square; Swone-one
Sloane Square: King's Road
Slough: Watford
small-town life: Main Street
Smith, Betty: Brooklyn
Smith, George "Brides in the Bath": Old Bai-
   ley
Smith, Jack: Los Angeles
Smith, Seba: Uncle Sam
Smithfield: Bart's
Snowden, Ethel: Iron Curtain, the
snuff: anatomist's snuffbox
Social Democratic Party: Limehouse
social work: Hull House
Soho: Chinatown, 2; Greek Street; Holy
   Land, the, 2; Seven Dials; SoHo; Tin
   Pan Alley; Wardour Street; West End,
   the
Soho Square: Greek Street; Soho
Solingen: Sheffield of Germany
Solomon Islands: Melanesia
Solomon, King: Sheba
Solomon, temple of: Wailing Wall, the
Somalia: Horn of Africa, the; Ogaden, the

Somerset: Camelot, 1; Cheddar; Glaston-
   bury; Isle of Athelney, the; Southwest,
   the, 2; West Country, the
Songhai: Sudan, the
Sorbonne University: Latin Quarter, the, 1
Sothern, Edward A.: dundrearies
sourdough: Fisherman's Wharf
Sousa, John Philip: Stars and Stripes
South, the: Mason-Dixon Line; Midlands,
   the; North, the, 3
South Africa: Highveld, the; Joburg; Karoo,
   the; Mafeking; Namibia; Rand, the;
   Subcontinent, the; Table Mountain;
   Third World, the; Zululand
South Africa, Republic of: Azania
South America: banana republic; El Dorado;
   Gondwanaland; Guiana; Neogaea; Third
   World, the; Tierra del Fuego; West,
   the, 1
South America, northern coast of: Spanish
   Main, the
Southampton: Hamptons, the; Hants; Island,
   the, 1; New Forest; Solent, the
South Atlantic Ocean: Seven Seas, the
South Atlantic States: Atlantic States
South Audley Street: Mayfair
South Bank: Waterloo
South Boston High School: Southie
South Britain: Britain
South Cadbury: Camelot, 1
South Carolina: Atlantic States; Deep South,
   the; Game-cock State; Grand Strand;
   Harry Percy of the Union; Hilton Head
   Island; Iodine State; Keystone State of
   the South Atlantic Seaboard; Palmetto
   State; Rice State; Sandlapper State;
   South, the, 1; Swamp State; Thirteen
   Original Colonies
South China Sea: Seven Seas, the
South Dakota: Artesian State; Bad Lands,
   the; Black Hills, the; Blizzard State; Co-
   yote State; Land of Infinite Variety;
   Land of Plenty; Middle Border, the;
   Outlaw Country; Sunshine State; Twin
   Sisters; West, the, 3
South Dearborn Street: Loop, the
South Downs: Hambledon; Weald, the
Southeast, the: South, the, 2
southeast Asia: Cambodia; East Indies, the;
   Farther India; Golden Triangle, the, 1;
   Indochina; Land of a Million Elephants,
   the; Orient, the; Siam
"southern oceans, the": South Seas, the
Southern Uplands: Lowlands, the
Southey, Robert: Lake District, the

Stone Age: Wolds, the
Stork Club: "21" Club
Story, Sidney: Storyville
Stour, River: Constable Country; Isle of
    Thanet, the
Strachey, Lytton: Bloomsbury
Strand Bridge: Waterloo
Strand, the: Adelphi, the; Broadway, 1; Ca-
    rey Street; Covent Garden; Drury
    Lane; Fleet Street; Golgotha, 1; Law
    Courts, the; Savoy, the; Simpson's (in
    the Strand); Somerset House; West
    End, the
Strategic Defense Initiative: Star Wars
Streatham: Lambeth
"Street of Ink, the": Fleet Street
"Street of Shame, the": Fleet Street
"Strip, the": Sunset Boulevard
Stromboli: Atlantis
Stuart, Charles Edward: Black Friday, 1
submarine service: Silent Service
suburban housing estate: subtopia
Sudeten Mountains: Sudetenland, the
Suffolk: Constable Country; East Anglia;
    Newmarket
Suffolk County: Island, the, 2
Sugar Loaf Mountain: Copacabana, 1
Sulawesi: East Indies, the; Spice Islands, the
Sullivan, Anne Mansfield: City of Kind
    Hearts
Sullivan, Ed: Stork Club
Sullivan, Louis: North Side
Sultan's Palace: Sublime Porte, the
Sumatra: East Indies, the
Sumeria: Fertile Crescent, the; Mesopotamia
Sumner, John: Minsky's
Sun Also Rises, the: Pamplona
"Sunken Forest": Fire Island
'sunrise, orient': Japan
Sunset Boulevard: Beverly Hills Hotel
Sunset Boulevard: Sunset Boulevard
Sunset Strip: Strip, the, 2
Suomenlinna: Gibraltar of the North
"Super Chief": Union Station
supercontinent: Gondwanaland; Laurasia;
    Pangaea
Supreme Court (London), Bankruptcy De-
    partment of,: Carey Street
Supreme Court of Judicature: Law Courts,
    the
Surinam: Guiana
Surrey: Bagshot; Camberley; Epsom; Home
    Counties, the; London; Southeast, the;
    Waterloo
Surrey Commercial Docks: Dockland

Surrey Cricket Club: Oval, the
Sussex: Bognor Regis; Brighton; Costa Geria-
    trica, the; Greenwich Observatory;
    Hambledon; Hastings; Peacehaven;
    Rapes; Southeast, the; Weald, the
Sutherland: Highlands, the
Sutton Place: East Side
Sveaborg Fortress: Gibraltar of the North
Swaledale: Dales, the
Sweden: Land of the Midnight Sun, the;
    Lapland; Northland, the; Scandinavia;
    Scandinavian Shield, the; Sodom and
    Gomorrah, 2; Sound, the; Venice of
    the North
"swinging London": King's Road
"swinging '60s": Carnaby Street
Swiss Tavern: Swiss Cottage
Switzerland: Bernese Oberland, the; Helve-
    tia
swords and foils: Sheffield of Germany
Sydney: Bondi Beach; Botany Bay; King's
    Cross, 2; Paddo; Pitt Street; Smoke, the
Sydney Harbor Bridge: Coat Hanger, the
Symphony Hall: Back Bay; Broadway, 1
Syracuse, New York: City of Isms; City of
    the Plains; Convention City; Salt City
Syria: Levant, the; Middle East, the; Near
    East, the

T

Tabard, the: Borough, the
"table cloth": Table Mountain
Tacoma: Galloping Gertie
Taff River: Valleys, the
Taft, William Howard: Mother of Presidents
Tahiti: Polynesia
tailoring: Savile Row
Taiwan: Formosa
Tamesis: Isis
Tampa: Alligator Alley
Tanglewood: Jacob's Pillow
Tanzania: East Africa
Tappan Zee: Hudson River
Tarpeian Hill: Capitoline, the
Tartars: Tartary
Tartary: Mongolia
Tasman, Abel: Van Diemen's Land
Tasmania: Apple Isle, the; Tolpuddle; Van
    Diemen's Land
'tatty': Brum
Taunton: Isle of Athelney, the
'tawdry': Brum
Taylor, Deems: Round Table at the Algon-
    quin

Taylor, Tom: dundrearies
Taylor, Zachary: Mother of Presidents
Taylor Street: Hull House; West Side
tea trade: Mincing Lane
Teesdale: Dales, the
television networks: Manhattan
television studios, Britain's first: Ally Pally
Temple Bar: Golgotha, 1
Temple Emanuel: Fifth Avenue
Temple Place: Combat Zone
Ten, the: European Economic Community, the
Tennessee: Appalachia; Appalachian Mountains; Athens of the South; Bible Belt; Big Bend State; Bluff City; Deep South, the; Dimple of the Universe; Gate City; Hog & Hominy State; Lion's Den State; Monkey State; Mother of Southwestern Statesmen; Queen City of the Mountains; Rock City; Silver City; South, the, 1; Volunteer State
Tennessee River: Big Bend State; Muscle Shoals Area
Tenth Avenue: Broadway, 1; Chelsea, 2; Hell's Kitchen; Third Avenue
terra sancta: Holy Land, the, 1
Terre Haute, Indiana: Sycamore City
test cricket: Ashes, the
Texas: Alamo City; Alamo, the; Alligator State; Banner State; Beef State; Bible Belt; Big Bend; Big D; Big Inch; Blizzard State; City of Homes; Dallas Book Depository; Golden Triangle, the, 3; Gulf, the; Jumbo State; Lone Star State; Magnolia City; Metropolis of the Magic Valley; Mission City; Oleander City; Panhandle, the; Port of the Southwest; Rio Grande Valley; Silicon Prairie; Southwest, the, 1; West, the, 3; West Point of the Air; Where Mexico Meets Uncle Sam
Texas State Fair: Big Tex
textile mills: Spindle City
Thailand: Golden Triangle, the, 1; Indochina; Siam; Southeast Asia; Venice of the East
Thames River: Adelphi, the; Alsatia; Bankside; Battersea; Bedlam; Bermondsey Market; Blackfriars; Blackwall Tunnel; Bray; Caledonian Market; Chelsea, 1; Clink Street; Dockland; East End; Embankment, the; Gravesend; Henley; Isis; Isle of Dogs, the; Lambeth; London Bridge; Nine Elms; Pimlico; Pool of London, the; Runnymede; Savoy, the;

South Bank, the; Temple, the; Thames Valley, the; Tower Bridge; Tower, the; Vauxhall; Waterloo; West End, the; Whitefriars; Woolwich
Thames River, River: Covent Garden
Thames Valley: Wessex
Thaw, Harry K: Madison Square Garden
theater: green room
theaters: Leicester Square
Theatre Royal, Drury Lane: Drury Lane
Theocritus: Arcadia
Thera: Atlantis
Thessaly: Aetolia
Third Avenue: Bowery, the
Third World: Free World, the
Thirlmere: Lake District, the
thirteen colonies: Rebel Capital
Thomas, Dylan: Fitzrovia
Thompson sub-machine gun: Tommy gun
Thoreau, Henry David: Walden Pond
Thoresby Hall: Dukeries, the
Thousand Guineas race: Newmarket
Thrace: Balkans, the
Thracian peninsula: Golden Chersonese, the
Threadneedle Street: Bank, the; Old Lady of Threadneedle Street, the; Throgmorton Street
"Three Princes of Serendip, The": Ceylon
Throggs Neck Bridge: Hell Gate
Throg Street: Throgmorton Street
Through Bolshevik Russia: Iron Curtain, the
Through the Dark Continent: Dark Continent, the
"Thyrsis": City of Dreaming Spires
Tibet: Forbidden City, the; Roof of the World, the
Tibullus: Eternal City, the
Tiergarten: Unter den Linden
Tiffany: Fifth Avenue
Tigris River: Fertile Crescent, the; Mesopotamia
Tilbury: Dockland
Time, Incorporated: Rockefeller Center
Time-Life Building: Rockefeller Center
Times, The: Dockland; Printing House Square; Thunderer, the; Turnabout, the
Times Square: Broadway, 1; Clock at the Astor, Biltmore; Gaiety, the; Great White Way; Herald Square; Jack Dempsey's; Strip, the, 2
"Times Square of the West, the": Hollywood and Vine
Timor: East Indies, the
Timaeus: Atlantis

"Tinseltown": Hollywood
Titusville, Pennsylvania: Oil Dorado
Todd River: Alice Springs
Todd, Sir Charles: Alice Springs
Tokyo: Ginza, the; Megalopolis; Orient-Express
Toledo, Ohio: Corn City
"Tolpuddle Martyrs": Tolpuddle
Tom Brown's Schooldays: Rugby
Tombs, the: Bridge of Sighs, 2
Tompkins Park: East Village, the
Tondo Foreshore: Little Vietnam
"Tonight Show": Burbank
Tonkin: Indochina
Topanga Malibu Sequit land grant: Malibu
Toronto: Bay Street; Hogtown; Parkdale; Queen City, the; Queen Street West; Rosedale; Strip, the, 2; Track, the
Torquay: Cornish Riviera, the
Torremolinas: Costa del Sol
Torrio, Johnny: Holy Name; Loop, the
torture: Skevington's daughter
Tory: Turnabout, the
Totable Tornado Observatory: TOTO
Tottenham: Seven Sisters
Tottenham Court Road: Centre Point; Fitzrovia; Warren Street
Toulouse-Lautrec, Henri de: Montmartre; Moulin Rouge
Touraine: Garden of France, the
Tower, the: Blackpool; Tower Bridge
Tower Bridge: Bermondsey Market; Caledonian Market; London Bridge
Tower of London: Tower Bridge
toy business: Chelsea, 2
Trafalgar Square: Aldermaston; Charing Cross; Number 10; Pall Mall; Soho; Whitehall
Trail of the Lonesome Pine, the: Blue Ridge Mountains, the
transportation: Botany Bay
Trans-Siberian railway: Siberia
Transvaal: Highveld, the; Joburg; Rand, the; Zululand
Transylvania: Balkans, the
Travancor: Native States, the
Travellers Club: Pall Mall
Travis, William Barret: Alamo, the
Treasury: Whitehall
Tredegar: Valleys, the
Tree, Beerbohm: RADA
Tree Grows in Brooklyn, A: Brooklyn
Tremont Street: Combat Zone
Trent: Arden

Trent River: Backbone of England, the; Burton upon Trent
Treorchy: Valleys, the
Triboro Bridge: Hell Gate
Tribune Company: Wrigleyville
Tribune Tower: Magnificent Mile, the
Trinity Church: Back Bay
Trinity College: Backs, the; Broad, the
Tripolitania: Barbary Coast, the
Trollope, Anthony: Barset
Troy, New York: Collar Capital of the World; Collar City
Trucial Coast: Trucial States, the
Trucial Oman: Trucial States, the
Truman, Harry S.: Camp David
Trumbull, Jonathan: Brother Jonathan
"Tube": Drain, the; London Underground
Tulsa, Oklahoma: Oil Capital of the World
Tunbridge Wells: Pantiles, the
Tunisia: Barbary Coast, the; Maghreb; North Africa
Tunstall: Five Towns, the
Turkey: Anatolia; Angora; Asia Minor; Balkans, the; Golden Horn, the; Middle East, the; Near East, the; Orient-Express; Sublime Porte, the
Turkish empire: Balkans, the; Sick Man of Europe; Sick Man of the East
Turner, J. M. W.: Chelsea, 1
Turnhill: Five Towns, the
Tuscaloosa, Alabama: Athens of Alabama; Druid City
Tuscany: Leghorn
Tuscarawas County: America's Little Switzerland
Tuscumbia: Muscle Shoals Area; Tri-Cities
Tuva: Mongolia
Tuvalu: Polynesia
Twain, Mark: Frogtown
Twelve, the: European Economic Community, the
"Twentieth-Century Limited": Union Station
Twickenham: Middlesex; Strawberry Hill
Two Thousand Guineas race: Newmarket
Tyburn: Marylebone
Tyler, John: Mother of Presidents
Tyne and Wear: Northeast, the, 1; Tyneside
Tynemouth: Tyneside
Tyne River: Jarrow; Tyneside
Tyneside: Northeast, the, 1; North, the, 1
Tyre: Queen of the Sea
Tyrone: Six Counties, the

U

Uganda: East Africa
Ullswater: Lake District, the
Ulster: Province, the
ultima Thule: Thule
Umm al Quaiwain: Trucial States, the
underground: twopenny tube
"Underground": London Underground
underground railroad: Casa Oscar Romero
UNESCO: Abu Simbel
Union Carbide: Bhopal
Union of Soviet Socialist Republics: Russia;
    Soviet Union, the
Union Square: Broadway, 1
Union Stockyards: South Side
Union Street: Cobble Hill
United Arab Emirates: Arabia; Gulf, the;
    Trucial States, the
United Fruit Company: banana republic
United Kingdom: European Economic Com-
    munity, the
United Kingdom of Great Britain and North-
    ern Ireland: Britain; United Kingdom,
    the
United Nations: 42nd Street
United States: City of Five Flags; French
    Quarter, the; Middle Border, the;
    North, the, 2; Northeast, the, 2; North-
    west, the, 2; Uncle Sam; West, the, 3;
    Wild West, the; See also *U.S.*, and *USA*
    in the Index.
United States, Constitution of: First State;
    Triple-headed Monster
United States, Constitution of the United
    States: Constitution State
United States military establishment: Penta-
    gon, the
United States Subtreasury: Wall Street
universities: redbrick
University College: High, the
University of Illinois: West Side, 2
Unter den Linden: Kurfürstendamm, the
Upper East Side: East Side; Gimbels
"Upper East Side": East Side
Upper Guinea: Guinea
Upper Midwest: Middle Border, the
Upper New York Bay: Bedloe's Island
Upper Palatinate: Palatinate, the
Upper Peninsula, Michigan: Land of Hiawa-
    tha
Upper Pool: Pool of London, the
Upper Regent Street: Piccadilly Circus
Upper West Side: West Side, 1
Uptown: Aragon Ballroom; North Side

Ural Mountains: Siberia
Ursa Major: Big Dipper; Charles's Wain
Ursa Minor: Little Dipper
U. S.: East, the, 1; House, the; Main Street
    of America, the; South, the, 1; Tin Pan
    Alley; See also *United States*, and *USA*
    in the Index.
USA: East, the, 2; See also *United States*,
    and *U.S.* in the Index.
"Use of Sarum": Old Sarum
U. S. Military Academy: West Point
U. S. Open: Forest Hills
Uspallata Pass: Christ of the Andes
U. S. S. R.: East, the, 2; Land of the Mid-
    night Sun, the
U. S. Treasury: Uncle Sam's Crib
Utah: Beehive State; City of the Saints; Des-
    eret State; Land of the Saints; Mecca;
    Mormon City; Mormon State; Salt Lake
    State; Southwest, the, 1
Utrecht, Treaty of: Acadia

V

"Valley girls": San Fernando Valley
"Valley, the": Rio Grande Valley; San Fer-
    nando Valley
vampires: Transylvania
Van Buren, Martin: Albany Regency
Van Cleef and Arpels: Tiffany's
Van Cortlandt Park: Broadway, 1
Vancouver, George: Northwest Passage, the
Vandiver, Willard D.: Show Me State
Varna, Bulgaria: Orient-Express
Vauxhall Gardens: Vauxhall
Velásquez, Diego de Silva y: Prado, the
Venezuela: Angostura; Guiana
Venice: Bride of the Sea; Bridge of Sighs, 4;
    Jewel of the Adriatic, the; Orient-Ex-
    press; Rialto
Venice Simplon Orient-Express: Orient-Ex-
    press
Ventnor: Boardwalk
Ventura: Malibu
Vermont: Appalachian Mountains; East,
    the, 1; Green Mountain State; Mohawk
    Trail; New England; Northeast King-
    dom
Verne, Jules: Reform Club, the
Versailles, Treaty of: Polish Corridor, the
Vesuvius: Atlantis
Via Condotti: Rodeo Drive
vicar of Bray: Bray
Vichy France: Vichy

Vicksburg, Mississippi: Gibraltar of America; Key City

Victoria: Pimlico; Scotland Yard

Victoria, Queen: Island, the, 1; Royal Borough, the; St. James's; Tunbridge Wells; Victoria

Victoria and Albert museum: Kensington; V & A, the

Victoria Embankment: Embankment, the

Victoria Station: Orient-Express

Vienna: Mistelbach

Vietnam: Indochina; Southeast Asia

Vikings: Vinland

"Village, the": Greenwich Village

Village Vanguard, the: Greenwich Village

Villanova: Main Line

Viminal: Seven Hills, the

Vine Street: Hollywood and Vine

Vineyard Sound: Cape, the

Vinland Map: Vinland

Virginia: Atlantic States; Blue Ridge Mountains, the; Cavalier State; Commonwealth; Delmarva Peninsula; Dismal Swamp, the; Down Where the South Begins; Mother of Presidents; Mother of States; Old Dominion; Outer Banks; South, the, 1; Thirteen Original Colonies

Virginia, General Assembly of: House of Burgesses

Virginia, Minnesota: Queen City of the Iron Range

Virginia City, Montana: Bozeman Trail

Virginian: *Monitor* and *Merrimack*

Vistula: Polish Corridor, the

Vizcaya: Guernica

Vladivostok: Siberia

W

Wabash River: Indian-Appian Way

Waco, Texas: Athens of Texas; Queen of the Brazos (River)

Wagner, Richard: Bayreuth

Waikiki: Banzai Pipeline

Walden, or Life in the Woods: Walden Pond

Waldorf-Astoria Hotel: East Side; Park Avenue

Waldorf Towers: East Side

Wales: Britain; Cambria; Coal Metropolis of the World; England; Lake District, the; Law Courts, the; Little Britain; Llanfairpwllgwyngillgogerychwyrndrobllllantysiliogogogoch; Marches, the, 1; Paddington; Principality, the;

Royal Borough, the; Seven Sisters; Snowdonia; United Kingdom, the

"Wales and the West": West, the, 2

Wales, Prince of: Brighton; Principality, the

Wall Street: Broadway, 1; Manhattan; Street, the, 1

Walpole, Horace: Strawberry Hill

Walsall: Black Country, the

"Waltz King, the": Aragon Ballroom

Walworth: Old Kent Road, the

Wantsum, River: Isle of Thanet, the

wapentakes: Rapes

Wapping: Dockland; Pool of London, the; Printing House Square

Warden, the: Barset

"Wardour Street English": Wardour Street

War of the Spanish Succession: Blenheim Palace

Warwickshire: Arden; Coventry; Midlands, the; Rugby; West Midlands, the

Washington: Chinook State; Evergreen State; Far West, the; Galloping Gertie; Inland Empire, the; Minneapolis of the West; Northwest, the, 2; Pacific Northwest, the

Washington, D. C.: Camp David; Connecticut Avenue; Embassy Row; Foggy Bottom; Ford's Theater; Hill, the; Megalopolis; Northeast Corridor; Northeast, the, 2; Pentagon, the; Tidal Basin

Washington, George: Brother Jonathan; Bunker Hill; Featherbed Lane; Mother of Presidents

Washington Heights: Broadway, 1; Featherbed Lane; West Side, 1

Washington Park: South Side

Washington Square Park: Bughouse Square; Fifth Avenue; Greenwich Village

Washington Street: Combat Zone

Wash, the: Fens, the

Wastwater: Lake District, the

'watchtower': Barbican, the

waterfront: Embarcadero; Fisherman's Wharf

Waterloo: Bakerloo; Cockpit of Europe, the; Old Vic, the

Waterloo and City Line: Drain, the

Waterloo Bridge: South Bank, the; Waterloo

Waterloo Place: Athenaeum, the

Waterloo station: Drain, the

Water Tower: Magnificent Mile, the

Water Tower Place: Magnificent Mile, the

Watford: Bakerloo

Watson, Dr.: Baker Street

Waugh, Evelyn: Azania; Metroland

Wayne: Main Line
Wealden oaks: Weald, the
Weavers, the: Greenwich Village
Webb, Captain Matthew: Channel, the
Webster, Daniel: Great Dismal
Wedgwood, Josiah: Etruria
Wednesbury: Black Country, the
Weimar Republic: Weimar
Weiss, Hymie: Holy Name
Welfare Island: Manhattan
Welland River: Fens, the; Wash, the
Wellbeck Abbey: Dukeries, the
Wellington, Duke of: Number One, London;
    Peninsula, the; Waterloo
Wellington Museum: Number One, London
Wellington Place: Hyde Park Corner
Wells, H. G.: Burton upon Trent
'Welshmen': Cambria
Wensleydale: Dales, the
Wessex: Dorset; East Anglia
Wessex Region: Wessex
West: East, the, 2; Midlands, the
West, the: Bamboo Curtain, the; Chelten-
    ham; Free World, the; Iron Curtain,
    the; North, the, 3; Paddington; V & A,
    the; West Country, the
West Africa: Guinea; Middle Passage, the;
    Senegambia; Slave Coast, the; Tim-
    buktu; White Man's Grave, the
West Berlin: Kurfürstendamm, the
West Britain: Britain
West Bromwich: Black Country, the
West Bromwich Albion: Albion
Westchester County: Grand Central; Scars-
    dale Syndrome
West Country: Mummerset; Southwest,
    the, 2; West, the, 2
West End: Albany; Belgravia; Berkeley
    Square; Bond Street; Bow Street; Car-
    naby Street; City, the; Clubland, 1;
    Drury Lane; Eisenhower Platz; Fitz-
    rovia; Harley Street; Islington; Jermyn
    Street; Knightsbridge; Leicester Square;
    London; Mayfair; Oxford Street; Pall
    Mall; Park Lane; Portland Place; Re-
    form Club, the; Savile Row; Seven Di-
    als; Shepherd Market; Soho; St.
    James's; Tyburnia; Wardour Street;
    Warren Street; Wimpole Street
western frontier: Wild West, the
Western Hemisphere: New World, the;
    West, the, 1
Western Sahara: Western Desert, the
Western Samoa: Australasia

West Germany: Berlin Wall, the; European
    Economic Community, the; Prussia;
    Reeperbahn, the; Ruhr, the
West Glamorgan: Seven Sisters
West Ham: East End
Westhampton: Hamptons, the
West Hollywood: Boystown
West India Docks: Billingsgate; Isle of Dogs,
    the
West Indies: Indies, the
West Midlands: Black Country, the;
    Bourneville; Bullring, the; Burton upon
    Trent; Etruria; Lincolnshire; Salop;
    Spaghetti Junction
Westminster: Lambeth; Mother of Parlia-
    ments, the; Thorney Island; Vauxhall;
    Whitehall
Westminster, monks of: Covent Garden
Westminster, Palace of: Star Chamber;
    Westminster
Westminster Abbey: Thorney Island; West-
    minster
Westminster Bridge: London Bridge
Westminster chimes: Big Ben
Westminster College: Iron Curtain, the
Westmoreland County: Athens of Virginia
Westmoreland County, Virginia: Athens of
    Virginia, the
West Orange: Oranges, the
West Riding: Ridings, the
West Side: Chelsea, 2; Tribeca
West Village, the: East Village, the; Green-
    wich Village
West Virginia: Appalachia; Atlantic States;
    Mason-Dixon Line; Mother of States;
    Mountain State; Panhandle State; Swit-
    zerland of America
Westwood: Sunset Boulevard
West Yorkshire: Ridings, the
Wharfedale: Dales, the
Wheeling, West Virginia: Nail City
Whig: Turnabout, the
whirlpool: Maelstrom, the
Whistler, James McNeill: Chelsea, 1
Whitechapel: East End
"Whitechapel murders": Whitechapel
Whitefriars: Alsatia
Whitehall: Charing Cross; Downing Street;
    Number 10; Scotland Yard
White House: Camelot, 2; Oval Office; 1600
    Pennsylvania Avenue
White Mountains: Appalachian Mountains
White Otter Lake: White Otter Castle
White Peak: Peak District, the
White's: Clubland, 1

White Sea: Karelia
White, Stanford: Madison Square Garden
Whitestone: Queens
White Tower: slider; Tower, the
Whittington, Dick: Highgate
Wicker Park: West Side
Wieland, Christoph: Weimar
Wigan: Neasden
"Wigan Pier": Wigan
Wight, Isle of: Island, the, 1; Needles, the;
    Solent, the
Wilberforce, Bishop: Timbuktu
Wilcox, Horace: Hollywood
Wilde, Oscar: Père Lachaise
Wilder, Billy: Sunset Boulevard
Wilhelm (William II), emperor of Germany:
    Sick Man of Europe
Willamette Valley: Oregon Trail
William III: gentleman in black velvet, the;
    Glencoe
Williamsburgh: Brooklyn
Williams, Shirley: Limehouse
Wilmington: Chemical Capital of the World;
    New Sweden
Wilshire Boulevard: Beverly Hills; Miracle
    Mile
Wilson Dam: Muscle Shoals Area
Wilson, Edmund: Minsky's
Wilson, Woodrow: Mother of Presidents
Wiltshire: Avebury; Old Sarum; Porton
    Down; South, the, 2; Wessex; West
    Country, the
Winchell, Walter: Stork Club
Winchelsea: Cinque Ports, the
Winchester: Barset; Camelot, 1
Winchester rifle: gun that won the west
Windermere: Lake District, the
Windmill Girls: Windmill Theatre, the
Windsor: Royal Borough, the; Runnymede
wine trade: Mincing Lane
Wisconsin: America's Dairyland; Badger
    State; Belle City (of the Lakes); Blonde
    Beauty of the Lakes; Copper State;
    Cream City; Deutsch-Athens; Four Lake
    City; Land of Lakes; Midwest, the;
    Mother of States
Witham, River: Fens, the
Witwatersrand: Rand, the
Wizard of Oz, the: TOTO
Wollsend: Hadrian's Wall
Wolverhampton: Black Country, the
Woods Hole: Cape, the
Woolcott, Alexander: Round Table at the
    Algonquin
Woolf, Virginia: Bloomsbury

Worcester: Mercia; Midlands, the
Worcestershire: Garden of England, the;
    West Midlands, the; West, the, 2
Wordsworth, William: Lake District, the
workingmen's clubs: Clubland, 2
World's Columbian Exposition of 1893: Mu-
    seum of Science and Industry; White
    City, 1; Windy City
"world series": Ashes, the
Worthing: Costa Geriatrica, the
"Wot Cher": Old Kent Road, the
"Wreck of the Hesperus": Gloucester
Wren, Christopher: Greenwich Observatory
Wright, Wilbur and Orville: Birthplace of
    Aviation
Wrigley Building: Magnificent Mile, the
Wrigley Field: Wrigleyville
Wrigleyville: Near North Side
Wye River: Offa's Dyke
Wynnewood: Main Line
Wyoming: Black Hills, the; Equality State;
    Middle Border, the; Northwest, the, 2;
    Sagebrush State

Y

Yahveh: Adonai
Yankee Stadium: House that Ruth Built
Yazoo River: Gibraltar of America
Yeager, Chuck: Glamorous Glennis
Yeardley, George: House of Burgesses
"yellow peril": Chinatown, 2
Yemen: Arabia; Middle East, the; Sheba
Yeomen Warders: Tower, the
YHWH: Adonai
Yonghy-Bonghy-Bo: Coromandel Coast, the
Yonkers: Broadway, 1
York: Ridings, the; Shambles, the
York, Duke of: Albany
Yorkshire: Broad Acres, the; Dales, the;
    Northeast, the, 1; North, the, 1; North-
    umbria; Wolds, the
Yorkshire Dales: Dales, the
Yorkshire Moors: Ridings, the
Yosemite: Land of Little Rain
"You Bet Your Life": Grant's Tomb
"Youngest County, the": London
"Young Pretender, the": Black Friday, 1
Ypres: Cockpit of Europe, the; Flanders
Yucca Flat: Nevada Proving Grounds
Yugoslavia: Balkans, the; Iron Curtain, the;
    Rumelia
Yukon Territory: Rockies, the; Territories,
    the

Z

Zaire: Copper Belt, the
Zambia: Copper Belt, the
Zealand: Sound, the

Zeeland: Low Countries, the
Zittau: Oder-Neisse Line, the
Zurbarán, Francisco de: Prado, the